CONSULS AND THE INSTITUTIONS OF GLOBAL CAPITALISM, 1783–1914

PERSPECTIVES IN ECONOMIC AND SOCIAL HISTORY

Series Editors: Andrew August
                      Jari Eloranta

TITLES IN THIS SERIES

Forthcoming Titles

CONSULS AND THE INSTITUTIONS OF GLOBAL CAPITALISM, 1783–1914

BY

Ferry de Goey

Routledge
Taylor & Francis Group
LONDON AND NEW YORK

First published 2014 by Pickering & Chatto (Publishers) Limited

2 Park Square, Milton Park, Abingdon, Oxfordshire OX14 4RN
52 Vanderbilt Avenue, New York, NY 10017

Routledge is an imprint of the Taylor & Francis Group, an informa business

First issued in paperback 2020

BRITISH LIBRARY CATALOGUING IN PUBLICATION DATA

Goey, Ferry de, author.
Consuls and the institutions of global capitalism, 1783–1914. – (Perspectives in
economic and social history)
1. Imperialism – Economic aspects. 2. Capitalism – Political aspects. 3. Diplomatic and consular service – Influence. 4. Economic history – 1750–1918.
I. Title II. Series
338.9'1'091719-dc23

ISBN-13: 978-1-84893-316-3 (hbk)
ISBN-13: 978-0-367-66912-6 (pbk)

Typeset by Pickering & Chatto (Publishers) Limited

CONTENTS

LIST OF TABLES

INTRODUCTION

In 1911 Major Joseph Orton Kerbey (1841–1913) published *An American Consul in Amazonia*. In the book he added a poem 'What People Think about a Consul', by an unknown author.[1] The poem reviews the many functions and duties of consuls, but despite this he is not much respected by society, not even after his death.

> In fact, a consul must know and do everything, or
> The general cry is, 'What's a consul good for?'
> He must not be old, or young, single or married;
> And I really believe that when he is buried
> They will still continue to vent all their spleen
> Denying him heaven, Sambo or Fiddler's Green.[2]

Kerbey was consul for the United States in the Brazilian port Belém do Pará.[3] As Kerbey explains in the following extract, he was appointed in 1891 by Secretary of State James G. Blaine (1830–93):

> 'I think you are the right man to send out there, as you are a telegrapher and a practical electrician, and we want to know something about the rubber insulation in this electric age, in its relation to reciprocity.' When I intimated that I did not know anything of Para, he replied: 'That's the trouble with all of us. I am sending you out there to learn something about it, as you have a good nose for news and your training as a newspaper scout qualifies you for collecting and reporting intelligently on the prospects for American business.'[4]

After his appointment Kerbey went to Para and contacted the acting consul. 'My conclusion was, after the first few days, that the United States consul at Para is located in the hottest, unhealthiest, and most expensive place in all the consular list.'[5] Despite this negative impression, Kerbey believed that Amazonia was the *Land of To-morrow*.[6]

The experiences of Kerbey as consul are not exceptional. In the nineteenth century, many consuls were appointed without any previous involvement in consular work; they received little training and were sent to their post with only a printed leaflet containing the consular regulations. Many believed that society did not reward them enough for all the hardships they had to endure. Most consulates in the nineteenth century, certainly those in South America, Africa or East Asia, were in remote places, with unhealthy conditions and poor means of transport and communication. Compared to the early nineteenth century, however, much had already improved. Steamships and the telegraph made transport and communication faster, cheaper and more reliable. More consuls received at least a basic training and were selected after examinations. The number of salaried or professional consuls had increased. The total number of consuls, salaried and unsalaried, grew tremendously in the nineteenth century. Apparently, Western states were convinced that consuls made an important contribution to their foreign policy.

Institutions and Consuls

The fact that D. C. North was awarded the 1993 Nobel Memorial Prize for Economics shows that institutions play a vital role in explaining the different historical developments of states. Recent examples are the works of the economists D. Acemoglu and J. A. Robinson and the historian N. Ferguson.[7] Although both of these books, and many similar publications, deal with international relations and politics, they do not discuss the institutions of diplomacy, the treaties of friendship and commerce or their role in the development of global capitalism. Old institutions like ambassadors and consuls are almost completely lacking, except for a cursory talk of the failed mission of Lord Macartney to China in 1793.

Why did the US appoint Kerbey in Para, although he admitted to lacking knowledge and business experience? Why was the institution of consuls developed? Entrepreneurship is often linked to risk-taking, but equally important is minimizing risk. Businessmen must have some sense of security that suppliers will deliver the ordered goods, consumers will pay their bills and contracts are enforceable in court. They need to know that courts will punish fraud and that when called upon, the state will protect their property. This need for security is even more important in the case of international business, like Western businessmen in Muslim countries, as discussed by Windler, because these entrepreneurs operate in different institutional, political, cultural and religious settings.[8] A. Greif reminded us that foreign states may not subscribe to the same idea of property rights or protection of commerce; clients may have different attitudes regarding settling debts or attach different values to impersonal written contracts.[9]

Entrepreneurs have developed several institutions to mitigate the risk of international business: commercial treaties; merchant guilds; merchant laws and courts for handling disputes between traders; bills of exchange; and written contracts. A. B. Hibbert mentions the use of special warehouses and other buildings.[10] This study will, however, focus on another institution: the consuls. To be able to function properly, consuls depend on many other institutions. An important institution was extraterritoriality: foreigners receiving 'exemption from the local laws and jurisdiction of the country where they reside'.[11] This is based on the idea of personal law: 'the laws of the nation to which an individual belonged followed him wherever he went and ... he was entitled to their protection and benefits without reference to the laws of the state in which he sojourned'.[12] In 1303, King Edward I (1239–1307) of England presented the *Carta Mercatoria*, promising foreign merchants protection and freedom to trade, besides exemption from tolls. They were allowed to lodge where they pleased and disputes between native and foreign merchants were settled by mixed courts.[13]

As Liu has shown, extraterritoriality was known in many parts of the world: in Europe, the Middle East, North Africa and East Asia.[14] Communities of foreign merchants were allowed to reside in certain places, usually ports or important commercial centres, to trade (economic privileges). This included the right to appoint a representative to settle disputes among themselves (judicial privileges) and to communicate with the authorities of the state (political privileges). These representatives were known under various names, but by the late eighteenth century, consul was the most familiar name. Rulers willingly relinquished some of their sovereignty to the consuls to attract foreign merchants and to stimulate foreign trade. In return, they hoped and expected other states to do the same: this principle is known as reciprocity.

The privileges were codified in bilateral treaties concluded between states. States are usually defined as having a permanent population, a defined territory, a government and the legal capacity to enter into relations with other states.[15] Following this definition, there were many states in the nineteenth century throughout the world. The wish to establish diplomatic and commercial relations prompted European rulers to conclude treaties with other rulers long before 1800. To these general criteria of a state, the Europeans gradually added a number of additional principles. The number of recognized states at the beginning of the nineteenth century that conformed to the European ideas of a state, was perhaps about a dozen. Through the treaty of friendship, commerce and navigation, they began to spread their idea of a state. This general treaty established ground rules for day-to-day relations between two states and was, says Coyle, the 'medium *par excellence* through which nations have sought in a general settlement to secure reciprocal respect for their normal interests abroad'.[16] They were an essential institution for consuls because they contained provisions for appointing representatives. The treaties in addition often contained a Most Favoured Nation (MFN) clause: any privileges given to a country would automatically become available to other countries with a MFN clause. This mechanism ensured that all countries in the end received the same privileges and guaranteed equal opportunities and fair competition.

From the mid-seventeenth century, rulers in Europe no longer granted full extraterritoriality to foreigners, because it conflicted with the notion of sovereign states. The principle of personal law was therefore exchanged for territorial law: the state is sovereign within a certain territory and this applies to all people, including foreigners. As a consequence, the consuls in Europe lost their political and judicial powers, keeping only their economic powers. In this more limited form of extraterritoriality, the political powers were handled by resident ambassadors who conducted diplomacy. Political and economic interests became separated in Europe and handled by different state representatives. Whereas in Europe extraterritoriality was no longer acceptable for the rulers, in their relations with non-Western states they insisted on having full extraterritorial powers for their representatives. Their main argument was that non-Western states were not civilized. By insisting on extraterritoriality in non-Western states, the European rulers reintroduced the idea of personal law they had previously abandoned. They furthermore claimed the right to appoint their consuls, thus ending the system of self-rule by merchants and introducing the system of patronage: rulers selected candidates for a consulate based on favours and friendship and political relations.

These changes were part of a particular form of international relations in Europe.[17] The European system of states was based on sovereignty, nominal equality between states, the rule of law (including protection of property and the idea that treaties and contracts were binding), and non-interference in domestic affairs. Because it was based on equality with no leader, the European system of states was in principle anarchic.[18] The European states observed the law of nations (now called international law), that was derived from Roman law and its handling of foreigners in the Roman Empire. Later it became a set of principles regulating the affairs and conduct of nations and sovereigns in Europe. Several European scholars contributed to the development of the law of nations, including Hugo Grotius (the Dutch Hugo de Groot, 1583–1645) and his concept of open seas. It should be pointed out, however, that non-Western states, such as the Muslim states, also made important contributions.[19] The European system of states furthermore contained the idea of shared norms and values or the standard of civilization: how states were internally organized and conducted international relations. The standard of civilization, says Bowden, was primarily based on Christianity, the presence of a state organization and acceptance of the rule of law.[20] States that in the opinion of European rulers met this standard were next admitted to the Family of Nations: they were invited to international conferences to settle disputes between states.[21]

The European system of states that began to take shape after the Treaty of Westphalia (1648) was fully developed in the early nineteenth century when the Concert of Europe was introduced after the Congress of Vienna (1814–15). As A. Osiander explains: 'It was not before the nineteenth century that the state as we know it finally established itself'.[22] Relations between European states and non-Western states also changed: Western states began to dictate the rules of international relations and this demanded much more of the consuls. During the nineteenth century, the consular institution was modernized by most Western governments. This development can be linked to the Institutional Revolution, as analysed by D. W. Allen.[23] Transport and communication improved considerably, reducing the role of nature: variability decreased and predictability increased. Old customs, including patronage, gradually disappeared. By the mid-nineteenth century, Allen explains, they were replaced by selection based on merit and more formal qualifications. However, in the case of the consular institution, this was not completed until the early twentieth century. The modernization of the consular institution coincided with the growth of industrial and military power. They demanded more privileges from non-Western states, without always granting the same privileges in return, as had happened before the late eighteenth century. Ambassadors, naval commanders and consuls were dispatched to non-Western states to conclude new treaties. These missions were often supported by the display of military and naval power: gunboat diplomacy.

The European system of states was one of many other systems, including the Islamic and the Sino-centric systems. During the nineteenth century different norms and regulations existed on how to handle consuls, depending on the prevailing system of international relations. This affected the duties and functions of consuls in regions that were not part of the Family of Nations because they did not (yet) comply with the standard of civilization: the Middle East, North Africa and sub-Saharan Africa and East Asia. In these regions the Western states insisted on providing their consuls with full extraterritoriality: political, judicial and economic powers. The role of consuls in these regions was therefore quite different from what they did in Western countries. This was very important to the development of global capitalism. Without full extraterritoriality the consuls would not have been able to protect the economic interests of Western states and businessmen in the Middle East, North Africa and East Asia. During the nineteenth century, the European system of states expanded across the globe until the world was 'united into an international society by the global acceptance, outwardly at least, of common rules and assumptions for the conduct of international relations'.[24] The growth of the number of consuls coincided with the globalization of the European system of states, colonialism and imperialism and the expansion of capitalism. M. Lang asserts that Western states played an active role in the globalizing economy of the nineteenth century. Most researchers ignore the complementarity of politics and economics. Lang argues that this denial is related to the Westphalian model that 'treats the economy as either contained within a state, and therefore secondary to the system itself, or outside state power, supraterritorial, and therefore a threat to the state's sovereignty'.[25]

The global economy, measured by world trade and foreign direct investment, was much more international in 1900 than in 1800.[26]

The main argument of this study is that the institution of consuls was indispensable for the development of global capitalism during the nineteenth century. By appointing consuls, governments extended their protection beyond the state borders. When conflicts arose consuls acted as intermediaries between various groups, including their fellow citizens, other Western and non-Western people, and local and national authorities in foreign countries. From an institutional perspective, it means that the many services of consuls reduced transaction costs for businessmen and they monitored the bad behaviour of foreign governments and citizens and compatriots. Transaction costs are here defined as the cost of establishing and maintaining rights.[27] This is precisely what many consider to be the main duty of consuls. It is, however, very difficult to determine whether consuls really reduced transaction costs for businessmen. After considering the available evidence and pointing out the difficulties of determining transaction costs, L. Müller and J. Ojala believe it is 'probable'.[28] Apart from the problem of having reliable statistics, there is the additional difficulty of the merchant-consul: consuls who were also active traders. Once appointed consul, they had a personal stake in stimulating trade. In the following chapters, cases are presented to demonstrate how consuls stimulated economic transactions, but it will become clear that appointing a consul did not guarantee a growth of trade and investments. The development of foreign trade depended on many factors, not only the presence of a consul.

We could ask what alternatives were available to governments wanting to protect their merchants in foreign places and to stimulate trade. A first option was for the foreign government to take care of this, but they would most likely privilege their own merchants and monitoring foreign governments would increase agency costs. A second solution was to allow merchants to rule themselves. The problem here was the exit option for merchants: they could ignore or evade the rules. Research had shown that shirking did happen, but not as frequently as one might expect. Merchants residing in foreign places formed small communities (nations), with certain rules of behaviour.[29] The emergence of social norms and social control by the group were an effective mechanism to force compliance. Dodging these rules would be very difficult and could be very costly: the merchant, says A. Greif, was ostracized.[30] Self-rule by merchants was the preferred solution for many centuries, until European rulers claimed the right to appoint consuls.

Besides the economic duties of consuls, it is necessary to include the many non-economic duties as well, because the difference is often academic. Negotiating new tariffs for customs duties had important economic effects for individual merchants and the economy at large. Already in the beginning of the nineteenth century the duties of consuls were extremely wide-ranging and at the end of the century they had grown even more. It is this combination of so many duties, economic, political, social and cultural, in one official representative that explains why states appointed consuls and why their number increased so rapidly during the nineteenth century. By combining so many different duties the consul was a relatively efficient, reliable and cheap institution. It furthermore explains why small states in particular appointed many more consuls compared to the number of inhabitants than large states.

Consuls in International Relations

A consul is an official representative of a state who is entitled to exercise consular functions in the territory of another state.[31] In contrast to a consul, an ambassador is the official representative of the head of state to another head of state and his main duties are political. While there is only one ambassador, there are usually several consuls from a state in a foreign state. Until the early twentieth century, the diplomatic and consular services of Western states remained separated. While the diplomatic service was primarily the domain of the nobles, the consuls mostly came from the upper class of society, including wealthy merchants.

The main peacetime tasks of a consul are to assist fellow countrymen, to further the development of trade, and to foster the friendship between the two states. He is appointed by mutual agreement, usually after ratification of a commercial treaty or consular convention. A state can refuse a foreign consul or ask for a replacement. The appointment is formalized when the sending state requests an exequatur and the receiving state provides one, although this was not the case everywhere.[32] An exequatur, also known as *lettre de provision, commission consulaire* or *letter patent*, is a formal document authorizing the consul to perform his duties. These consular duties and powers are limited to a certain place or region and the geographical limits are specified in the exequatur. Outside his place or region the consul has no formal authority.

Once a consul is accepted, he is entitled to certain privileges, exemptions and immunities, although these are not the same as those of ambassadors or other diplomatic representatives.[33] The consular privileges include the right to display the national flag on the consulate; exemption from certain (local) taxes, customs duties and military service; and protection from the receiving state. The consul and the consulate are furthermore protected against visitations by authorities of the foreign government. Entering a consulate without permission is considered a major breach of trust and a violation of the international law.[34]

At the Congress of Vienna the attending Western states agreed on the hierarchical ranking of diplomats, but they did not consider the ranking of consuls. During the first half of the nineteenth century, there was much confusion about the precise title, duties and powers of the consuls. This led to many deliberations between states, making the work of consuls rather difficult, especially in non-

Western states. After the 1850s, the privileges and authority of the consuls were gradually codified and by 1900 most recognized states accepted these. The hierarchy of diplomats in the nineteenth century was as follows: ambassador (legate or nuncio), envoy, minister plenipotentiary, minister resident, Chargé d'Affaires (replacing the ambassador during his absence).[35] For the consuls the hierarchy was: consul general, consul, vice-consul, consular agent and commercial agent. The lower-ranking vice-consuls reported to the consuls, who kept the consul general informed. The consul general communicated with the ambassador, who maintained contact with his own government and the foreign government. During the nineteenth century, however, this hierarchy was not always obeyed. Consuls and consuls general sometimes wrote directly to their government, even when there was an ambassador present. In many states in the Middle East, Africa and East Asia, and even South America, Western governments did not appoint an ambassador during the nineteenth century, because it was too expensive or the economic interests too unimportant. They wholly relied on their consuls general, and when no consul general was appointed, even on their consuls. States preferred appointing compatriots, but when no suitable candidate was available, they selected non-nationals: either a native or a foreigner, often from another Western country. At the end of the nineteenth century, appointing foreigners became less usual because of the growth of nationalism in many Western states. In addition to consuls there existed in the nineteenth century a whole range of officials with similar tasks bearing different names: consular agent, commercial agent, special agent, executive agent and even secret agent. They were often seen and addressed as consuls, but in many cases they had not received an exequatur and were therefore not officially consul according to the law of nations.

There are two categories of consuls: the salaried consul (*consul missi* or professional consul) and the unsalaried consul (*consul electi* or honorary consul). In the nineteenth century the distinction was not absolute: some consuls received a salary, but because it was considered insufficient to maintain a decent living were allowed to conduct business. Consuls that were also active traders were called merchant-consuls. Consuls general did not trade, at least not officially, while vice-consuls usually traded.[36] During the nineteenth century, many businessmen complained about unfair competition from the merchant-consuls. In 1835, Thomas de Grenrier de Fonblanque, British consul in East Prussia, remarked:

> The priority of intelligence which, especially at distant stations, has often been afforded to British consuls is still remembered as a cause of many unfair advantages being gained over other merchants. For example, a war announced with one country, revived intercourse with another; an increase of duty upon a particular kind of merchandize, or a premium on its importation, amounted to a faculty of pre-emption, and enabled the favoured individual to take the largest benefit, and to reject the loss upon the uninformed mass of merchants.[37]

These complaints convinced governments to replace merchant-consuls with salaried consuls. The process and pace of modernization of the consular services differed per country. As A. Broder explains, France introduced salaried consuls, examinations and training before 1800.[38] In other Western countries this took much longer, often until the 1910s or 1920s.

The status of consuls and especially merchant-consuls was usually low, but normally a sufficient number of candidates applied for a vacancy. Businessmen valued the status associated with the consular function and many believed that it would be beneficial for their own business activities. Their real motives may have been much more mundane, like becoming rich or securing a stable income. The growth of the civil service in Western states increased the opportunity for government employment with salaries and allowances. Once appointed, most consuls found it hard to live off the salary, mainly because they were not prepared to give up their lifestyle. They frequently complained and requested a higher salary, but often their letters remained unanswered.

According to a publication of the US Department of State (1922), the duties of consuls 'are so varied and multifarious that it is impossible to describe them briefly', because the consular regulations contained 'upward of 3,000 paragraphs'.[39] The duties and functions of consuls during the nineteenth century can be summarized in three main categories: (a) in relation to their own government, (b) in relation to their fellow countrymen and (c) in relation to the foreign government.[40]

The duties and functions in relation to their own government were most varied and consisted of writing reports (at least annually, sometimes on special requests), keeping records of all communication to and from their government, recording the arrival and departure of ships, and registering all seamen (shipped, discharged, sick and deceased) and collecting fees for their services. An additional task was to show the flag to defend the status and honour of one's country.[41] During war consuls furthermore gathered political and military intelligence, such as the movement of naval ships and the commissioning of new battleships. During the Napoleonic Wars in Europe, Thomas Barclay (1753–1830), British consul general for the Eastern States in New York, reported on the arrival and departure of French naval ships, including the whereabouts of Jérome Bonaparte (1784–1860), Napoleon's younger brother, during his short stay in the US.[42] The annual reports not only provided news about political and economic developments, besides statistics on trade and shipping, but additionally suggestions for new commercial activities or for improvements of existing products.[43] The US consul in Frankfort, Germany made several suggestions to bicycle manufacturers that increased the export of US bicycles.[44] His colleague in Scotland explained that the harvesters produced in the US had to be adapted, as 'they cut on the right side while the Scots wanted one that cut on the left'.[45]

The consular reports in addition made entrepreneurs receptive to differences in customs, standards (e.g. weights), and preferences in style and culture (e.g. colour, tastes and smells):

> In Columbia there is no sale for quiet patterns, and bright purple is the favourite color, as is the case in Venezuela where fancy prints on a white ground have a vast sale. In Hayti mauve is the popular color; in Singapore fast Turkey red.[46]

There existed numerous differences on how trade was conducted and different methods of packaging and transport. The Chinese carried cargo on a bamboo pole, but in Persia packaging needed to be convenient for transport by camels. The reports of the consuls naturally varied in quality and detail and much depended on how much time the consuls spent on collecting the necessary information. Robert Creighton Murphy (1827–88), the US consul in Shanghai, went to great lengths to describe the current situation in this port in 1855. He furthermore reported on the problems of American traders in other Chinese treaty ports, the need for treaty revision, and Chinese attitudes towards Western merchants.[47] To improve their contents governments changed the consular regulations and stipulated on which matters the consuls needed to report.[48] The annual reports, or summaries thereof, appeared in newspapers and magazines or were printed by the government. They contained an enormous amount of information, although not all of them were up to date or provided reliable statistics. This was not always the fault of the consul: they often depended on the cooperation and quality of statistics provided by foreign governments.

The second category consisted of functions and duties in relation to their fellow countrymen. It included issuing passports and visas, and various notary acts, like registering marriages (including mixed marriages), births and deaths, and property. Consuls furthermore frequently acted as a post office, accepting letters and parcels to be sent home or coming from home to be distributed. Many duties related to matters of trade, although not all nationals were traders, but additionally included sailors, soldiers, tourists, clergy and missionaries, and artists. Consuls vigorously guarded the provisions contained in the commercial treaties, including the duties on import and export, the use of bonded warehousing and free ports, measurements, weights and scales, coinage and payments, the right to lease or buy land, build houses and storage facilities and the use of burial grounds. An important duty of consuls was the consular courts and in some cases acting as policemen, although most had no legal training. According to the British consul in Shanghai, Harry Parkes (1828–85), this did not pose a real problem, because settling business disputes required only common sense.[49] Besides these normal activities, consuls were required to look after troublemakers (e.g. drunks), stranded seamen, bankrupt traders and sick and other destitute countrymen. In serious circumstances, they required prisons, but most consulates were not equipped with these. Instead, consuls used handcuffs to temporarily detain criminals. In most cases the offenders were simply sent back home, but consuls could hardly prevent them from returning on the next available ship.

The third and final group of duties is related to the foreign government. Although most people associate consuls solely with economic matters, in the nineteenth century they had important political and judicial powers. This, as was already explained, applies mainly to the Middle East, Africa and East Asia where consuls enjoyed full extraterritoriality. Consuls often dealt directly with local authorities and, when there was no resident ambassador, sometimes even state officials. In some cases, they cooperated with other consuls, because this was more successful, particularly when backed by some naval force. In some instances they even concluded treaties with foreign states, although these duties are usually connected to ambassadors.

Research Questions and Structure of the Book

Although the 'origin of the consulate antedates the establishment of permanent embassies', its history is far less studied.[50] Diplomatic historians are predominantly interested in ambassadors and have neglected the consular service, because it is believed that they only deal with minor subjects like business, and not high politics. The existence of consuls is acknowledged but not seriously studied.[51] Scholars of international relations deal with diplomacy, mostly with ambassadors, but few are intrinsically interested in history. The exception is here the English School of international relations. These scholars have studied the global expansion of the European system of states.[52] World historians and global historians have shown surprisingly little interest in the tools of diplomacy, and especially in consuls.[53] T. Kuran devoted the last chapter of his book to discuss the lack of consuls in Islamic countries. He argues that because they did not use consuls, Islamic businessmen lacked consular protection when travelling to foreign countries and this hindered economic growth, particularly foreign trade.[54] This is, however, difficult to prove.

Business historians have equally neglected the role of consuls, certainly as far as international business in the nineteenth century is concerned. In 1981 the British journal *Business History* contained several contributions based on consular reports as a possible source for business historians, but this had little effect. Until the 1970s, the history of consuls was a neglected subject, except for the early modern period.[55] During the Seventh International Economic History Congress (IEHC) of 1978 in Edinburgh, a session was scheduled on the consuls, but most of the papers were never published.[56] From the 1990s a growing number of articles appeared in journals dealing with consuls or using their reports as a source. Recently J. Ulbert, G. Le Bouëdec and L. Prijac edited two volumes on the history of consuls: one volume is devoted to the early modern period and the other to the nineteenth century.[57] In early 2011, J. Melissen and A. M. Fernández published an edited volume on the history of consular services in several countries.[58]

The present study builds on the existing publications, but broadens the perspective geographically. Although consuls received a copy of the existing consular regulations of their country when they were appointed, their precise function and duties depended on where they were posted. In 1842 Lord Palmerston (1784–1865) explained that 'the duties varied according to the place and the country in which the consul had to act, and from time to time, according to the circumstances under which he might be placed'.[59] Because the consuls and the system of international relations in Europe are already well studied, this book will look at consuls in the Middle East and North Africa, East Asia, the Americas and sub-Saharan Africa. Western countries in the nineteenth century mainly include Europe and the new republics in the Americas, while non-Western countries include the Middle East, East Asia and Africa.[60]

A second difference is the multidisciplinary approach. This book blends insights from academic specializations, particularly business history, world history and international relations, because I believe that they can contribute to a better understanding of the role of consuls. The main research questions are: did the institution of consuls contribute to the development of global capitalism between 1783 and 1914? What changes occurred in the consular services of Western states in this period? What role did consuls play in the development of international relations? How did consuls cope with the different environments and systems of international relations? To answer these research questions a variety of sources has been used. The primary sources include archives (mainly for the history of Dutch consuls), contemporary publications such as published reports, consular regulations, memoirs, diaries and governmental records.[61] Secondary sources include scholarly books and articles in journals and edited volumes.

This study will concentrate on the 'long nineteenth century': *c.* 1783 until 1914.[62] During this period European states lost most of their colonies in the Americas, except for the Caribbean, but they gained new colonies and possessions in the Middle East, Africa and East Asia. Business historians, like G. Jones, have analysed how the global economy and international business, particularly trading houses and multinational firms, expanded with the opening of new markets.[63] This period also witnessed the rise of several new states that eventually became empires. The periodization is additionally related to the focus on consuls from Great Britain, the Netherlands, the US and Germany. These countries were selected to provide a geographical range, besides offering an opportunity to discuss countries that already employed consuls before the nineteenth century (Great Britain, the Netherlands and the separate German states before the unification in 1871) and a country that was relatively unfamiliar with consuls: the US. While Great Britain and the Netherlands were already states and maintained large empires before 1800, the US and Germany were young states and would not become empires until 1900. The relative power of these states and empires changed in the long nineteenth century and this affected their consuls. Specific cases on consuls provide a more in-depth analysis. The selection of these cases was determined by the availability of sufficient (primary and secondary) sources, their national background and the difficulties consuls faced in different conditions.

Chapter 1 starts with a short introduction on the history of consuls before 1800, and then provides an overview of the consular services of Great Britain, the Netherlands, the US and Germany in the nineteenth century. A major transition before 1800 was related to the appointment of consuls. Before the mid-seventeenth century they were selected by merchants as their representative, thereafter the state began appointing consuls and they came to represent the state and no longer a specific group of merchants. In the nineteenth century, other important changes took place in the consular services: the selection of consuls was more and more based on qualifications (merit) and examinations and not on political patronage, a growing number received some training and they received a state salary. The modernization of the consular services during the nineteenth century exemplifies the growing importance states attached to the consuls.

The next four chapters discuss consuls in different parts of the world. Chapter 2 covers the Ottoman Empire and its dependencies in Northern Africa (the Barbary Coast) and Egypt. In this region consuls operated under the Islamic system of international relations that was quite different from the prevailing European system. In the Far East, discussed in Chapter 3, consuls confronted yet another system of international relations: the Sino-centric system. Consuls were not recognized until the opening of East Asian states for international trade and the treaties signed after the 1840s. The specific conditions in East Asia demanded much of the consuls, particularly protecting the treaty provisions on free trade. Chapter 4 discusses North and South America. This was yet another environment, although institutionally much more similar to Europe than the Middle East and East Asia. Decolonization, first in North America and from the 1810s in the Spanish possessions in South America, opened up these areas for international trade. As a result, many new consulates were opened and the number of consuls expanded. In sub-Saharan Africa, as discussed in Chapter 5, the anti-slavery campaign and the colonization of African territory by European powers were the main developments, practically ending with the Berlin Conference (1884–5). By the mid-nineteenth century, Western states accepted consuls from other Western states in their colonies. This further stimulated the growth of the number of consuls, although the position of foreign consuls was not always easy.

1 THE HISTORY OF THE CONSULAR INSTITUTION

This chapter traces the history of consuls in Europe. Before the nineteenth century, a major change in the consular institution occurred in Europe after extraterritoriality was limited. While consuls were previously elected by their fellow traders, after about 1650 rulers increasingly claimed the right to appoint consuls, although advice from traders was still sought. Consuls in Europe in addition lost their political and judicial powers, keeping only their economic duties. In the nineteenth century, further changes occurred when European governments modernized their consular services. They introduced examinations to select candidates, provided some basic training and merchant-consuls were gradually replaced by salaried consuls. The goal of the modernization was to make the consular service a more professional instrument of government policy.

Consuls before the Nineteenth Century

The origins of consuls or representatives with similar duties are hard to determine, because they are found in many parts of the world where groups of foreign merchants temporarily resided to trade. These traders, as J. Zourek reminds us, enjoyed extraterritoriality, making it possible to choose a representative.[1] Apparently, the Egyptians in the thirteenth century BCE offered foreign merchants protection and allowed them to worship their own gods. King Amasis (579 BCE–526 BCE) tempted Greek merchants to settle in the port of Naucratis (Nile Delta) by offering them the right to be judged by their own magistrates and according to their own laws and customs. The Greek institution of *proxeni* resembled the modern consul in some functions, because these Greek officials looked after foreigners.[2]

The growth of international trade during the Commercial Revolution (950–1350) in Europe increased the need to appoint consuls.[3] Italian city-states appointed consuls, carrying different names like provost, syndics or *bailo*.[4] The use of consuls spread to other parts of the Mediterranean and during the Crusades (1095–1291) to the Levant.[5] In the thirteenth and fourteenth century consuls appeared in northern Europe, including the Hanseatic League (known as *Ältermänn*) and England. By the sixteenth century, consuls were present in the major European ports and commercial towns. From the middle of the seventeenth century European rulers claimed sole sovereignty and jurisdiction within their realm and accepted no higher authority, including foreign consuls with extraterritorial powers.[6] The merchants no longer selected their representatives, but the ruler claimed the sole right to appoint consuls. From the seventeenth century, the consular institution became more public and national in character.[7] At the same time, the diplomatic corps gained in importance following the Treaty of Westphalia that eventually established the European system of states, the law of nations, including permanent embassies and territorial sovereignty.[8] As a result the main duty of consuls in Europe was related to commerce.

The Modernization of the Consular Services

After losing most of their colonies in the Americas from the 1780, in the nineteenth century the European states expanded their empires in Africa and Asia. Control of foreign trade became more important than occupying territory. The area under colonial rule in 1830 was 8.2 million square kilometres and in 1913 it had increased to 53.2 million square kilometres. The total number of people under colonial rule increased in the same period from 205.6 to 724.2 million.[9] New imperial powers, besides England, France, Spain, Portugal and the Netherlands, included Belgium, Italy and Germany. Before 1914, the United States and Japan joined the group of colonial powers.[10] Until about the mid-nineteenth century, the European powers perceived their colonies as exclusively promoting the economy of the motherland, and merchants from the motherland were therefore privileged above foreign merchants. Foreign traders were welcomed, but paid higher duties on imports and exports. Most Western states did not recognize foreign consuls in their colonies. This policy changed when the number of Western colonies in Africa and Asia expanded and the need to appoint consuls in these colonies grew.

To gain access to markets Western states used different instruments, ranging from diplomacy to military force. The diplomatic instrument used was the negotiation of bilateral treaties of friendship (or amity) and commerce that contained provisions for the appointment of ambassadors and consuls. For the globalization of business in the nineteenth century, this was of vital importance, but the social status and reputation of consuls were often low compared to ambassadors. Three problems in particular, which were gradually resolved, affected the consular service in the nineteenth century. First, the selection process was based on patronage: rulers appointed personal or political friends, who were sometimes recommended by relatives and these were not necessarily the best possible candidates. The second problem was the almost complete lack of formal instruction and training. Lastly, there was the problem of remuneration: should they receive a state salary or were they allowed to trade while they acted as consul? Imperialism, the growth of international trade and strong competition between Western states increased the importance of having qualified and professional consuls. Western governments consequently modernized their consular service to better meet the requirements of the time.

Great Britain

The British consular service, write A. W. Ward and G. P. Gooch, grew 'largely unperceived like most English institutions'.[11] Despite its global trading interests, the British Foreign Office wasn't founded until 1782 and only from 1825 did it assume responsibility for all British consuls. In 1830 the Foreign Office created a Consular Department to handle the growing number of messages, requests and instructions sent to and coming from British consuls. In 1740 there were only fifteen consuls, eleven working in the Mediterranean, but fifty years later the number of consuls had increased to forty-six, including eleven in Western Europe and three in the US.[12] Between 1814 and 1824 the number of consuls rose from 57 to 107, including consuls in the new independent states in South America. By 1900 their number had risen to 710: 260 salaried and 450 unsalaried consuls.[13]

The growth in the number of consuls was accompanied by the establishment of specialized branches: the General Consular Service, the Levant Consular Service and the Far Eastern Service. The consuls of the General Consular Service were located in Western countries, and their main task was therefore economical. They had no political or judicial powers and this branch numbered a large number of unsalaried or honorary consuls.The General Consular Service, says P. Byrd, had by far the lowest status and it was considered as a place of refuge for 'the lazy and incompetent who had some claim on the Secretary of State's patronage'.[14] The consuls of the Levant Service and Far Eastern Service usually received a salary and more attention was paid to their training, including mastering several foreign languages. They had a higher status and enjoyed more privileges within the Foreign Office.

The consuls of the Levant Service were the successors of those originally appointed by the Levant Company (1581), a chartered company taken over by the British government in 1825. The Levant Service expanded in 1836 after the Foreign Office took over the consulates on the Barbary Coast from the Colonial Office. The Levant Service itself was not formed until 1877, but soon became the most expensive and largest branch. The functions of these consulates, D. Platt explains, 'were mainly political and judicial, and the consulates in Morocco commercial to some extent, but again very largely political and judicial'.[15] The Middle East gained in geopolitical importance after the 1870s when Britain focused its foreign policy more on Egypt and the Suez Canal to preserve the connection with India and was less interested in maintaining the integrity of the Ottoman Empire.

The Far Eastern Service was established in 1834 after the abolition of the East India Company. Consuls selected for the Far Eastern Service were first appointed as student-interpreters for two years, before they could become consuls. They received a salary and were not allowed to trade. Because British investments in China were very large and many important companies were engaged in this trade, they 'relied heavily on the consuls for protection'.[16]

The social background of British consuls remained rather diverse and included 'dandies, explorers, archaeologists, soldiers, and men of letters'.[17] One explanation was the lack of formal requirements, but the main cause was the prevailing system of patronage or political appointments of consuls. This led to many complaints about incompetent people being appointed. The Consular Advances Act (1825) attempted to create a single civil service with qualified and salaried officials, but the changes were suspended in 1829 because of the need to economize on the budget. Most consuls complained that they could not live off the state salary (if they received one). Much depended, however, on the standard of living they preferred. English gentlemen, Platt notes, were usually not prepared to adapt to local conditions, although this would have been much cheaper.[18] In 1914 consul Ernest Holmes in Shimonoseki (Japan) wrote: 'One cannot live in Japanese style. That is impossible for Europeans.'[19] To supplement their income, British consuls were allowed to work as an agent for the London insurance company Lloyds, the post office or the major shipping lines.[20]

Despite the low status of the consular service, compared to the diplomatic service, the meagre salaries and limited possibilities for promotion, the British government had no difficulty finding sufficient applicants.[21] Obviously, certain posts were more popular than others: Lisbon was considered one of the most interesting posts and a vacancy for the post in Bordeaux attracted 130 candidates. This depended on the prevailing climate and the workload of each post, and also on business opportunities, if the consul was allowed to continue to trade.

Several parliamentary committees investigated the consular service and recommended changes: new regulations, selection based on formal qualifications, offering state salaries, formal training, examinations and regular inspections of the consulates. The Select Committee of the House of Commons on Consular Establishment (1835) advised amending the existing instructions to include the submission of a full report at least every six months. Selections of these reports were to be printed and made available to the general public. In March 1842, the House of Commons again debated the Consular Service. Benjamin D'Israeli (1804–81) believed that the distinction between political and commercial functions, split between diplomats and consuls, had 'no foundation; that it was fanciful and arbitrary; incapable of definition, and defying analysis'.[22] In Britain, commerce was the principal source of wealth and a public interest of the highest class, and therefore the two functions constantly blended, with consuls performing economic and political duties. D'Israeli supported his argument with examples from the Ottoman Empire and the new Spanish American republics. He proposed merging consular and diplomatic services, but other speakers disagreed and saw no reason for fundamental changes. Lord Palmerston (1784–1865) felt that 'taking the consular body as a whole, there was not a more able or efficient body in the service of any country in Europe'.[23]

After the 1870s the pressure to reform the consular service increased because of the general economic depression, the growing competition with Germany and the US, and declining British exports to the colonies. In 1872 the Foreign Office took over the main responsibility for overseas commerce from the boards of trade and created a Commercial Department. British businessmen more frequently contacted their consuls for commercial information on unprotected markets, but they felt that many consuls were not up to the task.[24] The Report of the Committee of the House of Commons of the Consular Service (1872) created two groups: salaried and unsalaried consuls. Salaried (or career) consuls were barred from trading. However, by 1900 there were still British consuls and vice-consuls that received a salary and traded on their own account. Most of the unsalaried consuls were foreigners in British service. With the rise of nationalism at the end of the nineteenth century, the position of these foreigners raised many protests. The Foreign Office, however, reported in 1903 that most of them provided useful services 'and, being almost always themselves businessmen, furnish excellent reports on commercial subjects'.[25]

In the early twentieth century, the growing separation of consuls from the business community led to much criticism from British businesses.[26] The Walrond Committee, chaired by Sir W. H. Walrond (1849–1925), recommended several changes that were incorporated in the law of 1903 regulating the British Foreign Office. This included a system of inspection, rationalization of salaries, and admission to the service by limited competition with a preference for men with commercial experience. This improved the awareness of consuls for the needs of British business. Increasingly they helped individual British firms that were competing with European companies in foreign markets. The Consular Instructions of 1914, however, did not allow consuls to provide information to a British company that was competing with other British companies. The President of the Associated Chambers of Commerce complained that the Consular Service lacked men with commercial experience. The Royal Commission on the Civil Service, however, concluded in 1914 that no further reorganizations were necessary. It did recommend introducing open competition in all branches of the service and improving the salaries, because the low payment did not encourage businessmen to enter the Consular Service. In 1943 the Consular Service and the Diplomatic Service merged into one Foreign Service.[27]

The Netherlands

J. Ulbert and L. Prijac see the Dutch consular service as a newcomer because the United Kingdom of the Netherlands (1814–30) was a new state.[28] However, as A. E. Kersten and R. van der Zwan have shown, the Dutch were using consuls from the early days of the Republic of the Seven United Netherlands (1581–1795).[29] The Dutch Republic maintained a dense consular network, although its foreign trade and political status gradually declined in the eighteenth century. In 1795 there were about seventy-seven consuls. The French Revolution (1789) and the Napoleonic Wars severely disrupted Dutch commerce and shipping. From 1806 until 1813, the Netherlands was part of France and in 1810 all consuls and ambassadors lost their commission. After the establishment of the United Kingdom of the Netherlands, the number of consuls quickly increased. According to C. B. Wells, King William I (1772–1843) appointed many new consuls 'to present his country to the outside world as a near-great power'.[30] In January 1814 the government issued new consular regulations that were altered in 1816, 1818 and 1846, when consuls were appointed in ports along the Rhine (e.g. Frankfort, Mannheim and Strasbourg).[31] In 1830 the number of consuls had increased to about 140 and in 1848 the Netherlands had 15 permanent diplomatic posts, some covering more than one country, and about 170 consulates. In 1887 there were 505 consuls and in 1900 there were 537.[32] Their chief duty was to protect Dutch shipping and commerce. They were expected to report regularly, but this was not enforced. Throughout the nineteenth century, the Netherlands mostly employed consuls that received no pay but lived on the fees and private trade. Applicants therefore had to be wealthy or commercially active. They also needed some status within the business community, because most consuls were appointed after consulting business organizations like the Chambers of Commerce.

The supervision of Dutch consuls was shared until 1862 by two ministries: Foreign Affairs and Colonies. The majority of the Dutch consuls in Europe and the US were administered by the Ministry of Foreign Affairs. They received no salary, but were allowed to trade and collect fees from captains and traders for their services. Depending on their post, whether a demanding port or quiet town, the fees could form a substantial part of their income. The Ministry of Colonies was responsible for consuls in the Middle East, Africa and South-East Asia. In 1814 there were about eleven consuls in the Ottoman Empire (including the Barbary Coast). They received a salary and had diplomatic and judicial duties based on the treaties negotiated with the sultan from 1621 onwards. From the 1850s, new consuls were appointed in China, Japan and Siam. These were predominantly merchant-consuls and in the beginning included many foreigners, because few Dutch merchants resided in these areas. These consuls enjoyed extraterritoriality after the negotiating of commercial treaties: they not only had economic powers, but in addition political and judicial powers. This eventually led to the appointment of more salaried consuls from the 1870s. In 1830 there were furthermore about sixteen consuls in Central and South America resorting under the Dutch governor on Curaçao. After the separation of Belgium in 1830, their numbers declined. These consuls had some diplomatic duties, because ambassadors in South American states were not appointed until much later in the nineteenth century.

After 1849, excerpts of the consular reports appeared in the *Nederlandsche Staatscourant*, the official magazine of the Dutch government, and later in separate printed volumes. The reports, frequently a few pages with statistics on the number of arriving and departing ships, were often inaccurate and the information outdated. This led to many complaints by members of Parliament, the Chambers of Commerce and businessmen. Given the sorrowful state of affairs of the Dutch economy in the first half of the nineteenth century, the number of consuls was much too large. Attempts to reduce their number came to nothing because of the successful lobbying of the Chambers of Commerce and politicians in Parliament. One explanation for this was the relatively low costs of the consular service in contrast to the diplomatic service. While the former continued to grow after the 1850s, the number of embassies hardly increased.

From 1862 the Minister of Foreign Affairs was made responsible for all Dutch consuls. Foreign Affairs invested little in training consuls: they only received a written instruction, the printed consular regulations and sometimes an interview with the Minister of Foreign Affairs before they departed. The consular regulations of 1864 required consuls to report at least annually on agriculture, industry, shipbuilding, mining, commerce, shipping, emigration and miscellaneous subjects. Not all consuls regularly sent in their reports, or did so only after many months of delay. The reports, published for sale to businessmen as separate leaflets and volumes after 1865, were written in Dutch, English, French and German. Most unsalaried consuls were foreigners, who could often not write in Dutch, or Dutch citizens living abroad. Kersten and Van der Zwan believe that the consular reports lost their economic value at the end of the nineteenth century.[33] The growing number of complaints from Dutch businesses and Chambers of Commerce seems to confirm this, but the reports were often the only and still the most reliable source of information about many places.

On 18 April 1874 a new act regulated the functions and duties of consuls. Dutch businessmen blocked a further professionalization for another three decades, because the government proposed to cover the salaries of consuls by increasing the fee businessmen had to pay. The act did, however, introduce a compulsory entrance examination, followed by a short period of training at the Ministry of Foreign Affairs. Candidates had to be at least twenty years old and

Dutch citizens. The examination tested their language skills (French, German and English were required); law (private and commercial); history; geography; mathematics; and knowledge of agricultural, industrial and trade products. The Dutch consular service had become an opportunity for a career in government service for educated young men.[34] A new attempt to modernize the consular service in 1906 came to nothing because of differences of opinion between the Ministry of Agriculture, Industry and Trade and the Ministry of Foreign Affairs.[35] The Dutch Consular Service and Diplomatic Service were not combined until after the Second World War.

The United States

For most people in the US, domestic affairs were of paramount importance during the nineteenth century. The share of foreign trade in the US economy was relatively small and as a result of this, the Department of State, including the consular service, remained rather feeble except in periods of political crisis. Many politicians believed that new means of transport and communication, including steamships, telegraphy and underwater cables, would soon render most of the diplomatic and consular service obsolete. Others felt that maintaining numerous permanent embassies and consular posts was simply too expensive. This attitude is clearly reflected in the institutional history of the American consular service and in the lack of scholarly interest in the subject. J. F. Matthews attributes this also to the nature of the consular powers and duties: they deal primarily with the more mundane commercial and maritime matters in seaports, in contrast to the high politics and related social intercourse of ambassadors located in the capitals.[36]

After the American Revolution (1776–83) the US was heavily in debt and to survive as a sovereign state it was necessary to stimulate foreign trade. Their traders were, however, no longer protected by the British Navy and consuls. The US government was required to develop a diplomatic and consular service and to conclude commercial treaties. Before 1800 it concluded treaties with France (1778), the Netherlands (1782), Sweden (1783), Prussia (1785), Morocco (1786), Great Britain (1794), Spain (1795), Algiers (1795), Tripoli (1796) and Tunis (1797).[37] E. Youngquist believes that these treaties were important instruments to protect US merchants from foreign discrimination and privateering.[38] The treaty of amity and commerce between the US and France of 1778 included the right to appoint consuls, vice-consuls, agents and commissaries in each other's ports.[39] In January 1781 Congress appointed Thomas Barclay (1728–93), a merchant from Philadelphia but resident in France, as the first US consul in Europe.[40] In 1783, Barclay became consul general with the authority to appoint vice-consuls and consular agents in French ports. He furthermore negotiated a treaty of peace and friendship with Morocco (1786), which clearly demonstrates the mixture of commercial and political duties of American consuls in these early years. The first consuls received salaries, but already in 1786 this policy was abandoned when Congress appointed an unsalaried consul for Canton in

China: Major Samuel Shaw (1754–94) (see p. 63). A problem for the US consuls was that they represented a republic. Few royals in Europe, Africa or Asia appreciated or understood the republican system. As a result, the status of the US consuls has usually been lower than those of Great Britain or France.[41] Nonetheless, by January 1795, there were five consuls general, twenty-five consuls, eight vice-consuls and two commercial agents in twelve countries. The number of consuls continued to grow: in 1830 there were 141 (including two consuls general) and in 1846 there were 178. In the early twentieth century the number of US consuls had increased to 566: 63 consuls general, 241 consuls and 262 consular agents. In 1922 there were about 457 consuls.[42]

Between 1775 and 1789, a committee was responsible for American foreign affairs, but from 1789 the Department of State, headed by a Secretary of State, assumed responsibility. After the reorganization of the department in 1836, a Consular Bureau was established until 1870, along with a Diplomatic Bureau and Home Bureau. John Jay (1745–1829), Secretary for Foreign Affairs from 1784 until 1790, reported to Congress on the need of a consular service on 19 September 1785. He proposed to appoint a small number of salaried consuls general that were not allowed to trade. The consul general could appoint consuls who received no salary but were allowed to trade. Jay furthermore suggested supplying a resident US minister with the additional powers of consul general, because that would save even more money. Nationality was not important, because there were few resident US merchants in foreign countries.

In November 1788 the US Minister in France, Thomas Jefferson (1743–1826), signed a consular convention with France. Before his appointment as Secretary of State in 1790, Jefferson had become familiar with the commercial and other duties of consuls in France and valued their work for US businessmen abroad.[43] After only three months in office as Secretary of State he appointed eight new consuls, 'and by the latter part of August, 1790, sixteen consular officers, six consuls and ten vice consuls had been appointed'.[44] The US was very keen to appoint consuls in the European possessions in the Americas, Africa and Asia, but the European powers did not accept foreign consuls in their colonies. In late 1790 Jefferson reported to Congress that 'the experiment of establishing consuls in the colonies of European nations has been going on for some time, but as yet we cannot say it has been formally and fully admitted by any'.[45] In November 1792 the US appointed Benjamin Joy (*c.* 1755–1828) as consul in Calcutta, India. The British East India Company, G. Bhagat notes, simply refused to recognize him, although he was allowed to stay as commercial agent.[46] For the US, gaining access to Western colonies remained a problem, because, at least until the late nineteenth century, it did not have colonies to offer in exchange. In 1815 Congress passed the Reciprocity Act and the US signed treaties based on limited reciprocity with Great Britain (1815) and the Netherlands (1818).[47]

Although Congress passed an act for a diplomatic service (An Act Providing the Means of Intercourse between the United States and Foreign Nations) on 1 July 1790, no funds were assigned for a consular service until 14 April 1792 (An Act Concerning Consuls and Vice-Consuls). This act, altered in 1796 and 1803, regulated the duties of consuls, the fees they could collect and the bond that was required of them. The act remained in force until 1856. Except for those on the Barbary Coast, the consuls did not receive a salary and they were allowed to trade. R. Kark believes that these merchant-consuls were hardly supervised by the Department of State and many 'regarded their jobs primarily as a means for advancing their personal business and commercial activities at the expense of other merchants'.[48] Communication with the Department of State proved difficult for the consuls: in 1836 only 3 clerks worked at the Consular Bureau handling reports and letters from more than 180 consuls. Daniel Strobel Jr (1768–1839), the former US consul in Nantes and Bordeaux, was asked to investigate the complaints of shipping masters in 1831.[49] In his report Strobel noted that many compatriots applied for a consular office hoping to increase their personal wealth only to discover that the post they occupied would cost them money. This led them to engage in all kinds of commercial activities and fraudulent behaviour. Strobel advised providing all consuls with salaries and prohibiting them from engaging in any kind of trade.

Congress did not act on the Strobel Report, but two years later Secretary of State Edward Livingston (1764–1836) wrote an extensive report on the consular service. 'To a nation essentially commercial like the United States, the consular functions are highly important'.[50] The Livingston Report also recommended providing salaries to consuls because it would aid in the protection and extension of commerce. Livingston furthermore hoped, as R. E. Armstrong Hackler writes, that the office of consul would henceforth be filled by 'men of talent, education, and respectability of character, who would be the protector, not the rival of our merchants'.[51] Congress declined to take action on the Livingston Report. A Select Committee of the House of Representatives prepared a new report in 1846 with similar proposals to those of Livingston, but again, Congress did not act. Meanwhile, the expansion of trade with Europe and Middle and South America led to a growth in the number of consuls: from 6 in 1790 to 131 (including only two consuls-general) in 1830 and 160 in 1846.

After the election of President Andrew Jackson (1767–1845) in 1829 the appointment of consuls became part of the spoils system. Each new president would replace consuls (and other civil servants falling under the spoils system) with his own candidates, although in the 1850s and 1860s this did not necessarily mean a political affiliation.[52] From the 1830s the merchant-consuls were thus joined by, as Hackler calls them, the political-consuls, whose appointment would only last four or perhaps eight years. Merchant-consuls usually remained much longer on their post, sometimes even decades. Thomas Aspinwall (1786–1876) was US consul in London from 1815 until 1853 and Alexander Hammett of Maryland held the post in Naples between 1809 and 1861.[53] Many criticized the spoils system, believing that it only produced mediocre consuls. The number of consuls rose not only because of expanding trade relations, but the need to find posts for political friends. Testimonials for a candidate from existing merchants and hints that replacing a non-US consul would stimulate foreign trade, often led to new consuls being appointed. Between 1828 and 1861 many newly appointed consuls indeed replaced non-nationals.[54] Applicants furthermore presented other arguments, including personal interests, knowledge of certain places and language skills, the desire for travel and adventure, and the readiness to endure hardships in remote places. Despite the obvious problems of political appointments, many felt that consuls were important instruments to foster trade. Most consuls were recruited from the major commercial centres and ports in New England and the Middle Atlantic states. Their social background was related to this: they often came from merchant families, although this gradually became less important after the 1860s when other qualifications became more important, like language skills and knowledge of commercial law. Besides merchant-consuls and political-consuls, the number of salaried consuls steadily grew. They viewed the work of consul as a profession and strove to be promoted to higher positions, perhaps even dreamed of becoming an ambassador.[55]

In 1854, the Committee on Foreign Affairs presented a comprehensive report on the consular service and recommended paying salaries to all consuls. In important places they were forbidden to trade, but in minor places they could continue their business, although their salary would then be adjusted accordingly. These proposals were met with much critique from the consuls and led to some modifications. The Act of 18 August 1856 introduced fixed salaries and classified consuls according to their remuneration. The highest groups, Schedule A and B, received a salary and were prohibited to trade, but Schedule C consuls could trade. At the bottom of the list were commercial agents (Schedule C, Class 7). New consular regulations were also introduced (revised in 1857), including the obligation to write an annual report (from 1880 also monthly reports) and maintain consular records and an archive. Excerpts of the reports appeared in print after 1857. Consuls in addition received better instructions and some basic training. These measures were an attempt to improve the quality of the consuls and to create a consular service capable of aiding businessmen to expand their foreign commerce. But before the Civil War (1861–65), Matthews writes, the main motive to apply for a consulship was to increase one's personal wealth and many believed that the title of consul would enhance their social status and business prestige.[56]

In 1868 a joint Select Committee of Congress decided to publish the complete annual reports. Although not all reports were up to date, some consuls went to great lengths to collect relevant information. R. J. Salvucci concludes that 'the U. S. consuls, whatever their personal financial interests, were reasonably unbiased reporters of economic information, or that their biases and interests did not significantly affect the reliability of the information they reported'.[57] In 1894 the State Department distributed copies of consular reports to about 1,200 newspapers and journals, 600 libraries, 150 boards of trade and 3,000 individuals.[58] These reports were frequently referred to in newspapers and periodicals aimed at businessmen.[59]

The Pendleton Civil Service Reform Act (1883) introduced examinations for jobs in the Civil Service, but this did not apply to the diplomatic and consular service. Calls for reform of the Consular Service became louder and more frequent in the 1890s.[60] Between May 1898 and June 1905 fifteen attempts were made to enact bills for consular reorganization.[61] Businessmen, Paterson notes, feared that domestic markets had become saturated after the closure of the frontier, the general depression of world markets and the strong competition from Great Britain and France.[62] The calls for reform were stimulated by the excesses of the spoils system during the presidencies of Grover Cleveland (1837–1908) and William McKinley (1843–1901).[63] In 1897 McKinley replaced 238 of the 272 consuls that were appointed by his predecessor Cleveland. E. Johnson, writing in 1898, complained that until the consular service was reorganized 'it will be impossible for the United States to secure the benefits of as efficient consular services as our commercial rivals in Europe have built up by adhering to the merit system'.[64] Elihu Root (1845–1937), Secretary of State between 1905 and 1909, felt that because of the spoils system the consular service was only used to get rid of 'broken down politicians and to take care of failures in American life whose friends were looking for some way to support them at government expense'.[65] Consuls possessed 'no hope for the future, no enthusiasm in their calling, and rather resented the idea that they were expected to do anything'.[66] Research by H. E. Mattox demonstrates that they were not nearly as incompetent as contemporaries and critics have portrayed them. Many consuls had above average levels of education and possessed 'worldly experience', which was still very low for the majority of US citizens in the 1890s. Most consuls adapted quickly to their new environments and performed their duties under often very difficult circumstances.[67]

In September 1895, President Grover Cleveland (1837–1908) issued an executive order that introduced examinations for consular positions, provided they were salaried from $1,000 to $2,500 annually. Unfortunately, the quality of the examinations was very low and almost every candidate passed. The Lodge Bill (April 1906), prepared by Root and Senator Henry Cabot Lodge (1850–1924), to reorganize the consular service was finally passed by Congress. Root received powerful support for his reform plans from President Theodore Roosevelt (1858–1919).[68] The Lodge Bill introduced numerous changes, including seven consular classes, a system of inspections, examinations and, most importantly, appointments and promotions based on merit. It completely abolished the payment of consuls based on fees and replaced it with state salaries. The Consular School began training consuls from 1907. The Rogers Act (May 1924) merged the Diplomatic Service and Consular Service in one Foreign Service.[69]

Germany

The German Confederation (1814–66) numbered some thirty-nine states. In 1866 several states, including Prussia led by Chancellor Otto von Bismarck (1815–98), formed the North German Confederation (*Norddeutscher Bund*) until they were joined by the southern states in 1871 to establish the German Empire. Before 1871 there was no unified consular service. Most of the larger German states, particularly the trading cities belonging to the Hanseatic League (Lübeck, Bremen and Hamburg), each had their own consular service. The Hansa towns cooperated where and when it was profitable for them to do so, but otherwise upheld their independence. This cooperation was, however, as B. Becker explains, particularly puzzling for foreign states.[70] Although most consulates of the Hansa towns were located in the European seaports and major trading cities, before 1790 they had some consuls in the Ottoman Empire (including the Barbary Coast) and the US.[71] The Hansa towns used consuls because they were much cheaper than permanent embassies. The consuls received no salary, but lived off their own business or accumulated riches.

From the 1820s, the number of Hansa town consulates steadily increased. In 1820 Lübeck had twenty-eight consulates, Bremen twenty-four and Hamburg thirty-one. They showed little interest in opening consulates in the other major German cities. Only Hamburg had a consulate in Berlin and Vienna since the 1820s. The expansion was mainly directed towards the new states in Central and South America, besides the consulates in the US. After Brazil became a kingdom in 1815, the Hansa towns were quick to establish commercial relations. This was important to the towns during the slow process of German unification and the ever growing importance of Prussia. Prussia itself appointed a large number of consuls in Europe and the Americas, including Brazil. Between 1818 and 1865 the number of Prussian consuls increased from 80 to 422.[72] Having consuls in the Americas was beneficial after the middle of the nineteenth century with the start of mass migration from German ports. By 1867 the number of consulates had grown substantially: Lübeck had 202 consulates, Bremen 217 and Hamburg 286. The large number of consuls from the Hansa towns shows that consuls were particularly employed by small states. The Hansa towns lost some of their independence after they joined the *Norddeutscher Bund* which became responsible for the consuls. The idea was to hand over responsibility for the consuls to the new Ministry of Foreign Affairs of the *Norddeutscher Bund,* but some states (including the Hansa towns) opposed this plan. Instead the consular service was supervised by the office of the chancellor (Bundeskanzleramtes). At the same time, I. B. von Berg writes, the office became responsible for all matters of trade and customs in the *Norddeutscher Bund*.[73]

The *Norddeutscher Bund* appointed its own first consuls in early December 1867 and in 1870 there were 438 consuls (salaried and unsalaried) in thirty-eight countries.[74] The *Norddeutscher Bund* enacted new consular regulations in November 1867 and in the following years incorporated most of the consulates of the Hansa towns and all other states.[75] Some consulates of the Hansa towns, however, continued for some time because nobody knew they still existed: their consuls had never produced an annual report. The Consular Law of 1867 required each consul to report annually on trade, shipping and other consular matters, including the number of visas issued, and the death and births of Germans abroad.

After the southern German states (e.g. Baden, Württemberg, Bavaria) joined the *Norddeutscher Bund* to form the German Empire, the last phase of the history of the consular service began. Establishing consulates was, according to the politician B. E. von Bülow in November 1871, 'absolutely necessary'.[76] It was strongly supported by the Hansa towns, who had established extensive trading relations with other parts of the world. Between 1872 and 1914 the total number of German consuls grew from 494 to 688, the number of unsalaried consuls increased from 461 to 533, while the number of salaried consuls increased from 30 to 155. Although the unsalaried consuls still outnumbered the salaried consuls in 1914, the share of the latter increased much faster.[77] The main duty of the consulates was, as Chancellor Bismarck explained in 1881, not only to protect German trade but to promote it where and whenever possible. Initially, the regulations of the *Norddeutscher Bund* were maintained, but in June 1871, the German Empire published its own revised instructions (*Allgemeine Dienst-Instruktion für die Konsuln des Deutschen Reichs*). The German Emperor was made responsible for all German consuls, although he delegated this responsibility to the Ministry of Foreign Affairs. Some previously appointed consuls were transferred to the new service, but many new consuls were selected.

Discussions about the negative impact of having unsalaried consuls combining the office with private trade had already begun in the 1860s. In most places the number of German merchants and size of trade simply did not justify the appointment of salaried consuls.[78] The direct effect of consulates on trade is hard to measure, but Von Berg notes that after 1871 both continued to increase, although this hardly proves that it was related to the work of consuls.[79] Besides trade, foreign investments of the German companies likewise increased and this often stimulated the establishment of new consulates.[80]

The growth in the number of consuls was primarily motivated by political and economic motives, but prestige and status certainly played a role. It was deemed essential for the German Empire to have consuls where other Great Powers had appointed consuls, even if there were no German merchants on the spot and the direct trade was small. This was particularly true for consulates in distant places like China, Japan, and Central and Southern America. Prestige and status furthermore required consulates in some non-Western countries (e.g. the Ottoman Empire and Siam) to be much more luxurious and costly than in Europe, because the social position of consuls was related to their style of living and overall appearance.[81] The German consular service was cheap compared to the diplomatic service. In 1875 the costs of one embassy were 126,923 Mark and one consulate 2,527 Mark and in 1914 these costs were 117,500 Mark and 9,738 Mark.[82] The increase in the number of salaried consuls was mainly in the rank of the consuls. Consuls general were usually placed in major cities and ports, while consuls were selected for less important trading areas. Von Berg notes that existing consulates were often promoted to consulates general when other major countries did the same.[83]

From 1871 until 1914 the Consular Service resorted under the second bureau of the Ministry of Foreign Affairs (the Handelspolitische Abteilung). This separation was criticized because diplomats showed little interests in matters of trade, while the consuls were often poorly informed about political matters that affected foreign trade.[84] The separation between the diplomatic service and consular service reflected and sustained the social background between these groups. Although some consuls, particularly consuls general, were recruited from the German nobility, it was rare for a consul to be promoted to a diplomat. Diplomats had a higher social status than consuls throughout the period before 1914. From the 1890s, the German consuls lost some economic duties to trade specialists (Handelssachverständigen) to stimulate foreign trade in the period of growing international rivalry. Before the First World War, the number of these trade specialists attached to consulates numbered about twelve, including New York, Mexico, Rio de Janeiro, Sidney, Yokohama, Calcutta and Johannesburg.

The Rise of the Career Consul

The preceding analysis of the development of the consular service in Great Britain, the Netherlands, the US and Germany has established the growth of the number of consuls during the nineteenth century (see Table 1.1).

Table 1.1: The number of consuls in selected countries (1790–1914)

	Great Britain	United States	The Netherlands	Germany
1790	46	10	77	
1800		52		
1810		60		
1813				
1814	57			
1818				80*
1820		83		83**
1824	107			
1830		141	140	
1841		152		
1846		178		
1848			170	
1851		197	196	
1860		282	216	
1865				422**
1867				703*
1870				438***
1872				494 (incl. 30 salaried)
1887			505	
1890				
1900	710 (incl. 260 salaried)	566	537	
1905			542	
1914				688 (incl. 155 salaried)

*   Prussia
**   Hanseatic League (Lübeck, Bremen and Hamburg)
***   *Norddeutscher Bund* (from 1872: German Empire)

Sources: Great Britain: D. C. M. Platt, *The Cinderella Service: British Consuls since 1825* (London: Longman, 1971), pp. 10, 14, 54–5. For 1931: G. Stuart, *American Diplomatic and Consular Practice* (New York: Appleton-Century-Crofts, 1952), p. 289; United States: J. W. Rooney Jr, *Belgian-American Diplomatic and Consular Relations 1830-1850: A Study in American Foreign Policy in Mid-Nineteenth Century* (Louvain: Bibliothèque de l'Université, Bureaux du Recueil; Publications universitaires de Louvain, 1969), pp. 16, 229. Includes vice-consuls and consular agents. 1890: R. Kark, *American Consuls in the Holy Land: 1832–1914* (Jerusalem: The Magnes Press, 1994), pp. 51–3. 1931: G. Stuart, *American Diplomatic and Consular Practice* (New York: Appleton-Century-Crofts, 1952), p. 289; The Netherlands: C. A. Tamse, 'The Netherlands Consular Service and the Dutch Consular Reports of the Nineteenth and Twentieth Centuries', *Business History*, 23:3 (1981), pp. 271–7; Germany: I. B. von Berg, *Die Entwicklung des Konsularwesens im Deutschen Reich von 1871–1914 unter besonderen Berücksichtigung der außenhandelsfördernden Funktionen dieses Dienstes* (Cologne: Hundt Druck, 1995), pp. 9, 47–9, 86.

Besides their numbers, the geographical spread increased following the opening of new markets in America, Africa and Asia. Although the available statistics are not wholly reliable, the overall trend is clear. In the first half of the century the unsalaried or merchant-consul dominated the consular service. The selection mechanisms of consuls varied, but patronage was fairly common in many countries. Complaints from other merchants about the poor quality of their consuls and government policy to offer better protection led to attempts to reform the consular service. At the end of the century, the number of salaried consuls had markedly increased, although unsalaried consuls continued to be used. Consuls not only were (better) paid, but in addition received training through special schools. Examinations replaced the selection based on patronage. Most countries furthermore began to inspect their consulates regularly to improve the impact and efficiency of the service. Consuls performing poorly, were corrupt or behaved badly towards local officials were replaced. In most Western countries this professionalization of the consular service was completed before the 1920s.

2 THE MIDDLE EAST AND NORTH AFRICA

Over the long period of its existence, the relationship between the Ottoman Empire (1299–1922) and Western Europe went through different phases depending on their relative strengths. Modern historiography, as presented by D. Gofman and others, presents a more positive view of the Ottoman Empire during the nineteenth century.[1] In the nineteenth century, however, European views of the empire were predominantly negative. Until the mid-nineteenth century, the Ottoman Empire was not considered a civilized state, according to the European standard of civilization, and was excluded from the Family of Nations.[2] This was, says D. Rodogno, sufficient reason for several military interventions for the sake of humanity, civilization and Christianity.[3] Ottoman relations with Europe were guided by Islamic law and customs, but additionally by much pragmatism. This becomes clear from the relationship between natives and foreigners and the role of consuls in Muslim states. Consuls, because they were Christians, were forced to cope with a different system of international relations in the Middle East and North Africa. The Islamic system was based on inequality between states and a clear hierarchy existed, with the sultan in Istanbul at its head. International relations were conducted after concluding treaties that were binding only for as long as the ruler lived. To obtain the privilege of trading, vassal states paid tribute to the sultan or one of his replacements. This required not only paying large sums of protection money, but additionally presenting gifts to the rulers and performing different ceremonies to show submission. At the beginning of the nineteenth century Western states and their consuls accepted these rules, but from the 1820s this was no longer the case. US consuls played an important role in bringing about this change by forcing Islamic rulers to accept Western rules.

Capitulations and Consuls

Islam divides the world in the *Dar ul-Islam* (the House of Islam) and the *Dar ul-Harb* (the House of War). In reality the division is not absolute and many economic, political and cultural contacts have existed throughout history. Non-Muslim merchants, S. Faroqhi explains, could enter the Ottoman Empire without much difficulty and received certain privileges.[4] They were semi-autonomous nations (*millets*), administering and organizing their own education, justice, religion and social activities.[5] Christians wanting to trade could either convert to Islam or obtain a pass (*amān*) that was valid for one year and offered protection and exemption from taxes as a *musta'min* (or bearer of *amān*). However, A. H. de Groot notes that many Westerners stayed longer without obtaining a new pass and by the eighteenth century this had become accepted practice.[6] For certain non-Muslim residents in the Ottoman Empire, including Zoroastrians, Orthodox Greeks, Armenians, Jews and Christians, the situation was different: they were Peoples of the Book (*dhimmīs*). Because they shared prophets and holy places with Islam, they were allowed to live permanently in Islamic societies, but under certain restrictions: they paid a poll tax (*jizya*), besides wearing a sash or belt.[7] In the late 1830s, these restrictions were abolished when all Christians were granted formal legal equality with Muslims, although everyday practice, R. Kasaba reminds us, remained rather different.[8]

The specific conditions of Christians under Islam affected the position of their representatives, including the ambassadors and consuls. Despite objections from the Pope, several Italian city-states concluded commercial treaties with Islamic empires before the thirteenth century. These treaties provided for the stationing of consuls and granted Western merchants a level of extraterritoriality. Later, other Western states concluded similar treaties with the Ottoman Empire. The treaty between France and the Ottoman Empire (1569) guaranteed 'complete freedom of commerce between the two peoples'.[9] It furthermore offered legal equality and protection, freedom of worship and exemption from certain taxes, besides a MFN clause. The ambassador and consuls received patents (*berats*) empowering them to administer their community and adjudicate disputes between their fellow countrymen. The treaty served as a model for subsequent treaties with England, the Netherlands, Prussia and Russia.[10] Faroqhi argues that, besides the desire for foreign commodities, the need for bullion of the Ottoman Empire to finance international transactions explains to a large extent why these privileges were given.[11]

From the perspective of the Ottomans, the treaties were temporary agreements, granted freely and unilaterally, that could be withdrawn at any time and were binding only for as long as the sultan lived.[12] The Europeans, however, C. R. Pennell says, saw the treaties (called Capitulations) as contracts that were legally binding.[13] Renewing and renegotiating the treaties allowed the European states to gradually demand more privileges.[14] Although the treaties were based on reciprocity, Muslim merchants visited the Italian city-states, but rarely northwestern Europe and only a few remained permanently in Christian lands, writes N. Matar.[15] We have already seen that the Ottoman Empire did not use consuls until after the 1850s and the sultan dispatched only ad hoc embassies to Europe because a permanent ambassador would infer equality.[16] It wasn't until the late eighteenth century, T. Naff shows, when the balance of power had already shifted to Europe, that the Ottoman Empire appointed permanent ambassadors.[17]

The nineteenth-century Capitulations contained almost similar regulations regarding the personal, judicial and economic privileges granted to the Western merchants. Personal privileges included the permission to reside in Islamic lands (except the holy cities of Mecca en Medina), freedom to travel by land and sea (including the ports) and freedom of custom, habit and religion. Economic privileges were freedom of some taxes (except merchandise for import and export), and freedom to establish any number and type of business. The judicial privileges included the right to be adjudicated by their ambassador or consul in cases between foreigners of the same nationality; in mixed cases (natives and foreigners) jurisdiction was reserved for Islamic courts, but with the consuls (or his translator, the dragoman) being present.[18] Only written documents could settle disputes between foreigners and natives; oral or verbal agreements in matters of business would no longer suffice. In international business, written contracts slowly replaced trust in people.[19]

Before the nineteenth century, the Capitulations were seen as a sign of the superiority and strength of the Ottoman Empire, but as the empire grew weaker and the Western states became stronger it was more and more regarded as a symptom of political weakness and moral decay.[20] T. Kuran says that the Capitulations contributed to the economic decline of the Middle East after 1800, but Ş. Pamuk disagrees.[21] In 1869 the Sublime Porte, the government of the sultan, presented a memorandum to the Western diplomats in which it was stated that the Capitulations were obstructing the development of Islam. It was an ill-fated attempt to limit the growing power of Western states in the Ottoman Empire. Two years later, the sultan was forced to sign the following protocol:

> That it is an essential principle of the Law of Nations that no Power can release itself from the obligations of a Treaty or modify its stipulations without the consent of the contracting parties by means of an amicable understanding.[22]

The decline of the Ottoman Empire, the result of domestic and foreign developments, contributed to the growing weight and status of the consuls in the nineteenth century.[23] Many consuls lived in stately mansions in centuries old Frankish quarters, near streets called Rue de Consul or large squares named Place des Consul. P. Mansel believes that their behaviour reflected this outer appearance. 'Consuls in Alexandria, and other Levantine cities, behaved as if they were the Emperor of Russia. They were "above everything": their watches, it was said, controlled the sun'.[24] Although commercial relations became increasingly important, a large number of consulates in the Middle East and North Africa existed for mainly political reasons. In 1870, Charles M. Kennedy of the Commercial Department of the British Foreign Office admitted that there were only 551 resident British in 'Asiatic Turkey'. This contrasted sharply with the large number of consulates: in 1852 Great Britain had forty-nine consuls and twenty vice-consuls in the Ottoman Empire.[25] These consuls performed three tasks: preventing violence against Christians, reporting on political unrest with potential wider repercussions, and providing an example for reform of the Ottoman administration.[26] The British consul William R. Holmes believed his duties were: 'to watch over the various movements and impulses of the mixed and hostile races which form the population, and whose condition is a matter of European importance'.[27] Although many Westerners believed that the presence of consuls could prevent potential religious insurrections, they did not stop outbursts of violence. This included the Damascus Massacre in 1860 (see p. 51) and the Bulgarian Horrors in 1875. Increasingly, however, the reports of consuls attracted international attention. The reports of the acting British consul Gerald Henry Fitzmaurice (1865–1939) in Smyrna and Adana on the forced conversions to Islam and massacres of Armenians between 1894 and 1896 received international media coverage and political attention.[28] Extraterritoriality, the bases of Western interference, was not abolished until 1923.[29]

The following cases provide a more in-depth analysis of the role of consuls in the Middle East and North Africa and its very different system of international relations. Although consuls were required to perform a vast amount of different duties, they often found plenty of time to pursue their own interests (e.g. collecting flowers or making excursions). The British consul general Henry Salt (1780–1827) became a passionate collector of Egyptian antiquities that he could sell to European museums. Salt arrived in Egypt during turbulent political times, but he did not find his normal consular duties very inspiring. On the Barbary Coast, part of the Ottoman Empire since the early sixteenth century but becoming practically independent a century later, conditions were rather difficult for consuls. Because Western states already had diplomatic relations with the sultan in Istanbul, they could not appoint ambassadors for the Barbary Coast. The consuls thus performed political, judicial and economic duties, but despite concluding treaties with the rulers in Tunis, Tripoli and Algiers, their position remained precarious. The arrival of consuls from the US eventually led to major changes in the system of international relations, as the case of US consul William Eaton (1764–1811) will demonstrate. From the mid-nineteenth century, Western states frequently intervened in the domestic politics of the weakening Ottoman Empire. This included another duty: protecting Christians, as the case of the Prussian consul Johann Gottfried Wetzstein (1815–1905) will show. Although consuls enjoyed extraterritoriality in the Ottoman Empire, this did not include the holy cities of Mecca and Medina in the Hedjaz. The growing number of pilgrims to the Hedjaz from Western colonies, after the opening of the Suez Canal in 1869 and the introduction of steamships, created problems for Western states wanting to control their colonial subjects when they went on pilgrimage. The Netherlands established a consulate in Jeddah in 1872 to keep an eye on the pilgrims of the Dutch East Indies, but this proved very difficult for the consuls.

Egypt: Henry Salt, Antiquity Hunting and Politics

Napoleon appointed Bernardino Drovetti (1776–1852) as Deputy Commissioner of Commercial Relations of Alexandria in October 1802.[30] In May 1805, he received instructions from his government to abstain from interfering in the political affairs because he was not a diplomat.[31] These instructions, R. T. Ridley reminds us, must have struck him as puzzling because since his arrival, Drovetti had been heavily involved in politics and would continue to be until his departure in 1829.[32] After the defeat of Napoleon, Drovetti was temporarily replaced by Pierre Paul Thédénat-Duvent in November 1815 until his reappointment as consul general in 1821.[33] From 1815 until 1821 Drovetti remained in Egypt as a private citizen and associated himself with French businessmen, while collecting Egyptian antiquities for sale in Europe. This is where he first encountered his British colleague and rival collector Henry Salt.

Drovetti arrived after the failed French attempt to occupy Egypt and Palestine in June 1798 to control the Eastern part of the Mediterranean and the link with India and Asia.[34] A combined British-Ottoman Army forced the French Army to surrender in June 1801 and they left Egypt at the end of 1801, followed by the British Army in 1803. The French occupation and British intervention demonstrated to the European countries the military weakness of the Ottoman Empire.[35] After 1803, Turkish, Albanian and Mamluk forces (a military caste in Egypt and former rulers) tried to gain the upper hand, creating a chaotic and dangerous situation. Consuls and consulates were frequently fired at, forcing their temporarily retreat to the safety of warships in the harbour of Alexandria.[36] Out of this chaos Muhammad Ali (*c.* 1770–1849) emerged as the new leader in June 1805 when the sultan appointed him pasha (viceroy), but his position remained fragile until at least 1815. He ruled Egypt until 1849 and established a new dynasty that would last until 1952.[37]

The French consuls were particularly interested in the British machinations because of their support of the Mamluks. Colonel Ernest Missett (d. 1820), the British consul general in Cairo from 1802 until 1815, was instructed to mediate between the Mamluks and the sultan in Istanbul.[38] Drovetti believed that Muhammad Ali preferred the British 'because they flatter his ambition and satisfy his avarice', besides guaranteeing his political independence.[39] In May 1809 Britain and Egypt concluded a commercial treaty that was very favourable for British traders.[40]

During his long reign, Muhammad Ali courted the major European countries, 'for he was quite erratic in his dealings with European diplomats'.[41] He started an ambitious programme of modernization along Western lines.[42] This was not only advantageous to Egypt and Western businessmen, but also for Muhammad Ali, since he monopolized the most important economic activities (e.g. the sale of cotton). Mansel says that by 1811 he was believed to be 'the richest Pasha in the Ottoman Empire'.[43] But Muhammad Ali's ambitions went much farther than modernizing Egypt; he wanted to create a large empire. In 1831, this already included the Hedjaz (Arabia), the Sudan, Syria and Lebanon. In December 1832 Egyptian forces even reached Kütahya in Anatolia, about 200 kilometres from Istanbul. Russia and France intervened and this resulted in the Treaty of Kütahya (May 1833). Muhammad Ali gave up his possessions in Turkey and in exchange the sultan appointed him pasha in the territories of Hejaz, Crete and Syria. However, in 1838 Sultan Mahmud II (1789–1839) again went to war over Syria. The consuls did their bit. The British consul Richard Wood (1806–1900) is said to have organized a revolt of Syrians, mainly Maronites and Druzes, against the Egyptians.[44] In July 1840 Muhammad Ali surrendered Syria. The Straits Convention (1841) finally settled the Egyptian challenge and the Ottoman Empire had survived its greatest danger supported by European countries that wanted to keep the empire intact.[45]

When the English consul general Henry Salt arrived in Egypt in 1816, the political situation had become more orderly, but he too would interfere in politics. Like other consuls in the Mediterranean, Salt was a passionate collector of antiquities.[46] Manley and Rée even believe that consuls were obliged to go on expeditions to increase British knowledge of other cultures. Collecting antiquities by the consuls was endorsed by Western governments, but certainly not included in the formal list of consular duties.[47] The quest for antiquities, Gunning notes, was stimulated by the opening of national museums (e.g. the British Museum in 1759 and the Louvre in 1793) and the growing rivalry between European states.[48]

Salt, trained as a portrait artist, had visited Egypt during the expedition to the East (1802–6) of Henry George Annesley, Lord Valentia, after he was enlisted as secretary and painter.[49] The expedition took him to India, Ceylon (Sri Lanka), the Red Sea and Abyssinia.[50] Salt returned to Abyssinia (Ethiopia) in 1809 and 1810 on an official government mission to counter the growing French interests in East Africa. Because of these travels Salt was 'better fitted to be a Consul in an Eastern land than most diplomats'.[51] When Missett resigned in 1815 because of failing health, Salt immediately asked some influential friends, including the Sir Joseph Banks (1743–1820) and Lord Valentia, to write to Lord Castlereagh (1769–1822) of the Foreign Office to support his application. According to his friend and biographer John James Halls (1776–1834), the Foreign Secretary 'made up his mind very quickly' after he received strong recommendations in favour of Salt.[52] His appointment is a clear case of patronage: Salt had no prior experience as a businessman and did not have much contact with the British business community. His main interest in a government appointment was the salary that guaranteed financial independence.

On 22 August 1815 Salt bid farewell to his friends, but contrary to his instructions to go directly to Egypt, he embarked on 'a very delightful tour on the Continent'.[53] While waiting in Malta for his passage to Egypt, he noticed the arrival of six vessels from Alexandria belonging to Muhammad Ali laden with grain and beans.

> The trade in corn, which he monopolizes, appears to be enormous. He had several fine vessels of his own, both in this sea and in the Red Sea. With such a man, I should think that a great deal may be done.[54]

On his arrival in Alexandria in late March 1816, Salt was much impressed by the changes he saw since his visit in 1806. There were more than one hundred sailing ships in the port, about one-third of them British. After being briefed by Missett, Salt expected significant trouble from Muhammad Ali, who was 'daily becoming more difficult to treat with and less inclined to pay attention to the rights of European Nations'.[55] He believed that 'it will be a very difficult matter to prevail upon the Pasha to attend to the capitulations, without some interference on the part of the Government'.[56] Salt attributed this to the physical weakness of Missett and the temporarily replacement of the French consul Drovetti.

Because of the plague season in Cairo, Salt had to wait until June 1816 before he had his first interview with the pasha. He got on very well with Muhammad Ali,

> a sensible, and, for a Turk, an extraordinary man. He has taken all the produce of the country in his own hands, and is himself the greatest manufacturer and merchant in the state. His revenue is enormously increased ... and fresh European adventurers are daily flocking in to the country.[57]

He discussed the joint venture of the pasha with the British company Briggs & Company in the trade with India. Muhammad Ali referred to the rebellious Wahhabis in Arabia that interrupted his commerce and asked for British naval protection in the Red Sea. Salt was apparently diplomatic enough not commit to this without further instructions from his government.

Salt rented a home in the Frankish Quarter near Ezbekiah Square that also served as British consulate. He soon discovered that his annual salary of £1,500 would hardly cover ordinary expenses and keep up a certain standard of living as British consul general in Egypt.[58] His expenses included gifts for the servants to celebrate the birthday of King George III. Salt was furthermore forced to entertain and house a growing number of British visitors to Egypt 'whom it would be disgraceful to the National Character to leave in the miserable auberges of Cairo'.[59] In early 1817 Salt complained to the Foreign Office that his salary was 'barely equal to the establishment requisite to support the British character and consequence in this country'.[60] The sudden death of his father in May 1817 left him with £5,000 to settle some of his debts and, more importantly, pursue his hobby: searching for antiquities.[61]

Before his departure, the Society of Antiquaries had asked Salt to search for other fragments of the Rosetta Stone (in British possession since 1801) or similar stones, and to make drawings and casts of interesting objects.[62] Likewise, his previous employer, Lord Valentia, asked Salt to collect antiquities for his home.[63] Gunning explains that Salt had 'no clear or specific indication that part of his official duties should be to help gather antiquities for the British Museum'.[64] For his explorations Salt engaged the Italian Giovanni Battista Belzoni (1778–1823), but the two later disagreed over the discoveries they had made.[65] Besides his own activities as collector, Salt provided many services to British travellers, explorers, scientists and archaeologists, by giving detailed information, securing the required permits and organizing transport facilities. Salt also entertained many British guests, including nobility, civil servants, sea captains, naval and army officers, missionaries and ordinary tourists. In September 1817 the Earl of Belmore, his wife and two sons visited Egypt. Salt wrote that 'I am now setting out with Lord and Lady Belmore up the Nile, on a voyage to Nubia, and expect to be absent three or four months'.[66] Salt took them to see the Pyramids and the pasha. Some colleagues believed that Salt abused his position as consul general to gain permission to excavate solely for his own advantage, 'engaging in a kind of trading monopoly in conjunction with Sig. Drovetti in a manner not very creditable to either the individuals or their Governments'.[67] George Gliddon (1809–57), US vice-consul and merchant in Alexandria, felt that Salt was busier with his 'literary studies, poetry and pictorial sketches' or battling the French consul Drovetti over a 'mummy pit or an idol than with Mehemet Ali's [Muhammad Ali's] Monopolies'.[68] From 1819 Salt started sending his collection to Europe, but the British Museum rejected Salt's asking price. He next sold several objects to the Louvre, but in 1835 an unsold part of the collection was bought by the British Museum for its Gallery of Egyptian Antiquities.[69]

Salt's expeditions to Giza, Thebe, Abu Simbel and Luxor lasted several weeks or months and the daily business of the consulate was apparently taken care of by someone else. Unfortunately, neither Halls nor Manley and Rée discuss his consular work extensively. For Salt his consular duties must have been less exciting than the excavations. In Cairo Salt had under his jurisdiction about 300 British citizens, including many non-Westerners (e.g. Maltese, Ionians), besides a number of Muslims under British protection. Peter Lee, the British consul in Alexandria, handled about the same number of British, but being in a busy seaport he was required to receive numerous sea captains and settle disputes between sailors and captains. Salt did not like the consular work: 'We do our best, sometimes proceeding as far as imprisonment, fining and whipping; but you may be sure we never, however hardened the criminal, or terrible the offence, proceed to the extremity of hanging'.[70] In June 1819, Salt wrote:

> Public business has much increased upon me since I have had the appeals from Alexandria, owing to the great influx of Ionian and Maltese subjects resident here; so that I have been fagged to death, and am not very stout.

In 1820 he provided some more details, writing that he passed not a single day without having to settle an argument or business dispute, and sometimes a more serious offense. After being consul general for several years, Salt had formed a clear opinion about his office and concluded that it was very different from what it is in Europe. He questioned the system of extraterritoriality: 'in these barbarous regions the Consuls are a sort of Kings. Every Consulate *here* is a little Government, and all those residing in the country are considered to be under its exclusive protection'.[71] Only in very severe cases did the pasha interfere by beheading a European, 'but otherwise he leaves everything that concerns our subjects ... to our *wiser* jurisdiction'. The system of Capitulations was strange, one that 'was certainly never in the contemplation of the Government at home'.[72]

The domestic situation increasingly forced Salt in a diplomatic and political role, and his opinion of Muhammad Ali had changed. In June 1818 he wrote: 'The Pasha here talks of conquering Abyssinia some day or other; but *that will never do*; for though bad Christians, that is better than being Mussulmans'.[73] In late 1820 Salt received permission to return to England for his first leave since his arrival to settle some private affairs and to recover his health. But the political disorder, the Greek Rebellion against the Ottoman Empire, made it impossible for him to abandon his post. He blamed the Russian Emperor Alexander I (1777–1825) for stirring up Greek sentiments that might have repercussions for the British:

> the Turks have taken a high tone that will soon make a residence in the Levant scarcely supportable to a European. And what thanks does England get for her kind interference? – None; she is, they say, a true trader, and knows her commercial interests.[74]

In September 1824, Consul Lee suddenly died and Salt was forced to take over his duties in Alexandria. He now had to deal with quarrels between sea captains and sailors, issuing passports and visas, checking ship's papers, collecting consular fees, and settling other disputes between members of the English community. Salt supervised a growing number of protected subjects, including Egyptians, Greek, Maltese and Ionians. Some of them were employed by the British (e.g. as translators), but others simply wanted to benefit from the privileges of the consuls in Islamic countries, including tax exemption. The Foreign Secretary George Canning (1770–1827) instructed Salt to treat them as 'His Majesty's natural born subjects'. Salt found the consulate in Alexandria

> by no means an agreeable post, the duties being more like those of a Bow-street mag-
> istrate[75] than any other Christian office: gales of wind daily, and *gales* among the
> seamen and captains – I have no less than seven seamen in prison at this moment.[76]

He additionally maintained contacts with British companies, including Briggs
& Company and Gliddon & Hayes.

Lee was eventually replaced by John Barker (1771–1849) in October 1826,
a highly experienced consul who had served in Aleppo between 1799 and 1825.
Salt eagerly awaited his arrival: 'that might, perhaps, be the best occasion to talk
about a pension; I have now been here, you will recollect, ten years, amid plague
and amid all sorts of ills'.[77] The appointment of Barker released Salt from the
routine consular duties in Alexandria and he returned to Cairo. By 1827 Salt's
health had deteriorated severely and on 30 October 1827 he died at the age of
forty-eight. In the presence of most of the foreign consuls he was buried in the
garden of his home in Cairo. A cenotaph recalled his mission to Abyssinia, his
explorations in Egypt and his publications.[78]

The Barbary Coast: William Eaton, Changing the Rules

The North African coast, called al-Maghreb ('the west') in Arabic, is better known
in European history as the Barbary Coast.[79] The Ottoman Empire conquered the
area in 1517, except for Morocco that remained an independent kingdom.[80] The
sultan in Istanbul appointed a pasha to rule in his name, assisted by a corps of
Janissaries (elite troops of the sultan). In the early seventeenth century the sultan
lost control over the three provinces and their capitals: Tunis, Tripoli and Algiers.
The Janissaries selected their own rulers and founded their own dynasties with the
sultan as a ceremonial and religious figure. The relationship was never officially
broken and the North African rulers continued to pay tribute to the sultan.[81]

In Europe the Barbary Coast was feared for its pirates, known as corsairs, and
the problem of white slavery: Christians captured and enslaved by Muslims.[82] R.
C. Davis estimates that the total number of white slaves between 1530 and 1780
was about 1 million or perhaps 1.25 million.[83] White women slaves were especially valued because they sold at higher prices than white males. In 1816 there
may have been about 1,600 white female slaves in Algiers alone.[84] Slavery in the
Mediterranean was a consequence of the numerous confrontations between
Christians and Muslims and, as K. Fleet reminds us, was a profitable business
for both sides.[85] Christian slaves could improve their situation by converting to
Islam and some indeed did, including sailors and sea captains joining the corsairs. The life of those that did not convert depended on the willingness of family
members, religious groups or their government to provide the requested ransom.
Some Christian slaves were able to improve their position because they spoke
Arabic, English or French, knew European maritime law or possessed special
skills like shipbuilding, weaponry or engineering.

To deal with the Barbary Coast, European states used diplomacy and concluded treaties; they paid tribute to the rulers and ransom to free slaves and occasionally deployed naval force.[86] Because the rulers on the Barbary Coast were still considered part of the Ottoman Empire, the Europeans always had to take the Ottoman Empire into account. According to the law of nations, treaties could be negotiated between rulers of sovereign states. The Dutch scholar Hugo de Groot, one of the founding fathers of international law, argued that because the North African rulers could declare war they were sovereign states.[87] This allowed the Europeans to negotiate treaties with them, but they decided to call them regencies and not sovereign states. European merchant vessels normally sailed in convoys escorted by several navy ships, but this was rather costly. It was cheaper to buy protection by concluding a treaty and pay an annual tribute, besides presenting gifts to the rulers. C. Windler says that these treaties differed from the Capitulations because the former were 'real treaties, sealed and ratified by the two parties'.[88] The treaties, however, were hardly respected by the Barbary rulers and, as Panzac demonstrates, had to be renegotiated and renewed repeatedly by the Europeans.[89] The menace of the Barbary Coast could have been solved easily if the Europeans had joined their naval forces, but the strong rivalry among European states prevented this.[90]

Although treaties of friendship and commerce were signed, the Western states could not appoint ambassadors because of their diplomatic relations with the sultan. They relied on consuls who, besides their economic duties, received political as well as jurisdictional powers. The consuls, J. Black says, 'played a crucial role in relations with the Barbary states of North Africa'.[91] Despite their extensive powers, the position of the consuls remained difficult because they lived in societies that did not acknowledge the equal status of Christians.[92] The consuls were frequently loathed, beaten, imprisoned and some were even put to death. During meetings with the Barbary rulers the consuls were expected to show their submission.[93]

From the early nineteenth century, however, the attitude of consuls changed and they no longer accepted their inferiority. On 3 January 1805 the English consul Richard Cartwright arrived in Algiers, but departed on 22 February 1806. 'What I have experienced since my stay here has literally been a summary of all the horrors and indignities that have been offered to the British nation for the last thirty years'.[94] He was constantly insulted and the water supply was frequently cut off. R. L. Playfair furthermore writes: 'The residence at Algiers has, I believe, ever been considered the most disagreeable and difficult of all others, and few men of independent fortune will ever be found to occupy it'.[95] During his first interview with Henry Stanyford Blanckley (1752–1828), the British consul general in Algiers from 1806 until 1812, the ruler as usual offered his hand to be kissed. Blanckley 'respectfully, but in the firmest manner declined, doing so, as being an homage he only felt due to his own Sovereign'.[96] While his dragoman nervously translated Blanckley's answer, the ruler at first looked at him very seriously, but then shook hands with Blanckley. The gifts Blanckley had brought on behalf of Great Britain, including an expensive watch, were less appreciated.[97] According to C. S. Kennedy, the suffering endured by the consuls on the Barbary Coast persuaded their governments to provide better training, besides giving them a salary.[98]

The arrival of US merchants and consuls contributed much to the changing relationship between the consuls and the rulers of the Barbary Coast. The US consuls forced the Barbary rulers to respect existing treaties and end the system of paying tribute. After the American Revolution, the US relied heavily on its foreign trade, particularly with Europe and the Mediterranean. In August 1784 John Adams (1735–1826) and Thomas Jefferson went to Paris to seek recognition of the US and conclude commercial treaties with European states and the rulers on the Barbary Coast. In late 1785 Jefferson instructed the US consul in France, Thomas Barclay, to negotiate a treaty with Sultan Muhammad III (*c.* 1710–90) of Morocco.[99] Although the sultan had expected the US to send an ambassador, Barclay was only a consul because, as Jefferson explained, whatever the custom of the Old World, 'it is not ours; that we never sent an ambassador to any nation'.[100] The US and Morocco concluded a treaty of peace, friendship and ship-signals in June 1786. Article 23 granted the US the right to appoint consuls in any Moroccan seaport. They had judicial powers to settle disputes between citizens of the US, while in mixed cases Islamic courts were used with the consul present.[101] After the death of Sultan Muhammad III, Congress again directed Barclay to Morocco for obtaining recognition of the existing treaty.[102]

It took almost ten years after signing the treaty with Morocco, before the US concluded a treaty with one of the Islamic rulers on the Barbary Coast.[103] During this period US vessels were frequently raided by their corsairs and trade with the Mediterranean suffered tremendously. Algerian corsairs captured the *Dauphin* and the schooner *Maria* in July 1785. The captain of the *Dauphin*, Richard O'Brien (1758–1824) and the crew and passengers were enslaved for over ten years. O'Brien desperately addressed churches in 1795 in an attempt to collect money for their release, 'and by every possible exertion of godlike charity, to restore us to our wives, to our children, to our friends, to our God and to yours'.[104] The crew and passengers of the *Maria* were likewise enslaved. One of the crew was James Leander Cathcart (1767–1843). For eleven years, he was a slave in Algiers, but improved his position by becoming Christian chief clerk.[105] At the end of 1793 the number of US captives in Algiers was about 119 and in December 1795 it had risen to around 150.[106]

Jefferson reviewed the matter in December 1790 in his 'Report of the Secretary of State Relative to the Mediterranean Trade'. He began by pointing out the importance of this trade for the US economy: 'that that commerce loaded outwards from eighty to one hundred ships, annually, of twenty thousand tons, navigated by about twelve hundred seamen'.[107] To restore this important trade he considered three possibilities: establishing a safe port in the Mediterranean, obtaining peace by purchasing it, or using force. The first option was considered unobtainable, while the second posed a problem: how much would peace cost? Captain O'Brien, writing from his prison in Algiers, estimated this to be $322,000, but another source suggested $1,000,000. It was believed that Great Britain paid an annual tribute of $80,000. 'But it must be noted that these facts cannot be authentically advanced; as from a principle of self-condemnation, the governments keep them from the publick eye, as much as possible.'[108] Jefferson wrote that after the death of the ruler, 'respectable presents must be made to the successor, that he may recognize the treaty; and very often he takes the liberty of altering it'.[109] The third option was to use force, but the US did not possess a strong navy in the early 1790s. Jefferson concluded: 'Upon the whole, it rests with Congress to decide between war, tribute, and ransom, as the means of re-establishing our Mediterranean commerce'.[110]

Congress decided to follow the existing European practice: conclude treaties and pay tribute to buy protection for the merchant vessels. In September 1795 a treaty was concluded with Algiers after lengthy and very difficult negotiations. The treaty with Algiers committed the US to paying $585,000 and a yearly tribute of maritime stores worth about $21,600, besides personal gifts for the ruler every two years.[111] The US concluded a similar treaty with Tripoli in November 1796.[112] Joel Barlow (1754–1812), an American living in Paris, was appointed agent plenipotentiary to negotiate a treaty with Tunis, but he apparently left the task to a Frenchman: Joseph-Étienne Famin (1762–1806).[113] A treaty with the ruler of Tunis was concluded a year later and ratified by Congress in March 1798, except for article 14: the duties on cargo. Secretary of State Timothy Pickering (1745–1829) appointed William Eaton (1764–1811), a former US officer, as US consul to Tunis.[114] His first duty was to renegotiate article 14 of the existing treaty. Eaton left in December 1797 accompanied by Cathcart, appointed US consul to Tripoli, and four fully laden ships that served as the annual tribute for Tunis.[115] The first stop was in Algiers, where the two consuls were joined by O'Brien, appointed US consul general for the Barbary Coast. On 22 February 1798 the three Americans met the ruler of Algiers. Eaton, who had not met an Islamic ruler before, recorded the meeting in his journal.

> We were shown to a huge, shaggy beast, sitting on his rump, upon a low bench, covered with a cushion of embroidered velvet, with his hind legs gathered up like a taylor, or a bear. On our approach to him, he reached out his fore paw as if to receive something to eat. Our guide exclaimed, 'Kiss the Dey's hand!'. The consul-general bowed very elegantly, and kissed it; and we followed his example in succession ... Having performed this ceremony, and standing a few moments in silent agony, we had leave

to take our shoes and other property, and leave the den, without any other injury than the humility of being obliged, in this involuntary manner, to violate the second commandment of God, and offend common decency. Can any man believe that this elevated brute has seven kings of Europe, two republics, and a continent, tributary to him, when his whole naval force is not equal to two line of battle ships? It is so![116]

After arriving at his destination in Tunis on 26 March, Eaton complained about the heat and being surrounded by 'brutal Turks, swindlers, jews. Perfidious Italians, miserable slaves, lazy camels, churlish mules, and savage Arabs – without society and without amusement'.[117] After observing slavery in Tunis he felt outraged because the US did not have the 'fortitude to resist it',[118] a remarkable opinion considering the widespread slavery in the US. Eaton and Cathcart next started the negotiations to revise article 14 of the existing treaty, but that took much longer than anticipated.

> The Barbary courts are indulged in the habits of dictating their own terms of negociation. Even the English, as the Consul himself informed me, on his arrival and reception here, had furnished him a present in cash and other articles valued in England at seventeen thousand pounds sterling.[119]

In his reports and letters Eaton did not hide his contempt for the ruler of Tunis, nor his preference for military action: 'The United States sat out wrongly; and have proceeded so. Too many concessions have been made to Algiers. There is but one language which can be held to these people; and this is terror.'[120]

Eaton not only reported about his tiresome negotiations that lasted until January 1800, but in addition supplied information about the export trade of Tunis, including hides, wax, wheat, barley and oil. According to Eaton the trade was wholly in the hands of Jews, organized in a guild-like organization called Giornata, for which they annually paid the ruler $17,142. He informed the US government about the corsairs, the number of ships they had, the major seaports, and their defences. He wrote how the present ruler seized the regency from Sidi Mahmoud, the rightful heir, who had since lost all hopes of reclaiming his position.

The US government, much to the horror of Eaton, continued to pay tribute.

> You are authorized to inform the Bey of Tunis, that a vessel is now preparing to take in the cargo, which will complete the regalia due to him, and that no time will be lost in getting her on her voyage. The jewels, to the amount of 40,000 dollars, have, as you know, been ordered to be prepared in London.[121]

Peace with the rulers on the Barbary Coast remained fragile even after concluding treaties, paying tribute and presenting gifts. In 1800 the USS *George Washington* with Captain William Bainbridge (1774–1833) arrived in Algiers with the annual tribute. The ruler of Algiers complained that the presents were unsatisfactory and ordered Bainbridge to bring his tribute to Istanbul.[122] When this news arrived in

Washington, the US government and Congress were exasperated. At about the same time, Tripoli felt severely neglected by the US and demanded more tribute and presents. When the US consul declined, the ruler had the flagpole of the consulate cut down and ordered the corsairs to hunt for US vessels.[123]

President George Washington (1732–99) and his successor, John Adams, preferred concluding commercial treaties, paying tribute and presenting gifts, but Jefferson was more opposed to the whole idea, although, as Oren comments, he seems to have been rather inconsistent in his views.[124] As Secretary of State he followed the European practice, but during his presidency (1801–9) Jefferson was able to procure funds for the construction of a sizable navy. When it was completed, he first used it against the Barbary rulers and corsairs. This, says R. J. Allison, convinced Europe that the US 'was a new kind of nation, one that would not follow the corrupt practices of the old world'.[125] It took the US two wars against the Barbary rulers and even a (failed) coup to achieve its goal.

The first war began in 1801 and lasted until 1805.[126] A squadron of the US navy, joined by the Swedish navy, blockaded Tripoli. In early 1803, a second squadron under Commodore Edward Preble (1761–1807) was ordered to attack vessels belonging to the ruler of Tripoli.[127] In a daring move, USS *Philadelphia* entered the harbour of Tripoli in October 1803 chasing a corsair, but it ran aground. The ship was easily captured by corsairs and Captain William Bainbridge and his crew of about three hundred men were imprisoned. Fearing that the modern and heavily armed ship would be added to the corsair fleet, it was set ablaze on 16 February 1804 by Lieutenant Stephen Decatur (1779–1820).

Consul Eaton then proposed an even more daring plan.[128] This amounted to nothing less than a palace coup: replacing Yusuf Karamanli (1766–1838), the ruler of Tripoli, with his deposed brother Hamet Karamanli. Eaton explained:

> The idea of dethroning our enemy, and placing a rightful sovereign in his seat, makes a deeper impression on account of the lasting peace it will produce with that regency, and the lesson of caution it will teach the other Barbary states.[129]

Jefferson next appointed Eaton as secret agent to complete this mission. Eaton went to Egypt with a small army to meet the deposed ruler Hamet, and took him all the way overland to Tripoli, eventually reaching the port of Derne. News of their arrival persuaded Yusuf to quickly sign a new, and for the US more favourable, treaty with Consul General Tobias Lear (1762–1816) on 4 June 1805.[130] Although Eaton felt betrayed by his fellow citizen Lear, he afterwards admitted:

> Our peace with Tripoli is certainly more favourable – and considered separately, more honourable than any peace obtained by any Christian nation with a Barbary regency, at any period within a hundred years; but it might have been more favourable and more honourable.[131]

The treaty still contained an annual gift of $60,000, to be supplemented by the usual gifts for the rulers.[132]

After the Napoleonic Wars the Western states increased their efforts to crush the corsairs and enforce existing treaties with rulers on the Barbary Coast.[133] In February 1815, one week after the US and Great Britain made peace to end the War of 1812, Congress decided to declare war on Algiers.[134] President James Madison (1751–1836) appointed Stephen Decatur, the hero of Tripoli in 1804, commander of the US fleet. Decatur captured several corsairs, weakening the already declining fleet of the ruler of Algiers. The US signed a new treaty with Algiers on 28 June 1815. Article 2 of the treaty stated:

> It is distinctly understood between the Contracting parties, that no tribute either as
> biennial presents, or under any other form or name whatever, shall ever be required
> by the Dey and Regency of Algiers from the United States of America on any pretext
> whatever.[135]

The treaty, Abulafia notes, impressed the European powers: 'they viewed the United States with far greater respect than ever before'.[136] William Shaler (1773–1833) (see p. 91), previously secret agent in Cuba and Mexico and a member of the peace delegation in Ghent, was appointed consul general to Algiers.[137]

During the Congress of Vienna, the participants condemned Barbary slavery and a British fleet sailed to the Barbary Coast in early 1816 to convey the resolution, but this did not stop the corsairs. In August 1816 a joint British-Dutch fleet bombarded Algiers, later also Tunis and Tripoli.[138] After his defeat the ruler of Algiers was forced to make a public apology in the presence of all consuls. Over 3,000 Christian slaves were freed. The practice of paying tribute and presenting gifts was finally abolished, although piracy in the Mediterranean continued for some decades.

After the 1830s Western relations with Muslim rulers in North Africa changed completely. When French payments for Algerian grain fell behind, the Algerian trader, the house of Bacri, turned to their ruler for help. During a meeting on 20 April 1827 with Pierre Deval (1758–1829), French consul general to Algiers from 1814 to 1827, emotions ran high and the ruler used his fly whisk to hit the consul. France demanded satisfaction to restore its honour, but when the ruler refused to do so France declared war on Algiers and blockaded the harbour from the summer of 1829 until July 1830. The treaty of 1830 between France and Tunis ended the remaining humiliating ceremonies during receptions with the rulers.[139] France took control of Algiers, mainly to support French businessmen in North Africa. It marked the beginning of a new phase of Western presence in North Africa. This culminated in the French protectorate in 1881 over Tunis and the British occupation of Egypt in 1882.[140]

Syria: Gottfried Wetzstein, a Humanitarian Intervention

In 1516 the Ottomans conquered the area presently known as Syria. In the seventeenth and eighteenth century some parts achieved a level of autonomy similar to those in Egypt and the Barbary Coast. Between 1831 and 1841, Syria was occupied by the Egyptian ruler Muhammad Ali (see p. 37). During the Egyptian occupation, Ibrahim Pasha (1789–1848), his eldest son, ruled Syria. Ibrahim Pasha centralized administration, effected conscription for the army and promulgated the legal equality between Muslims and non-Muslims. By reforming the tax system and defeating a number of Bedouin tribes, he stimulated the settlement of Christian and Jewish traders.[141] The Egyptian occupation endangered the European policy of maintaining the integrity of the Ottoman Empire and they supported the Ottomans in conquering Syria in 1840/1. In return for British support, the Sublime Porte concluded a new commercial treaty in 1838 that abolished existing state monopolies, thus further opening the empire for Western capital and traders.[142]

In 1761 Prussia and the Ottoman Empire concluded a treaty of friendship and commerce that made the appointment of consuls possible. From 1806 until 1848, Prussia was represented by the native Jewish trading family of Picciotto, but thereafter by the British consul Richard Wood. In April 1849, however, the first Prussian consul arrived in Damascus. Damascus was the third largest town of the Ottoman Empire after Istanbul and Cairo. It was an important marketplace and terminal for the caravan trade coming from Bagdad, connecting India and Persia with the Middle East. From Damascus the caravans continued to Palestine, but also to the Hedjaz and its holy cities Mecca and Medina and the port of Jeddah.[143]

Johann Gottfried Wetzstein (1815–1905) studied theology and Semitic languages, later also Turkish and Persian, in Prussia. Wetzstein was 'a dreamer, an optimist, an entrepreneur, a humanitarian and, alas, an imperialist'.[144] E. von Mülinen writes that he became one of the most knowledgeable experts on Syria.[145] His travels and explorations were in the best tradition of Johann Ludwig Burckhardt (1784–1817) and he corresponded with other Orientalists, like the Dutch scholar Christiaan Snouck Hurgronje (1857–1936). After living in Syria for almost ten years he had become, in his own words, almost an Arabian.[146] His fluency in Persian and modest character made it relatively easy to establish friendly relations with Syrians. Wetzstein did not receive a state salary for his consulate, but certain expenses were reimbursed by the Prussian Department of Foreign Affairs. He rented a part of a grand palace in the Muslim quarter of Damascus, near the covered bazaar (or suq) al-Arwam and engaged about fifteen Syrians to serve in his household. His income to support this large household derived from publishing articles on the history and culture of Syria, collecting old Arabic manuscripts for sale to Prussian university libraries, working as a commission agent for Prussian firms and, after 1855, managing several farms in nearby villages.

Wetzstein in the beginning concentrated on his economic duties, hoping to stimulate direct trade between Prussia and Syria. He contacted several Prussian companies to arouse their interests to trade with Syria and offered his assistance. This included the firms of F. C. Herrmann & Sohn (textile fabrics) and A. Wilhelm Solbrig (jewellery). Some firms contacted Wetzstein asking for his help, like Bilstein & Höfkers (metals). He furthermore tried to establish business relations between Syrian and Prussian businessmen trading in Persian carpets, silk and porcelain. Despite these efforts, direct trade between Prussia and Syria remained modest. Most Prussian goods were exported to Syria on British, French or Austrian ships. According to Wetzstein this demonstrated the importance of having a direct shipping line, which was lacking until 1890,when the *Deutsche Levant Linie* was founded. The poor results of Wetzstein, I. Huhn writes, were due to the disruption during the Crimean War (1853–6), the economic recession in Prussia between 1857 and 1860 and international monetary instability.[147] Wetzstein furthermore had no experience as a businessman, he was foremost a scholar and Orientalist. Huhn concludes that Wetzstein was 'unable to really influence the trade between Damascus and the German Zollverein'.[148]

During his first leave to Prussia Wetzstein wrote a long memo of thirty-six handwritten pages about the consulate in Damascus.[149] He argued that Damascus was 'die Seele Syriens' (the hart of Syria), connecting many different places in the Middle East.[150] The main reason for opening a Prussian consulate was to offer protection to humanity, not because Islam or Syrians were intolerant, but because of the rather weak legal position of Christians. Despite the large number of courts (from national to local), the legal position of Europeans remained poor, 'and without consular protection, no large trading house would be willing to open business here'.[151] Wetzstein believed that the main duties of the Prussian consul were political, not economical, and this required the appointment of a salaried consul, like the British, French and Russians. Wetzstein's recommendations were not followed up: trade between Prussia and Syria was still too unimportant to appoint a salaried consul.[152]

The poor results of Wetzstein's efforts to stimulate trade, his general disappointment in Damascus, and the rejection of his proposal to appoint a salaried consul may have contributed to his request to be relieved from his consulate in 1850. His letter of resignation was, however, upheld and Wetzstein continued as Prussian consul until August 1861. He married again in 1853, but from 1857 his wife decided to remain in Berlin with the children. In the period from 1850 to 1861 he went on leave to Germany three times and made seven extensive expeditions in Syria, including a trip in early 1858 to the Hauran area, south-west of Damascus. For these travels he received permission from his superior: Count

Robert Heinrich Ludwig von der Goltz (1817–69), the Prussian ambassador in Istanbul. During his travels, Wetzstein presented himself as Prussian consul because of the protection that was associated with this function, although it forced him to travel with a large entourage, including several Bedouins.[153]

Wetzstein arrived in Syria during a period of rising agitation after the promulgation by Sultan Abdülmecid I (1823–61) of new regulations during the *Tanzimat* era, including the legal equality of Christians and Muslims in 1856 and subscription for the army. The tensions between Christians, Jews and Muslims worsened after the growing economic and political power of the Western states and their consuls from the 1840s onwards. Besides representing their fellow countrymen, the consuls offered protection to a large number of natives, whether Christian, Jew or Muslim. Consular protection offered several advantages, including exemption from certain local taxes and lower tariffs on import and export of goods.

From 9 to 16 July 1860, Wetzstein witnessed the massacre of Christians in Damascus.[154] The jealousy of non-protected Damascenes, as well as religious and political discontent, contributed to the Damascus Massacre,[155] though Fawaz believes that the main cause of the massacre in Damascus was economical and not religious.[156] The precise number of deaths is unknown: estimates range from 2,000 to 12,000 deaths. Wetzstein himself believed that there were 6,000 victims, including men, women and children.[157] Riots between Christians, Jews and Muslims in Syria were not uncommon before 1860. In May and June 1860, Christian Maronites were attacked and killed by Druzes in several villages in Mount Lebanon.[158] These attacks and killings led to official protests from their protector countries, notably Russia and France. On 8 July, the sultan appointed Mehmet Fuad Pasha (1815–69) to investigate the murders and restore order. A day later the Christian quarter in Damascus was attacked by about 20,000 Druzes and Muslims.[159]

The massacre came as a surprise to many consuls, although the British consul James Brant (d. 1861) and his Russian colleague wrote alarming reports to their foreign ministers. After his leave in Prussia in late 1859, Wetzstein returned to Damascus in February 1860. A few weeks later he began preparing for a journey in eastern Jordan. During the expedition, he noticed nothing out of the ordinary, but after his return to Damascus ten weeks later, the tension was already building. On 27 June he expected riots to start at any moment. The consuls discussed the matter with the governor of Damascus, but all he did was to forbid Christians to carry weapons. The next day and on 2 July, Wetzstein wrote messages to Von der Goltz in Istanbul and the Foreign Office in Berlin. He proposed an immediate foreign military intervention to protect the Christian population.[160] When the riots and killing started, the Russian, French, Dutch, Austrian, Belgian and American consulates in the Christian quarter of Damascus were attacked first. This demonstrates how unpopular the consuls were; the US consul and native

Damascene, Abdu Costi, was almost beaten to death. The acting French consul and Belgian vice-consul hurriedly disguised and found, together with the Russian and Greek consul, refuge in the home of the Algerian exile Amir Abd al-Qadir (1808–83). The Christians entered the citadel of the city en masse to seek protection. Churches and homes of Christians were pillaged and burned; several missionaries were attacked and killed. Captured Christians were carried off; some were forced to convert to Islam. After a week of killings and riots, the Christian quarter of Damascus was destroyed.

The Prussian and the British consulates were attacked but not destroyed. Both were located in the Muslim quarter, and after the riots began were protected by armed guards of important local Muslims. During the riots, several hundred Muslims offered assistance and protection to Christians.[161] Wetzstein immediately opened the Prussian consulate and harboured several dozen Christians, mostly women and children, at his own expense. His superior Von der Goltz warned Wetzstein not to interfere in domestic political affairs, because he was only a consul without political powers. Wetzstein, however, continued to offer relief because he saw it as humanitarian aid and not a political act. The refugees stayed within the consulate building until order was sufficiently restored. Many Christians, however, moved to Beirut and again Wetzstein offered help by organizing their transport.

When information on the massacre reached Istanbul, the sultan was horrified, fearing that this might lead to further Western encroachments on the Ottoman Empire. Russia and France were in favour of an international intervention, but Great Britain was reluctant. It was weary of the growing influence of France (e.g. French involvement in constructing the Suez Canal), in the Middle East. Eventually the five major powers, France, England, Russia, Austria and Prussia agreed to send an expeditionary force of about 6,000 French soldiers under the command of General Charles de Beaufort d'Hautpoul.[162] They would stay for no more than six months. Fuad Pasha arrived in Beirut on 12 July with almost unlimited powers to restore peace. He proceeded quickly and within a few weeks restored order, returned the possessions of Christians, supplied medical treatment and food, requisitioned several hundred homes of Muslims for Christians, and prosecuted hundreds of murderers in special tribunals, including the previous governor and several high ranking officers. Most accused were hanged or shot; this included a guard employed by Wetzstein. Because of the instant measures taken by Fuad Pasha, the Ottoman Empire was able to limit further foreign interference.[163]

Wetzstein was disappointed that the expeditionary force remained in the area of Beirut and did not enter Damascus. In September and October 1860 the remaining Christians in Damascus, particularly the Greek Christians, suddenly turned against the Jews, accusing them of having murdered and plundered in the Christian quarter during the massacre. The Greek consul accused the Jews of actively participating in the killings.[164] Ottoman authorities next drew up lists of incriminated Jews to be arrested. The Jews turned to the consuls for help. Baron says that 'only the Prussian representative, Dr. Johann Gottfried Wetzstein, seriously took up the defence of the Jews'.[165] Wetzstein wrote to Von der Goltz on 24 September 1860: 'The fear which arose among the Jews has induced me to open the Consulate Building once again this morning'.[166] The ambassador again warned Wetzstein not to interfere in domestic politics: by offering protection to the Jews in the Prussian consulate he obstructed Ottoman jurisdiction and violated their sovereign rights. Wetzstein neglected these instructions and protected fourteen Jewish refugees, mostly women and children, for several weeks 'in the interests of humanity'.[167] The incriminations brought against the Jews by the Greek Christians were in his view not primarily religious, but only intended to extort money from them.

Conditions in Damascus did not improve until early 1861. A new governor was appointed and he organized festivities to improve the relationship between Christians, Jews and Muslims.[168] One result of the attacks on Christians in Syria was that Western governments, with the help of their consuls, more closely monitored the position of Christians and other religious minorities in the Ottoman Empire. In June 1861 Sir Henry Lytton Bulwer (1801–72), the British ambassador in Istanbul between 1858 and 1865, sent a questionnaire to all British consuls in the Ottoman Empire. To form an opinion about the position of Christians in the Ottoman Empire, the ambassador needed local knowledge and for this he depended on the consuls. The twenty-four questions covered various items, from facts (e.g. the number of Christians in certain places), to their treatment by the authorities and the native population. Reports arrived in the following months. In August 1860 James Henry Skene (1812–86), consul and later consul general in Aleppo from 1855 until 1877, reported that

> The Christians of Aleppo are a keen, money-making people, clever in trade, miserly at home, abject without support, and insolent when unduly protected. The great mass of them live in a state of chronic terror. This was merely a reflex of what they suffered in the massacre of 1850, and their panic is now enhanced by the disasters of Mount Lebanon and Damascus.[169]

In August and September 1860 the major European powers signed conventions urging the Ottoman authorities to take measures to improve to conditions of the Christians throughout the empire.[170]

Wetzstein believed that Syria could survive only if it separated from the Ottoman Empire and became an independent state.[171] This was, however, not the policy of the major European powers, who wanted to preserve the integrity of the empire. After the massacre in November 1860, Wetzstein again wrote a letter of resignation. His desire to return to Prussia was related to his wife remaining in Berlin after 1857 and the horrors he had just witnessed. His request was accepted and in August 1861 the new Prussian consul, Wilhelm von Herford, arrived in Damascus. Wetzstein remained a few more months to settle his affairs and returned in early 1862 and accepted a position as lecturer on the history and culture of the Middle East. In 1870, during the Franco-Prussian War, he was asked to join Gerhard Friedrich Rohlfs (1831–96) on a secret mission to Algeria. Their task was to stimulate locals to start a revolt against France and force it to send its North African troops from Germany back to Algeria.[172] Wetzstein died in Berlin in January 1905.

The Hedjaz: Dutch Consuls and the Pilgrim Business

The Suez Canal, administered by the *Compagnie Universelle du Canal Maritime de Suez* (Suez Canal Company) was opened for international shipping on 17 November 1869. It marked the beginning of a new phase in the history of the Middle East, when 'the Indian Ocean and Mediterranean became a passageway'.[173] The construction of the Suez Canal was part of the modernization programme of Egypt, but would eventually lead to the occupation of Egypt by British troops in 1882. The canal had become too important to leave under the control of the Egyptians. As Schölch demonstrates, the British Consul-General Sir Edward Malet (1837–1908) kept his government well informed of French policy regarding Egypt. Although he made clear that the French would not intervene in Egypt, the British Prime Minister Gladstone (1809–98), basing his views on the reports from Malet, thought that they would.[174] However, Halvorson argues that the main motive for the British occupation of Egypt was not economical, but prestige *vis-à-vis* the other major powers.[175]

The opening of the canal affected economies in a wider area: the important caravan trade from Damascus to the Hedjaz declined from the 1870s (see p. 49).[176] K. McPherson believes it was 'an event of far-reaching importance. It revived the Red Sea as a major international shipping artery.'[177] On certain shipping routes (e.g. London to Bombay) the canal cut the distance by almost 40 per cent and it was therefore an immediate success.[178] The number of ships entering the canal rose from 485 (436,609 net tonnage) in 1870 to 3,624 (5,767,656 net tonnage) in 1886. In the same period the number of passengers carried increased from 26,758 to 171,411.[179] Passengers included colonists, convicts, coolies, civil servants and soldiers, besides businessmen and tourists. A special group was Muslim pilgrims. To make a pilgrimage (hajj) to Mecca at least once during a lifetime is one of the five pillars of Islam.[180] The journey to Mecca and back could take several months or, in the early modern period, even years to complete.[181] The number of pilgrims from North Africa and the Ottoman Empire fluctuated strongly, due to political conflicts, economic conditions and epidemics. The introduction of steamships in the Red Sea from the 1840s operated by the Peninsular and Oriental Steam Navigation Company (P&O), later joined by other shipping companies, disconnected the transport of pilgrims from the regularity of the monsoon that previously determined the schedule of sailing vessels.[182] Western steamship companies soon dominated the transport of pilgrims, says M. B. Miller, because they had the knowledge and resources to apply business methods for handling large volumes of passengers.[183] Carrying pilgrims to and from Jeddah, the main port of the Hedjaz, was a very profitable business for the European shipping companies.[184]

The total number of pilgrims arriving in the port of Jeddah by sea rose from about 112,000 in 1831 to almost 300,000 in 1910.[185] Most pilgrims travelled in groups and during their stay native guides took care of them. However, because of the low costs of travelling by steamship and sponsorship by wealthy Muslims, a growing number of pauper pilgrims went on pilgrimage. This increased the danger of epidemics, particularly cholera, and led to several international sanitary conferences between 1851 and 1894. Quarantine measures, inspections of pilgrim ships and limits on the number of pilgrims per ship were introduced to improve conditions.[186] The pauper pilgrims often had insufficient means to support their stay in Mecca or pay for their return ticket. Many were forced to offer their services to Muslim money lenders and virtually became their slaves. This, R. Singha remarks, required the interference of the consuls when they were colonial subjects.[187] Equally important were growing Western fears of Muslim activism. A few days after the Sepoy Mutiny (1857–58) in India, twenty-two people in Jeddah were killed; all except one were Christians or foreigners under consular protection.[188] Among the victims were the French consul and his wife and the British vice-consul. Presumably more killings took place in Sulawesi and Borneo in the Dutch East Indies.[189]

Between 1852 and 1858 about 2,000 Muslims annually went on pilgrimage from the Dutch East Indies to Mecca, but after the opening of the Suez Canal their number rose to 5,000, reaching 20,000 in 1900.[190] Travelling from the Dutch East Indies to Mecca had become much easier after the establishment in Amsterdam of a regular steamship line between the Netherlands and Batavia: the *Stoomvaart Maatschappij Nederland* (*SMN*, Steamship Company Netherlands). Supervision of the large number of pilgrims from the Dutch East Indies was handled by a British commercial agent, but in 1872 the Dutch government decided to open a consulate in Jeddah.[191] The two main duties of the Dutch consul, M. Witlox explains, were to stimulate trade between the Dutch East Indies and the Netherlands and to keep a watchful eye on potential political activities of pilgrims from the Dutch East Indies.[192] The Dutch consul and his foreign colleagues in Jeddah had extraterritorial powers inside the town, but not beyond the city gate and walls. In addition, non-Muslims were forbidden to enter the holy cities Mecca and Medina. Supervision of the pilgrims was therefore not possible in these cities and this created anxiety amongst the consuls. The British consul in Jeddah, James Ernest Napoleon Zohrab (1830–91), reported in 1879:

> The annual meeting at a fixed time ostensibly for the purposes of the Pilgrimage of Representatives from every Mussulman Community affords a means without creating suspicion to exchange opinions, to discuss plans, to criticize the actions of the European Governments and form combinations to resist the supremacy of the Christian Powers.[193]

The consuls hired native spies that could go to Mecca and Medina and, E. Tagliacozzo adds, European governments introduced a system of visas or passports and 'compulsory return tickets'.[194]

The first Dutch consul in Jeddah, Rudolph Willem Johan Cornelis de Menthon Bake (1811–74), was not a success. He supplemented his salary by taxing pilgrims additionally for stationary and administrative duties when they applied for a visa. He was ordered by the Minister of Foreign Affairs to stop this practice in February 1873.[195] In May 1873, Bake went on leave to Germany without awaiting permission and he was dishonourably discharged as Dutch consul in July.[196] His successor was Willem Hanegraaff (1839–78), consul between 1873 and 1878. In his first annual report Hanegraaff discussed several investment opportunities for Dutch entrepreneurs and provided valuable advice on how to proceed in Jeddah.[197] Dutch businessmen wanting to trade had to associate themselves with a local merchant because of differences in language, culture and business practices. It furthermore 'neutralized religious conflicts'.[198] He saw great potential for Dutch steamships sailing to Java via the Suez Canal because during the pilgrim season about 40,000 to 45,000 pilgrims entered the port of Jeddah. 'Without the pilgrim business, Jeddah would be a dead city', wrote Hanegraaff.[199] The business of transporting pilgrims did not require large investments from the shipping companies, because they only needed shelter, wood and water, and kitchens to cook their food. He admitted that transporting pilgrims was perhaps not very a pleasant business, 'but the money was good'.[200]

After the unexpected death of Hanegraaff in 1878, Johannes Adrianus Kruyt (1841–1927) was the new Dutch consul in Jeddah until 1888. After only a few months in his new post, Kruyt reported that the most important European and Arabian firms participating in the pilgrim business had come to some kind of agreement, terminating 'the endless quarrels and disputes, besides the unfair competition that gave so much troubles for the consuls in Jeddah'.[201] In 1883, ten years after Hanegraaff's first report, Consul Kruyt observed in his annual report: 'The proposal, by Dutch shipping companies, to participate in the transport of pilgrims from and to the Dutch-East Indies, had not yet commenced, but they will, so I hope, begin next year'.[202] The near absence of Dutch shipping companies in the pilgrim business until 1883 is puzzling, since in 1882 Dutch shipping through the Suez Canal ranked third after Great Britain and France. The main explanation was the failed attempt by a Dutch and local businessman to monopolize the pilgrim business.

In 1873 the Dutch entrepreneur Pieter Nicolaas van der Chijs and the Arabian merchant Omar Nassir Effendi, emir in Jeddah, operated *Le Compagnie Hollandaise*, an import and export business. Van der Chijs, later Dutch vice-consul in Jeddah, was in addition agent for the Ocean Steamship Company of Alfred Holt (1829–1911).[203] From 1877 Van der Chijs had frequent contact with the two main Dutch shipping lines: the Amsterdam-based *SMN* and the *Rotterdamsche Lloyd* (*RL*) in Rotterdam. Both companies were eager to enter the pilgrim business. *Le Compagnie Hollandaise* was to handle the pilgrims who voluntarily deposited their money at the Dutch consulate to secure their return passage with the Dutch mails. For these services *Le Compagnie Hollandaise* received a commission from the Dutch shipping companies. Although the pilgrims' money was deposited at the consulate and Van der Chijs kept some office space in the building, the acting consul claimed that he had nothing to do with the arrangement. The deal of 1877 only worked for six months, when it was cancelled by Omar Nassir, perhaps because it was unfavourable for the existing Arab middlemen in Jeddah.

It wasn't until 1883 that a similar contract was negotiated between Van der Chijs and the Emir of Java. From 1883 the two Dutch shipping companies *SMN* and *RL* started a weekly service to Java via the Suez Canal. Together with the *Koninklijke Paketvaart Maatschappij* (*KPM*), established in 1888 by *SMN* and *RL*, to maintain links between islands in the Dutch East Indies, these companies organized the transport of pilgrims from North Africa and South-East Asia to Mecca. For this they handed out return tickets to pilgrims through Van der Chijs at the consulate in Jeddah. In 1888 Van der Chijs sold 6,316 tickets to pilgrims, but this profitable arrangement was strongly criticized by local Muslim authorities, because it competed with their own interests. From 1895 the Dutch shipping companies used modified freight ships to transport pilgrims. These ships had simple kitchens and berths that were removed once the pilgrim season was over. By 1914, Miller writes, transporting pilgrims had become a large and profitable business for the European shipping lines.[204] In the 1920s the Dutch companies entered into an agreement with Alfred Holt's Ocean Steamship Company, thus further expanding the business to include pilgrims from Singapore and Malaysia.

3 THE FAR EAST

In the Far East, the consuls and traders encountered a totally different system of international relations than in Europe: the Sino-centric system.[1] Whereas in Europe, the sovereign states were sovereign and nominally equal, creating an anarchic system of international relations, in Asia states were placed in a hierarchy with China, the Middle Kingdom, at the top. All other states were considered vassals and were inferior because they had not become Sinicized. The hierarchy was based on the level of absorption of Chinese culture, including Confucianism. Nearby states, like Korea, the Kingdom of Ryukyu, Japan and Vietnam, had become more Sinicized than faraway states like Siam or India. To acknowledge the superiority of the Chinese emperor, the vassal states were obliged to send delegations and pay tribute.[2] The frequency of missions and the size of the accompanying group depended on the distance to the Middle Kingdom and thus the level of civilization.

Over the centuries, the Sino-centric system of tributary relations had become well-structured and organized; the elaborate ceremonies, including the kowtow during the reception with the emperor, had become familiar to all. After paying tribute and receiving gifts from the Chinese in return, the foreign mission was allowed to stay for several weeks or months to trade at selected places and ports before returning to their homeland. Despite this hierarchy, international relations were usually cordial and frequent. The Chinese fostered friendly relations with other states, because this would allow their culture to spread more quickly. The Asian states accepted Chinese superiority, because this allowed them to enter the Chinese realm and opened the possibility of trading directly with the Chinese. In the Sino-centric system international trade was highly regulated by the Chinese state because of is large revenues. In addition to the exchange that was part of the tribute missions and the subsequent period of legal trade, there was always a considerable illegal trade with China by smugglers and pirates.

The dominant position of China was occasionally challenged by other Asian states wanting to develop their own regional system of tributary relations, for example Cochin-China (Vietnam), Japan or Siam.[3] As long as they did not directly challenge China's position and continued to send delegations to the

Emperor, T. Hamashita says, the Chinese accepted this. Tributary relations were common in Asia and existed not only in relations with China but in addition between other Asian states (e.g. Cambodia paid tribute to Cochin-China and Siam).[4] Although China was forced to open more ports after the First Opium War (1839–42), this did not end the existing Sino-centric system of international relations. The Chinese continued to believe in this until they were defeated in the Sino-Japanese War (1894–5).

An important role in the Far East was played by the treaty ports, opened after concluding commercial treaties.[5] In the treaty ports Westerners enjoyed extraterritorial rights, making the consul, according to J. K. Fairbank, the central figure.[6] The consuls performed political, judicial and economic duties, but as time progressed the political duties were taken over by ambassadors and the judicial duties by special courts. Extraterritoriality in China ended only in 1943, in Japan in 1899, and in Siam some of the Western countries relinquished their extraterritorial rights after the First World War.

Tribute, Trade and Treaty Ports

When the Portuguese arrived in China in 1517, their request to trade was initially denied.[7] After several failed attempts, the Portuguese traders were finally allowed to set up a small trading post on Macao in 1557. Although the Portuguese considered the island their colony, as it was administered by an appointed governor and a *senado* (senate) according to their own laws, the Chinese saw the Portuguese as just another group of foreigners. For the privilege to reside and trade, A. Ljungstedt explains, the Portuguese annually paid 500 silver taels (one tael was about forty grams of silver) and were obliged to send tribute missions to the Chinese emperor.[8] European states arriving in China after the Portuguese, like the English, French, Dutch and Danes, were also incorporated into the Sino-centric system.

In 1715 the emperor decided to further limit the foreign influence and he concentrated all foreign trade in the southern port of Canton, near the Portuguese settlement on Macao. From 1715 until the First Opium War, Canton remained the only Chinese place that Westerners were allowed to visit. After 1759 new regulations were introduced to further control foreign trade and became known as the Canton system.[9] Trade was allowed only during the summer (from October to May) and conducted in several stages in Macao, Whampoa (the main anchorage in the Pearl River) and, finally, Canton. Each stage involved Chinese intermediaries, including government officials (customs officer or *hoppo*), Chinese merchants (organized in a guild: the *Co-Hong*), a translator/purchaser (*comprador*) and Chinese porters to bring the cargo into Canton. Outside the city gates of Canton the Westerners were allowed to construct offices and warehouses (called *hong*).[10] They were forced to leave Canton during the winter months (June to October) when no trading occurred. They left for home or retreated to Macao until the next trading season started. Some Western states appointed consuls in China prior to the First Opium War, but these were never recognized by the Chinese and did not receive an exequatur. They were at best spokespersons without consular powers, and their ability to offer protection to fellow countrymen was therefore limited.

Opening East Asian states was done by concluding commercial treaties, if necessary accompanied by gunboat diplomacy. Siam was the first country to sign commercial treaties with Portugal (1820), Great Britain (1826), the United States (1833) and other Western countries. Siam opened its economy only to a certain extent: until the 1850s the state continued to control international trade through monopolies. Other East Asian states were less willing to open their ports freely. Three military conflicts were required to force the Chinese government to open the country, while a threat of force by the US Navy opened Japan in 1853 to 1854. Korea, however, remained firmly closed for Western traders until it was forced to open some ports by the Japanese in 1876.

After the opening of East Asian countries the Western merchants were mostly confined to purpose-built foreign settlements in selected treaty ports and commercial cities. In contrast to the consuls appointed before the opening of East Asian states, these consuls operated with full powers according to international law. Their position was confirmed by the receiving government, which provided an exequatur. After the 1850s, many foreigners in the Chinese treaty ports were still without a consul of their own and British merchants were quite willing to become consul because they 'derived from their official status a very pleasant degree of prestige in Chinese eyes'.[11] Most consuls, whether salaried or unsalaried, had little knowledge of East Asia: only two out of five British consuls appointed after the First Opium War spoke a little Chinese. In contrast to the British, the French appointed experienced consuls who had acquired a basic knowledge of Chinese. R. Israel writes that the French consuls complained that most French entrepreneurs were very reluctant to invest in China, due 'to their prejudices, misinformation, and ignorance'.[12]

In their dealings with East Asian authorities the consuls were convinced of their superiority and they almost 'conducted a daily battle against Chinese ways'.[13] The US consul in Shanghai, Edward Cunningham (1823–89), agent of the firm Russell & Company, stated that the Asian had a 'childish character', and needed Western guidance and education.[14] Western merchants showed little interests in East Asian countries and like the consuls, they felt superior. Commenting on the British community in China, Platt says that their arrogance 'increased rather than diminished with the passage of years'.[15]

Living conditions in the growing number of foreign settlements in East Asia could be perilous because of xenophobia, wars and uprisings, bad housing and the climate. The Dutch consul in Bangkok, Peter Simon Hamel (1845–1900), complained that he could not light a lamp at night because of the 'amazing number of mosquitoes and other insects'.[16] In September 1882 he wrote about the 'terrible heat and cholera epidemics' and proposed to move the consulate to Singapore.[17] Many consuls (not to mention their wives and children) died of tropical diseases and infections. In 1859, fifteen years after the opening of the first Chinese treaty ports, eleven of the twenty-five British consuls and vice-consuls had already died.[18] Most salaried consuls found it hard to live off their pay because they were not prepared to adapt their style of living. George S. Morrison (c. 1830–93), British consul in Nagasaki, Japan, between 1859 and 1863, complained about the high cost of living because most products had to be imported from China or elsewhere. He requested compensation

> in consideration of an exile to the extremity of the earth, of banishment from society
> and from the relations of home, and exposure to discomfort and privations difficult
> to depict and cruel to endure, I say nothing of the climate.[19]

He believed the merchants only endured these poor conditions 'in the hope of speedily acquiring a fortune and quitting these scenes for ever'.[20]

The problems of the consuls were exacerbated by the great distance from their home country and the slow means of transport and communication. When the mail from Shanghai arrived in Yokohama on 11 November 1864, its distribution was delayed by the illness of the postmaster and an angry mob gathered in front of the French consulate general, throwing sticks at the building. Armed forces were called in to control the crowd. To avoid repetition of these events, the consul general published a notice in the *Japan Herald* that in the future the hour of distribution of mail would be posted outside the gate of the consulate. Y. A. Honjo says that the incident clearly illustrates 'the fragility and isolation of treaty-port life; it was life on the periphery, far away from the metropolis'.[21] The introduction of steamshipping from the mid-nineteenth century and the telegraph after the 1870s improved conditions, but this only applied to the important consulates in the treaty ports and cities. The large number of small and less important consular posts in East Asia remained isolated for most of the nineteenth century. This required the consuls to cooperate with their colleagues from other countries, if there were any. In the larger ports and cities, the consuls from different nationalities usually lived in the same quarter and frequently met during the day and at parties and other social events like national holidays. These occasions were important to strengthen the bond between the relatively small numbers of Westerners and to accentuate their presence in East Asia.

To investigate how consuls coped with the different conditions in East Asia, in particular the Sino-centric system of international relations, the following case studies have been selected. From the beginning the US was very eager to establish commercial relations with East Asia. The first ships that left for East Asia and safely returned attracted much media coverage. This included the voyage of the first vessel to reach China: the *Empress of China*. Its supercargo, the individual responsible for purchasing and selling cargo, Major Samuel Shaw became the first US consul in China appointed by Congress in 1786. Because he was never recognized by the Chinese, his powers remained limited as was clearly demonstrated during the trial and death sentence of a Western sailor. In Siam the Dutch consuls struggled to contain Chinese colonial subjects from the Dutch East Indies trading in Bangkok and Siamese traders under Dutch protection. This led to many trade disputes and clashes with the Siamese government. The opening of Japan from 1 July 1859 was eagerly anticipated by Western traders, who crowded in the few open ports. This included a number of traders from Prussia and the Hanseatic Cities. The first Prussian consul, Max von Brandt (1835–1920), arrived in 1862. His position was hampered by his title: Prussian consul for Japan. Most consuls were appointed to a port or city, not a whole country. Von Brandt furthermore received little support from his government, because of the German unification: domestic affairs were considered to be more important than what happened in Japan. As a result, Von Brandt was mostly excluded from discussions with his Western colleagues, who were soon promoted to Ministers Resident. After he had become Chargé d'Affaires in 1868 and after the German unification in 1871, the position of Von Brandt in Japan improved. Because of his long tenure in Japan and later China, he became an expert on East Asian matters. In 1895 he warned the West of the growing Japanese influence in the region. After the abolition of the slave trade, Western planters wanted to recruit labourers from British India and China. From the beginning the coolie trade involved the consuls. The first salaried Dutch consul general in China in 1872, Jan Helenus Ferguson (1826–1908), was instructed to secure from the Chinese government the free and direct emigration of Chinese labourers to the plantations in the Dutch East Indies. This would substantially reduce the costs of hiring coolies for the Dutch planters. Ferguson did not succeed in his mission until 1888. Dutch planters accused him of obstructing their plans and believed that Ferguson hated the coolie trade on moral grounds. This was not true: his efforts were thwarted by the Chinese government who demanded the reciprocal right to appoint a consul in the Dutch East Indies. The Dutch government was able to block this until 1912.

China: Samuel Shaw, the Difficulties of the Canton System

After the American Revolution, the merchants of the US lost access to the British colonies, particularly the Maritime Provinces and the West Indies, and this forced them to seek new markets all over the globe.[22] Their dealings in the

Mediterranean have already been discussed in the previous chapter. Another promising market for the US was China. The problems of the US merchants in China before the First Opium War were similar to those of European merchants: the restrictions of the Canton system, the lack of tradable products and the rivalry between Western countries. The merchants from the US had at least one important advantage: their trade in the early nineteenth century was not hampered by monopolistic chartered companies.[23]

In February 1784 Major Samuel Shaw sailed to China on the *Empress of China*, with Captain John Green (1736–96).[24] Shaw made four journeys to Canton between 1784 and 1794 and recorded his experiences in his journal.[25] A. O. Aldridge argues that the first voyage was 'a testing ground for negotiating diplomatic relations and foreign trade'.[26] The ship was owned by the trader and financier Robert Morris (1734–1806) of Philadelphia and several traders from New York represented by the firm of Daniel Parker & Company. Shaw's assistant was Thomas Randall (d. 1811), like Shaw a former officer in the Continental Army. The *Empress of China* sailed to Canton via the Cape of Good Hope, arriving in Macao on 23 August. Shaw reports that the French, Danes, Dutch and the British were happy 'to welcome your flag to this part of the world'.[27] To temporarily reside in Macao, they needed the permission of the Portuguese governor, and to continue to the anchorage at Whampoa, they required a permit (a passport called *chop*) from the Chinese authorities. The day after their arrival, Shaw met Philippe Vieillard, French consul in Canton, who took him to the Portuguese governor, 'but his Excellency not being at home, he left a written report of our visit'.[28]

During his first meeting with the Chinese customs officer (*hoppo*), Shaw apologized for not having brought a *sing-song* (a mechanical clockwork) as a gift. Despite this mistake, he was allowed to trade after promising to bring an extra gift on his next visit.

> Ours being the first American ship that had ever visited China, it was some time before the Chinese could fully comprehend the distinction between Englishmen and us. They styled us the *New People*, and when, by the map, we conveyed to them an idea of the extent of our country, with its present and increasing population, they were not a little pleased at the prospect of so considerable a market for the productions of their own empire.[29]

In Canton, Shaw established a provisional factory (warehouse), next to the other European factories. He noted that most Europeans traded by chartered companies, while the French had no such company (until a new company was established in 1785). The British in addition had a large number of country traders, ships sailing between India and China licensed by the British East India Company, but owned by private traders. He added that the Dutch, 'by their resources from their settlements on Java, Sumatra, Malacca, and other possessions in India, are enabled to manage their trade with China under equal, if not superior, advantages to any other people'.[30]

The Europeans were not the only foreigners. Shaw mentioned Armenians and Muslims as active traders in pearls and other merchandise. Shaw found life in Macao comfortable: 'When the gentlemen of the several nations are all there, the state of society is not bad. Each house has a billiard-table, many individuals keep pleasure-boats, and there is a public concert twice a week.'[31] A number of 'social parties' tended to promote 'a harmony and good-fellowship'. These occasions were important to strengthen the bond between the relatively small numbers of Westerners and to accentuate their presence in Asia.

During the first visit, Shaw became involved in what he exaggeratedly called 'the Canton War', but is more commonly known as the Lady Hughes Affair.[32] The conflict began on 25 October 1784 when the *Lady Hughes*, a British country trader, fired a salute killing a Chinese official and wounding two other Chinese in the boat alongside. In his journal, Shaw recollects that in 1780 an almost similar incident had occurred. Two sailors from the same ship, a Frenchman and a Portuguese, had a fight in which the latter was killed. On hearing about this offense, the Chinese, wanting to uphold their laws, demanded that the Frenchman should be given up and face trial before a Chinese court. The Chinese tribunal found the Frenchman guilty and strangled him in sight of the Western factories outside Canton, to set an example and demonstrate their power to uphold Chinese law.[33] In the same year a Dutch sailor murdered a countryman and fellow sailor, but was not handed over to the Chinese. The Dutch sailor was tried on board the vessel, found guilty and executed in sight of the Chinese officials. They strongly objected because, as E. P. Scully says, 'the Europeans have not the power of punishing a criminal'.[34]

After the Lady Hughes Affair, the Chinese authorities demanded that the British hand over the gunner, but they refused because his punishment was most surely death.[35] The Chinese at first agreed that the British should investigate the case themselves and prosecute the man, but two days later they suddenly seized George Smith, the supercargo of the *Lady Hughes*. After his arrest, the Western traders stopped doing business and used armed boats to protect their warehouses. The Americans, along with the Danes, Dutch and French, supported the British. During the crisis, Shaw acted as spokesperson for the US merchants. The Chinese explained that Smith would only be released in exchange for the gunner. In the meantime about forty Chinese warships gathered in front of the Western warehouses. At a meeting with the head magistrate of Canton, the Westerners declared that the seizure of Smith 'was considered, not as a matter affecting the English only, but as nearly concerning every foreign trader in Canton, whose property or person could no longer be considered secure'.[36] The Chinese magistrate again declared that the gunner must be given up within three days and promised a fair trial.

The British in the end decided to hand over the gunner and Smith was released by the Chinese authorities. The gunner was tried, found guilty and strangled to death. Shaw believed that his death could have been prevented by stronger cooperation between the Westerners, but private trading interests were considered more important. Another possible explanation for this lack of unity may have been that the gunner was a Filipino, and not a Westerner.

The *Empress of China* left Canton on 26 December with a cargo consisting of tea, silk, porcelain and nankeen (yellow cloth made of cotton). The sale in the US produced a profit of $30,727, or about 25 per cent of the costs for fitting out the ship, but more importantly, its success stimulated other ship owners to try their luck in the China trade. Between 1784 and 1814 the number of US merchant vessels calling at Canton was about 300 making a total of 618 voyages.[37] The Napoleonic Wars offered a window of opportunity for US merchants in the Far East. A large quantity of the Chinese silk and porcelain they bought in China was re-exported to Europe, because demand in the US was still relatively small. American traders with China benefitted from the Act Imposing Duties on Tonnage (1789) which discriminated against foreign vessels arriving in US ports with cargoes of tea or other Chinese products. Because the Americans used smaller ships, the value and tonnage of British trade with China were still much larger. Six days after his return, Shaw wrote a detailed report to Jay, the Secretary of Foreign Affairs. The conduct of Shaw during the Lady Hughes Affair impressed Congress and he was appointed Consul of the US for Canton in China on 27 January 1786. He was to exercise the duties and functions of consul at Canton: 'and we do hereby pray and request his Imperial Majesty the Emperor of China ... to permit the said Samuel Shaw fully and peaceably to enjoy and exercise the said office'.[38] The consulate was unsalaried, but Jay added: 'yet so distinguished a mark of confidence and esteem of the United States will naturally give you a degree of weight and Respectability, which the highest personal merit cannot very soon obtain for a stranger in a foreign land'.[39] He asked Shaw to collect all possible information regarding the trade in Canton and on China more generally.[40]

Shaw departed for his second voyage to Canton in February 1786, stopping first at Batavia in the Dutch East Indies. The Dutch–American Treaty (1782) made no references to trade in Batavia, but US vessels were usually welcomed, although they were not allowed to appoint a consul in the Dutch colonies. Like the Europeans before them, the Americans discovered that the products they brought to China were not much in demand. Initially they traded ginseng, but as trade expanded they were forced to use bullion, although they continued to search for other products, like furs, sandalwood, Bêche-de-mer, exotic products (e.g. pearls), cotton and, eventually, opium. Calling at Batavia allowed the US merchants to buy spices for the Chinese market: 'A profit may sometimes be made on merchandise carried from Batavia to Canton'.[41]

Shaw does not mention any reception with the Chinese authorities in Canton to present his commission as US consul. He may have contacted the Portuguese governor instead, although, as has already been explained, the

Portuguese had no authority to provide exequaturs in China. Shaw was never recognized by the Chinese government and until the First Opium War the position of a US consul, and all other consuls, remained unofficial.[42] The Chinese saw him as a taipan: the chief foreign businessmen who acted as liaison between the Americans and Chinese to settle disputes.[43] From his journal it seems that Shaw performed few regular consular duties. The bankruptcy of the Chinese merchant Howqua (aka Wu Ping-chien, 1769–1843) in late December 1788 required him to render some services to compatriots that had traded with this important Chinese merchant. In criminal cases, however, the Chinese insisted on their right to prosecute foreigners, as happened in the Lady Hughes Affair. On his second visit, Shaw noted the fierce competition between Western traders and discovered four other vessels from the US. After a residence of six months, Shaw had collected sufficient information on the Canton system and China for his report to Jay. Shaw wrote two official reports in his capacity as US consul: on 31 December 1786 and 21 December 1787. His assessment of the conditions of the Westerners in China was not very positive.

> On the whole, the situation of the Europeans is not enviable; and considering the length of time they reside in this country, the restrictions to which they must submit, the great distance they are at from their connections, the want of society, and of almost every amusement, it must be allowed that they dearly earn their money.[44]

On 25 January 1789, Shaw returned to the US and in March 1790 departed for his third voyage. The *Massachusetts* (about 800 tons) was the largest American vessel in the China trade and built for the firm Shaw & Randall according to the specifications of Shaw. The construction and voyage of the ship are recorded not only by Shaw, but additionally by the second officer Amasa Delano (1763–1823).[45] T. Dennett believes that building such a large ship was a sign of the profitable development of the trade with China, but is seems more likely that Shaw and his partners had decided to build it because all ships at Canton were required to provide the *cumshaw* (a substantial gratuity) to the Chinese customs officer.[46] The amount was fixed and not related to the size of the ship. On the smaller vessels employed by most US merchants this represented a very large duty.[47] On his way to China, Shaw again stopped at Batavia, hoping to trade. Delano notes that the Dutch governor was surprised to find that the US had appointed a merchant as consul because he believed that they 'only hurt the commercial interest of other commanders and supercargoes, as they naturally had every advantage over the man who had not the confidence of his own government to help him'.[48] The Dutch did not allow the Americans to trade and this was a major blow for Shaw. The ban on trade in Batavia prompted Shaw, in his capacity as US consul, to write an official letter of complaint. This had little effect because Shaw was US consul to China and not Batavia.

The arrival of the *Massachusetts* attracted many visitors, says Delano, but the ship was already rotten. This was caused by the cargo of green masts and spars loaded immediately after felling the trees after which the hold was caulked down. When the hatches were opened in Canton, the air was full of moisture and 'the inside of the ship was covered with a blue mould more than half an inch thick'.[49] Shaw was nevertheless able to sell the *Massachusetts* to the Danish Asiatic Company (*Asiatisk Kompagni*) for $65,000 and used the proceeds to buy cargo to be sold in Bombay. In Bombay, however, he decided to split the cargo: one part went to the US, while the other part was placed on board a chartered Danish ship to Ostend.

Shaw returned to the US in January 1792, intending to leave again for China before the trading season began. His departure was delayed by his marriage in August 1792, but in February 1793 Shaw departed for what turned out to be his fourth and final voyage. Typhoons lengthened the voyage and Shaw did not arrive in Canton until early November 1793. During his stay in Bombay on his previous voyage, he had contracted a disease of the liver and decided to return to the US, but died at sea on 30 May 1794. Shaw was succeeded by other US consuls to China, however until the American–Chinese Treaty of 1854 these were merely merchants 'whose only compensation was the fees of the office, the dignity of the position', and the information on business transactions from his competitors made available in official reports.[50] The US consul in Asia, says Dennett, 'was not an imposing functionary'.[51] The support from their government was minimal and only occasionally did a man-of-war enter Asian waters before the 1850s.[52]

Despite the many obstacles, the trade of the US with China flourished in the pre-treaty period. From the 1820s, trade with China was mostly handled by several large trading houses, including Russell & Company, Olyphant & Company and Augustine Heard & Company. The US merchants could call on their consul if one was present: a consul was only available for fourteen of the first fifty years. In retrospect we may conclude that in the nineteenth century the Chinese market promised more to Westerners than it delivered. Westerners have, much to their disappointment, continually overestimated the magnitude of the Chinese market in the nineteenth century. The number of Western merchants in some Chinese treaty ports by 1900 was smaller than it had been in the 1840s.[53]

Siam: Dutch Consuls, Managing Colonial Subjects

Siam (Thailand after 1939) was part of the 'Asian Mediterranean' long before the arrival of Western traders in the sixteenth century. It maintained relations with other states in the region, including tributary relations with vassal states in the north.[54] Siam was a major producer of rice and other valued commodities that were traded with China and other Asian countries, including Japan.[55] Chinese junks dominated the port of Bangkok and a large community of Chinese mid-dlemen handled most of the foreign trade of Siam. Besides the Chinese, there were Muslim traders from Persia and Arabia, along with merchants from India and other south-eastern Asian sultanates, kingdoms and empires.[56] The King-dom of Ayutthaya concluded commercial treaties with several European nations, namely the Portuguese (1516), the Dutch (1604), the British (1612), the Danes (1621) and the French (1662). Their traders and consuls received only limited religious and commercial privileges.[57]

After the fall of the Kingdom of Ayutthaya in 1767, the Westerners left until 1818, when the Portuguese returned to Bangkok, the new capital of Siam. In November 1820 they concluded a commercial treaty that allowed them to set up a trading post (or *feitora*) 'and with the privilege that all Portuguese could come to trade as before as His Majesty favours the Portuguese Nation more than all others'.[58] They were allowed to appoint a consul: the first consul was the mer-chant Carlos Manuel da Silveira, a trader in tropical wood and weapons.[59] Other Western states followed the Portuguese. The first British mission by John Craw-furd (1783–1868) in 1821/2 was a failure. Captain Henry Burney (1792–1845) was more successful and signed a treaty of amity and commerce (Burney Treaty, 1826), but it concerned mostly political matters and few economic conces-sions. The Burney mission was followed by the American expedition of Edmund Roberts (1784–1836) in 1832/3.[60] The American–Siamese Treaty of 1833 was almost identical to the Burney Treaty. Roberts next went to Muscat and signed a treaty with the sultan on 21 September 1835 (see p. 126).[61]

After the First Opium War, Siam became a vital link for Great Britain between Calcutta, Penang, Singapore and Hong Kong.[62] Pressed by British merchants and manufacturers, the government decided to send James Brooke (1803–68) to Bang-kok in 1850. His mission failed completely, as did the American mission of Joseph Balestier (1788–1858) in April 1850.[63] The fiasco of these two missions was partly the result of the illness of King Rama III, who died in 1851, but also Siamese resist-ance to Western advances. During the reign of two progressive kings, Rama IV (Mongkut, 1804–68) and Rama V (Chulalongkorn, 1853–1910) Siam opened its economy. This prevented formal colonization of Siam by Western powers, like Burma or Vietnam. D. Rajanubhab believes that the pro-Western attitude of King Mongkut was strongly influenced by the defeat of China in the First Opium War.[64] A. Webster, however, argues that endogenous factors were more important, partic-ularly the long tradition of international trade. This made the Siamese elite 'more attuned than has been recognized to the demands of international commerce, and therefore better able to manage the international pressures'.[65]

In 1855 Sir John Bowring (1792–1872), the British governor of Hong Kong, went to Siam to negotiate a new treaty. Bowring succeeded after just one month of negotiations with King Mongkut. M. R. Auslin notes that Mongkut 'was a realist who had witnessed the British use of force in Burma'.[66] The treaty of friendship and commerce between Siam and Great Britain (the Bowring Treaty, 1855) resembled previous treaties with China (1844) and Japan (1854). These were essentially unequal treaties with the Western states dictating the provisions.[67] Tagliacozzo says that the Bowring Treaty granted the British 'such wide commercial privileges in the kingdom that it is difficult not to see in Siam a huge breach of economic sovereignty'.[68] All ports in Siam were opened for British subjects. The treaty furthermore abolished the complicated system of taxes based on the size of ships for one fixed duty of 3 per cent of traded goods. The trade in rice and opium was liberalized and all existing state monopolies were abolished. The British received extraterritoriality in Bangkok and were allowed to appoint a consul with judicial powers. They could travel freely in Siam and were allowed to buy property, although they could reside only in Bangkok. The Bowring Treaty served as a model for later treaties between Western countries and Siam.[69] The US consul Townsend Harris (1804–78), on his way to Japan, concluded a similar treaty on 29 May 1856.

The reform policy of King Mongkut was continued by his successor Chulalongkorn. Between 1850 and 1868 the value of Siamese foreign trade almost doubled. Export of rice grew from 60,000 tons in 1857, to 475,100 tons in 1890. The export trade was dominated by British traders in Bangkok. At the turn of the twentieth century about 93 per cent of import and export was controlled by British merchants.[70] The natural resources of Siam spurred British foreign direct investment, particularly in teak.[71] Siamese and Chinese middlemen performed an essential role because of their knowledge of inland markets and international networks. Their presence, Webster writes, was 'key to the Siamese survival'.[72]

The Netherlands and Siam concluded a treaty of amity and commerce in December 1860, although there were only a few Dutch traders in Bangkok. Direct trade between both countries was non-existent, but some traders from the Dutch East Indies visited Siam. The first Dutch consul in Siam in 1860 was Paul Pickenpack (d. 1903), a merchant from the Hanseatic town of Hamburg and working for the firm Pickenpack, Thies & Company (established in 1858).[73] Pickenpack was a well-known family business in Penang.[74] He remained consul for about ten years. When Paul Pickenpack returned to Hamburg in late 1870, he proposed that his brother Vincent be appointed as his successor. In the annual report of 1871, Vincent Pickenpack noted that, although the Siamese King Mongkut had recently visited Java, trade between Siam and the Netherlands, including the Dutch East Indies, had not increased because of bad rice harvests and lack of regular shipping. He added that taxes in Siam remained high and the 'local government in its dealing with Western nations, is very cautious and extremely circumlocutions in coming to any understanding'.[75] In 1874 the Dutch government felt that relations with Siam warranted the appointment of a Dutch citizen as consul. The Siamese government had previously expressed their aversion of merchant-consuls and the Dutch government appointed a salaried consul: Walter Hugo Senn van Basel (1843–93). Van Basel was a former civil servant in the Dutch East Indies and spoke the Malaysian language.[76]

Van Basel arrived in Bangkok on 24 May 1875 and temporarily stayed in Vincent Pickenpack's home, because the existing hotels were 'inhospitable and houses were unavailable'.[77] He presented his credentials to King Chulalongkorn on 5 June, who showed his appreciation to the Dutch government for appointing a salaried consul and not a merchant-consul. However, complaints by the Siamese government about Van Basel began almost immediately after he received his exequatur. The main issue was the consular protection of Dutch colonial subjects, especially the numerous Chinese traders from the Dutch East Indies. The Chinese merchants engaged Siamese traders as their middlemen, but these middlemen also applied for Dutch protection, primarily to evade the high Siamese taxes and benefit from other privileges. The Siamese government seriously doubted whether all Chinese traders registered as Dutch subjects were actually from the Dutch East Indies and thus entitled to consular protection. After the arrival of Van Basel, the number of Chinese under Dutch protection rose from about 15 to 174. The question of who was and who was not a Dutch subject in Siam was investigated in 1877 by the Dutch government. It decided that in future Chinese traders from the Dutch East Indies wanting to do business in Siam under Dutch protection had to be born in the Dutch East Indies and had to have lived there for at least six years without interruption. This special arrangement with Siam was in force from May 1877 until 1903.[78]

Despite this arrangement, Van Basel had made himself hugely unpopular in Bangkok and in August 1877 he asked for an honourable discharge as consul.[79] The Dutch consulate was temporarily taken over by the US consul David B. Sickels and the vice-consul J. W. Torrey. But Torrey soon ran into trouble with the Chinese traders under Dutch protection. To the Dutch consul general in Singapore, the British merchant William Henry Macleod Read (1819–1909), he wrote in March 1878:

> The large number of Chinese, as well as other natives, under the protection of the Netherlands Government, coupled with the police and other judicial functions, with which the consular officer at this Port is invested, provide abundance of employment for an official having no other matters to divide his attention.[80]

In March 1878 the Dutch government appointed J. Salmon, previously an officer in the Navy and Dutch consul in Aden. Before he left for Bangkok, Salmon visited Batavia to study documents from Van Basel. He organized meetings with representatives of the Dutch Chamber of Commerce in Batavia and the Samarang Trade Association. From these meetings he learned that few Dutch traders were active in Siam, 'because this trade was wholly controlled by Chinese merchants, and the European traders were mostly ignorant of trade in Siam'.[81] Salmon arrived in Bangkok on 14 July and found the consular archive in complete disarray. In a private letter to the Minister of Foreign Affairs Salmon wrote about his daily work.

> Since my arrival here, I have been overloaded by work; I start at seven AM and continue until four or five PM; it is impossible to imagine the chaos and disorder of the consulate on my arrival, although the situation has much improved; however, work is not lessening because activities of the subjects, particularly the Chinese, require my full attention and the two assistants.[82]

He lived in the former home of Van Basel and Pickenpack, built on wooden poles near the river. Good houses were extremely difficult to get in Bangkok, and all transport was done by boat. Salmon furthermore wrote that relations with Siam had already improved and deplored his predecessor for bringing down the status of the Dutch consulate.

In October 1878 Salmon presented draft regulations for a *Chineeschen Raad* (Chinese Board) consisting of Dutch-Chinese from Java, appointed by the consul. The goal of the Chinese Board was 'a proper respect for the treaty of friendship, trade and shipping' between the Netherlands and the Empire of Siam.[83] The Chinese Board supervised the Dutch-Chinese from Java in Bangkok that were registered as Dutch colonial subjects at the consulate and fell under consular protection. The board members could not punish members of the Dutch-Chinese community, but had to report criminal cases to the consul. The Dutch Ministry of Colonies, however, objected to some of the draft regulations. It believed that the Dutch-Chinese were not the real problem anymore since the new criteria issued in 1877. Most problems arose from the Siamese middlemen in the service of the Dutch-Chinese. The Ministry of Colonies argued that these Siamese middlemen were not entitled to Dutch consular protection, but the Ministry of Foreign Affairs disagreed on legal grounds.[84] Similar rules applied in the Middle East concerning natives working for Western traders.

After some modifications of the regulations, Salmon appointed members for the Chinese Board. But the board did not relieve Salmon of his many duties and created even more problems. In his annual report of 1878, Salmon noted that he handled eighty-one judicial cases between July 1878 and December 1878; between January 1879 and February he already counted thirty-seven cases. Settling all these cases required a tremendous amount of time, because of the necessary correspondence with many different Siamese government officials. The heavy workload and the climate began to affect Salmon's health. In October 1879 he requested leave to recuperate in China. His physician explained that 'for many months past he [Salmon] has been suffering from great depression & the nervous system, which [is] aggravated by the relaxing nature of the climate in Siam'.[85]

Salmon left Bangkok in June 1880, but would not return. He was replaced by Peter Simon Hamel in May 1881, who was previously consul general in Elmina, West Africa. Shortly after his arrival in early October 1880, Hamel reported: 'As far as I can ascertain, the prestige of the consulate has suffered from abuses, especially related to judicial matters; these abuses I will rectify with all my abilities, but I must be careful in this'.[86] Hamel proposed to abolish the Chinese Board and the existing police instruction for Dutch citizens. He felt that the instruction was 'unnecessary as long as the number of Dutch citizens in Siam does not substantially increase'.[87] According to his information there were only three Dutch citizens in Bangkok, besides the consulate, but about 190 Dutch-Chinese subjects under Dutch protection, with 250 assistants and 265 Malaysians.[88]

> Quarrels between these peoples or with Siamese, occur every day. For each small case, the consul is informed. This requires a long investigation and much correspondence in English and Siamese or Malay. Because of corruption, a personal meeting with the Siamese government or even King is often necessary.[89]

Hamel believed, however, that his presence was much welcomed by the Dutch-Chinese traders.

> The Chinese merchants are very grateful for the protection they are offered, because this allows them to trade, which is mostly trade on credit. Without interference from the consulates it is very difficult for them to receive justice at Siamese courts apart from bribery, which requires large amounts of money.[90]

After his arrival Hamel limited the number of Dutch-Chinese under consular protection: it decreased from 212 to 112 and this reduced the workload of the consulate and the tensions with the Siamese government.

A month after his arrival Hamel proposed upgrading the consulate in Bangkok to a consulate general.[91] He admitted that direct trade between the Netherlands and Siam was still unimportant, but that was not true for trade with the Dutch East Indies. His calculations showed that in 1880 exports from Bangkok to Batavia amounted to about $1,500,000 and imports to $60,000, around $2,100,000 in total. About 72 Dutch vessels came from the Dutch East Indies to Bangkok, while 102 ships left from Bangkok to Batavia.[92] The proposal to create a consulate general in Bangkok was accepted in mid-1881 and on 17 May Hamel was promoted to consul general. In June 1887, however, Hamel was forced to leave his post because of failing health.[93] In a memorandum of the Ministry of Foreign Affairs the question was raised whether the high costs of the consulate general in Bangkok, almost 17,000 Dutch guilders annually, was justified because trade between Siam and the Netherlands hardly existed, while trade with the Dutch East Indies had declined since the early 1880s. It proposed to downgrade the consulate general to a consulate or even appoint a merchant-consul.[94]

Japan: Max von Brandt: Defending the Interests of Prussia

Although the Chinese regarded Japan as a vassal state that was part of the Sino-centric system, after 1600, starting with the rule of the Tokugawa, Japan developed its own regional tributary system. This included the Kingdoms of Korea and Ryukyu, and 'Dutch Barbarians' on Deshima (Nagasaki).[95] After 1640 all foreign trade was concentrated in Nagasaki and the country was effectively closed to Western states, except for the Netherlands.[96] Attempts by Western countries to open Japan and end the Dutch monopoly increased after 1800. The Russians, British, French and the Americans all tried several times to open diplomatic and economic relations with Japan, but before 1853 their missions failed.[97] In 1853 the US despatched Commodore Matthew Calbraith Perry (1794–1858) with four men-of-war to negotiate a treaty. On his second visit in early 1854 he succeeded, not only because of his stubbornness and willpower, and gunboat diplomacy, but also because the Dutch informed the Japanese about the humiliating defeat of China.

The treaty of amity and friendship (Treaty of Kanagawa or Perry Treaty, 31 March 1854), allowed American vessels to enter the ports of Shimoda and Hakodate for provisioning. According to the treaty, ships and sailors in distress would receive better treatment when they landed in Japan. The treaty did not contain any provision for trade, although article 6 seemed to offer this possibility.[98] Perry furthermore secured the provision for the appointment of consuls (based on reciprocity). On 4 August 1855, Townsend Harris, a New York merchant in chinaware, was appointed US consul general in Japan.[99] Hammersmith summarizes his previous experiences as 'modest achievements and frequent disappointments'.[100] Between 1849 and 1855 he visited many countries in East Asia.[101] His main duty as consul general was to conclude commercial treaties with Siam and Japan. He engaged as his interpreter Hendricus (Henry) Conradus Joannes Heusken (1832–61), who in 1853 migrated from the Netherlands to the US.[102]

After their arrival in August 1856, Harris and Heusken remained secluded in an old Buddhist temple in the town of Shimoda because the Japanese refused to start negotiations. On 25 December Harris wrote in his diary:

> Merry Christmas! How happy are those who live in lands where these joyous greetings can be exchanged! As for me, I am sick and solitary, living as one may say in a prison – a large one it is true – but still a prison.[103]

Negotiations did not begin until late February 1857 and in June, Harris was able to conclude the Convention of Shimoda, but he was not satisfied: 'I have not made a commercial treaty that would open Japan as freely as England is open to us'.[104] Subsequent negotiations resulted in the treaty of amity and commerce (29 July 1858). Japan next concluded similar commercial treaties with Russia, the Netherlands, Great Britain and France (collectively called the Ansei Treaties). The treaties opened three ports for international commerce: Nagasaki, Yokohama and Hakodate. After several years, additional ports and commercial cities would be opened, including Kobe/Hyogo, Osaka and Edo (known as Tokyo after 1868).

Already before the opening of Japanese ports in July 1859 a countermovement started to revise the Ansei Treaties and to expel the Western barbarians. This movement gained momentum after the emperor, previously a symbolic and religious figure, openly opposed the policy of the shogun (the military and de facto leader) and the government (*bakufu*), while the feudal landlords (*daimyo*) were divided and mostly tried to strengthen their own position. Disgruntled warriors (samurai) attacked and killed several Westerners in the foreign settlements in the open Japanese ports.[105] Before the official opening of Yokohama on 1 July 1859, Harris met the Dutch vice-consul Dirk de Graeff van Polsbroek (1833–1916) and the British consul general Rutherford Alcock (1809–97), arriving from his previous post on the China coast. In September, they were joined by the French Minister Gustave Duchesne, Prince de Bellecourt (1817–81). The first Prussian consul, Max August Scipio von Brandt, arrived on 28 December 1862.[106] These men played an important role in Japan during 'the Bloody 1860s'. Although their relationship was initially friendly, nationalistic rivalries and differences of opinion on how the deal with the Japanese soon led to conflicts and antagonism. The chaotic and unruly conditions during the first years forced them to cooperate.

Von Brandt, the son of a Prussian general, was Germany's representative in Japan between 1863 and 1875. From 1875 until 1893 he was Minister Resident to China for the German Empire. Because of his long tenure in the Far East, he became an expert on Asian affairs. Von Brandt's consular career in Japan was strongly influenced by the rise of Prussia in Europe and the process of German unification, culminating in the founding of the German Empire. These domestic developments meant that foreign affairs were less important. The isolated position of Von Brandt was worsened by the long distance and slow means of communication.

Von Brandt first visited Japan as attaché to the *Preußische Ostasien-Expedition* (Prussian East-Asian Mission, 1859–62), led by Friedrich Albert Count von Eulenburg (1816–81).[107] The goal of this large mission was to conclude commercial treaties with Siam, China and Japan.[108] When the Prussians arrived in the Bay of Edo in September 1860, V Von Brandt already noticed the political tensions. R. Wippich notes that von Brandt believed that the attacks on Westerners served two goals: to satisfy personal hatred and to weaken the position of the shogun.[109] Because of the political situation, the Prussian request to commence negotiation was at first rejected. The Japanese government was particularly horrified when Von Eulenburg explained that he had come to negotiate a treaty not only on behalf of Prussia, but twenty more German states.[110] With the help of Harris and Heusken the Prussians finally succeeded, although the Japanese refused to sign separate treaties with the other states of the *Norddeutscher Bund* and the cities of the Hanseatic League. On 24 January 1861 the Prussian–Japanese Treaty of Friendship, Commerce and Navigation was signed. The treaty was mainly important for Prussia in the European context: to establish itself as a major power. Six days before signing the treaty, Heusken was buried. He was killed by samurai after attending a party organized by the Prussians to celebrate the conclusion of the treaty. The murder of Heusken, Wippich says, was a key factor in forming Von Brandt's opinion of the Japanese.[111] Von Brandt believed that, because the Japanese were Asians and therefore uncivilized, they should be treated differently. The Japanese would listen only to force, military power or gunboat diplomacy, and it was necessary for the Westerners to cooperate.[112] A united front of Western powers proved difficult to maintain, however, because of diverging interests.

Von Brandt was appointed Prussian consul in Japan on 8 May 1862. His commission was not limited to a certain port, city or area. Prussia hoped to combine the economical duties of a consul and the political powers of an ambassador, but it soon turned out to be a mistake, because the other Western representatives and the Japanese authorities only saw him as a consul. Until 1868 Von Brandt was mostly excluded from the negotiations of Western treaty powers with the Japanese government. In political affairs he kept a low profile.[113] This was not necessarily a weakness, because it earned him sympathy and respect from the Japanese authorities. H. Stahncke notes that Von Brandt mostly agreed with the political views of the British and French representatives, but he had more friendly relations with the Dutch, Italians and Americans.[114]

From 1 January 1863 Von Brandt settled in Yokohama and officially began to work as Prussian consul. After 1865 he also maintained a residence in Edo, although Japanese authorities usually tried to avoid him and instead arranged a meeting with low-ranking officials such as the governor of Kanagawa. Being excluded from most meetings with his foreign colleagues as far as politics was concerned, meant that Von Brandt could focus on the normal consular duties. Direct trade between Germany and Japan was of minor importance; most German products were exported on British vessels. According to K. Meissner, only about ten or twenty Prussian merchants resided in Nagasaki, Yokohama and Hakodate.[115] An important German trader in Nagasaki was Louis Kniffler (1827–88), who was appointed vice-consul for Prussia.[116] Kniffler and the Bremer merchant Martin Hermann Gildemeister (1836–1918) founded the trading firm of L. Kniffler & Company in Nagasaki; it is still operating today in Japan as Illies & Company.[117] At first the Prussian traders preferred remaining under British, French or Dutch protection, but within almost a year most German merchants had placed themselves under the protection of their own consul.[118] Von Brandt had earned their respect and usually was quick to respond to emergencies. When fire destroyed the warehouse of Kniffler in December 1863, he kept order by drawing his gun to prevent any looting.[119]

Conditions in Japan worsened after the murder of a British merchant in September 1862 near Namamugi by samurai from the domain of Satsuma in southern Japan. The British demanded financial compensation and when the ultimatum was not met in April 1863, the tension in Yokohama almost erupted. Von Brandt believed that Great Britain wanted to wage war against Japan and feared that the confrontation would completely disrupt trade. Together with his Dutch and Italian colleagues, he tried to mediate. In December 1863, after the British bombardment of Kagoshima, the capital of Satsuma, an agreement was signed and the atmosphere in Yokohama and Nagasaki relaxed. However, it became clear to the Western representatives that the emperor wanted to expel all foreigners by 25 June 1863. While the shogun and *bakufu* ignored the order, the landlord of Choshu remained loyal to the emperor and bombarded Western ships passing his domain when they entered the Strait of Shimonoseki.

In the midst of this turmoil the Prussian consul general Guido von Rehfues (1818–94) arrived from China in August 1863 on board of the warship *Gazelle*. The purpose of the visit was to exchange the ratified treaties. This was, however, totally unnecessary, because according to the provisions of the Prussian–Japanese Treaty it would automatically be ratified on 1 January 1863.[120] The visit seems to have been mainly motivated by the wish to show the Prussian flag in Japan. At the same time a Swiss mission wanted to conclude a commercial treaty with Japan, while the US started negotiations on new tariffs. Unsurprisingly, Rehfues had difficulty persuading the Japanese government to exchange the ratified treaty and his visit certainly did not help Von Brandt. Von Brandt was relieved to see his fellow countryman depart at the end of January 1864, although he would have liked the *Gazelle* to remain in Yokohama. Germany could not take part in the Western naval expedition to punish Choshu in early September 1864. Afterwards the opening of Osaka (near Kyoto, the residence of the emperor) and the ports of Hyogo and Niigata became a major problem. Prussia did not take part in these discussions, because it had agreed not to demand the opening of these ports and cities in the first place. In the end, it was decided that these ports and cities would be opened on 1 January 1868, as was previously agreed in the London Protocol (6 June 1862).

In late summer 1866, Von Brandt went on leave to Germany and was promoted to consul and *Chargé d'Affaires* (*Geschäftsträger*) on 11 February 1867. Wippich argues that Bismarck's diplomatic experiences were critical for this promotion, because he was well aware of the low status of a consul in international relations. Bismarck believed that to maintain the status of Prussia in Japan a *Chargé d'Affaires* was required. After the establishment of the *Norddeutscher Bund*, Von Brandt was promoted to consul general and *Chargé d'Affaires* (20 July 1868).[121]

Von Eulenburg's original instructions included searching for possible colonies in Asia, but because of the difficulties of the mission to conclude a commercial treaty, Von Eulenburg never investigated this plan. The idea of founding a German colony in Asia was taken up by Von Brandt. Before his leave in 1866 to Germany, he revealed a rather ambitious plan to colonize the northern island of Japan: Hokkaido. He explained that occupying Taiwan, another possibility, would require at least 20,000 soldiers. He recalled the difficulties of Portugal and the Dutch Republic to establish a foothold in Taiwan during the seventeenth century. Von Brandt believed that Hokkaido offered excellent opportunities for Prussia to establish a naval base to protect its growing interests in East Asia. It had abundant supplies of coal, an agreeable climate and space for about 1 million colonists. Von Brandt believed that the island could be bought from Japan, but more simply conquered with eight corvettes, eight battleships and 5,000 soldiers.[122] The natives, the Ainu, would not pose a threat, while there were only a few Japanese. Berlin was, however, not interested because domestic developments, namely the unification of Germany, were more pressing. In the summer of 1868, Von Brandt revised his original plan and mailed it to Berlin, but again no official response came. Berlin did, however, establish a naval squadron called the *Ostasiatischen Schiffstation* (East Asian Squadron), although this lacked a permanent naval base in the area.[123] German interests were focused more on China after the Triple Intervention of Germany, Russia and France; following the Sino-Japanese War (1894–5), Japan was forced to retrocede the Liaotung Peninsula it had acquired from China. Germany occupied the Bay of Kiaochow (also Kiautschou) that became a naval base and colony.[124]

When Von Brandt was promoted to consul general and *Chargé d'Affaires* in July 1868, the political situation in Japan had changed completely. A civil war ended the reign of the Tokugawa, ruling Japan since 1600, and the shogun had resigned. The new head of state was the young Emperor Meiji (1852–1912). The government met the Western representatives on 9 January 1868, including Von Brandt, and guaranteed full compliance with the existing commercial treaties and protection of Western property. During his second leave in Germany in May 1871, the Franco-Prussian War started and Von Brandt enlisted as an officer to serve his country. After the war, he was promoted to Minister Resident of the German Empire in Japan. Von Brandt was sceptical about the Meiji Restoration: the modernization of Japan after 1868.[125] He believed that the new Japanese leaders selectively introduced Western ideas and technologies to give the country the outer appearance of a modern state. In reality Japan, according to Von Brandt, remained a typical conservative Asian state. Japanese interests in Germany increased after the 1870s because they saw it as a model for Japan, particularly the army and the constitution. The Germanophilic trend ended in 1895 after the Triple Intervention. By that time, Von Brandt was no longer in Japan, but promoted to Minister Resident in China. Before Von Brandt left for China, however, he was confronted with the murder of the German consul in Hakodate. Ludwig Haber (1843–74) was a German businessman from Brief (Silesia). On 11 August 1874, Haber was brutally murdered by Tazaki Hidechika, a Japanese soldier from the Akita prefecture. It was the first killing of a consul in Japan and one of the last attacks on Westerners.[126]

As Minister Resident in China, Von Brandt warned the West about the rapid industrialization of Japan that would disrupt the existing balance of power in East Asia. His most anti-Japanese publication was *Die Zukunft Ostasiens* (The Future of East Asia, 1895). He pointed to the growth of Japan's economic and military power. Von Brandt's views on Japan as the Yellow Peril became a reality in the Sino-Japanese War and the Russo-Japanese War (1905). Von Brandt did not witness these wars in China. In April 1893 he married Helen Maxima Heard (1868–1937), the daughter of the US Minister Resident in Korea and well-known merchant Augustine Heard (1827–1905). Apparently the marriage was against the wishes of the German Emperor and Von Brandt was recalled. He returned to Weimar and until his death continued to write about Japan and China in German newspapers and books.

China: J. H. Ferguson, Organizing the Coolie Trade to the Dutch East Indies

Although the treaties concluded in the 1840s opened several ports and commercial towns, the Chinese continued to believe in the Sino-centric system at least until the Sino-Japanese War. In 1861 the Chinese government reluctantly acknowledged equality with the Western states and it established a Foreign Office (*Zongli Yamen*) to handle foreign relations, while the kowtow was officially abolished in 1873. From the 1870s, China tried to modernize its economy and adopted other Western institutions, but only on a limited scale.[127] China and the West continued to quarrel over several issues including the labour of Chinese in Western colonies.

The anti-slavery campaign from the early nineteenth century increased the demand for labour in Western colonies and to meet this demand, Western merchants turned to British India and China. According to Chinese laws, emigration – including emigration under contract – was illegal, but from the 1830s large numbers of contract labourers, known as coolies, left China. In the mid-nineteenth century the coolie trade was unfavourably compared to the transatlantic African slave trade. The public anger forced Western countries to regulate trade from the 1860s. The Chinese government became more active and insisted on reciprocity: the right to appoint Chinese consuls in Western colonies. Most Western governments, however, objected to this, including the Dutch government.

In 1862, the Dutch consul in Canton, Jan des Amorie van der Hoeven (1825–77), an agent of the Dutch Trading Company (NHM) since 1855, was instructed to negotiate a commercial treaty with the Chinese government.[128] The first Dutch–Chinese commercial treaty of 1863 (Treaty of Tientsin) provided the Dutch with all the rights and privileges that were contained in treaties concluded between China and the other Western powers. In June 1872 the Dutch government appointed the first salaried consul general to China: Jan Helenus Ferguson. Ferguson was born in Curaçao and pursued a military career before becoming Governor of Aruba and Bonaire, in the Dutch Antilles, and thereafter in Elmina on the Coast of Guinea, until this last Dutch possession on the Gold Coast was handed over to the British in 1872. According to his instructions, Ferguson was not only consul general, but also *Chargé d'Affaires* although only on a personal basis.[129] Ferguson was instructed to secure from the Chinese government the free and direct emigration of Chinese coolies to the Dutch colonies in the East and West Indies (mainly Surinam).[130]

The growing demand for Chinese coolies coincided with the economic liberalization of the Dutch East Indies from the 1860s. On the east coast of Sumatra and its main port Deli, a large number of smaller and larger tobacco plantations developed from 1863, one of the most important being the *Deli Maatschappij* (the Deli Company), established in 1869 as a free-standing company with headquarters in Amsterdam but operations in the East Indies.[131] With the growth of tobacco production, the number of labourers increased and this could not be solved by contracting more natives from Sumatra. Most planters even considered the natives unsuited for this kind of work and the main source of labour came from China.[132] The number of plantations grew from fifteen in 1872 to twenty in late 1875, providing work for some 4,476 Chinese, besides a few hundred natives.[133] The plantation owners organized themselves in 1879 in the *Deli Planters Vereniging* (Deli Planters Association) that was a powerful pressure group. Their primary concern was the steady supply of cheap labour, meaning Chinese workers, for their plantations. Since emigration under contract was banned by the Chinese government after 1876, the Deli Planters Association requested and received the help of the Dutch government.

Chinese attitudes towards the coolie trade changed in the 1870s. After first ignoring the trade, the Chinese government became more active. In return for concessions to Western states, they wanted to appoint Chinese consuls in Western colonies. This new policy complicated the mission of Ferguson, because he had to confront the Chinese government, besides the parties most interested in the coolie trade: the Chinese coolie brokers and the British merchants and shippers in the Straits Settlements. Ferguson knew that the Dutch government opposed the demand of the Chinese to appoint a consul in the Dutch colonies, certainly the East Indies. To complicate matters even more, Ferguson gradually became convinced that the coolie trade was not much better than the African slave trade. F. van Dongen even calls him 'a sworn enemy of the trade'.[134] In December 1874, Ferguson wrote a long handwritten Report on the Governmental Situation of China for the Ministry of Foreign Affairs in The Hague. On p. 90 he discussed the Dutch commercial interests in China and explained these were modest, but 'the extent and status of our East Indian possessions necessitate the Netherlands to protect the same interests, the same duties and expectations, as any other major power in Europe'.[135] During the period 1872 to 1880 Ferguson made little progress in the matter of the coolie trade. The trade in coolies was controlled by Chinese and British middlemen in treaty ports like Amoy and Swatow and the coolie markets in Singapore and Penang. Transport was dominated by British shipping companies. Dutch plantation owners went to these markets to offer the coolies a labour contract. For each labourer the Chinese middlemen charged a commission, making the coolies rather expensive. The plantation owners wanted to contract Chinese labourers directly in China without the interference of the Chinese middlemen or the British shipping companies. These attempts were frustrated by negative publicity following a number of scandals on Dutch plantations on Sumatra in the 1870s. In 1880 Dutch Parliament promulgated the Coolie Ordinance to regulate labour relations on the plantations. This included labour under contract (three years) and the duty of the employer to treat the worker decently (providing water and food, medical care and regular payment), but in addition contained a number of penal sanctions for the coolies in case of misconduct, refusal to work diligently and desertion.[136]

In 1886 Ferguson still had not made much progress in his negotiations with the Chinese government. The Chinese did not allow the Dutch to offer free Chinese emigrants a contract to work on plantations and directly ship them to Sumatra or any other colony. Ferguson believed that pressing the matter would only result in Chinese demands to appoint consuls in Dutch colonies, which was still unacceptable to the Dutch government. In August 1886 a Chinese fact-finding mission went to South-East Asia to investigate the conditions of all overseas Chinese, not just coolies. The mission, consisting of two Chinese delegates, lasted twelve months and they visited over twenty ports and cities. Initially Deli was not included, but was added after news of serious abuses there. In their report, they concluded that of the Chinese in the Dutch East Indies, the coolies of Sumatra were 'the worst treated group'.[137] There were about 50,000 to 60,000 coolies working on plantations owned by Dutch nationals. Interviews confirmed the maltreatment. Coolies were flogged when they did not work properly, some even died from this, and sacked when they became ill. Without a job and home they depended on the goodwill of natives and other Chinese. The Dutch planters had appointed Chinese supervisors with ranks like *majoor* (major), *kapitein* (captain) and *luitenant* (lieutenant), but the delegation found that these leaders were intimidated by their Dutch employers. The Chinese delegation concluded that better protection of the overseas Chinese was required and recommended the appointment of consuls and vice-consuls, including one in Deli. Lack of funds and obstruction by Western governments, however, delayed the development of Chinese consulates in Western colonies for many years.[138]

To assist Ferguson to complete his mission, the Dutch government asked Dr J. J. M. de Groot (1854–1921), a sinologist and linguist, who was familiar with conditions on the coast of Fujian, to do some research on the coolie trade.[139] His assignment was strongly supported by the Deli Planters Association because by then they had completely lost their faith in Ferguson. They even suspected him of actively obstructing the coolie trade to the East Indies.[140] De Groot arrived in June 1886 in Amoy, but as a private person with hardly any support from his government he achieved little during the first months. On 8 March 1887 a first group of Chinese contract labourers was scheduled to sail for Sumatra, but the departure was delayed by angry Chinese middlemen. In May, Ferguson appointed de Groot as his deputy, to provide him with some authority to conduct negotiations. After the failed first attempt, de Groot completely avoided the involvement of British merchants. He telegraphed the *Deli Maatschappij* that in the future German traders would act as middlemen. These included the firms of Lauts & Haesloop in Swatow and Pasedag & Company in Amoy. He furthermore enlisted the help of the German consuls: in Canton Hermann Budler (d. 1893) and in Swatow E. Freiherr Von Seckendorff. With their help de Groot secured the support of the Chinese Imperial Commissioner for Foreign Affairs (the *daotai*) in Tianjin. A few days later the first group of Chinese coolies departed from Swatow and on 14 August 1888, the steamer *Dubourgh* unloaded sixty Chinese in Deli. Zwi Werblowsky notes that 'the costs per coolie by direct shipping from Fujian was 60% of that paid in the Straits'.[141] According to the chief administrator of the Deli Company, Hendrik Cornelis van de Honert (1854–1916), the price per coolie in Singapore or Penang was between $90 and $100. The free and direct emigration of Chinese to Sumatra reduced this to $20 or $25. Total savings for the planters in Sumatra would be about $70,000 monthly or $800,000 annually, assuming a monthly supply of 1,000 coolies.[142] Obviously the financial gains for the plantation owners were huge and would increase even more when more coolies would be contracted. Ferguson was ordered by the Minister of Foreign Affairs to go to Swatow in person to finalize the last details on this deal. He was even to temporarily move the consulate to Swatow until his mission was completed. In a letter to The Hague, Ferguson noted that, although the German consuls had been very helpful, their main interest was helping German shipping companies. He believed that this was not in the interest of Dutch shipping companies and traders.[143]

It would not take long before this emigration scheme to Sumatra was again interrupted by protests from Chinese coolie brokers and British businessmen in Singapore and Penang. In April 1889, the German steamer *China*, transporting 272 coolies to Sumatra, entered the port of Singapore when the Chinese suddenly revolted. They claimed to have been kidnapped and never wanted to go to Sumatra. The case was investigated by the German consul, and according to the Dutch consul general in the Straits Settlements, the revolt was orchestrated by Chinese coolie brokers in Singapore.[144] In late 1889 the transport to Sumatra was again stopped. The Chinese authorities had received complaints about the payment of coolies on the plantations, but according to the Deli Planters Association these allegations were false rumours.

That year Ferguson published his book *A Philosophy of Civilizations: A Sociological Study*.[145] Zwi Werblowsky, Blussé and Van Luyn, argue that it was one long complaint against the coolie trade in China.[146] In fact, only a few pages are devoted to the coolie trade. Archival records demonstrate that Ferguson was not against the hiring of Chinese labourers to work on foreign plantations or mines. He disapproved of the existing coolie trade: the kidnapping, the abuses, the coolie markets, and the miserable conditions on the ships, the plantations and in the mines. He wanted to modernize and improve the system of contract labour. He was very much in favour of the free and direct migration of Chinese, because this would break the monopoly of the coolie brokers and their accomplices, including the British merchants in China and the Straits Settlements. To improve the coolie trade Ferguson pleaded for more government regulation. In China, the government could organize coolie depots in the ports instead of the barraccoons (the wooden sheds) of the coolie brokers. Contrary to the opinion of the Dutch government, Ferguson believed that the Chinese government should be allowed to appoint consuls in Western colonies to protect their countrymen. This would only improve labour conditions of the Chinese on plantations and in mines. His ideas were hardly original, because already in the 1850s British authorities in China suggested regulating the coolie trade. In the British Straits Settlements several committees investigating the coolie trade in the 1870s made recommendations similar to Ferguson. In 1890 a British commission in Singapore again investigated the conditions of Chinese labourers. It proposed to establish depots under government control and introduce licenses for the coolie brokers.[147]

Ferguson was on leave in the Netherlands when his book was published. The British consul in Swatow wrote to the governor of Singapore about 'an unjust attack made by the Netherlands Minister at Pekin on cooly-emigration from China, occurring in his work "Philosophy of Civilization".[148] The governor expected that the book would have a negative impact on the attitude of the Chinese government regarding the coolie trade. The Dutch consul general in Singapore explained that Ferguson's remarks were addressed against the abuses of the coolie trade, not the principle itself. The former director of the Deli Company and founding member of the Deli Planters Association, Jacob Theodoor Cremer (1847–1923), at the time an influential member of the Dutch Parliament, expressed his anger and frustration about Ferguson in a private letter to the Minister of Foreign Affairs.[149] Ferguson mailed copies of his book to a number of people, including the British and Dutch Ministers of Foreign Affairs. In late January 1890 the Governor General of the Dutch East Indies contacted the Minister of Colonies about the book. He believed that Ferguson should avoid any action that might persuade the Chinese government to make new demands concerning the coolie trade, like appointing Chinese consuls in the East Indies. The Minister of Colonies concurred and informed the Minister of Foreign Affairs.

Before Ferguson left The Hague to return to his post in Peking, the Minister of Foreign Affairs had a personal interview with him. Ferguson explained that he was not against the trade, but against its many cruelties. The minister replied that although Ferguson was fully entitled to express his point of view in a book, he was not pleased. The matter was closed, but it may have speeded up the process of appointing a salaried Dutch consul general in the ports of Southern China in 1890. His main duty would be to protect Dutch interests, like the free and direct migration of Chinese to Sumatra and other Dutch colonies. The new consul general was Pieter Simon Hamel, previously consul general in Elmina (Africa) and thereafter Bangkok (see p. 73). His official title was Consul General of the Netherlands in Southern China, residing in Amoy. Ferguson immediately noted to the minister in The Hague that he was consul general, and also Minister Resident, for the whole of China. Hamel remained in China for only a very short period: he became ill in 1892 and a year later requested and received an honourable discharge.

The demand for Chinese labourers to work in Western colonies continued to grow. Until 1923, about 250,000 Chinese went to Deli.[150] The development of the oil industry in the Dutch East Indies on western Sumatra and other islands in South-East Asia provided new employment for Chinese workers.[151] Not until the Dutch–Chinese Consular Convention of 1910 did the Netherlands allow the Chinese government to appoint consuls in the Dutch East Indies and other colonies. The first Chinese consul general, Su Jui-chao, arrived in August 1912 in Batavia.[152] The Dutch, however, did not regard him as a consul according to international law, but only as a trade representative.[153] In 1911, China already had forty-six consulates in foreign countries, including Western colonies.

4 NORTH AND SOUTH AMERICA

Whereas in the Middle East and the Far East, the consuls played an import role combining political, judicial and economical duties, in North and South America conditions were completely different. The role of consuls remained much more limited to economic matters and in some places, mainly South America, political affairs. European countries were eager to establish diplomatic and commercial relations with the United States of America after 1783 and the new republics in Central and South America after the 1820s. It was equally important for these new states to conclude treaties of friendship and commerce because it would ensure their political and economic survival. The system of international relation in the Americas was familiar to the Europeans. Both were based on European ideas about equality, sovereignty, the rule of law, the law of nations, the standard of civilization and the Family of Nations. For consuls this meant that their role was easier in comparison to the conditions encountered in the Middle East and Far East. The Europeans introduced different institutions in North and South America from the sixteenth century, based on different 'institutional blueprints' related to the system of government and property. In North America democracy and private property were introduced, in South America monarchic absolutism and state property ruled. In the long run, this created a divergence between the northern and southern part of the Western hemisphere.[1]

European states appointed ambassadors first to the US and much later to the republics of South America. In many states in the Americas, particularly in South America, consuls thus remained the only official representative for several decades. In South America consuls often combined political and economic duties, but they did not possess judicial powers because extraterritoriality was not included in the treaties and consular conventions.

Decolonization and Consuls

After the Thirteen Colonies revolted and proclaimed their independence, their economic survival depended on acquiring land for agricultural production, and accessing new foreign markets where they could sell their agricultural surplus and buy necessary consumer products. Overseas trade was hampered by the loss of the privileges they had possessed under the Navigations Acts, including access to markets of the British Empire, particularly the British Maritime Provinces and the British West Indies. They furthermore lost the protection of the British Navy and credit from London-based trading houses. Trade with the West European colonies in Central and South America was obstructed by regulations that privileged their own merchants.

The Treaty of Paris (1783) doubled the territory of the Thirteen Colonies, providing new land for agricultural production.[2] Equally important was the securing of fishermen's rights of access to the Grand Banks near Newfoundland and other areas in the North Atlantic. The geopolitical situation remained precarious, as the new republic was surrounded by British, French and Spanish possessions and territorial claims. Political survival depended on becoming recognized as a sovereign state by concluding bilateral treaties and establishing diplomatic relations with the major European countries. These would secure the sovereignty of the US and accord it a place in the European system of states. The leaders of the revolution were well aware of this and they soon appointed representatives to start negotiations with European governments.

On 6 February 1778, the US concluded a treaty of amity and commerce with France followed by a treaty of alliance. L. J. Sadosky notes that after signing this treaty 'every power in the Atlantic world was now forced to deal with the American states in this new way, and in doing so, they had to rethink the structure of the Atlantic world itself'.[3] Article 31 of the former treaty granted both parties the right to appoint in each other's ports 'Consuls, Vice Consuls, Agents and Commissaries, whose functions shall be regulated by a particular Agreement'.[4] It took ten years before a consular convention between the US and France was concluded.[5] The delay was caused by differences of opinion about the privileges of consuls. Jefferson initially expressed as his opinion that the US did not need consuls. It was important in ancient times and perhaps still in countries that had not yet emerged from the state of barbarism, but in civilized states commerce had become so important that they already provided sufficient protection to traders. The agents of the trading houses were well equipped to look after their business without consuls. Jefferson soon changed his point of view and the US concluded consular conventions and appointed consuls like the European states.

Becoming recognized as a sovereign state, the treaties with France were important, but not sufficient, and Congress appointed several agents in a number of European cities, including Berlin, Vienna, Madrid, Amsterdam and St Petersburg, to conclude similar treaties. Most European states were reluctant to recognize the independence of the Thirteen Colonies for a number of reasons: fear of retaliation from Great Britain, loss of trading opportunities, and uncertainty about the outcome of the American Revolution. This explains why the Netherlands, although providing money and provisions (e.g. via St Eustatius in the Dutch Antilles), did not conclude a treaty until 1782. The Treaty of Paris between Great Britain and the North American colonies ended the struggle for independence. Articles 4 and 5 regulated the restitution of war debts and debts from commercial transactions before the war. British merchants were eager to recover much of their debts and for this purpose they lobbied Parliament to appoint commercial agents or consuls to the US. The British Foreign Secretary Lord Carmarthen (1775–1838) appointed Sir John Temple (1732–98) as consul general and George Miller (d. 1798) as consul for the southern states of North Carolina, South Carolina and Georgia. Phineas Bond (1749–1815) was a candidate as consul for the middle-Atlantic states. Because the US and Great Britain had not signed a commercial treaty or consular convention, appointing consuls was problematic. When Temple arrived in New York in late November 1785, Secretary of State John Jay asked Congress: should we receive Temple de jure or de gratia?[6] According to Emer de Vattel (1714–67), the leading scholar on international law, a nation was not obliged to accept a foreign consul. The US was therefore not obliged de jure to receive Temple, but Jay argued that a rejection would certainly irritate Great Britain: 'In my opinion, therefore, this Consul should be received, but in such a manner as to be and to appear as a matter of favor, and not as a matter of course'.[7] Congress accepted Jay's point of view and recognized Temple as consul general on 2 December 1785.

The refusal of the US government to discuss political matters with the British consul general induced Carmarthen to provide Bond with a second commission: commissary for commercial affairs for all the US. This second commission was ambiguous in international law and hardly used. Some scholars regarded these as ministers of second rank, with 'the authority to negotiate with both local and federal governments on all commercial matters'.[8] Although Bond had doubts regarding this second commission, he accepted his appointment and sailed for the US in early September 1786. Bond presented his credentials to Jay, but because Congress was not in session, he could not receive Bond until Congress had accepted his credentials.[9] Congress did not decide on Bond's commissions during its next session (4 December 1786 to 2 February 1787), but asked for a new advice. According to Jay, on 29 March, although no treaty of commerce and navigation existed, the US could accept Bond as a favour but not as a right. Jay still rejected Bond's second commission, because it was very unusual and the precise limits of powers undefined. 'Your Secretary suspects that this appointment was made to supply, in some sort, the place of a Minister; and in his opinion, it will be more prudent not to let it take effect'.[10] The government was afraid that other countries would follow the British example and appoint consuls with added powers instead of regular ministers or ambassadors. That would harm the status of the US in international relations. A month later, Bond had a new meeting with Jay and finally Congress accepted his appointment as consul, but rejected his second commission. Bond replied that the second commission was more important for British business, but Jay answered that such a commission was impossible without a treaty of commerce and navigation.[11] During his consulship in the US between 1786 and 1814 Bond was never recognized as commissary for commercial affairs for all the US.

The first European consuls were appointed in major US ports and cities along the east coast, including New York, Boston, Philadelphia, Charlestown, Savannah and New Orleans. The number of consuls and particular vice-consuls rapidly increased with the expansion to the west coast when consulates were opened in San Francisco in the 1850s. The consuls reported on many different topics. When the Habsburg Empire appointed Alois J. X. Baron von Lederer (1773–1842) as consul in New York in 1820, his instructions were to report on the development of the country 'and to report on all institutions, ordinances and inventions which could be reasonably of any use to the Austrian monarchy'.[12] The European consuls, L. A. White notes, furthermore discussed demography, geography, agriculture and manufacturing, the educational system, the position of women, migration, quarantine measures and the issue of slavery in the southern states. Robert Bunch, the British consul in Charlestown, reported on the 'frightful atrocities of slave holding'.[13] More worrisome was the growing participation of the US in the revival of the transatlantic slave trade from the 1850s. This included schemes, similar to French policies in the West Indies and the Indian Ocean, to import free Blacks to the southern states. British consuls living in the US in the 1850s were 'astounded at the American West', the energy and restlessness of the Americans.[14] The Belgian consul in Savannah, Laurent Marcellin Joseph de Give (1828–1910), wrote: 'This country is immense; it can feed a hundred million people. It is already very rich, but its present wealth can give no idea of its future riches.'[15] Some predicted a separation between the North and the South over the issue of slavery and even suggested a split between the states on the Atlantic and the Pacific.

The position of the European consuls, especially those in the southern states, was precarious during the Civil War. Direct communication with their embassy in Washington was no longer possible after 1863. After the war, the rapid industrialization and the enormous growth of European emigration to the US were a major concern for the consuls. The consular duties did not end when the migrants were admitted to the US, because as long as they remained compatriots they could apply for consular protection. The British consul in Chicago reported in 1856 that immigrants were often victims of fraud after landing in New York, while the trip to Chicago depleted their resources before they could continue their journey to one of the new states like Iowa.[16]

Before independence came to the colonies in South America, Portugal and Spain followed mercantilist policies. The main purpose of the Spanish colonies was to contribute to the wealth of the metropolis. All import and export first went through Madrid or Lisbon, creating a strong dependence of the colonies on the motherland. The colonies, says J. M. Viana Pedreira, were the exclusive domain of the motherland and both Spain and Portugal therefore tried to limit the number of foreign traders.[17] They certainly did not accept the appointments of foreign consuls in their colonies. 'The basic goal, B. Fausto argues, was '"exclusivity" – colonies should trade with their imperial capital and with no one else'.[18] Spain introduced controls to regulate trade, including merchant fleets, a *Casa de Contratacion* (Chamber of Commerce) and *consulado* (merchant's guild).[19] By the late eighteenth century, neither Spain nor Portugal was able to completely enforce this policy. Colonials evaded the existing regulations and smuggling was widespread. Rebellions broke out in different parts of the colonies (in Pernambuco in 1710 and Minas Gerais in 1789) as manifestations of a desire for independence and growing nationalism. These movements gained momentum after the American Revolution and the French Revolution. Both revolutions created a crisis in the existing colonial system of Spain and Portugal. Until 1816, the Spanish government maintained, according to F. L. Paxson, that 'the Laws of the Indias' were still in place and they did not permit any foreign vessel to approach or carry on commerce with the port of Buenos Aires in Argentina.[20]

After proclaiming their independence, the South American leaders were eager to become recognized as a sovereign state. The struggle to achieve full independence and become a sovereign state was hampered by a division in the colonial elite (the creoles) between those that remained loyal to Spain and those that wanted to pursue their own destiny. The result was a long succession of juntas, making it difficult for outsiders to determine who was in power and whether the colonies had already achieved independence. To protect their economic and political interests, Britain and the US began to appoint consuls. However, before the formal independence of the South American states their position remained unofficial, although they were cordially received by the juntas. Their unofficial character is reflected in their commission and the title agent instead of consul, although their duties were not very different. After the Napoleonic Wars, G. R. Andrews explains, the deposed king of Spain, Ferdinand VII (1784–1833), was restored to the throne and the Spanish government tried to regain possession of the colonies because they were of vital importance to the economy.[21] These attempts were blocked by other European powers, joined in the Quintuple Alliance after 1815 (Great Britain, Austria, Prussia, Russia and France), because it was not in their interests. Great Britain, however, favoured monarchism, not republicanism, and wanted to preserve the Spanish Empire by giving the Spanish colonies some degree of autonomy. But Great Britain also favoured free trade and wanted to abolish the restrictions and monopolies on foreign trade.

1x156 - PB - 13mm - 0 - 1858426-6 - 1 - 9780367669126 - 2UP-450mm-Web-TECNAU 2025/05/01 13.11.17

The policy of the US was not very different from the Europeans. The revolts in Central and South America were supported because it would end European colonialism and open up the countries for US businessmen.[22] But the alliance of European powers and the actions undertaken since the Congress of Troppau (1820) worried the US. Would this also affect the American hemisphere where similar revolts were happening? As far as the US government was concerned, retrocession of Latin American republics to one of the European powers was out of the question. This policy was incorporated in the Monroe Doctrine (1823) that warned European powers not to interfere in the Western Hemisphere.[23] M. T. Gilderhus writes that the message of President James Monroe (1758–1831) was received in Europe without much excitement, except for strong Spanish objections. The Russian Tsar Alexander I (1777–1825) and the Austrian Minister of Foreign Affairs Von Metternich (1773–1859) believed that it was arrogant, because the US lacked the maritime and military power to enforce it.[24]

The US closely monitored developments in Central and South America and appointed dozens of special agents, sometimes titled consuls, to report on the developments. As soon as the US government was convinced that the new republics had secured their independence, W. S. Robertson says, it would recognize them as sovereign states and immediately start the process of concluding treaties of friendship and commerce regulating the appointment of consuls and ambassadors.[25] The US believed that because of its own history, it possessed an advantage over the European states. In the 1780s American politicians already referred to their special relationship, based on geography and the struggle for independence, with the Spanish and Portuguese colonies. This eventually culminated in the idea of Pan-Americanism that was present in some of the despatches of the US agents in the 1810s and 1820s. The South American republics initially gravitated towards the US, but from the 1840s tried to stimulate trade with Europe to counteract the growing influence of their powerful northern neighbour. European trade and foreign direct investments in South America (including mines and railways) expanded, but the financial instability of the South American republics led to much political instability.

The position of consuls in the Americas is clarified by looking at the following cases. The experiences of William Shaler and Joel R. Poinsett (1779–1851) demonstrate the strong interests of the US in the decolonization of South America and its eagerness to establish diplomatic relations. Both men played a very active role, in the case of Poinsett even joining the army of Chile, and promoted republic ideas. European states were equally interested in establishing diplomatic and commercial relations with South American republics, as the case of the Prussian consul Carl Wilhelm Theremin (1784–1852) shows. This case furthermore illustrates that the presence of a consul alone did not necessarily stimulate foreign trade: direct trade between Prussia and Brazil remained small. From the mid-nineteenth century migration from Europe to North America increased quickly, creating all kinds of additional duties for the consuls. They mediated between the European shipping companies, migrants and the US government. Consul provided relief to fellow citizens and assisted their own governments in tracking down criminals that had escaped to the US. The Civil War disrupted the migration business only on a limited scale, as the case of the Dutch consul Rudolph Christian Burlage (1809–83) demonstrates. But the war created new problems for consuls, because they were supposed to maintain the neutrality of the country. The case of Leonard Burlington Smith (1839–98), the US consul on Curaçao for many years, shows that foreign consuls often developed an interest where they resided. As a merchant-consul, Smith was primarily busy developing his own business, but at the same time he was a member of the local community. He introduced several new products and technologies on the island. The globalization of business in the nineteenth century left few places undisturbed. The investigations of the British consul general Roger Casement (1864–1916) into the rubber industry in the Upper Amazon region, and previously in Congo Free State, involved the governments of Peru, Great Britain and the US. His reports helped to set limits on the exploitation of the natives by Western companies and contributed to promoting the humanitarian cause in the nineteenth century.

South America: William Shaler and Joel R. Poinsett, Promoting Republicanism

During and immediately after the American Revolution, the Continental Congress appointed secret agents in the Caribbean, several European countries, the East Indies and Asia. They were often merchants residing in foreign countries and after their appointment continued to mix business and politics, without worrying about morality.[26] After the adoption of the Constitution in 1787, the US continued to employ private persons in public functions.[27] Their titles varied: special agent, secret agent, agent for commerce and seamen or commercial agent. H. M. Wriston labels them executive agents, while R. F. Nichols calls them advance agents, 'men who were missionaries preaching the gospel of the new and enlightened republican way of life'.[28] They were appointed by the president without consulting Congress (hence, executive agents) and they did not receive an exequatur from the receiving government, nor did the US government ask for one. The instructions these executive agents received were similar to those of US consuls in Europe, but they were not consuls according to international law. These were informal and unofficial appointments, 'informal from the point of view of international law, and unofficial from the point of view of constitutional law'.[29] Executive agents were mainly employed to open relations with new states or states not yet recognized, to reopen relations with states that were broken off, send to

colonial and dependent states, to represent the US during international conferences, or send to states lacking diplomatic officers, and for many other purposes.

The US appointed a large number of these executive agents to Central
and South America between *c.* 1810 and 1824. Although the US government
supported the rebels for emotional, ideological and political reasons, their
official policy was neutrality and non-recognition until full independence was
achieved.[30] The main tasks of the executive agents were: to collect information
and report on the progress of the revolution, promote trade, explain the US
policy of neutrality and to propagate republican ideas and democracy. Although
the executive agents usually went in secret, they were received by the ruling juntas, but exequaturs were not requested nor provided because this would imply
formal recognition by the US government.[31] These executive agents thus represented the US in Central and South America until formal relations could be
established and consuls could be appointed.[32] Most of the executive agents operated alone, and many used this freedom to propagate republican ideas based on
the model provided by the US.

In 1810 President James Madison appointed William Shaler as agent for commerce and seamen at Vera Cruz in Mexico, but he was in addition instructed to
collect information about the Spanish colony of Cuba. His life in the first decades of the nineteenth century was a characteristic mixture of mercantile activities
and governmental functions.[33] Shaler freely talked about the political role of the
US in the world, despite the ideology of isolationism.[34] While some of his ideas
could be interpreted as Pan-Americanism, he was, as J. C. A. Stagg argues, also
very much rooted in the eighteenth century and supported notions like mercan-
tilism and the law of nations, including the standard of civilization and the rule
of law.[35] From 1794 until *c.* 1803, Shaler worked in France as agent for the New
York firm Phoenix, Ingraham & Nixen. In January 1799 he went as supercargo to
the Spanish ports in La Plata, touching at Montevideo and Buenos Aires. After his
return to Europe in September he sailed to the Île de France (Mauritius), where
his vessel was captured by French privateers during the quasi-war between the US
and France. Shaler was forced to stay, lodging temporarily at the home of the US
consul and here befriended Richard Jeffry Cleveland (1773–1860). Shaler and
Cleveland became business partners, making several voyages to South America,
the north-west coast of America, China and Europe between 1800 and 1810.

The appointment of Shaler as agent for commerce and seamen was secured
through his friendship with powerful men like Robert Smith (1757–1842), Secretary of State between 1809 and 1811. His task was to promote trade in the
Gulf region and to collect information about the revolt in Mexico and Cuba.[36]
Shaler first went to Cuba to investigate whether it would be willing to become
part of the US, while at the same time he was to stress that the US government
would not accept foreign rule, excluding Spain. Shaler arrived in Havana in

the summer of 1810 and began collecting information. He was arrested by the Spanish authorities on 8 November 1811 on suspicion of collaborating with the revolutionaries and ordered to leave the island. Shaler moved to New Orleans and between January and March 1812 wrote several reports on Cuba for the Secretary of State. Shaler pointed out that Cuba was of great geopolitical and strategic value because of its proximity to Florida and the Gulf Coast. If Great Britain or France would conquer Cuba, they would be 'masters of the American coasts from Charlestown to Darien. Havana would become a great naval station, that would give them the complete command of those seas; not a boat could leave the Mississippi and enter it without their License.'[37] Shaler continued: 'If Cuba came under the influence or direct control of the United States, no major power could wage war and the Union would be safe'.[38]

When in 1811 the Cortes (the Portuguese Parliament) in Madrid discussed the possibility of abolishing the slave trade, Shaler reported that the Cuban planters panicked and proposed to separate from Spain, while some discussed the possibility of joining the US.[39] Shaler concluded that Cubans would not accept any other European power to take control of the island. In his fourth report, he discussed the racial division and the dominant role of the Catholic Church on the island.[40]

After being ousted from Cuba in November 1811, the consulate of Shaler was transferred to Natchitoches, Louisiana to report on the Mexican revolt against Spain. Shaler contacted Bernardo Gutiérrez de Lara (1774–1841), who attempted to recruit soldiers.[41] Shaler supported the idea:

> It is thus indispensably necessary that the American people interfere in this interesting Struggle; their honor, their interests, humanity, require it. It is time to set a boundary to the Ambition of Europe: this continent was not created for their sole convenience: much nobler destinies I trust await it.[42]

Shaler joined Gutiérrez in the revolt against Spain when the latter travelled to Texas until the Gutiérrez–Magee Expedition proclaimed the independence of Texas. For this action he was reprimanded by President Madison. In his last report, Shaler discussed Mexico and its many valuable natural resources and important mining industry.[43] In the remainder of the report he elaborates on the possible expansion of the US across the northern continent, from the Atlantic to the Pacific, including California. Having made a visit to California during his wanderings with Cleveland, he was well aware of its geographical location and natural advantages for the US.

In 1814 Shaler travelled to Belgium to assist the US Peace delegation in the negotiations ending the War of 1812 between the US and Great Britain (Treaty of Ghent, 1814). He next went to Algiers with Stephen Decatur and Captain William Bainbridge to secure a peace treaty with the ruler of Algiers to end the Second

Barbary War between the US and Algiers (see p. 48).[44] After concluding this treaty, he was appointed US consul general in Algiers and served for almost fourteen years. In 1828 he returned to Cuba, accepting a post as US consul general in Havana, after Spain had finally agreed to recognize foreign consuls in her colonies. Shaler joined his old business partner Cleveland, who served as US vice-consul on Cuba. Shaler died in Havana when a cholera epidemic struck the town in 1833.[45]

On 24 May 1810 the United Provinces of Rio de la Plata elected a provisional government in Buenos Aires. A month later, Joel Roberts Poinsett was appointed commercial agent for South America, especially Argentine and Chile.[46] According to Paxson, Poinsett 'seems to have been one of the ablest and best representatives of the United States in South America'.[47] He was born into a wealthy Protestant family in Charlestown, but from 1796 until 1800 studied at the University of Edinburgh. He toured extensively in Europe between 1801 and 1806. C. L. Chandler says that this gave him 'more knowledge of the world than any degree from Harvard, Yale or Princeton'.[48] Dyer and Dyer claim that Poinsett was 'among the best, if not himself the best, of American observers abroad during the first quarter of the nineteenth century'.[49]

According to the instructions from Secretary of State Robert Smith, Poinsett was to travel to Buenos Aires, and later to Lima in Peru or to Santiago in Chile, or both, and to report on the struggle for independence without jeopardizing 'the neutral character and honest policy of the United States'.[50] He was to stress 'that the United States cherish the sincerest good will towards the people of South America as neighbors, as belonging to the same portion of the globe, and as having a mutual interest in cultivating friendly intercourse'.[51] Smith wrote: 'The real as well as ostensible object of your mission is to explain the mutual advantages of a commerce with the United States, to promote liberal and stable regulations, and to transmit seasonable information on the subject'.[52] In a separate letter, Smith explained that the commerce between the US and Buenos Aires was substantial enough to appoint a consul: the US was the second largest exporter to South America in 1810.[53] Poinsett was therefore asked

> to attend to the Commercial and other concerns of our Citizens in all the cases where they would fall under the patronage of a Consul, and you may appoint Deputies wheresoever it may be found necessary in your District, being yourself responsible for their acts.[54]

Poinsett received printed instructions and circular letters for US consuls and even a cypher to send coded messages if necessary. If Poinsett felt that the revolutionary governments were sufficiently established, he could furthermore negotiate a commercial treaty on behalf of the US. Poinsett presented himself much more as a consul than Shaler, receiving all the instructions (his written commission from the US government and any personal instructions received from the Secretary of State or president) as well as the stationery of a US consul, although that was not his official title. It was clear that the purpose of Poinsett's mission was to secure trading rights for the US.

On 13 February 1811 Poinsett was received by the junta in Buenos Aires. He was allowed to gather information, although the junta expressed disappointment that his letter of credentials was not addressed to it and not even signed by the American president.[55] Poinsett wrote a detailed report about the commerce of Buenos Aires, including geographical and statistical data. Chandler writes that Poinsett made some policy suggestions that can be understood as Pan-Americanism.[56] In a letter to the new Secretary of State, James Monroe, on 24 October, Poinsett explained that the struggle for independence could only succeed when the South American colonies united to create a powerful blockade against European powers and 'to solicit the aid and protection of the United States and make one great simultaneous movement of the whole continent'.[57] He discussed these ideas with the junta. Monroe, writing to Poinsett in April 1811, urged caution:

> The destiny of these provinces must depend on themselves. Should such a revolution however take place, it cannot be doubted that our relation with them will be more intimate, and our friendship stronger than it can be while they are colonies of any European power.[58]

When Poinsett discovered that Great Britain had negotiated lower tariffs on import and export with Buenos Aires, he asked to be given an official appointment as US consul to negotiate a commercial treaty with similar conditions. In April 1811 Poinsett was indeed promoted to consul general for the Spanish provinces of Buenos Aires, Chile and Peru.[59] Luis Goddefroy (1774–1860), a long-time resident merchant of Montevideo, was to be US consul, while William Gilchrist Miller, an American businessman, became vice-consul in November. Because Congress did not approve the appointment of Goddefroy, he was replaced by Thomas Lloyd Halsey (1777–1845) between 1812 and 1819.[60] It is not clear why the US government appointed a consul general, consul and vice-consul, because they were not officially recognized by the junta, no exequatur was requested or received, and it clearly contradicts the policy of neutrality of the US. Perhaps the US government wanted to present a counterweight to the strong British influence in the region, particularly in Brazil. After Poinsett protested against the existing preferential duty on British shipping to Buenos Aires and demanded similar conditions for American ships, the *junta* replied that any commercial privileges for British commerce would be extended to the US or any other country.[61] According to D. M. Parton, Poinsett and the junta did agree on new commercial regulations allowing the US to export some of its produce duty free.[62] C. J. Stillé notes that he signed commercial treaties with Argentine and Chile, but these were never ratified by Congress.[63]

Poinsett next shifted his attention to Chile and moved to Santiago in December 1811. The Chilean junta looked towards the US as a model. The first Chilean National Congress began symbolically on 4 July 1811 and a year later the new Chilean flag was presented. Trade was liberated, the import of slaves banned and several ports were opened for foreign shipping in February 1811, including Valparaiso, Talcahuano, Coquimbo and Valdivia.[64] The revolutionary government of President José Miguel Carrera (1785–1821) was eager to recognize Poinsett as US consul general because they hoped that it would lead to full diplomatic relations with the US. Poinsett offered his services for drafting a new constitution to cement the US–Chile relationship and appointed Mathew Arnold Hoevel (1773–1819), of Swedish-American descent, as US consul to Santiago.

The Chilean Revolution was countered by Spanish Royalists and the Spanish viceroy in Lima in the summer of 1812. Several foreign ships in Chilean ports, including those of the US, were seized. Poinsett took an active interest in the fate of Chile and accepted a post as commander of a division in the Chilean Revolutionary Army.[65] Revolutionaries and Royalists clashed at San Carlos and Talcahuano in the Bay of Conception, Peru. Poinsett was able to free eleven American vessels, mostly whalers. Spanish Royalists again went on a counter-attack from March 1813 and finally recaptured Santiago. They imprisoned Carrera, who later managed to escape. Poinsett first tried to leave Chile in March 1814 on board of a US warship, but the Royal Navy ships *Cherub* and *Phoebe* opened fire, sinking the vessel and killing most of its crew. Poinsett returned to Buenos Aires by crossing the Andes, but because of the War of 1812 was not able to return to Charleston until May 1815.

On 9 July 1816, the United Provinces of Rio de la Plata proclaimed their independence from Spain. President Monroe appointed Colonel Joseph Devereux as agent to collect information, but his mission was a complete failure.[66] According to Wriston, Devereux 'engaged in unwarranted financial negotiations involving the United States, and his authority was withdrawn'.[67] He was succeeded by Special Agent William G. D. Worthington on January 1817. Soon after his arrival, Worthington presented, on his own initiative, a draft commercial treaty based on full reciprocity, including the exchange of consuls, but the treaties were never ratified, 'as an exchange would have been tantamount to recognition and a direct violation of the United States policy of neutrality'.[68] When Worthington proceeded on the same course in Chile he was dismissed as US consul.[69] J. C. Pine says that his 'personal desire to excel and a wish to assist the patriot cause led him into this major diplomatic blunder'.[70] In 1817 Monroe asked Poinsett for a second mission to Buenos Aires, but when he declined the US government appointed the South American Commission (1817–18) for the mission.[71]

In 1822 several Spanish colonies in the Americas had secured their independence and the US proceeded to grant them formal recognition.[72]

On 8 March President Monroe recommended that Congress acknowledged the independence of Colombia, Chile, Peru, Buenos Aires and Mexico. He furthermore recommended establishing diplomatic missions to these states. Instructions were sent to the US executive agents to present themselves as US consul or *Chargé d'Affaires*.[73] In the remaining Spanish colonies, including Cuba, the US continued to appoint agents baring various titles.[74] Poinsett was appointed as special envoy to Mexico in 1822 and three years later became US Minister.[75] In 1829, however, the Mexican government asked for his removal because Poinsett had frequently interfered in domestic politics. He left Mexico in January 1830 and returned to South Carolina. From 1837 until 1841 Poinsett served as Secretary of War under President Martin Van Buren (1782–1862). Initially, the South American republics welcomed the Monroe Doctrine and quickly established diplomatic and economic relations with the US, but from the 1840s their enthusiasm declined as many experienced financial and economic problems. Instead they began cultivating stronger relations with European states and increasingly employed tariffs and other measures to protect their domestic trade and industry.[76]

Brazil: Carl Wilhelm Theremin, Promoting Prussian Trade

During the Napoleonic Wars Portugal sided with Great Britain and this led to the occupation by France in November 1807. Prince Regent Dom João (1767–1826), acting on behalf of his demented mother, Queen Maria I, and a following of about 10,000 or 15,000 people fled to set up their residence in Rio de Janeiro in early 1808.[77] During the crossing they were escorted by the Royal Navy. Lacking the protection of their own navy, the Portuguese continued to rely on them, allowing Great Britain to demand commercial privileges. This included the opening of Portuguese ports in Brazil and a pledge to end the slave trade between Africa and Brazil.[78] The arrival of the large royal retinue gave an enormous boost to the development of Rio de Janeiro, which became the capital of the Portuguese dominions. This was further stimulated on 28 January 1808 when Dom João proclaimed the *Carta Régia*, ending the monopoly system that had existed for three centuries. It opened the ports to all foreign shipping of friendly nations, but British traders benefited most from this. The number of foreign trading houses in Rio in 1808 was about three hundred, including almost a hundred and fifty British traders.[79]

The influx of British merchants led to complaints of Brazilian traders and this prompted Dom João to issue a new law in June 1808 to limit free trade to a number of ports: Belém, São Luis, Recife, Salvador and Rio de Janeiro. Great Britain concluded a secret treaty of navigation and commerce in February 1810, supplemented in 1817, and at the same time a treaty of alliance and friendship. The maximum tariff on British goods entering Brazil was fixed at 15 per cent ad valorem (this was previously 26 per cent), while Portuguese goods paid 16 per cent. Britain was furthermore allowed to appoint *judges conservatores*, special magistrates responsible for legal cases between British subjects. This was not the same as extraterritoriality, but it provided the British with judicial powers in Brazil.

On 16 December 1815 the United Kingdom of Portugal, Brazil and Algarve was proclaimed. The former colony of Brazil was now a kingdom and equal to Portugal and Algarve. It stimulated aspirations for full independence following earlier revolts. Insurrections in some cities in Brazil in 1817 remained unsuccessful and were crushed with British support. After the death of Queen Maria I in March 1816, Prince Regent João was crowned King João VI in 1818, but he remained in Rio de Janeiro. Between 1813 and 1820, the British William Carr Beresford (1768–1856) acted as pro-consul of Portugal with full military and political powers. His rule triggered the Portuguese Revolution of 1820. King João VI returned to Lisbon in 1821 and appointed his son Pedro de Aleantara (1798–1834) as regent of Brazil.

When the Cortes issued unfavourable tax laws, Brazil declared independence in January 1822. On 22 October Dom Pedro I took on the title of Emperor of Brazil (*Emperador Constitucional e Defensor perpetuo do Brasil*). The independence of Brazil was not recognized by Portugal until August 1825. During the first years insurrections broke out in several Brazilian provinces, including Bahia, Minas Gerais, Maranhao and Pará, that strove for independence but most attempts failed. In 1828, however, the southern state of Banda Oriental became the independent state of Uruguay, after mediation by the British and French governments. The dominant British position in Brazil was challenged by other Western countries, including the US, France and Prussia.

The special relationship between Great Britain and Portugal was equalled by Prussia and Portugal. Crown Prince Pedro had married Maria Leopoldina (1797–1826), daughter of Austrian Emperor Franz I (1768–1835), and this stimulated many Germans to migrate to Brazil.[80] Although Prussia had shown interest in trade with Brazil previously, as part of the Holy Roman Empire and because of its adherence to the principle of legitimacy of governments, it was difficult to support the independence movements in the Americas. The principle stated that only governments possessing a historical right to govern were legitimate.

In 1817 Prussia appointed Count Von Flemming as *Chargé d'Affaires* in Brazil to investigate possibilities to stimulate trade. His mission remained largely unsuccessful because Brazil was afraid to relinquish its trade relations with Great Britain and was initially unwilling to grant the same trading privileges to other Western countries. On the recommendation of Von Flemming, the Prussian King Frederick Wilhelm III (1770–1840) in January 1820 appointed a consul: Carl Wilhelm Theremin.[81] Before his appointment, Theremin was a merchant trading in Antwerp and in 1815 he became Prussian consul in that town. A year later he applied for a position as salaried consul general in Rio de Janeiro. His motives remain unclear, but it seems likely that he saw a better business prospect in South America than in Europe. The Prussian Minister of Foreign Affairs was positive about Theremin because he had proven himself as consul in Antwerp, but his colleague in the Ministry of Finance was against the appointment. In 1817 Theremin travelled to Brazil for the Antwerp trading house of A. Saportas. This first encounter with Brazil much impressed Theremin. In March 1818 he submitted a private report to the Minister of Foreign Affairs in Berlin about the good prospects for trade between Prussia and Brazil. After his return to Berlin in July 1818, he reminded the minister about his earlier application. He requested compensation for the high costs of a public position as consul in a foreign country, because without this he could not possibly accept the post as his own funds were already exhausted. Despite a recommendation by Von Flemming, the Minister of Foreign Affairs was adamant: no Prussian consul received a state salary. Because of the unclear state of affairs in Brazil the matter remained unsettled until early 1820. In the end Theremin reluctantly accepted the position of unsalaried Prussian consul on 15 January and in August sailed to Rio de Janeiro. After his arrival, Von Flemming returned to Europe, leaving Theremin behind as the only official representative of Prussia. Theremin soon complained to the Minister of Foreign Affairs that his political duties were very costly, mainly because Brazilians valued much pomp and circumstance, forcing him to spend large sums of money on clothing, housing, furniture and organizing social events, like dinner parties. The Prussian government awarded Theremin financial compensation in 1824, 1825 and 1826 because he performed duties similar to a consul general and ambassador.

In Rio de Janeiro, Theremin established W. Theremin & Company, a commission house working for European traders. Little is known about the commercial activities of Theremin & Company, but Theremin did rather well as a businessman.[82] He possessed a ranch and estate in Flamengo and was a well-respected person, co-founder of the German association *Germania* (1821), and an active member in the German Evangelic Church.[83] Most of the business consisted of commission trade for other firms, like Joh. Bernh. Hasenclever & Söhne in Remscheid (Rhenish Prussia) and Gebrüder Adrianus und Abraham Saportas in Antwerpen and Amsterdam. After his employee Ferdinand Ziese started his own business, Theremin asked his son Leon, working for a trading house in Liverpool, to come to Rio de Janeiro. In 1835, Theremin & Company was renamed Theremin, Saportas & Company until the expiration of the partnership contract in August 1838.

After Brazil and Great Britain concluded a new commercial treaty on 17 August 1827, other European states were eager to follow the British. Theremin asked the Prussian government to dispatch a diplomatic mission to Brazil and in 1827 Ignaz Franz Werner Maria von Olfers (1793–1871) arrived in Rio de Janeiro. The Brazilian Minister of Foreign Affairs, Marquês de Queluz (João

Severiano Maciel da Costa, 1769–1833), was reluctant to negotiate a treaty, because he questioned the economic importance of Prussia for Brazil. On 9 July 1827 the treaty was signed and only a few months later, on 17 November, the Hanseatic cities concluded an almost similar treaty with Brazil. Other Western states followed, including the US, the Netherlands and Denmark.[84]

In November 1827, Theremin journeyed to Berlin to ratify the Prussian–Brazilian Treaty. He confessed that, now that there was a commercial treaty, his duties and workload as consul would increase. Without a salary, he no longer wanted to remain Prussian consul in Rio de Janeiro. The Prussian government agreed and in December 1827 Theremin was appointed consul general and received an annual salary of £350. Compared to other consuls general his salary was rather small, but then trade between Prussia and Brazil was almost non-existent. Between 1825 and 1840, says W. Penkwitt, the average number of Prussian ships entering the port of Rio was no more than two per year.[85] More important was the trade between the Hanseatic towns and Brazil. They imported Brazilian sugar, coffee and other products, and exported mainly industrial goods (see Table 4.1).

Table 4.1: The number of ships entering the port of Rio de Janeiro in 1820 and 1830

Year	1820	1830
Great Britain	173	229
United States	73	126
Portugal	0	71
France	31	27
The Netherlands	0	8
Sweden	12	21
Other	0	110
Including from		
Hamburg:		18
Bremen:		2
Pruisen:		2

Source: W. Penkwitt, *Preußen und Brasilien. Zum Aufbau des preußischen Konsularwesens im unabhängigen Kaiserreich (1822–1850)* (Wiesbaden: Franz Steiner Verlag GmbH, 1983), p. 83.

Theremin wanted to appoint his son Leon as vice-consul to assist him, but this was rejected by Berlin, because he was still too young and not engaged in business on his own account. Theremin next listed several other candidates for the post, all Prussian businessmen. None of these candidates were appointed before Theremin travelled to Europe in September 1835 to recover his health, and he temporarily appointed his son Leon as vice-consul. In Berlin Theremin discussed the affairs of the consulates in Brazil and suggested appointing himself as consul general and *Chargé d'Affaires*. According to Theremin there were about 10,000 or 12,000 Germans in Brazil, including 7,000 to 8,000 from Prussia, creating a large amount of work for the consulate. Because of his failing health, Theremin informed the ministry in July 1836 that he wanted to resign as consul general and proposed to appoint his son as his successor.

His son Leon continued to operate the family business until 1838, before starting his own firm and was appointed Prussian consul in 1840. The number of Prussian consulates in Brazil increased from one in 1820 to five in the 1840s: San Salvador, in Bahia; Montevideo; Rio Grande do Sul; Pernambuco, in Recife; and Santos. Trade between Brazil and Prussia had still not increased much. In 1838 the existing treaties between Brazil and European countries expired. Prince Adelbert of Prussia (1811–73), accompanied by Friedrich Theodor Alexander Graf von Bismarck-Bohlen (1818–94) and Alfons Heinrich, Count Von Oriolla, travelled to Brazil in 1842 to negotiate a new commercial treaty.[86] Brazil was unwilling to renew the existing treaties because the provisions were unfavourable, as the country was experiencing severe budgetary problems. In 1844 Brazil unilaterally raised the import duties from 15 to 30 per cent to raise tax revenues and protect domestic companies. German relations with Brazil increased in importance from the 1850s, when the number of migrants from Germany grew, and several colonies were founded in Brazil and other South American states.

North America: Rudolph Christian Burlage, the Civil War and Immigration

Rudolph Christian Burlage was born in Amsterdam and after an apprenticeship in Liverpool, moved to Remscheid to start an iron foundry. During the revolts of 1848, the foundry was demolished, and Burlage migrated to the US.[87] In New York he established Burlage & Company, a commission house. Burlage was a member of the New York Produce Exchange and active in the transport of grain and other products, including petroleum.[88] The journal *Deutsche Pionier* (German Pioneer) noted that he was highly regarded as an export trader.[89] He was associated with other merchants as well, including the banking firm Bunge, Burlage & Company with offices in New York and New Orleans.[90] When the Dutch consul general Johannes Christian Zimmerman died in 1855, several candidates applied for the position. The Minister of Foreign Affairs selected Burlage because of his knowledge of commerce in New York and his respectable family background. From 1855 until his death in 1883, Burlage served as Dutch consul general and because of his long tenure, he became the dean of the consular corps in the city. Johannes Edward Zimmerman (1832–72), the son of the former consul general, was appointed as vice-consul in 1855 and promoted to vice-consul general in 1860 because of the growing workload of the New York consulate general.

Dutch–American relations improved after a consular convention was concluded on 22 January 1855. Article 1 allowed the US 'to appoint consuls into all the ports in the transmarine possessions or colonies of the Netherlands, which are open to the vessels of all nations'.[91] Burlage served during the Civil War and witnessed the growth of immigration in the 1870s, including migrants from the Netherlands. After the start of the Civil War the immediate problem for European consuls in the South, E. H. Berwanger notes, concerned the legality of their exequaturs: did they still possess the consular privileges and immunities?[92] The solution worked out by the Confederate President Jefferson Davis (1808–89) was to recognize all consuls appointed before the outbreak of the war, 'so long as they confine themselves to the sphere of their duties, and seek neither to evade nor defy the legitimate authority of this government within its own jurisdiction'.[93] The Confederate States hoped to gain goodwill and be recognized as a new sovereign state, but most European states adopted a wait-and-see policy, besides declaring their official neutrality in the conflict. Maintaining this neutrality became one of the most important tasks of the European consuls and diplomats in the US.

The Civil War was fought as much on land as on the high seas, interrupting regular commerce with Europe. At the start of the war, the Confederacy, having no navy of their own, supplied letters of mark to privateers, although the Treaty of Paris (1856), ending the Crimean War, outlawed privateering. The US, however, had not signed this treaty. On 19 April 1861 President Lincoln announced a blockade of all major Southern ports, including Charleston, Mobile, Savannah and New Orleans. The Treaty of Paris stipulated the conditions of a naval blockade: it could not merely be proclaimed, but had to be rigidly enforced. The European consuls in the South were therefore asked to report whether the blockade had been carried through. During the first months of the war, the Union was not able to muster sufficient ships to blockade all Confederate ports and trade continued mostly uninterrupted. Even after one year the Union was not able to close all ports in the South.[94]

Blockade runners, fast ships trying to evade the patrolling warships of the Union, remained active throughout the war. In December 1864 the Dutch brig *Geziena Hillegonda*, under the command of Captain Bernardus Pieter(s) Jansen (1831–94), sailing from Liverpool to Matamoras in Mexico, was seized by the Union screw gunboat USS *Pembina* of the West Gulf Blockading Squadron. After the capture, the Dutch consul in New Orleans telegraphed Burlage, who informed Theodorus Marinus Roest van Limburg (1806–87). The Dutch ambassador protested against the unlawful seizure of the ship from a neutral country. Secretary of State Seward replied that the ship was taken while transporting contraband to the Confederacy. The vessel was taken to New Orleans, conquered by the Union in the spring of 1862, and after the release of the captain and crew, the cargo and the ship was to be sold at auction. The Dutch owners of the ship applied to their government in The Hague for help, insisting that that the cargo, including iron, clothes and medicine, was not contraband. According to the owners, the ship was destined for Rio Grande, but had drifted towards the blockaded southern ports on a calm sea, until stopped by the Pembina. During the trial, the ship was cleared of all charges, but the district attorney successfully appealed in a higher court. The *Geziena Hillegonda* was considered a legal prize following the Prize Act of 1864 and sold at auction on 10 June 1865.

After 1863, when the war turned against the Confederacy, the position of the European consuls in the South became more difficult. Direct communication with Washington was forbidden. This pushed the European consuls in the South into a more diplomatic role than before. They communicated directly with their own government and the authorities of the Confederacy.[95]

The position of the European consuls in the Union was less problematic. Their main concern was the arbitrary arrests of foreigners, damage to property belonging to their compatriots and attempts to enlist them as soldiers in the Union Army, particularly after the Enrollment Act of 1863. Nationals from neutral countries, including consuls, were exempted from military service. Many foreigners feared conscription in the army unless they could prove their nationality and they applied to their consuls for assistance. Burlage wrote to the Dutch ambassador in Washington, Roest van Limburg:

> Almost everyday Hollanders contact me to ask for a Certificate of Protection that will proof their Dutch nationality, which will prevent enlistment in the American army. Several persons have not yet decided whether they will apply for American citizenship or not, but even those who have already become American citizens demand the same protection.[96]

Another potential source for new recruitments was immigrants from Europe. Despite the Civil War, immigration continued: between 1861 and 1865 about 800,000 immigrants arrived, including almost 12,000 from the Netherlands. The number of men between the ages of eighteen and forty-five was about 533,000, and 183,448 were eventually enlisted as soldiers in the Union.[97] The US government asked their consuls in Europe to promote the US to prospective migrants by pointing out the good employment opportunities and high wages. The Contract Labour Law (1864) was intended to allow US citizens to hire foreign labourers. Some immigrants were offered a contract to work in the US as labourers, but during the Civil War many discovered that this 'work' meant joining the Union Army instead. During the Civil War, Burlage continued his own business activities and even travelled to the southern states for this.[98]

After the Civil War, immigration to the US increased quickly, stimulated by the establishment of new steamship companies that offered cheap and fast crossings. The number of shipping companies regularly calling (making at least five voyages each year) in New York, increased from four in 1855, to sixteen in 1873 and twenty-six in 1913.[99] The transport of migrants across the Atlantic was a major business in the European and North American ports between *c.* 1870 and 1920. According to A. A. Keeling, it was dominated by four shipping lines: from Great Britain the Cunard and the White Star Line, and from Germany the Hamburg America Line (*Hamburg-Amerikanische Packetfahrt-Actien-Gesellschaft*, or *HAPAG*) and the *Norddeutscher Lloyd*. These four companies carried almost 40 per cent of all migrants in the 1870s and two-thirds after 1900.[100] Other shipping companies included the Belgian Red Star Line (1873, owned by an American shipping company) and the French *Compagnie Générale Transatlantique* (1855), besides numerous smaller companies in South Europe.

Before the mid-nineteenth century, migration from Dutch ports to the US remained small. In 1871 merchants in Rotterdam established the firm Plate, Reuchlin and Company and succeeded in raising capital to buy two small steamships and open a direct connection with New York. Plate, Reuchlin and Company initially engaged Burlage as their agent. The partners in the firm believed that his position as consul general in New York and his reputation as a businessman in New York would be beneficial to them. The appointment of Burlage was brief: in 1874 he was replaced by H. Cazaux van Staphorst, who remained an agent until 1884. Feys notes that this was related to the expansion of the shipping business and the establishment in 1873 of the *Nederlandsch Amerikaansche Stoomvaart Maatschappij* (*NASM*), later adapted to Holland America Line (HAL).[101] The HAL probably felt that Burlage's own commercial activities intervened too much with their shipping business. He continued to be involved in the immigration business, however. In May 1878, Burlage was informed by the Commissioners of Emigration in New York that during the latest voyage of the steamship *Rotterdam* of the HAL on 10 April, one male adult and four children died and that no medical officer or doctor was available. After the arrival in New York, three children were admitted to the hospital because they were ill. Burlage requested a transcript of the minutes of the report and contacted Captain F. M. Lucas of the vessel. Lucas confirmed what had happened, but felt that the commissioners had misunderstood him. The deceased male adult had already been weak when he boarded the ship in Rotterdam. According to Lucas, 'the shipping company had in vain tried everything possible to hire a medical doctor until the last minutes before departure'.[102] Burlage asked the Dutch ambassador in Washington to report the case to the Dutch government, because newspapers had picked up the story and this was hurting the reputation of the HAL and Dutch shipping.

An additional duty of Burlage and of other European consuls in the US included finding migrants who had fled to escape criminal charges. In June 1867 the Dutch consul in London telegraphed Burlage to arrest a Dutch citizen, named Dirk Lunstroo, who had stolen 18,000 guilders in Amsterdam and fled to New York. Burlage asked for more detailed information, including the name of the ship Lunstroo had boarded. A few days later Burlage was able to report that 'with the help of detectives and by intimidating the thief, the money was recovered'.[103] Until the Extradition Treaty of 1872, the US was considered a safe haven for Dutch criminals. Equally time-consuming for the consuls was tracking down migrants on behalf of deceased relatives in the Netherlands when inheritances were involved. Dutch shipping companies frequently complained at the consulate in New York about runners operating in the US ports along the east coast. These runners tried to enlist sailors by offering higher wages, sometimes using threats or other means. Many sailors were tempted by the offer and deserted ship. Burlage contacted the Mayor of New York to discuss the problem, but the mayor could do little as long as wages in the US remained much higher than those offered in Europe. His only suggestion was that ship captains or masters put a gun against the head of the runners when they boarded the ship.[104] In his last published annual report, for the year 1882, Burlage reported a strong growth in manufacturing in New York and New Jersey. About 20 per cent of the estimated 15,000 workers in silk factories were from Dutch descent. 'They are preferred, because they are clean and show good behaviour'.[105] After his death in 1883, Burlage was succeeded by Jan Rutger Planten (1815–1912), who remained Dutch consul general until 1911.[106]

The Caribbean: Leonard Burlington Smith, Curaçao and American Trade

Article 21 of the treaty of amity and commerce (8 October 1782) between the Netherlands and the US 'grants to each other, mutually, the liberty of having, each in the Ports of the other, Consuls, Vice-Consuls, Agents and Commissaries of their own appointment'.[107] Their functions were to be regulated in a separate consular convention. The US merchants soon discovered that this treaty did not include the ports of the Dutch colonies. Mercantilist policies considered colonies the private property of a country and therefore national merchants enjoyed exclusive trading rights; foreign merchants were allowed to trade but paid higher duties on import and export. In the nineteenth century, the European states used their colonies to barter for access to the colonies of their main competitors, but since the US lacked colonies of its own it had little to offer.[108] Foreign consuls, often active merchants, were also not recognized in the colonies. This policy was continued by the Dutch–American Treaty of Commerce and Navigation of 19 January 1839.[109] The Convention of Commerce of 1852 confirmed existing policies. The US government strongly rejected these exclusive arrangements and in negotiations stressed reciprocity that would give US merchants access to European colonies on a more equal basis. The growing interest of the US in the Caribbean increased their desire to appoint consuls. In the meantime, the government tried to offer protection to US merchants by appointing executive agents. Having no exequatur, their position remained ambiguous.

The first US agent to Curaçao was Benjamin Hamnel Philips, of Pennsylvania, who served between 1793 and 1805.[110] He was on the island during the Dutch Batavian Revolt (1795) until the Netherlands became part of France.[111] During this period merchants from the US were able to increase their trade with Surinam and the Dutch Antilles, particularly when these were shut off from trade with the Netherlands during the Napoleonic Wars.[112] After Dutch authority in the West Indies was restored in 1816, conditions normalized, with Dutch merchants again receiving privileges not granted to foreigners. In 1815, Congress passed the Reciprocity Act: new commercial treaties (with Great Britain in 1815 and the Netherlands in 1818) abolished discriminatory duties and dues, but only on direct trade and it still did not include the European colonial ports. The US government countered by passing Navigation Acts that closed American ports for European ships coming from their colonies. This eventually led to the conclusion of new commercial treaties and consular conventions that opened most of the West Indies for US merchant vessels and allowed for the appointment of consuls in Western colonies.

The Dutch–American Consular Convention (22 January 1855) opened the ports in the Dutch West Indies for US merchants. The convention furthermore regulated the duties and privileges of US consuls in the Netherlands and Dutch consuls in the US.[113] The first US consul on Curaçao was not appointed until July 1875: Moses Jessurun was a native merchant of Jewish origins.[114] Like many other merchants on Curaçao, Jessurun traded primarily with nearby Venezuela. During the struggle for independence in South America, Curaçao became an important supplier of provisions and weapons. This continued after the republics achieved their independence, because of the political instability in Venezuela. Curaçao was traditionally a place of refuge for Venezuelan exiles and the centre of new revolutionary plots. This enraged the Venezuelan government, whether centralists (Liberal party) or federalists (Oligarca), and led to numerous political disputes with the Netherlands.[115]

During the 1870s, political tensions between Venezuela and the Netherlands increased and eventually all diplomatic relations broke down, frustrating commerce between the Antilles and Venezuela. Before he became president in 1870, Guzman Blanco (1829–99) was forced to flee to Willemstad on Curaçao when the centralists occupied Caracas in June 1869. From Willemstad Blanco launched attacks to regain power. Some of his letters to his allies in Caracas were intercepted by the Peruvian government who handed them over to the Dutch consul general T. D. G. Rolandus (1819–99) and demanded that the Dutch governor of the Antilles, Abraham Mathieu de Rouville, expel Blanco and his rebels.[116] According to the governor, opening personal mail was against all international laws and conventions. The Dutch should continue to give hospitality to foreigners and only expel them when they threatened the security in the Dutch colonies. The Dutch Minister of Colonies, however, disagreed and ordered him to expel the Venezuelans, but the governor refused to comply. After regaining power in 1870, Blanco demanded the replacement of Rolandus. The Dutch government replaced Rolandus with J. Brakel, a captain and quartermaster in the Dutch Army, and appointed a new governor on Curacao: H. F. G. Wagner. To further improve relations with Venezuela it embargoed the sale of weapons from Curaçao until 1 April 1872. The normalization of the relationship now seemed fully established. A major problem was the clandestine trade between Curaçao and Venezuela that had increased after Guzman had increased the duties on import and export for vessels from Curaçao. After the outbreak of a new revolt in Venezuela in October 1874, Blanco complained that several merchant ships from Curaçao, including those of Abraham Jesurun, illegally supplied the rebels. On 30 October one of the ships of Jesurun, the *Midas*, entered the port of Sucre, in Cumaná, and was seized and the crew imprisoned. Several ports were closed for Dutch vessels. Blanco appointed José María Rojas as Envoy Extraordinary and Minister Plenipotentiary of Venezuela in the Netherlands.[117]

Rojas arrived in The Hague on 1 June 1875 to start negotiations. The Netherlands government made it clear that negotiations could begin only after the return of the *Midas* and the release of the crew. To improve relations, the Netherlands was prepared to prolong the ban of the sale of arms from Curaçao until 1 October 1875. In September Venezuela returned the *Midas* and released the crew, but the ports remained closed, hurting trade from the Antilles. Blanco indicated that he was prepared to seek arbitration, preferably from Germany or Italy.

To solve the conflict, the US offered mediation, says R. van Vuurde.[118] It supported the proposal of Venezuela to buy the Dutch Antilles from the Netherlands, because that would fit within the Monroe Doctrine.[119] According to President Rutherford B. Hayes (1822–93), the US should expand its interests in Central and South America. Because of the politically sensitive nature of the matter, the US did not use their ambassador in the Netherlands, but one of their consuls. Instructions were sent to the US consul in Amsterdam, Charles Müller, to persuade the Netherlands to sell the Dutch Antilles to Venezuela.[120] The Dutch government received Müller, but answered to James M. Birney (1817–1888), the US ambassador in The Hague between 1876 and 1882. Selling the Dutch Antilles to Venezuela, or any other Dutch colony, was out of the question. The mediation of the US demonstrates that in the last quarter of the nineteenth century the Caribbean was increasingly seen as the American Mediterranean. This meant that the role of US consuls in this region became more important.[121]

In August 1876 Captain Leonard Burlington Smith (1839–98) entered St Anna Bay, the entrance to Willemstad, for the first time.[122] Despite the conflict with Venezuela, the economy of Curaçao prospered. Since 1872 Curaçao had been directly connected to Europe by the steamers of the *HAPAG*. Goods from Europe were shipped to Central American countries via Willemstad and in return tropical products were unloaded in Willemstad and shipped by steamer to Europe. This had boosted the economy and in particular the shipping business and shipyards on the island. In 1875 the governor ordered a deepening of St Anna Bay to accommodate more and larger ships. The projected canal through the Isthmus of Panama would surely improve the geographical location of Curaçao and boost the import and export trade. Curaçao could become an important coaling station and, soon, perhaps a storage place for crude oil from Venezuela.

The first impressions of Smith were positive, and he returned in December with a cargo of ice. Although the demand for ice did not meet his expectations, Smith decided to permanently stay on Curaçao in 1877 and brought his wife and their four children to Willemstad. A year later Smith obtained permission to construct a warehouse to store ice, but the demand for ice in a tropical place such as Willemstad remained much lower than Smith had anticipated. The islanders, says J. Hartog, believed that cold drinks were bad for your health.[123] Besides ice, Smith tried to sell wood that was much more in demand in the Dutch Antilles, but his first shipment of wood from Maine found few buyers. His main competitors, selling wood from the South American mainland were Gomart & Company and the firm S. E. L. Maduro & Sons, from 1890 also the *Handel- and Industrie Maatschappij*.[124]

Despite these austere beginnings, Smith continued and expanded his interests to shipbuilding. The shipyard Joseph Foulke & Sons was established in Willemstad in the beginning of the nineteenth century. Joseph Foulke (1769–1852) originally came from New York and in 1879 Smith became agent for Foulke & Sons, who would act as agent for Smith in New York. From the 1880s, the firm of Smith began to prosper. The demand for ice steadily increased, and Smith was able to sell ice boxes from the US in Willemstad. Besides ice and wood, Smith handled a variety of goods, including salt from Bonaire. He also worked as an intermediary in the shipbuilding industry, selling a newly built American ship to Surinam in 1882. A year later the *Koninklijke Westindische Maildienst* (*KWIM*, Royal West Indies Mail Services) started a direct steamer service between the Netherlands, Surinam and the Dutch Antilles.[125] The *KWIM* constructed its own coal station in the port of Willemstad. The growth in steamshipping and the related demand for coal offered new business opportunities for Smith. When he temporarily became US vice-consul in 1883 he reported to the US government on the prospects of setting up a coaling station. This could aid US merchant shipping with the Caribbean, but also the US Navy. His proposal was not supported by the US government and Smith, after being replaced as vice-consul by Jacob Wuister, decided to start his own coaling depot. In November 1885 he bought a slip dock near the existing sheds of his ice business to build a coaling station. From the mid-1880s, Curaçao had two coal depots: Smith and the *KWIM*.

After his period as vice-consul, Smith applied for the post of US consul to advance his business and social position. The previous consul, Almont Barnes, appointed in December 1880, was frequently on sick leave. On 30 March 1884 Barnes wrote to the Secretary of State that his salary was insufficient and he resigned from the consular service. Barnes explained that Curaçao was a difficult post and that it was best to appoint a resident American businessman. He believed that the new consul should be allowed to continue his business activities. Since few Americans lived on Curaçao and Smith had already proved himself as vice-consul, his appointment as US consul on 4 July 1884 was no surprise. Smith remained consul until December 1897, except for the brief period between January 1895 and October 1897 when Jervis Spencer was consul. When Smith was reappointed in October 1897, his annual salary was raised to $2,000, including an office allowance of $100.

The US consulate in Willemstad was in a poor state of affairs when Smith began his consulship. Its possessions included two wooden bureaus, two bookcases, eleven chairs, an iron chest, two consular seals, an old flag of the US and a copy of the Consular Regulations of 1881. Smith continued his business while he was US consul and the consulate was housed in a number of rooms in the office of his firm. Smith continued to introduce new ideas and technologies. In 1888 he proposed to construct a dry dock and in 1890 developed plans to build a modern resort hotel, anticipating a growth in tourism from the US to the Caribbean. He is, however, best remembered on Curaçao for building the first pontoon bridge, the Queen Emma Bridge, across St Anna Bay in 1888 and for improving the water supply in 1893. The latter project failed due to the corrosion of the tubes from the salt water, but the pontoon bridge was an immediate success. In 1893 he also introduced electric lightning on the island. Most of these business ventures were taken over by S. E. L. Maduro & Sons after Smith died in 1898.

Besides attending to the normal consular duties of registering American ships and helping sailors and distressed compatriots, Smith wrote many reports about Curaçao and potential business investments, which included shoes, leather, oranges, cattle-breeding and salt. Political matters surfaced often. In 1891 rumours circulated on Curaçao that Germany wanted to buy or take over the island. German firms were increasingly active in South America, including in Argentina, Brazil, Peru and Venezuela. To the Secretary of State, Smith wrote

the acquisition by purchase or otherwise of this little island by Germany, which, as is well known, has always been looking with a covetous eye on it, would give the entire control of Venezuela's commerce in their hands to the detriment of ours. The most intelligent people here fear the consequence to this island of a German victory in case of a European war, as they are so closely allied to the United States by its commerce.[126]

The German plan never materialized and Curaçao remained part of the Netherlands.

Leonard Burling Smith died on 16 December 1898, when the Spanish–American War (1898) had already begun. Curaçao and its coaling stations played an important role in this war. The arrival of a Spanish squadron on 14 May, with the intention of bunkering coal, was reported by Smith to the Secretary of State. As a neutral country, the Netherlands could not refuse this, although the governor allowed only two ships in St Anna Bay. After a few days the ships left for Cuba, where they were destroyed by the US Navy. One week before Smith died, the Treaty of Versailles ended the Spanish–American War. Spanish colonialism in the Caribbean ended and the US gained control of Cuba. Its important geostrategic position for the US had already been noticed by Shaler in the early nineteenth century (see p. 110). The war transformed the US into a colonial power and empire, with the possession of Puerto Rico, Guam and the Philippines.

The Amazon: Roger Casement, the Horrors of the Rubber Industry

After the 1860s the Upper Amazon area, known as Putumayo, experienced a rubber boom.[127] The natural or wild rubber was collected by native Indians in the forest. The main rubber markets at the end of the nineteenth century were Europe and the US. Explorers, adventurers and businessmen from neighbouring countries, but also from Great Britain, the US, Germany, and even a small group of Jews from Northern Africa, came to Putumayo. Here they encountered various groups of indigenous Indians and *mestizos* (descendants of mixed blood).

In 1907 the Peruvian Amazon Company (PAC), locally known as *Casa Arana*, was established by Julio César Arana (1864–1952), a former Panama hat-maker.[128] The PAC dominated the rubber business of Putumayo, controlling about 18.6 per cent of the rubber export from the province Iquitos. The PAC was a British-registered company with British members on the Board of Directors, while workers from Barbados, a British colony, were hired to oversee the native Indians who collected the rubber.[129] In Putumayo the PAC collected the rubber in a number of sections (depots) before it was transported to the two main stations: El Encanto en La Chorrera. Each Indian was forced to collect a certain number of kilos and when he failed to produce the quota was flogged and branded with the *marca de Arana* (the scars of whipping). The Indians were furthermore kept under a system of peonage or perpetual debt, akin to slavery.[130]

In December 1907 reports on the atrocities committed by the PAC appeared in local newspapers, but these attracted little attention outside the region. The US consul in Iquitos, Charles Christopher Eberhardt (1871–1965), informed his government in two reports.[131] While his first report was based on published sources, the second confidential report of 3 December was written after a six week visit to the region and clearly exposed the cruel treatment of Indians.

The Peruvians are seeking to get the benefit of the Indian's labour before he disappears entirely, and to that end do not hesitate to perform the most outrageous acts of cruelty. However, I do not pose as a reformer in this matter, the instances I have cited above, both hearsay and what I have personally seen, being intended only for the department's information, and it is hoped that the despatch, or, at least, the part pertaining to these cruelties, may be kept from the public.[132]

The second report was not published until much later and the government took no further action because no company from the US was involved.[133]

News of the appalling conditions in Putumayo was first reported in Great Britain in 1909 by the magazine *Truth*, known for its investigative journalism. 'The Devil's Paradise: A British-Owned Congo', and similar articles, exposed the conditions of the Indians. The magazine received its information from Walter Ernest Hardenburg (1886–1942).[134] Hardenburg, an engineer from the US, went to Putumayo in 1908 with his friend Walter B. Perkins, hoping to find work in the construction of the railway between Madeira in Brazil and Mamoré in Bolivia. During one of several clashes between Peruvian and Colombian rubber companies in the disputed border area, they were captured by employees of the PAC. After his release, Hardenburg collected as much evidence as possible to expose the crimes of the PAC.[135] In Iquitos, he contacted Guy T. King, the acting US consul, who had succeeded Eberhardt, but King explained that his government could do nothing. Tully claims that King refused to help because he feared for his life in Iquitos where Arana's political power was very strong.[136] Hardenburg left for England in September 1909 and in London contacted several newspapers, but they all declined to publish his story. He eventually established contact with Rev. John H. Harris (1874–1940) of the Antislavery and Aborigines Protection Society.[137] Harris eventually advised Hardenburg to approach the editors of *Truth*, who might be interested to report on Putumayo.

After the first articles appeared in *Truth*, the PAC denied all allegations. The articles resulted in oral questions in the House of Commons and in March 1910 the Secretary of State for Foreign Affairs, Sir Edward Grey (1862–1933), replied that he had contacted the PAC and suggested an investigation by the company. 'The locality is on foreign territory where we have no special Treaty rights, and is not within reach of any British representative from whom we could receive a report'.[138] In Lima, Leslie Combs, Envoy Extraordinary and Minister Plenipotentiary of the US between 1906 and 1911, reported in November 1909 to his government:

The articles recite numerous acts of outrage and brutality. It speaks of it as the Peruvian Kongo and declares the labourers are forced with the lash and at the point of the gun to perform the work of gathering rubber. There is no doubt, I think, that the rubber gathering is conducted with much brutality in the greater part of the Amazon district.[139]

In June 1910 Grey informed the House of Commons that the PAC had agreed to send a Commission of Inquiry to Putumayo. He added: 'I propose to suggest that one of His Majesty's Consuls and a Barbadian official should go with the Commission in case any British subjects are involved and require assistance'.[140] The Peruvian government also appointed a commission headed by two judges of the criminal court of Iquitos: Carlos A. Valcárcel and Rómulo Paredes.

Grey asked the British consul general in Rio de Janeiro, Roger Casement, to join the PAC Commission of Inquiry. Casement was a highly experienced consul serving in various posts in West Africa. His report on the atrocities committed in the rubber industry in Congo Free State (1903) had gained him international fame.[141] He next accepted a post in the Brazilian port Santos, but had already exchanged it in 1907 for Belém do Pará, the main port for the export of rubber. A few months later he received news of his appointment as consul general for Rio de Janeiro and surrounding states. It is important to note that the British had no extraterritorial rights in Peru and any possible misconduct of British subjects would thus fall under Peruvian jurisdiction. The British government asked their consul general in Rio de Janeiro and not the British Legation in Lima to join the PAC Commission of Inquiry. Peru made no objections to the inquiries of Casement. During his work in the Consular Service, Casement wrote many official letters, reports and notes on behalf of the Foreign Office, besides keeping a personal diary. The diaries have led to a debate about their authenticity and contents because of the frequent homosexual encounters (or, possibly, fantasies) and discrepancies between entries describing the same events.[142] His reports on Putumayo were published by the Foreign Office in 1912. Known as the Blue Book, its authenticity is beyond dispute, just like his report of 1903 on the Congo.

In July 1910, Casement was instructed to investigate

> whether any British subjects have suffered or are in distress, and if so from what causes, and whether they stand in need of relief. You should also report, in a separate despatch, any facts which may come to your knowledge in the course of your inquiry, in regard to the methods of rubber collection and the treatment of natives by the employés of the Company in the district which your visit.[143]

S. Ó Siocháin says that he was to exercise great caution, 'so as to afford no ground for possible objection being raised by the governments of the territory visited'.[144] He was obviously well aware of the fact that he had no formal authority and depended wholly on the cooperation of the Peruvian authorities. Although Casement accompanied the PAC Commission of Inquiry, he conducted his own investigations in Putumayo from 22 September until 29 October.[145] Casement inspected the compounds and interviewed several men from Barbados. They confirmed the cruelties and murders in which they themselves were implicated.[146] In his report, A. Mitchell writes, Casement concluded: 'There is no doubt that the Hardenburg papers are in the main true. There are lies and exaggerations, but the main facts and charges are substantially correct. Moreover, hundreds of crimes not recorded there have taken place.'[147]

Back in London, Casement penned a short preliminary report in early January 1911. 'The crimes charged against many men now in the employ of the Peruvian Amazon Company are of the most atrocious kind, including murder, violation, and constant flogging'.[148] By the end of January, he had completed his full report and in March finished his additional report on the methods of collecting rubber and the treatment of Indians by the PAC. This report was accompanied by a list of British subjects from Barbados employed by the PAC and interviewed by Casement. All their testimonies were added to the report.[149] Casement estimated that about 30,000 Indians out of an initial population of 50,000 lost their lives over a period of twelve years. Most Indians died because of the poor labour conditions, others because of Western diseases brought to the area. Between 1904 and 1910 they had extracted about 4,000 tons of crude rubber, valued in London at £966,000. The profits of the PAC had declined from £61,000 (1906–7) to £35,365 (1909–10), mainly because of the opening of new rubber plantations in East Asia. At an extraordinary meeting of shareholders on 13 September 1911 it was decided to liquidate the PAC and to restructure it.

Percy Falcke Martin (1861–1941), a correspondent for English newspapers in Mexico and Central America, writes that Peru 'instituted prompt and vigorous steps to arrest and prosecute those who were responsible for the offences mentioned'.[150] This has been so successful that 'we may therefore believe that the "Devil's Paradise" and "A British owned Congo" as the Company's estates were dubbed have either ceased to exist, or have been very considerably improved in regard to the management'.[151] However, after Casement submitted his reports it would take one year before they were made public to give the government of Peru the opportunity to arrest the criminals and demonstrate its good will. According to Grey, publication 'would exhaust the last remaining remedy, namely, an effort to focus on the toleration of such atrocities the indignation of the civilized world'.[152]

Casement, after receiving a knighthood for his humanitarian work in Congo and Putumayo, returned to Rio de Janeiro in mid-1911. From October until December 1911, however, he again visited Iquitos. The purpose of the second visit is unclear; perhaps it was only to pressure the government of Peru to take action.[153] On 31 December 1911, after finishing the second visit, Casement went to New York and met President William Howard Taft (1857–1930). Casement explained that he wanted to get the Americans in on the matter.[154] He returned to Great Britain on 20 January 1912 and reported to the Foreign Office that Peru 'made no really serious efforts to prosecute the parties responsible for the atrocities in the Putumayo'.[155]

The British informed the US government in April about the still confidential reports of Casement. M. E. Stansfield believes that Great Britain tried to involve the US in the scandal, but that they wisely kept a distance because it could hurt their important commercial interests in Peru.[156] This is, however, not supported by published correspondence and telegrams in which a 'harmony of action' was stressed from the beginning. Already on 15 September 1911, the Acting Secretary of State, Huntington Wilson (1875–1946), wrote: 'The department, feeling in entire sympathy with the humanitarian endeavours of the British Government, consented to instruct appropriately the American minister at Lima'.[157] Despite this combined pressure, Peru did not arrest the main culprits. The report of Judge Rómulo of September 1911 did not change their attitude, although in April 1912 they appointed a new commission to formulate reforms for Putumayo. In July 1912 the British government was no longer prepared to wait and published the official reports of Casement.[158]

The publication of the Blue Book prompted the US House of Representatives to request an additional inquiry.[159] Stuart Jamieson Fuller (1880–1941), the US consul in Iquitos, was instructed to investigate and report on the conditions and ascertain whether they had improved or not. He was to cooperate with the British consul George Babington Michell (1864–1936). Both consuls visited the area and interviewed employees, although they were constantly closely watched by employees of the PAC.[160] Their investigations showed some improvements, but the criminals had either fled or were simply not arrested.[161] In his final report of 28 October 1912, Fuller concluded 'that the horrible conditions laid bare by the testimony of observers in the past still exist in all their enormity'.[162] In Great Britain the Select Committee of the House of Commons on the Putumayo Atrocities started hearings in March 1913.[163] After thirty-six sittings and interviewing twenty-seven witnesses, including Hardenburg, Casement and Arana, the committee published their report in June.[164] The Select Committee censured the British directors of the PAC for their negligence with regard to the appalling labour conditions and felt that they had exposed the good reputation of England. Lloyds Bank stopped financing APC and on 19 March 1913 the company ceased to function. Not one of the major criminals was tried or convicted. The international interest in Putumayo and the fate of the Indians of the Amazon soon disappeared after the outbreak of the First World War. Casement did not return to Rio de Janeiro because of health problems and retired from the consular service to pursue the Irish Case.[165] After joining the Irish Volunteers in 1913, Casement travelled to Germany in 1914 to support Britain's enemy, hoping to receive their help in the Irish struggle for independence. Casement secretly returned to Ireland in April 1916 on a German U-boat, but was arrested during his landing just hours before the Easter Uprising in Dublin. He was found guilty of high treason and hanged on 3 August 1916. He is generally regarded as a pioneer in the international humanitarian movement of the late nineteenth century.[166]

5 SUB-SAHARAN AFRICA

In this chapter the role of consuls in sub-Saharan Africa is investigated. Unfortunately, little is known about the international relations in sub-Saharan Africa. G. W. Irwin, focusing on diplomacy on the African west coast, distinguishes three phases of international relations on the African continent: indigenous (before *c.* 1500), Afro-European (*c.* 1500–*c.* 1880) and European–African (after *c.* 1880).[1] Scholars even debate the existence of states in sub-Saharan Africa before the arrival of Europeans in the fifteenth century. N. Lante Wallace-Bruce, however, points out that Africa in the precolonial period certainly had states and practised diplomacy similar to European states.[2] In the nineteenth century, parts of sub-Saharan Africa came under Muslim rule. In these territories the consuls operated under the Islamic system of international relations, similar to those of the Middle East and North Africa. In non-Muslim territories the conditions remained more varied. Scholars distinguish two categories of African states: more centralized (e.g. Asante and Zulu) and more decentralized (e.g. Ibo and Nuer).[3]

Until the 1850s, there were no consuls in sub-Saharan Africa. Thereafter their number increased after the Europeans were able to conclude new treaties of friendship and commerce that allowed the appointment of consuls. It took longer to obtain extraterritoriality, which gave consuls judicial powers over their compatriots. Until about the 1870s, the African rulers offered protection and decided on civil and criminal cases when Westerners were involved. The number of consuls in sub-Saharan Africa also increased because the Western powers agreed to recognize foreign consuls in their African colonies. This allowed the Western states to monitor the colonial policy of their rivals much more directly, resulting in numerous conflicts, including Portuguese claims on the Congo delta.

Commerce, Colonies and Consuls

Long before the arrival of Europeans, sub-Saharan African states had diplomatic relations, concluded treaties and traded. These treaties, R. Smith explains, were cemented by exchanging gifts, planting trees, arranging marriages or giving hostages.[4] As also happened elsewhere, treaties were broken and this necessitated diplomacy. Treaties contained provisions for paying tribute, besides presenting gifts. This indicates that at least in certain parts of sub-Saharan Africa, hierarchical relations existed between African rulers. African traders relied on the protection of foreign rulers and some appointed one of the locals to take care of foreign merchants or selected a foreigner as their representative.[5] Smith believes that 'their functions seem to have been comparable to those of the early European consuls'.[6] Their powers were limited because the concept of extraterritoriality seems to have been unknown in sub-Saharan Africa, until it was introduced by Muslim traders. When the British consul Joseph Dupuis (1789–1874) went to Asante (Ashanti) to negotiate a commercial treaty, he met Muslims who had secured the privilege of appointing a pasha as the head of the Muslims in Kumasi.[7] Smith points out that the arrival of Islam furthermore introduced literacy and the keeping of records, including written treaties.[8]

From the mid-fifteenth century the Portuguese – followed by other Western European traders – arrived, bringing their own institutions. They dispatched ambassadors and special envoys to negotiate treaties with African rulers. J. Thornton points out that these early treaties were all based on reciprocity, including the exchange of envoys: the kings of Benin and Congo each had an envoy in Portugal at the beginning of the sixteenth century.[9] The early relationship was not tainted by racism. The main distinguishing features for the Portuguese were the appearance of nobility, dress, ceremonies and status accorded by the subjects.[10] Local African rulers saw an opportunity to increase their wealth and welcomed European traders as long as they paid tribute and presented gifts. They allowed the Western traders to trade and offered them protection, although their presence was usually restricted to a small strip of beach where trade was conducted. The Europeans were forbidden to trade in the interior.[11] This allowed the Africans to regulate the trade, but it stimulated a competition between the African rulers to occupy the beaches. The European traders were happy to remain on board of their ships or settle on one of the numerous islands and only went to the beach to trade. According to Smith, the first Europeans made no effort to introduce the idea of sovereign territorial states in Africa.[12] The trade between Europe and West Africa did, however, stimulate the process of state formation that had already started in some parts of Africa, including Mali and Songhai. J. E. Inikori says that the demand for slaves in the eighteenth century reversed this process. African warlords seized authority and established more militaristic states, for example in Dahomey, Asante and the Segu Bambara state.[13]

From the late eighteenth century the Europeans increasingly began to present themselves as superiors. While previous treaties were based on reciprocity, the nineteenth-century treaties were dictated by the Western states, as also happened in the Middle East and East Asia. By the mid-1860s, Great Britain had signed about 107 treaties with African rulers, mostly related to anti-slavery and commerce.[14] The British Foreign Secretary Lord Palmerston, however, banned the use of the word 'treaty', because African rulers were still barbarous chiefs and not part of the civilized Family of Nations.[15] Besides extraterritoriality the new treaties contained provisions for appointing consuls. Their duties were gradually taken over by governors in the growing number of protectorates and (Crown) colonies. After the partition of Africa at the Berlin Conference, the number of consuls continued to rise because Western states allowed the appointment of foreign consuls in their colonies.

The experiences of consuls in sub-Saharan Africa are investigated through the following case studies. Sierra Leone was one of the first British Crown colonies in Africa. Foreign trade was dominated by British merchants, and they were protected by their governor. Other European traders also traded in the colony and some Western states appointed consuls, but their position was difficult, as the case of the German consul Johann Gottfried Nagel (1813–64) will demonstrate. Lacking support from your own government made the position of a consul even more difficult, as the case of the US consulate in Sierra Leone shows. After a promising start, the consulate was downgraded to a commercial agent, until a new consul was appointed in 1879: Judson A. Lewis (1840–1913). From the early nineteenth century, and particularly after the 1830s, the anti-slavery campaign in West Africa became a significant factor. Consuls, certainly those of Great Britain, played an active role in suppressing the slave trade and stimulating legal trade: 'Consuls were an especially valuable source of information on local slave trafficking, and consular clerical staff sometimes made up for staffing deficiencies in the mixed commissions'.[16] This becomes clear from the case of the British consul John Beecroft (1790–1854) in West Africa. On the East African coast, the slave trade and slavery continued for much longer. The consuls even benefited from their existence, because many of them were also active businessmen, as the case studies of the US consul Richard Palmer Waters (1807–87) on Zanzibar and William Sunley (1820–86) on the Comoros Islands demonstrate. Claims of European states on African territory increasingly frustrated traders. Several Western states appointed consuls to protect their interests, but competition and rivalry made their work difficult, as the case of the Dutch consul Lodewijk Kerdijk on the African south-west coast shows.

Sierra Leone: German and American Consuls in a British Crown Colony

Sierra Leone, a peninsula located on the estuary of a river, was highly valued by European traders for its natural harbour, but the climate was horrible: mortality rates were very high and it was known as 'the White Man's grave'.[17] In 1787 a British settlement, Granville Town, was constructed to house a number of black and white immigrants. The settlement was not a success, and many immigrants died of malaria and dysentery. In 1791 the chartered Sierra Leone Company was formed to 'promote Christianity, commerce and Western civilization'.[18] The company reconstructed the settlement, renamed Freetown, and new immigrants arrived, including blacks from Nova Scotia and Jamaica.

In 1808 Sierra Leone became a British Crown colony: a colony under state control ruled by a governor. To generate more income from taxes, the governors of the colony stimulated foreign trade but at the same time they introduced regulations to protect British merchants. This made it an attractive location for British businessmen, besides offering an excellent naval base for the Royal Navy during the anti-slavery campaign of the first half of the nineteenth century. In 1818 the Court of Mixed Commissions was set up in Freetown to prosecute captains of captured slave ships.[19] Slavery in the British colonies was not abolished until the early 1830s and the British tried to persuade Africans to switch to legitimate trade, including groundnuts (peanuts), kola nuts, palm oil, palm kernels and timber. Despite the transition to legitimate trade, the slave trade in West Africa did not end; both expanded during the first decades of the nineteenth century.[20]

The Hamburg merchant Johann Daniel Eppfenhausen – calling himself John Eppfenhausen – settled in Sierra Leone in the early 1830s to trade in ivory.[21] He established a partnership with Ernst Caesar Hartung between 1838 and 1841. When the partnership was dissolved, Hartung continued on his own and became consul for Bremen in Freetown, while Eppfenhausen found a new partner: Johann Gottfried Nagel.[22] Nagel had previously worked in Pernambuco, Brazil for A. Schramm & Company. Before Nagel left Hamburg, he asked the Hamburg Senate to appoint him consul. German trade with Freetown was growing annually and although the Hanseatic towns had signed commercial and anti-slavery (1837) treaties with Great Britain, merchant vessels were often intercepted by the Royal Navy on suspicion of carrying slaves. Nagel's solicitation was supported by the *Commerz-Deputation* (commercial department), A. Schramm (his previous employer in Brazil) and Eppfenhausen. Nagel was appointed consul for Hamburg in Sierra Leone on 15 April 1842. To formalize his appointment, the Hamburg Senate requested an exequatur from the British government. He was instructed to support German citizens and send regular reports, including reports on the local health conditions, because of Freetown's bad reputation when it came to diseases. P. E. Schramm says that Nagel's consular reports contained valuable information for the Hamburg Senate because they were often the only source of information about places that were hardly known at the time, and they were fairly reliable. Nagel was a merchant-consul and was allowed to trade in Freetown.

Nagel arrived in Freetown on 9 September 1842 and presented his exequatur to the British governor. He reported that he was cordially received because 'the people of Hamburg are well regarded everywhere'.[23] Soon after his arrival Nagel reorganized and expanded the business of Eppfenhausen & Nagel. He enlisted the help of a clerk, the British citizen Henry Williams, and chartered three small vessels for the coastal trade. By 1843 the firm had already received seven vessels from Europe. Nagel's success in business resulted in several complaints and accusations from rival British traders. The firm Heddle & Company, owned by Charles William Maxwell Heddle (1812–88), complained to the Freetown Customs House that Nagel had violated existing regulations and the Navigation Act:

> Now these Germans have already done much mischief here and are likely to do more with such a man as Mr. Cormick (the director of the Customs House in Freetown), unless they are checked, and the best check will be to see, that the Customs House enforces the law.[24]

According to the complaint, Eppfenhausen & Nagel had imported coffee from the British West Indies to Freetown and re-exported it to Great Britain as British colonial goods to save on export duties. Eppfenhausen & Nagel were furthermore engaged in the coastal trade between Freetown and West Africa that was the preserve of British ships according to the Navigation Act.

Pending the investigation, the customs house seized a merchant vessel and some of Eppfenhausen & Nagel's trade goods. Heddle's allegations seriously damaged the reputation of the firm and Nagel's personal reputation. In the small community of Westerners in Freetown, his future as consul of Hamburg was in doubt. After first denying all allegations, Nagel later admitted that his clerk had made a mistake regarding the trade in coffee from the West Indies. To the Senate in Hamburg he wrote that the trade between Hamburg and Freetown was frustrated by the many new British regulations and he proposed to conclude a commercial treaty with Great Britain to provide Hamburg merchants with equal trading rights. The Hamburg Senate replied that, despite the accusations brought against Nagel, they supported him, because commercial relations between Hamburg and Sierra Leone had much improved since his arrival. The Senate furthermore instructed its representative in London, James Colquhoun (1780–1855), to address the matter with the Foreign Secretary.[25] Colquhoun pointed out that British and German relations had been cordial for many years and the best solution for the problems in Sierra Leone would be to make Freetown a free port. This would stimulate foreign trade and contribute to the British policy of promoting legitimate trade in Africa. He added that Hamburg had been already opened to all nations and reciprocity in international relations required the same of Freetown. But the Foreign Secretary rejected his proposals: the complaints against Nagel were too serious and required a thorough investigation.

In June 1846, almost three years after Heddle's complaints were made, the customs house in Freetown published its report. Eppfenhausen & Nagel had not committed an offense with regard to the customs duties. As far as the second complaint, the coastal trade in West Africa, was concerned, it had violated the

Navigation Act. This verdict destroyed the reputation of Nagel as a trader and consul of Hamburg. In late 1846 another Hanseactic town, Lübeck, requested the Foreign Office in London to appoint Nagel as consul in Freetown, but this was denied. In his reply to the Senate of Lübeck, Lord Palmerston suggested that Hamburg recall Nagel before the British government asked him to return his exequatur. On 24 January 1847, Eppfenhausen indeed asked the Hamburg Senate to discharge Nagel as consul. The Hamburg Senate complied, but out of protest decided not to appoint a new consul. Schramm argues that the position of Nagel as consul was already severely weakened after the accusations were made and he never stood a fair chance against the British firms and the authorities. He was the victim of British envy of the German commercial success and, according to Colquhoun, it was an 'act of meanness and selfishness' because the British policy in Sierra Leone was still guided by 'less liberal principles'.[26]

In his book on Sierra Leone, W. W. Shreeve noted that US merchants from New York, Philadelphia, Boston, Salem and other places frequently visited Sierra Leone. Their merchandise consisted mainly of provisions that sold well, including flour, tobacco, tea and butter. 'Manufactured goods, such as those of Manchester and Birmingham, they never import, showing their inability to compete with England in price and quality'.[27] After the United States industrialized, competition in industrial goods did increase and British traders started to complain about unfair competition. The trade of the US with Sierra Leone was mostly conducted through indigenous or European commission agents. Lack of protection and higher agency costs induced the US merchants to press their government to appoint a consul.

On 11 August 1853 Captain John E. Taylor (d. 1859), a merchant from Baltimore, became acting US consul in Sierra Leone.[28] Taylor did not receive a government salary for his consulship, but he was allowed to trade and collect fees from US merchant vessels visiting the port. I. Kargbo writes that Freetown became one of the few ports on the West African coast where the US had substantial commerce, particularly from the 1870s. In this development, the consulate played an important role, despite British attempts to protect their own interests.[29] Taylor was officially recognized as acting consul by the British governor, but he was not a consul according to international law because the US government had not requested an exequatur and London had not provided one.[30] His powers to protect the US merchants and sailors were therefore limited. In February 1855, Taylor requested that a vessel of the US African Squadron be sent to Sierra Leone once or twice every two months, hoping that this would enhance his position. Commander-in-Chief Isaac Mayo (1794–1861) declined the request: the US squadron consisted of only three vessels for the entire West African coast.[31]

Two years later, a number of US merchants petitioned their government, because of the very unsatisfactory position in which the representation of the American government stand in the colony of Sierra Leone. That notwithstanding the very important and extensive commerce between the United States and West Coast of Africa, and particularly with this colony, it is a singular fact that there has never been a Consul nor even Consular Agent appointed by the United States government as its representative here.[32]

The US government did not act upon the petition and in February 1858 Taylor again raised the issue in a letter to the Department of State. Although he was recognized as acting consul this meant little, because his powers could be revoked at any time when he complained to the British governor. He pointed out that all US vessels seized on suspicion of carrying slaves were taken to Sierra Leone for adjudication. Between April 1857 and May 1858, twenty-seven US vessels were seized and only one ship was returned. All other ships were condemned because they had fittings on board or actually carried slaves. Taylor added that since his appointment in August 1853, about 120 merchant vessels from the US visited Freetown. He therefore proposed that he be appointed consul 'to maintain the dignity of our great nation'.[33]

In contrast to Schramm's viewpoint on the importance of the consular reports of Nagel, G. E. Brooks says that the annual reports of US consular agents in West Africa were of little value. 'Since consular agents were themselves traders, they saw no advantage in disseminating knowledge valuable to others'.[34] This general statement is, however, not confirmed in the case of Taylor or any of his successors. Their reports contained many details on trading conditions and suggestions for improvements. Taylor's Annual Report for 1858 showed that twenty-five vessels (in total 4,374 tons) had entered the port, bringing about $400,000 in goods from the US, 'nearly all of which took return cargoes from this place'.[35] In his view Sierra Leone was 'the natural and most effective inlet for American foreign trade', and the major merchants of the colony, Kargbo notes, were obliged to keep a supply of American manufactures at hand because of the great demand.[36] The British governor of Sierra Leone remarked in his Annual Report for 1861 that the main reason for the increasing demand for American goods was their 'inexpensiveness and durability'.[37] No other reports were sent by Taylor after February 1859: he died during an epidemic in Sierra Leone.[38] C. Fyfe notes that 'one disease after another broke out – fever, yellow fever, measles. Smallpox ravaged the villages.'[39] After seven months 500 people had died, including forty-two Europeans.

Taylor was succeeded in 1860 by Henry Rider, a merchant from Salem and agent of Enoch Richard Ware and Company (New York). Rider was appointed consular agent, a position less important than acting consul.[40] Rider would frequently, but in vain, appeal to his government to promote him.[41] Despite his disappointment at not being promoted to consul, Rider helped several US companies wanting to trade with Sierra Leone. The Harter Medicine Company

(Dayton, Ohio) wrote to the consulate in 1860 for inquiries about a certain Creole merchant in Freetown, 'regarding his financial standings, business ability, and whether he would meet the business obligations'.[42] During the Civil War trade between the US and Sierra Leone remained fairly stable, but the statistics could be misleading because an increasing share of the imports from the US first went to Great Britain and were loaded onto British ships before being sent to Sierra Leone. The steady growth of US trade with Sierra Leone stimulated merchants of London and Liverpool, organized in the British Mercantile Association, to petition their government to better protect their interests. Between 1862 and 1872 a number of ordinances were published to protect British traders in Sierra Leone. In March 1862 the sale of weapons and ammunition, a major export article from the US, was restricted beyond Freetown. The following year the duties on the export of animal skins, hides and palm oil were increased.

Table 5.1: The value and share of United States trade with Sierra Leone

	Imports from US (value in £)	Exports to US (value in £)	Imports from US (%)	Exports to US (%)
1853	9,515	20,045	9.6	14.8
1855	14,547	26,630	12.7	15.6
1857	16,017	50,072	9.3	17.3
1859	20,210	50,203	11.9	20.3
1861	15,891	29,649	6	13.9
1863	41,126	58,073	19.6	19.6
1865	39,164	37,913	18.1	16
1867	42,064	63,483	14.7	21.4
1869	36,033	57,001	12.4	14.1
1871	30,894	46,242	10.1	10.5
1873	28,908	50,502	5.9	10.9
1875	39,183	18,366	12	5.2
1877	34,735	21,265	9.4	5.5
1879	29,750	19,775	7.8	5.1
1881	33,771	19,516	9.7	5.3
1883	31,061	19,595	7.9	4.4
1885	42,138	23,244	13.8	7.1

Source: G. E. Brooks Jr, *Yankee Traders, Old Coasters and African Middlemen: A History of American Legitimate Trade with West Africa in the Nineteenth Century* (Boston, MA: Boston University Press, 1970), pp. 305–9.

Despite these measures, total foreign trade between the US and Sierra Leone increased to $700,500 between 1865 and 1870, up 10 per cent from the period 1860 to 1865.[43] After the Civil War several merchant houses from the US established new agencies in Sierra Leone, including G. Amsick and Company (New York), Pingree Brothers (Salem), and H. Roberts and Justin Rideout (Boston). The US government, however, saw no reason to appoint a consul. The consulate in Sierra Leone gradually became less important because the representative was downgraded from acting consul, to consular agent and, finally, to commercial agent. In 1879 the US appointed Judson A. Lewis (1840–1913), agent for the firm of Joseph W. Yates and Robert Porterfield (New York), as consul and he remained in office until 1890.[44] After reorganizing the consulate, Lewis actively began to promote trade. In a despatch written in March 1880 he noted that many new products from the US sold well, including axes, hammers, chisels, cooking stoves, kerosene oil stoves, safes, sewing machines and other hardware. 'Many of the above articles have been introduced through the influence of the representation as made in the "Scientific American" and "The American Exporter", both of said journals being received regularly at this consulate.'[45] Despite the efforts of Taylor, Rider and particularly Lewis, the share of the US in the import trade of Sierra Leone declined from 20 per cent in 1863 to about 5 per cent in 1873 (see also Table 5.1).[46] Unites States export trade with the entire continent of Africa remained small: in 1840 it was 0.6 per cent and in 1870 it was 0.5 per cent.[47] Brooks says that despite this low percentage the trade was 'of considerable significance in the African context'.[48]

West Africa: John Beecroft and the Anti-Slavery Campaign

From the mid-eighteenth century, opposition to the slave trade and slavery became more prominent in Western countries. Following Denmark (1803), the US (1805) and Great Britain (1807) outlawed the slave trade.[49] Great Britain concluded numerous bilateral treaties with Western and African states in an attempt to stop the slave trade.[50] The treaties with African rulers allowed Great Britain to use force to put down the trade and subject the tribe to 'severe acts of displeasure'.[51] They contained provisions for financial compensation and it was hoped that this would stimulate the development of the legal trade in African produce. This transition proved difficult for those African states with a large stake in the slave trade, like Dahomey.[52] Besides the anti-slavery treaties, Great Britain concluded a large number of commercial treaties with African states.[53] K. O. Dike writes that the British views on these commercial and anti-slavery treaties were inconsistent and many were never ratified.[54] To enforce the anti-slavery treaties, the Royal Navy patrolled the west and later also east coast of Africa. Other countries, including France (1831) and the US (1842), ordered their navy to cooperate with the Royal Navy. Despite the joined naval efforts, the slave trade increased after the 1840s, particularly in Brazil and Cuba. A blockade of the Brazilian coast by the Royal Navy from 1850 to 1852 was most effective in stopping this trade. The focus next shifted to the Spanish colony of Cuba. The slave trade to the US ended when the Confederate Army was defeated in 1865, while the slave trade to Cuba stopped two years later.[55] In 1869 the Royal Navy's West Africa Squadron ceased to operate.[56]

Besides black slaves, Europeans traded in various African products. This included palm oil that was used to season meat and fish, as lubricant and lamp oil, and medical treatment.[57] Palm oil was 'the quintessential commodity of the era of so-called legitimate trade for large parts of West Africa'.[58] The major centres of production were the ports on the Bight of Biafra, including Bonny, Brass and Old Calabar. On the Slave Coast (or Bight of Benin), where the trade in slaves continued for some decades after 1807, the port of Lagos was an important exporter of palm oil after the 1850s. The system of trade used in West Africa was known as 'trust': Western merchants provided credit, usually trade goods, to brokers to buy palm oil from the inland producers. The system occasionally led to disputes over unfulfilled contracts. Sometimes Western traders randomly grabbed canoes carrying palm oil, or even native traders, to force compliance. The consuls tried to arbitrate, although their judicial powers on the mainland were initially limited. Increased competition following the introduction of steamshipping, the development of new production areas (in South-East Asia) and the discovery of Pennsylvanian petroleum in 1859, reduced the profitability of the palm oil trade from the 1880s. M. Lynn argues that the Western traders responded by employing more hulks (redundant sailing ships) to temporarily store palm oil, using resident agents and by establishing trading posts on land.[59] As a result, the number of Westerners living on the coast steadily increased, creating more work for the consuls as they had to settle disputes over business deals and other matters. Life in the delta of the palm oil rivers began to resemble other Western communes.

Until the appointment of a consul, British traders in West Africa were protected by local African rulers. After 1807 the Royal Navy offered some additional protection, but British traders preferred African rulers, because 'the Navy was ill-suited for handling disputes between Africans and British traders. It too easily resorted to force in issues that required diplomatic handling.'[60] In October 1827, Captain William Fitzwilliam Owen (1774–1857) of the Royal Navy arrived on Fernando Po (present Bioko in the Gulf of Guinea). Great Britain wanted to establish a permanent settlement and naval base for the suppression of the slave trade in the Bight of Benin and Bight of Biafra.[61] It was furthermore intended to house the Court of Mixed Commissions, at that time located in Sierra Leone (see p. 118).[62] Fernando Po was claimed by Spain, but the British were nevertheless allowed to construct a small settlement. After two years Owen was replaced by Lieutenant-Colonel Edward Nicholls (1779–1865), who appointed John Beecroft, an agent of the firm Richard Dillon & Co. (later Dillon, Tennant & Co.), as Superintendent of Works. Beecroft lived an adventurous life as merchant, prisoner of war between 1805 and 1814, and explorer. Shortly after his arrival on Fernando Po he organized two successful expeditions to Old Calabar on the mainland to restore friendly relations with the local African ruler. This established his reputation in the area. In 1832 the British abandoned

Fernando Po 'in consequence of the great mortality among the Europeans', but Beecroft remained on the island.[63] From 1833 he was 'uncrowned king of the island', until his appointment as Spanish Governor in 1843.[64] Beecroft operated the steamer *Ethiope* for the Liverpool merchant and shipbroker Robert Jamieson (*c.* 1791–1861).[65] He collected palm oil on the African coast and transported it to Fernando Po, before re-exporting it to Great Britain. Beecroft, like many other Western explorers, made several expeditions to find the main channel of the Niger to establish direct trade with the palm oil producers.

In June 1849, Beecroft was appointed British consul for the Bights of Benin and Biafra. Dike points out that his fame rests on two achievements: he began the era of empire building and familiarized Africans with the role of consuls as de facto rulers on the Bights of Benin and Biafra.[66] The British Commissioner and consul general for the oil rivers, Sir Claude Maxwell MacDonald (1852–1915), wrote in 1893 that Beecroft 'was instrumental in making many of the treaties for the suppression of the export slave trade'.[67] W. D. McIntyre sees in him 'an empire-builder in the tradition of Maclean of the Gold Coast'.[68] Beecroft's ability to intervene in domestic politics was rather limited under the existing treaties. In contrast to consuls in the Middle East and East Asia, consuls in sub-Saharan Africa enjoyed no extraterritorial powers until 1872.[69] Beecroft was nevertheless able to institutionalize consular authority, which was helpful for his successors.[70] In his instructions to Beecroft, Lord Palmerston referred to previous requests of British traders for a representative in the Niger Delta. Beecroft was chosen because of his general knowledge of African affairs and customs, 'and because of the influence which you appear to have acquired over the Native Chiefs'.[71] His commission was not intended to 'gain Possession, either by purchase or otherwise of any portion of the African Continent in those parts, not of any neighbouring Island'.[72] For his consulship Beecroft received an annual salary of £300, and was furthermore allowed to trade.

After his appointment, Beecroft visited Lagos, the Niger Delta, Old Calabar and the Cameroons. He intentionally made use of naval vessels to impress native chiefs and kings, who were invited to visit him on the deck of the vessel. Beecroft encountered little opposition from the states who were already active in the palm oil trade, but had more problems with Dahomey, Lagos and Bonny. British attempts from 1841 to persuade their rulers to give up the slave trade in exchange for financial compensation failed.[73] In May 1849 Lord Palmerston appointed John H. M. Duncan (1805–1849) as vice-consul for Whydah to monitor the slave trade in this region more closely. In early November Duncan died and was replaced by the zoologist, collector, curator and explorer Louis Fraser (1810–1866) until the arrival of Benjamin Campbell (*c.* 1802–59) in July 1853.[74] Campbell would remain consul until his death in April 1859; two years later Great Britain annexed Lagos and established a protectorate under a British governor.

After the appointment of Campbell in Lagos, Beecroft's commission was henceforth limited to the Bight of Biafra. Beecroft's second visit to Dahomey to persuade the king to stop the trade in slaves was a failure and it convinced Beecroft 'that nothing short of a major war could bring that kingdom into line with British policy'.[75] Beecroft believed that a military attack was necessary to 'renovate and reform Africa and pull it out of the awful darkness that overshadows it'.[76] The first British attack failed, but the second was successful and on 27 December 1851 they took possession of Lagos. Beecroft concluded a treaty in January 1852 with King Akitoye to suppress the slave trade and to stimulate legal trade. It is important to note that in this agreement the British consul and other foreign consuls were not mentioned at all.[77] The Western merchants on the mainland still operated under the protection of African rulers.[78] After settling the affairs with Dahomey, Beecroft turned his attention to King Pepple of Bonny. Despite several treaties with the British (in 1836, 1839 and 1841), the king continued to trade in slaves, because these treaties were not ratified by the Foreign Office until 1848, when a commercial treaty and an anti-slaving treaty were concluded.

Beecroft established Courts of Equity for handling disputes between African and European traders but their legality was questioned in the late 1850s by the Colonial Courts of the Gold Coast and Sierra Leone.[79] The anti-slavery treaties and commercial treaties had not provided the British consuls with extraterritorial powers in sub-Saharan Africa.[80] Attempts in 1859 by Beecroft's successor, Thomas Joseph Hutchinson (1820–1885, consul from 1855 until 1861), to conclude new treaties that would gave him jurisdiction over British subjects failed.[81] When Hutchinson was succeeded by Sir Richard Francis Burton (1821–90, consul between 1861 and 1864) he was again instructed to conclude new treaties, but there is no evidence that Burton ever attempted this. He preferred exploring Africa above his regular consular duties.[82] Charles Livingstone (1821–73), consul from 1864 until 1873, was equally unsuccessful.[83] The West African Order in Council (February 1872) finally provided the British consuls with jurisdiction to try and punish British subjects in civil and criminal cases. From 1884 Great Britain concluded treaties of protection that conferred 'full and exclusive jurisdiction, civil and criminal, over British subjects and their property' on Her Britannic Majesty, to be exercised by the consul.[84] This jurisdiction included all people under British protection.

Zanzibar and the Comoros Islands: American and British Consuls, Commerce and Slavery

In September 1833 the US and the Sultan of Oman and Zanzibar concluded a treaty of amity and commerce. The treaty with Said bin Sultan (1791–1856, also called Seyyid Said) was signed by Special Agent Edmund Quincy Roberts.[85] The treaty removed most restrictions, except for the trade in weapons and ammunition that could be sold only to the government. Duties on import and export were fixed at 5 per cent. The treaty offered protection to shipwrecked vessels and sailors and allowed US merchants to reside in any port or town of the dominions of the sultan. Article 9 stated that the US was allowed to appoint consuls, 'which shall be the exclusive judges of all disputes or suits wherein American Citizens shall be engaged with each other'.[86] The US thus obtained extraterritoriality in the Empire of Oman. Oman signed similar treaties with other Western states, including Great Britain (1839), France (1844) and in 1859 with the Hanseatic towns.

Said bin Sultan is considered 'one of the most important rulers of the Omani Empire'.[87] During his rule the empire included the nearby island of Pemba and parts of the Swahili coast bordering the area that was claimed by Portugal: from Cape Delgado to Delagoa Bay. Said bin Sultan modernized the economy on Zanzibar. This included the production of cloves from the 1820s, which led to a growth in the domestic demand for slaves. According to his daughter Sayyida Salme (1844–1924), her father owned forty-five plantations, each of which had 50 to 100 slaves, and on the largest plantation there were 500 slaves.[88] The British consul Lieutenant Colonel Atkins Hamerton (1804–57) wrote in 1841 that 'almost every one of the Sultan's subjects owns slaves, the poorer about five, and the wealthier from 400 to 1,500'.[89] The slavery, however, went against the British policy. In 1819–20 Great Britain supported Said bin Sultan in his struggle against the Wahhabis in Arabia and the Arab pirates in the waters near Oman. The two countries concluded a treaty on 10 September 1822 (the Moresby Treaty)[90] to suppress the slave trade between Zanzibar to the Mascarenes and India, but not between Zanzibar and Oman or Arabia.[91]

Zanzibar was part of the monsoon system, the seasonal pattern of reversing winds, connecting East Africa with Egypt, Oman, Persia and India. It exported ivory, rhinoceros horns and hides, ox hides, beeswax, miller, rice, coconut oil, gum copal, tortoise shell and slaves.[92] In 1840 Said bin Sultan moved his court from Muscat to Zanzibar to benefit from the growing trade with the African mainland.[93] His primary source of income was the customs duties, the collection of which was farmed out to the Banyans, a merchant class from British India living on Zanzibar.[94] The Banyans dominated the local economy and the foreign trade of Zanzibar, acting as middlemen, money lenders, and wholesale and retail traders.[95] To the embarrassment of the British government many were also active in the slave trade.

Merchants from New York, Boston and Salem had directed their vessels to the Indian Ocean, including the Red Sea and Oman, from the 1790s, and after the 1820s they began to regularly visit Zanzibar.[96] Besides merchants from the US, Zanzibar was frequented by British and French traders and those from the Hanseatic League.[97] According to the German missionary Johann Ludwig Krapf (1810–81), who was in Zanzibar in 1844, there were about twenty Europeans, mostly merchants.[98]

The first US consul on Zanzibar was Richard Palmer Waters of Salem, Massachusetts. His appointment was a clear example of the existing patronage or spoils system in nineteenth-century America. Waters, the owner of a general store, had not visited any other foreign country before and spoke only English. His appointment was nevertheless strongly endorsed by merchants of the Salem community, in particularly the firm Shepard & Bertram owned by Michael Shepard (1786–1856) and John Bertram (1796–1882). Their main rival was the Salem firm of Pingree & West owned by David Pingree (1795–1863) and George West (1810–52).[99] Shepard & Bertram engaged Waters as their agent on Zanzibar. The consular salary was insufficient to maintain a decent living and, like most other US consuls in the mid-nineteenth century, Waters was allowed to trade. Waters was a very religious man and in his letters strongly opposed slavery. During his stopover in Mozambique, he saw two slave ships with many young children on board: 'This sight called up many unpleasant feelings. What can I say to those engaged in this trade, when I remember the millions of Slaves which exist in my own country?'[100] On Zanzibar Waters witnessed a lively slave trade and widespread domestic slavery. According Sayyida Salme, even 'a good many Europeans in Zanzibar kept slaves themselves or bought some when their interests were at stake'.[101] G. J. Pierson argues that the merchants and the consuls from the US did little to stop the slave trade and slavery because of their own business interests. They saw the anti-slavery campaign of Great Britain and its European allies as another attempt to frustrate competition from American businesses and not at all inspired by humanitarian motives.[102]

When Waters arrived on 18 March 1837, he was saluted by one of the many vessels owned by Said bin Sultan. He met fellow merchants from the United Sates and was taken to the local officials. The merchants from Salem dominated the US trade with Zanzibar exporting unbleached cotton cloth, still known as *merkani* or *amerkani* on the Swahili coast, besides other products like clocks, shoes, various household items, and weapons.[103] One of the first consular duties of Waters was taking care of the estate of the deceased merchant James Devereux who died on Zanzibar in June 1831.[104] Zanzibar was frequented by merchant vessels and whalers of the US and one of the consul's more tiresome duties was to arbitrate disputes between sailors and masters. As John Ross Browne wrote in his journal while he was a sailor on a US whaler, there were many abuses on these ships. Desertion of sailors was a common problem that required the attention of consuls.[105] In December 1837 the whaling ship *London Packet* from Fairhaven arrived and the captain contacted Waters to complain about six sailors' mutinous conduct. Waters requested the help of the sultan, who supplied twenty-two armed guards. In his report to the US government, Waters wrote: 'I am ashamed of my countrymen when they conduct in such a manner as to bring disgrace upon themselves and their country. This trouble was all occasioned by rum.'[106] Waters appealed to the sailors to peacefully accompany him to the prison in the sultan's fort until he had investigated the complaint. According to Browne, two-third of the men died during their captivity because of the poor conditions. Browne himself was luckier: thanks to Waters he was able to arrange the discharge of the whaler *Styx* and was treated 'very humanely' by the consul.[107]

Not long after his arrival, Waters was confronted by the customs house manager Jairam Shivji (1792–1866), a Banyan from Kutch.[108] From 1835 until 1886, he farmed the customs on behalf of Said bin Sultan for $150,000 per year; it rose to $170,000 in 1854 and $196,000 or $220,000 in 1859.[109] Because of the high costs of obtaining the license, it was in Jairam Shivji's interest to make sure that all cargo went through the customs house. He not only managed the customs house, but in addition supplied the workforce (porters called *pagazi*) for loading and unloading ships for which he charged an additional fee of $100 to $150. Jairam Shivji apparently did very well, because he was one of the wealthiest Indians. He invested in commerce and plantations and offered loans to indigenous and foreign merchants and even to the sultan. Soon the sultan came to depend on the credit facilities offered by Jairam Shivji. To the Secretary of State, John Forsyth (1780–1841), Waters wrote that Jairam Shivji

> governs the whole business of the customhouse. This Master of Customs has continued the practice up to the present time of compelling the Americans to bring every article which they export to the Custom House, and making them pay the expense attending the transportation.[110]

Waters complained to the sultan arguing that it violated the commercial treaty with the US.[111] Said bin Sultan replied that he expected foreign merchants to bring their cargo to the customs house and pay for the work of the porters. He was, however, willing to change the treaty if the US government wanted to do so. Jairam Shivji responded by charging merchants from India when they landed cargo that was destined for US vessels. When Waters again complained about this to the sultan, the latter agreed to end the practice. These actions made the US consul very unpopular with local officials and merchants. Not much later Waters was physically attacked outside the consulate; the consulate itself, as well as Waters's residence, was molested at night several times when stones were thrown at the building.[112]

Waters's motivation for accepting the post on Zanzibar, and his willingness to endure these hardships, become clear from a letter written in August 1837. He states that he was willing to work hard for a couple of years

> if I can acquire a necessary portion of riches. Not that I mean to make gold my God, but feel that I am in the performance of my duty, while engaged in an honest business and acquiring riches. I want money for my own sake, for my dear Mothers, Sisters & Brothers sake.[113]

A few months later Waters and Jairam Shivji made a deal that proved very beneficial to both men. Waters directed all trade from US vessels to the customs house, while Jairam Shivji controlled the native merchants.[114] According to C. Goswami, the agreement allowed them to dominate the import and export trade at Zanzibar by 'excluding both the American and English traders who refused to trade through them'.[115] In December 1839 Waters wrote to his brother William that about 90 per cent of his business was with Jairam Shivji, who was making 'a great deal of money'.[116] According to M. R. Bhacker, the profitable partnership between Waters and Jairam Shivji did not last long, and 'by 1842, Waters succeeded in diversifying his local clientele and competed on a local level like any other merchant'.[117]

The commercial treaty between Great Britain and Oman (1839) did arouse the interest of some British businessmen, and a consul was appointed: Lieutenant Colonel Hamerton of the Indian Army. Hamerton soon clashed with Waters and Jairam Shivji, after British merchants complained about their business deal. The main British firm was Newman, Hunt and Christopher from London.[118] Their first resident agent on Zanzibar between 1833 and 1837 was Captain Robert Brown Norsworthy (d. 1845). Norsworthy complained to the sultan but he took no action. It was apparently impossible for British traders to bypass the Shivji–Waters combine and negotiate directly with merchants from the US or Zanzibar.[119] R. Coupland argues that Hamerton did little to promote trade and his main attention was with politics: protecting the independence of Zanzibar.[120] With the arrival of Hamerton the position of Waters changed because he was no longer the only foreign consul on Zanzibar. In 1841 Waters decided to end his agency for Shepard and Bertrand and began working for their rivals: the firm of Pingree & West. The deal between Jaraim Shivji and Waters fell apart after 1842. That year Waters did about one-third of his business with Jaraim Shivji and increasingly dealt with Indian and Arab traders.[121] Perhaps he had amassed enough money and already contemplated leaving Zanzibar. On 3 October 1844, Waters bade farewell to his compatriots and his other friends, including Jaraim Shivji and Said bin Sultan. Although Waters maintained contact with Said bin Sultan for some time after his return to the US, he never visited Zanzibar again.

Table 5.2: The import and export trade of Zanzibar for 1859 (£)

	Import from	Export to	Total trade
Great Britain	–	5,566	5,566
British India	99,606	105,888	205,494
United States	126,398	118,688	245,086
France	114,790	55,000	169,790
Germany (Hamburg)	101,296	35,777	137,073
Others	466,821	434,767	901,589
Total	908,911	755,686	1,664,598

Source: E. Hieke, *Zur Geschichte des deutschen Handels mit Ostafrika. Teil 1: Wm. O'Swald & Co., 1831–1870* (Hamburg: Verlag Hans Christians, 1939), p. 295.

Others include: Kutch (Gujarat, India), Singapore, Arabia, East Coast Africa, West Coast Africa and Madagascar. Author corrected the total for the US from the original source.

The US initially dominated the trade with Zanzibar in the 1850s (see Table 5.2), but its share fell to about 10 per cent in 1861 before recovering to 20 per cent in 1868. The opening of the Suez Canal in 1869, however, placed the merchants of the US at a disadvantage over their European rivals when sailing vessels were replaced by steamships.[122] After the American Civil War in 1865, it was hoped that slavery would be totally extinguished, but in many parts of the Middle East, Africa and East Asia it continued to exist. In early 1873, the British dispatched Sir Bartle Frere (1815–84) to Zanzibar to make an inquiry into the slave trade.[123] Zanzibar became a British protectorate in 1888, but slavery continued until their emancipation in 1897.[124] Frere also visited the island Johanna and saw 'a flourishing estate, chiefly for sugar cultivation, belonging to Mr. Sunley, an Englishman, carried on by free labour'.[125]

From the ninth century, the Comoros Islands came under the influence of Muslim traders from Oman, Persia and Arabia. The Portuguese were the first Europeans to arrive in 1529. Because of their favourable location in the Mozambique Channel, the islands became a hub between Portuguese East Africa, Madagascar and Goa in India. Besides merchant vessels and warships, the islands were often visited by pirates and buccaneers in the seventeenth century and whalers from the late eighteenth century onwards.[126] In November 1844, Great Britain concluded an anti-slave-trade treaty with Sultan Selim of Nzwani, one of the Comoros Islands.[127] British interests increased after the island Nosy Bé became a French protectorate in 1840, followed by Mayotte (or Mahoré, one of the four Comoros Islands) in 1841. France took these islands to compensate for the loss of Île de France in Mauritius to Great Britain after the Napoleonic Wars.[128]

To counter the growing French presence in the Indian Ocean, the Foreign Office decided to appoint a consul on the Comoros Islands. In August 1848, Josiah Napier (*c.* 1822–1850) became British consul for Nzwani, then known by the British name Johanna (or the French name Anjouan). Napier came to Johanna in 1845 to trade and later formed a partnership with H. E. G. Martindale. The latter also partnered with William Sunley, the son of a London merchant, who arrived on Johanna in 1847.

> Mr. Sunley came originally to the Mozambique with some command of capital, and with the intention of operating largely in the markets of its neighbourhood. He was accompanied or followed by four associates, of who two died, a third was lost at sea, and the fourth broke his back. His correspondents in London failed: his agents at Nossi Be and Zanzibar operated for him at a loss. His stores at Johanna were burnt down.[129]

It was decided that Martindale would return to London to buy merchandise that could be sold on the East African coast. At the end of 1849 Martindale returned to Johanna with the cargo, but Portugal claimed the area between Cape Delgado and Delagoa Bay and prevented foreign traders conducting their business. The ship and cargo of Martindale and Sunley were confiscated by the Portuguese.

On 3 June 1850 Consul Napier concluded a treaty of friendship and commerce with the sultan of Johanna. The treaty was based on full reciprocity and British subjects enjoyed protection for their person and property. It additionally contained a MFN clause, while article 8 regulated the appointment of consuls. In September, Napier died of phthisis (miliary tuberculosis). Because of the lack of consular protection and to prepare a claim against Portugal for the return of the confiscated cargo, Sunley returned to London. When he arrived in May 1851, he received news of his appointment as consul (18 February 1851). His annual salary was £150 and, because this was insufficient for a living, he was allowed to trade.

Before he returned to his post, Sunley wrote a report on the Comoros Islands for the Foreign Office on 16 July 1851. He noted that direct trade between Great Britain and the Comoros Islands did not exist. Most British trade concerned direct trade between Bombay, Zanzibar and Mozambique, touching on the Comoros Islands. The foreign trade on the Comoros Islands was dominated by merchants from the US. Sunley was confident that 'European energy and capital' could become more important because the sultan wished to attract more British traders. 'Property is now secure, the English language generally understood by the natives, the Anchorage excellent and much frequented by Whale ships and vessels bound to Aden and Bombay from Europe'.[130] The greatest obstacle was 'the claim of Portugal to the country from Delagoa Bay 25^0 South and Cape Delgado in Latitude 10^0 South. The Portuguese exclude trade from this area, though their authority is not acknowledged by many tribes'.[131]

After his return to Johanna, Sunley bought a piece of land to build a consulate. He interfered in local politics in 1855 by offering British protection to the sultan, who wanted his son to succeed him. Perhaps Sunley's most important decision after his return was to divert his business interests from trade into agriculture. For £45 annually he leased a few acres of land at Pomomi to develop a sugar plantation. When he died in 1886, his estate had grown to about 300 acres.[132] Because there were no free labourers on Johanna, Sunley was forced to use slaves, but he decided to pay them wages. Half of the wages were paid to the slaves, while the other half was for the slave-owner or master.

> He would not distil rum, nor allow tobacco to be grown; but he laboured early and late with his own hands to instil regular and orderly habits into his savage followers. He attended carefully to their complaints, both physical and mental. The results of his years of heavy labours are now (1861) visible in a most thriving estate: a contented, sober, and healthy looking body of negroes: and a heavy harvest of splendid cane, realising 28£ to 30£. per ton in the Mauritius market.[133]

In April 1861 Sunley was visited by David Livingstone (1813–73) after his mission to the Rovuma River. He was accompanied by his brother Charles, later British consul on Fernando Po (see p. 126), John Kirk (1832–1922), later consul on Zanzibar, and a number of missionaries of the Universities Mission to Central Africa (UMCA). Charles Livingstone noted that about 500 slaves (300 men and 200 women) worked on Sunley's plantation. Rev. Lovell J. Procter of the UMCA estimated the annual profit to be between £2,000 and £3,000, much more than his consular salary. Besides sugar, the plantations later produced coffee, cacao and vanilla. Captain Alan Henry Gardner (1817–78) of the Royal Navy called at the consulate on 2 September 1862. In his journal he wrote:

> Mr. Sunley is hard at work making his sugar and seems to be going on very prosperously, the sugar cane coming at a great pace. I was surprised to see how ably and intelligently the blacks (mostly slaves) do their allotted tasks. They drive the engine, make the wagons, break in cattle for draught and drive them and conduct all the different operations without any white overlooker besides Mr. Sunley.[134]

Two years later Captain Algernon de Horsey published an account of his visit to the Comoros Islands. He estimated the export and import of Johanna in 1856 at £10,000 annually, 'of which full half is accounted for by the produce of a sugar estate at Pomony, the property of H. M. consul of these islands'.[135]

News of the lucrative business of Sunley and his use of slaves reached British authorities in Cape Town in 1861 and they decided to investigate the matter. In 1843, the British Parliament had extended the Act of 1824, prohibiting slave-trading by British subjects 'in foreign countries and settlements not belonging to the British Crown'. The question was: were Sunley's workers slaves or paid labourers? The report sent to the Foreign Office in October revealed the extent of Sunley's operations and the Secretary of Foreign Affairs, Lord John Russell (1792–1878), asked for an explanation from Sunley. Although they praised him for setting an example by offering wages and recognized that it was impossible for Sunley to work the plantation with free labourers, employing slaves went against the British policy. The Foreign Office felt that 'our Principle as regards Employment of slaves must be adhered to'.[136] In his reply of 11 January 1862, Sunley explained that his workers were wholly free to come and go at any time. Some worked for only several weeks and then returned home, others stayed much longer. Besides the hired slaves, he employed thirty free labourers, but saw no real distinction between the two groups: on Johanna the difference between free man and slaves was small. 'They work for wages, are treated as free men, and think it is a great shame that they do not get all the wages they earn as their comrades do who have no master'.[137]

The matter was also debated in the British Parliament. In May 1862, Charles Buxton (1822–71) asked for Sunley's explanation for employing slaves on his x156 - PB - 13mm - 0 - 1858426-6 - 1 - 9780367669126 - 2UP-450mm-Web-TECNAU 2025/05/01 13:11:00

plantation.[138] During the same session Austen Layard (1817–94) remarked that 'Her Majesty's Government had under their consideration how far they ought to disapprove of the conduct of Consul Sunley in this matter'.[139] Lord Russell informed Sunley on 14 June 1862 that he must give up his plantations or his consulship. Sunley replied in late 1863:

> I am fully sensible of the honour of holding the appointment of Her Majesty's Consul at the Comoro Islands, but if it is imperative on me either to resign my commission or dismiss the labourers now employed on my estate, and thus put a ruinous termination to my undertakings here just as they are becoming remunerative, and after devoting many years and spending much money in prosecuting them, I beg reluctantly to place the resignation of my commission in your lordship's hands.[140]

The Foreign Secretary was adamant and informed Sunley that his name would be struck from the Consular List and his salary would cease to be paid.

> From reports received by Her Majesty's Government, I have every reason to believe that you have, by your example and enterprise, done much to promote the welfare and prosperity of the labouring classes in Johanna, both free and slave; but, as I have before explained to you, it is impossible that Her Majesty's Government can tolerate the employment of slaves by an officer holding Her Majesty's consular commission.[141]

In the end, Sunley decided to give up his appointment as consul and its small salary and continued to live on Johanna as a successful plantation owner. His plantations were still prospering in the 1870s and Sunley had even expanded his business to the island Mohilla (Mwali).[142] According to a member of the Frere Mission to Zanzibar, C. H. Hill, who visited Johanna in 1873, the sugar plantation of Sunley was about 700 acres and employed nearly 800 labourers. Hill noted that, because of the example set by Sunley, natives learned to love earning money from labour. An official of the Slave Trade Department in London admitted that Sunley had set a good example on Johanna and did an excellent job as a consul. He was 'a most active agent for the suppression of the S.T. [Slave Trade]'.[143]

Although in his last official letter he warned the Foreign Office about the growing influence of France in the region, Sunley was never replaced. In his last annual report, he noted that the trade of Johanna, and the Comoros Islands, was unimportant. G. W. Clendennen and P. W. Nottingham therefore believe that Sunley's dismissal as consul was additionally motivated by the declining importance of British trade and shipping to the Comoros Islands.[144] Johanna lost its attractiveness for British importers and exporters and offered little for manufacturers. As a station for the Royal Navy it retained some importance, besides the Seychelles Islands that were occupied in 1794, but merchant vessels no longer called at Johanna. After the opening of the Suez Canal and the introduction of steamships, the geostrategic position of the Comoros Islands became even less important. When Sunley died in 1886, the Comoros Islands became a French protectorate and in 1908 a French colony.

South-West Africa: Lodewijk Kerdijk, Opposing Portuguese Claims

In July 1849 two Dutch merchants, Henry P. Kerdijk (1822–89) and Lodewijk Pincoffs (1827–1911), formed a partnership in Rotterdam for trading in natural dyes for cotton and textiles.[145] This choice was probably related to the trading activities of their fathers, who had formed a partnership as well, dealing mainly in textiles. The two families were originally Jewish traders from Eastern Europe. In 1857 Kerdijk & Pincoffs expanded their business in South-West Africa. Simon Pincoffs (1812–1902), an elder brother of Lodewijk Pincoffs, had been living in Manchester since 1831 and worked as a textile trader.[146] In 1847 he set up a factory in Middleton for the production of garancine (a red dye) and his main client was Salis Schwabe & Co., calico printers in Middleton.[147] Until January 1852 he formed a partnership with Julius Robert Haus under the name of Pincoffs & Company.[148] Simon's business relations in Manchester included a British businessman, also of Jewish decent and a sometime resident of the Netherlands: Leopold Samson (b. 1813).

When Samson indicated that he wanted to sell his West African business, Simon contacted his brother in Rotterdam and Kerdijk & Pincoffs bought the business activities of Samson. What this deal precisely included is unknown, but it may have been some merchandise, (shares in) a number of sailing ships and trading posts in South-West Africa. In the summer of 1857, they directed Lodewijk Kerdijk, younger brother of Henry, to Manchester to familiarize himself with the trade in dyes and the West African trade of Samson. According to testimony of Henry Kerdijk from 1880, he received full cooperation from the British authorities to establish a trading post near Banana (also called Banana Point) at the entrance of the Congo River, because Kerdijk & Pincoffs pledged not to trade in African slaves. Whether British support was really required is doubtful, because most of the coastal region in South-West Africa was claimed by Portugal.

In August 1857 Lodewijk Kerdijk went to South-West Africa. There were already other Dutch traders on the West African coast, including the Rotterdam firm of H. van Rijckevorsel & Company.[149] In South-West Africa Kerdijk & Pincoffs competed with several European, American and Brazilian merchants. Lodewijk Kerdijk visited three factories (trading posts) of Kerdijk & Pincoffs: in Ponte da Lenha, Ambriz and Quisembo. In early 1861 another trading post was opened in Banana. This last trading post was expanded two years later, after taking over the activities of the French firm Régis.[150] The business activities of Kerdijk & Pincoffs continued to expand in the following years. According to Lynn, the firm was 'prominent on the South Coast by the 1860s'.[151] In the summer of 1859, Lodewijk Kerdijk returned to Rotterdam, but in December he was back in Banana. During 1860 he continued to expand the business of Kerdijk & Pincoffs.[152] On 31 May 1861, after a short illness, Lodewijk Kerdijk died in Banana. He was succeeded by D. P. Tavenraad Elkman, who became the chief agent of Kerdijk & Pincoffs in South-West Africa until 1869.

From October 1859 until October 1860, Lodewijk Kerdijk acted as Dutch consul.[153] The area was claimed by Portugal and this created political tension with several Western states. In June 1858 Kerdijk & Pincoffs wrote to the Ministry of Foreign Affairs in The Hague complaining about the unfair treatment of Dutch traders. They had opened in the past year 'several factories on the Southwest Coast of Africa to the north of S. Paul de Loando [present Luanda in Angola]'.[154] According to Kerdijk & Pincoffs, British traders paid lower duties on import and export than the Dutch. This was the result of a commercial treaty between Portugal and Great Britain that additionally demarcated the northern border of the Portuguese claims: the river Lodge (also Loge or Loze) about two miles north of Ambriz.[155] Kerdijk & Pincoffs requested the same privileges as the British traders and asked for the support of the Minister of Foreign Affairs. They stressed the importance of their business for the Dutch economy: 'The undersigned take the liberty to point out to your Excellency that the business they have established is completely new and that for the first time the Dutch flag is flying from their factories in this part of Africa'.[156] The Minister said that negotiations between the Netherlands and Portugal for a commercial treaty had been going on for some time. A Dutch proposal had not received a Portuguese response. In the meantime, the Dutch legation in Lisbon was instructed to obtain equal rights for Dutch traders from the Portuguese government.[157] In September 1858 Kerdijk & Pincoffs again appealed to the Minister of Foreign Affairs: 'despite the advantage of having sufficient and good stocks, trading of Dutch merchants on this part of the coast was almost impossible unless some agreement with Portugal was reached'.[158] Such an agreement, Kerdijk & Pincoffs continued, would stimulate trade between the Netherlands and the south-west coast of Africa. Although the Portuguese had since 1846 officially opened their colonial ports for foreign traders, they were forced to pay higher duties on import and export. To avoid these taxes, many non-Portuguese traders, including Kerdijk & Pincoffs, moved to the north of Ambriz. The Dutch ambassador in Lisbon reported in January 1859 that, after 'long and patient discussions', Portugal agreed to give Dutch traders equal rights until this matter was settled in a commercial treaty.[159] The ambassador added that the Portuguese were certainly not against concluding a commercial treaty with the Netherlands. During informal conversations they always expressed their willingness to sign a treaty, but their good intentions were never followed up by concrete actions.[160]

In early March 1859 Kerdijk & Pincoffs petitioned the Ministry of Foreign Affairs with a special request.

> It would be of great importance to us to appoint in these colonies a Dutch consul and because L. P. Kerdijk Esq. resides in Ambriz and is of Dutch nationality, we take the liberty to humbly ask your Excellency, to appoint him honorary consul general or consul for the Portuguese possessions on the South-west Coast of Africa. With this request we would confirm that Mister Kerdijk would be willing to provide assistance and information to all Dutch citizens as can be expected from his position.[161]

Although Kerdijk & Pincoffs and other Dutch traders had already received the same commercial privileges as British and French traders, it was obviously important for the firm to strengthen its position. Having an agent who was also an official Dutch representative would surely add to the status of Kerdijk & Pincoffs. It might furthermore aid in negotiations with local Portuguese officials in this remote area. Other major powers, including Great Britain, had already appointed consuls in this area.

According to the Minister of Foreign Affairs, appointing a Dutch consul was allowed according to the Consular Convention of June 1856, but he wanted to know from the Dutch Legation in Lisbon whether Ambriz was indeed Portuguese territory. He furthermore requested some information about L. P. Kerdijk.[162] The Dutch legation replied that Ambriz had indeed been Portuguese territory since May 1855.[163] Ambriz was a small town and foreign trade, particularly direct trade with Portugal, was still unimportant. However, by Royal Order of 6 October 1856, Ambriz was made an open port for all nations with special tariffs on import and export. An agent of a Portuguese trading house in Loanda provided information on Lodewijk Kerdijk. After receiving positive testimonies of the Portuguese trader Francisco Antonio Flores, a former Brazilian slave trader, Lodewijk Kerdijk was officially appointed consul by the Dutch king on 5 October 1859.[164] He did not receive a salary: he was a merchant-consul. The Dutch legation in Lisbon was instructed to obtain the exequatur from the Portuguese king, Dom Pedro, which was received on 18 November.[165]

The appointment of Lodewijk Kerdijk as Dutch consul coincided with the growing anxiety in Portugal over advances from foreign traders on the southwest African coast, especially the region near the entrance of the Congo River. Most non-Portuguese traders, including Kerdijk & Pincoffs, moved to this area to avoid Portuguese taxes. To claim this territory, Portugal ordered a detachment of soldiers to the Congo River, but this operation met with little success because of the fierce resistance of African tribes. After his return to Ambriz in late 1859, Lodewijk Kerdijk noted a growing hostility of the Portuguese towards European traders and increasing problems with African tribes. On 2 May 1860 Kerdijk wrote two letters to the Minister of Foreign Affairs. In the first letter, he acknowledged the arrival of his exequatur and Royal commission. He also informed the minister that he had moved to Quisembo (north of Ambriz) and wanted to change his commission because he no longer resided in Ambriz. In his second letter he explained the conditions in Ambriz and requested further instructions, on how to deal with the Portuguese claims on the south-western African coast. Should he present his exequatur to the Governor General Loanda or wait for further instructions? Kerdijk wrote that he resided in Quisembo most of the time, which did not belong to his district: he did not have consular powers beyond Ambriz. However, if the Dutch government allowed their consul to reside in Quisembo, it implied recognition of Portugal's claims in this area and this would offend Great Britain and other European powers.[166]

The letters of 2 May and 4 August, containing the latest information, arrived at the same time in The Hague, on 22 September.[167] Kerdijk still had not contacted the Portuguese Governor General, because the British consul in Loanda, H. V. Huntley, had advised him not to present his exequatur.[168] The Governor General might demand that Kerdijk return to Ambriz or accept his residence in Quisembo, but this would mean that the Dutch government recognized Portuguese claims. The Hague had not yet formulated its policy regarding these Portuguese claims, but the government informed Kerdijk & Pincoffs that a Dutch consul living in Quisembo and not in Ambriz would not benefit the trading interests of the Netherlands, including those of Kerdijk & Pincoffs.[169] On 28 September, Kerdijk & Pincoffs replied that they agreed and requested an honourable discharge of Lodewijk Kerdijk as Dutch consul.[170] Foreign Affairs accepted this proposal: Lodewijk Kerdijk was honourably discharged as consul on 9 October 1860.[171] After the death of Lodewijk Kerdijk in May 1861, no new Dutch consul was appointed until A. d'Angremond in 1870.[172] Like Kerdijk he was the agent of Kerdijk & Pincoffs between 1869 and 1875. When d'Angremond was presented as a candidate for a consulship by the *Afrikaansche Handels-Vereeniging* (*AHV*, African Trading Company), the Minister of Foreign Affairs accepted his nomination on the condition that the *AHV* would not participate, directly or indirectly, in the slave trade. In their reply, the *AHV* ensured the minister that the *AHV* had no connection with the slave trade. The firm referred to the White Books of the British government, where the *AHV* was always mentioned as contributing to the abolishment of the slave trade and promoting the legal trade in South-West Africa.[173] The *AHV* did not mention that they used slaves as workers in their factories. The chief agent D'Angremond was appointed on 23 February 1870 and received his exequatur in April.

Kerdijk & Pincoffs had many business relations with firms trading in West Africa, including James Hutton from Manchester and H. Müller Samuelson from Rotterdam. In 1863 Richard Francis Burton, British consul on Fernando Po for the Bight of Biafra (see p. 126), visited the trading post of Kerdijk & Pincoffs in Banana during one of his many excursions: 'In the rear stands the far more modest and conscientious establishment of Messrs. Pencoff and Kerdyk: their plank bungalow is full of work, whilst the other lies idle; so virtue here is not, as in books, its reward'.[174] He noted that the Western trading posts looked dull since the decline of the slave trade.

> The jollity, the recklessness, the gold ounces thrown in handful upon the montetable, are things of the past: several houses are said to be insolvent, and the dearth of cloth of causing actual misery. Palm and ground-nut oil enable the agents only to buy provisions; the trade is capable of infinite expansion, but it requires time – as yet it supports only two non-slaving houses, English and Dutch.[175]

In 1866 the West African business of Kerdijk & Pincoffs was separated from the partnership in the *AHV*. Three years later it was incorporated under Dutch law and 1871 it increased its capital by issuing a loan of 2.5 million Dutch guilders. Most agents of the *AHV* acted as Dutch consuls on the Portuguese south-west African coast.[176] By 1878 the *AHV* was in dire straits, mainly because of the fraud committed by Lodewijk Pincoffs. The losses of the *Rotterdamsche Handels-Vereniging* (*RHV*, Rotterdam Trading Company), another business of Pincoffs in Rotterdam, were covered by secret loans taken by the *AHV*. When the fraud was revealed, Pincoffs fled to the US with his family. No attempt was apparently made to trace him through the Dutch consul in New York, as happened with other criminals fleeing from the Netherlands. The *AHV* was liquidated and restructured in 1880 in the *Nieuwe Afrikaanse Handelsvereniging* (*NAHV*, New African Trading Company); later it was incorporated.

Portuguese claims in the area north of Ambriz, including the Congo River and beyond, continued to cause problems.[177] The explorations of Henry Morton Stanley (1841–1904) and the *Association Internationale Africaine* (International African Association) proved that the Congo River was the main route to Central Africa and thus of vital importance for stimulating legal trade in this area. If Portugal was allowed to establish its authority over the delta it would probably introduce a commercial tariff to privilege its own traders. In February 1884, Great Britain and Portugal signed a treaty that ceded the territory along the coast of the Congo to Portugal. The treaty raised a violent protest from merchants and politicians in Europe and was never ratified.[178] The international dispute was settled during the Berlin Conference. The area became part of the Congo Free State, privately owned and ruled by King Leopold II (1837–1921) of Belgium.[179]

Reports about the maltreatment of natives induced the British government to instruct their consul Roger Casement (see p. 110), to conduct an inquiry.[180] His report to the Foreign Office (15 February 1903) initially received little press coverage, but this changed after Casement and Edmond Dene Morel (1873–1924) established the Congo Reform Association (CRA) in March 1903.[181] The CRA organized public meetings, addressed politicians, published books and wrote articles for newspapers. King Leopold II first denied the accusations, but was forced to appoint an international commission of inquiry. Their report was published on 31 October 1905.[182] In general 'the evidence collected agrees in all essential details with Mr. Casement's reports on the subject'.[183] For his work in the Congo, Casement was awarded a Companion in the Most Distinguished Order of St Michael and St George in June 1905.[184] Negotiations between King Leopold II and the Belgian government over the Congo Free State were not concluded until 14 November 1908: Congo became a Belgian colony.

CONCLUSIONS

This study examined the history of consuls in different areas during the nineteenth century to answer the following questions: how did the consular services of Western states change in this period? What role did the consuls play in the development of international relations? How did the consuls cope with the different environments and systems of international relations? And, finally: did the institution of consuls contribute to the globalization of capitalism between *c.* 1783 and 1914?

During the long nineteenth century the number of consuls increased quickly to offer protection to their merchants. The main reasons for the growth in the number of consuls are the opening of new markets in the Middle East, East Asia and Africa; the growth in the number of recognized states after the decolonization of the Americas; the acceptance of foreign consuls in Western colonies; and the rivalry between Western states. States with a long consular tradition, like Great Britain and the Netherlands, were able to expand their network of consular posts existing before the Napoleonic Wars. New states, like the United States, had to start from scratch. Despite the rhetoric of isolationism, the US concluded commercial treaties and established a consular service. Small states, in particular, appointed many consuls. This was the case in the Netherlands and the German states before their unification in the German Empire.

Compared to resident ambassadors, consuls were much cheaper. This additionally explains why their numbers grew, because most governments were forced to economize on their budget. In the case of consuls, this was easily explained, because their contribution was regularly questioned by politicians. The solution adopted by most Western states was to appoint merchants as consuls. Merchant-consuls were allowed to trade while performing the duties of a consul. This combination of duties was much sought after by active merchants. Not because of the income, but they believed that the status of the office would enhance their standing as businessmen. They furthermore believed that the privileges of a consul would be beneficial for their company. This led to many complaints from their main competitors and forced the Western governments to reform the consular service. At the end of the nineteenth century, appointing merchants as consul was no longer accepted and instead states began to offer salaries to con-

Consuls and the Institutions of Global Capitalism, 1783–1914

suls. This made the consul even more of a state official, but the consequence was a growing influence of governments on the functions of the duties of consuls.

The third change of the consular institution in the nineteenth century was related to their selection. From the mid-seventeenth century, Western states began to appoint consuls instead of merchants, selecting their own representatives. The selection of rulers introduced the system of patronage: personal and political friends were appointed as consul. These were not necessarily the best possible candidates, and many had no previous business experience or appropriate knowledge of commercial laws and regulations. Increasing complaints about the poor quality of the consuls forced Western governments to revise the selection mechanism. From the 1850s, and particularly after the 1870s, they introduced new regulations and required higher qualifications from prospective consuls. They furthermore introduced schooling and training, besides examinations and regular inspections of the consulates. The social background of consuls was diverse. Many came from the upper middle classes and were active businessmen. The motivation to apply for a post as consul was equally varied. They often referred to promoting and protecting national interests and they pointed to the growth of trade that necessitated the better protection of merchants and compatriots. Some indicated that they were seeking adventure or wanted to travel to unknown places. Others mentioned their experience in trade with certain regions.

These changes in the consular institution during the nineteenth century were closely linked to the opening of new markets with different systems of international relations, especially in the Middle East, East Asia and Africa. To be able to function, the consuls depended on many other European institutions that were part of the European system of states, including the treaty of friendship and commerce, the MFN clause, the consular convention, the law of nations and the standard of civilization. Although the consuls had lost their political and judicial powers in Europe from the mid-seventeenth century, in non-Western states they usually enjoyed full extraterritorial powers. These were contained in the treaties of friendship and commerce, and also the consular conventions that Western states concluded from the 1810s. Western states insisted on extraterritorial powers for their consuls to be able to offer better protection to their merchants in foreign places, particularly areas with different systems of international relations. These regions did not have the same European ideas about the law of nations, the rule of law, sovereignty or the standard of civilization. Through the MFN clause, these treaties resembled each other and this helped to expand Western ideas to other areas.

The main duty of the consuls was to stimulate trade and protect the provisions contained in the commercial treaties: they protested when treaties were violated. If necessary, they could request assistance from their government who could dispatch a naval squadron to force compliance with the existing treaties. The role of the consuls in the nineteenth century became more demanding that it had been before 1800. Western governments responded by appointing more consuls, but additionally modernizing their consular services. At the end of the nineteenth century, the European system of states and its ideas about international relations had become generally accepted, although this did not happen without resistance from non-Western states. Consuls were important in forcing this transition and by doing so they were able to stimulate international trade and investment. The transition did not proceed at the same pace and along similar lines in all regions of the world. This affected the role consuls played in these regions.

Consuls often operated individualistically because of the remoteness of many locations, the slow means of transport and communication. However, because of these conditions they often depended on their fellow consuls. In difficult circumstances the consuls cooperated to increase their effectiveness. Consuls furthermore organized parties and frequently gave receptions. They usually celebrated important national holidays (e.g. the birthdays of the royal family). These occasions increased their sense of belonging to the same community, no matter where they were posted. The cooperation between consuls was made difficult because of conflicting characters and national rivalries.

Western states held different opinions about the sustainability of the Ottoman Empire and its dependencies, including Egypt and North Africa. From the Middle Ages they maintained trade relations with the empire, and their consuls were given extensive extraterritorial powers contained in the Capitulations. The frequent revision of the treaties, following the death of a sultan, allowed the Western states to demand more privileges. Throughout the nineteenth century, they increasingly interfered in the Ottoman Empire when they believed that it was in their interests to do so. This included offering support to local rulers, such as Muhammad Ali in Egypt, until he threatened the stability of the Ottoman Empire. In North Africa, the Western states used their navy to protect their interests and after the Napoleonic Wars forced the local rulers to respect existing treaties, besides ending the centuries' old system of tribute. In this the consuls, especially those of the US, played an important role.

In Syria in the early 1860s consuls offered protection to Christians, and later Jews. Protecting religious minorities in Muslim territories became an additional task of consuls on which they frequently reported to their government. They could, however, not prevent new outbreaks of violence against minorities in the 1880s and 1890s. As the Ottoman Empire became weaker, the power of Western states and their representatives, including ambassadors and consuls, grew stronger. Some areas, however, long remained beyond the reach of the consuls, such as the holy cities of Mecca and Medina in the Hedjaz. Even here they tried to extend their consular powers by hiring native spies to control pilgrims from the Western colonies. Many consuls in the Middle East and North Africa performed duties not directly related to economic matters, but were nevertheless considered of vital importance.

The system of international relations in the Far East was dominated by China in the early nineteenth century. Under the Sino-centric system, the consuls played a minor role, as the case of the US consul Samuel Shaw demonstrated. The Chinese government was able to uphold its sovereignty and judicial powers in criminal cases involving Western merchants in Canton. The Western states were able to change this system from the 1840s, using their naval and military force in China in a number of wars and threatening to do so in Japan in 1853/4. This display of military power was enough to convince Siam to open its ports to Western traders from the 1850s. In the East Asian treaty ports the consul played a central role as intermediary between compatriots, between foreigners, and between foreigners and natives. He furthermore maintained close relations with local and sometimes state officials, when no ambassador was present. Consuls performed all these duties because of the full extraterritorial powers (political, judicial and economical) included in the commercial treaties. These extensive powers allowed them to interfere in all matters they, or their own governments, considered important. In Siam, this for instance included protecting the interests of colonial subjects and natives under consular protection trading in Bangkok. In the case of the Dutch consuls in Siam, they chiefly protected Chinese merchants from the Dutch East Indies, because few Dutch traders were present in Bangkok.

Japan was relatively quick to abandon its regional tributary system of international relations and adopted Western ideas, including negotiating treaties of commerce and the use of consuls. Until 1868, however, the position of the consuls in the treaty ports remained precarious because of the resistance of some Japanese to the Western intrusion. The frequent attacks on Western merchants, sailors and soldiers forced the consuls to cooperate to effect a change of attitude from the Japanese state. Rivalry amongst Western states influenced the relations between their consuls. In the case of the German consul Von Brandt, his position was further weakened by limited support from his government because of domestic developments: the formation of the German Empire.

After the First Opium War, China opened several ports for international trade, but this did not immediately end the Sino-centric system. In the matter of the emigration of Chinese workers in Western plantations, however, it was not able to maintain Chinese laws because in the treaty ports Western laws prevailed. From the 1860s, the Chinese state tried to regain some of its power and insisted on appointing Chinese consuls in Western colonies and elsewhere. Most Western governments rejected this. The case of the Netherlands demonstrated how domestic politics and foreign politics mixed, making the duties of a consul even more complicated. Despite his hard work, Consul General Ferguson, apart from his personal views of the coolie trade, was not able to secure the free and direct emigration of Chinese coolies to the Dutch East Indies until the late 1880s.

The decolonization of British colonies in North America and, after the 1820s, the Spanish and Portuguese colonies in Central and South America, stimulated Western states to appoint consuls to secure their interests in these markets. Their appointment was simplified by the similar system of international relations. In North and South America the role of the consuls was more limited than in the Middle East and the Far East: they mostly performed political or diplomatic duties (when no ambassador was appointed), besides their economical duties. Even before they achieved their formal independence, and again, despite the rhetoric of isolationism, claiming some unity of interest based on geography and history, the US government appointed a large number of executive agents to protect the interests of its merchants. Although these agents were not officially consuls according to the law of nations, they often performed similar duties and in some instances were provided with the same title. They were to assess whether independence was already achieved and inform their government when diplomatic and commercial relations could be established. These agents operated very individually, sometimes interfering directly with domestic politics, as in the case of Shaler and Poinsett, and many promoted republican ideas.

European states were equally eager to establish diplomatic and commercial relations with the new republics in the Americas, even when no or few merchants were present in the 1820s. It was hoped that by appointing a consul direct trade would increase, but as the case of the Prussian consul Theremin demonstrated, trade did not always follow the flag, nor was the reverse always true. The possibilities of consuls to directly stimulate trade was limited; the ultimate decision to invest or trade with foreign markets depended on private merchants who usually considered many more factors. Most Western states soon appointed an ambassador in the US limiting the role of consuls to economic matters. But conditions can change, for instance, during rebellions or worse, as the case of the Dutch consul Burlage in New York has shown. During the Civil War the position of the consuls in the US dramatically changed, enhancing their political role. The consuls in the southern states could no longer correspond directly with their ambassador in Washington, but were forced to write to their governments instead. The main duty of the consuls was guarding the neutrality of their country, but the war at sea and land disrupted foreign trade and this created more work for the consuls: contraband, blockade runners and legal traders demanded their attention. Even during the war, immigrants from Europe continued to arrive, some involuntarily ended up in the army of the Union. After the war, the transatlantic migration created much additional work for the consuls: catching thieves who had fled to the US, tracing relatives of deceased nationals and assisting migrants after their arrival.

From the 1870s the US became more interested in the Caribbean, because of the plan to construct a canal through the Isthmus of Panama. Many islands in the Caribbean were still European colonies, including the Dutch West Indies. Until the 1850s, the US could not appoint consuls on Curaçao. The first US consul was a native, but thereafter nationals were appointed. They combined trade and the office of consul, as was the case of Captain Leonard Burlington Smith. Smith remained on Curaçao from 1877 until his death in 1898 and he served as US consul for almost thirteen years. During the consulship, Smith was not only able to expand his business, but actively tried to stimulate trade between Curaçao and the US. He promoted the development of the island by introducing new technologies (water supply and electricity) and improving its infrastructure (the pontoon bridge across the St Anna Bay).

Smith is still remembered on Curaçao, but never became as famous as the British consul Roger Casement. His fame rested on his reports on the rubber industry in Congo Free State (1903) and Putumayo (1912). The growth of international business at the end of the nineteenth century often implicated Western governments. In Putumayo the rubber industry was dominated by the Peruvian Amazon Company (PAC), a British-registered company with British members on the board of directors. When news of the atrocities committed by PAC against native Indians appeared in London magazines and newspapers, the British government acted. The investigation of Casement, then consul general in Rio de Janeiro, in Peru, revealed the extent of the maltreatment of the natives collecting rubber for the PAC. His powers to act in Peru were, however, limited, because Great Britain had no extraterritorial powers. Prosecution of the managers of the PAC thus depended on the cooperation of the Peruvian government. When they showed little intention to act, the British government published the report of Casement. The PAC, however, did not survive and was wound up in 1913.

In sub-Saharan Africa, the role of the consuls depended on whether they were located in places already dominated by Islam or not. In West Africa the impact of Islam increased, but was not yet dominant in the early nineteenth century as it was in East Africa. In West Africa, Western merchants continued to rely on protection from African rulers, as they had done since the early fifteenth century. From the early nineteenth century, Western states were able to negotiate more favourable treaties with the African rulers, giving them more privileges. This also included the cessation of African territory on the mainland, which later became Western colonies. These colonies, including British Crown colonies like Sierra Leone, were open to foreign merchants, but they paid higher duties on import and export than British merchants. Western states appointed consuls in these colonies, like German states and the US, and, although they were recognized by the British government, had only limited powers. British rivalry and jealousy of German business success frustrated the career of the Hamburg merchant and consul Nagel. In the case of the US, the representatives in Sierra Leone received little support from their government from the start, and were eventually downgraded to commercial agencies. Trade between the US and West Africa declined until the 1870s, when the first US consul, Judson A. Lewis, was appointed.

An important duty of the consuls in West Africa was to monitor the slave trade as part of the anti-slavery campaign. British consuls in West Africa actively interfered in local politics to stop this trade, often working on direct instructions from their government, as the case of John Beecroft demonstrated. The consular duties gradually increased as their powers contained in the commercial treaties expanded. Through their actions, Great Britain increased its control of territory in West Africa and this stimulated other countries to increase their claims to African territory. Although the transatlantic slave trade disappeared after the 1860s, domestic slavery continued to exist. Many consuls explained that introducing legal trade to replace the slave trade only increased the demand for slaves as labourers on African plantations.

Merchant consuls in East Africa could not do without slaves themselves. The consuls of the US, like Richard Palmer Waters, may have objected to slavery, but in Zanzibar they wholly depended on the labour of slaves. Waters adapted quickly to local conditions and was able to benefit from a favourable deal with a local merchant. On the Comoros the British consul Sunley engaged slaves to work on his sugar plantation. Although he paid the slaves half their wages directly, the British government objected to this arrangement and forced Sunley to give up his consulship.

On the south-west coast of Africa the claims of the various Western states resulted in a political conflict centring on the entrance of the Congo River. These claims made the work of consuls in the Portuguese area very difficult and they moved north to the area that was not controlled by Portugal. Politics and economics again mixed, because the territorial claims were related to gaining access to the African mainland. The Berlin Conference settled the dispute and partitioned most of Africa. In the colonies consuls continued to be used to the protect the economic interests of their country and compatriots, but also to address humanitarian questions, like the maltreatment of Africans in the Congo Free State that was revealed in the reports of the British consul Casement.

At the end of the long nineteenth century, world trade and foreign direct investments reached unprecedented levels. To claim that this was the work of the consuls would be imprudent. This study has provided examples of consuls who were able to stimulate trade, but also examples of consuls whose efforts remained unproductive. We have furthermore noted that it is difficult to prove that the consuls actually lowered transaction costs for businessmen. But to focus solely on the economic duties of consuls is equally wrong. In Europe and in some Western countries the duties of consuls were indeed mainly economical. But even here the consuls performed a large variety of duties and functions, some directly related to trade, some not. Their precise duties depended to a large extent on their geographical position. In many regions they possessed full extra-territoriality providing them with political, judicial and economic powers. In other regions, like North and South America, their powers were more limited, but conditions can change, as was the case during the Civil War. Distinguishing between economic and political factors is often arbitrary and many political or judicial duties had economic effects.

The main contribution of the consular institution to the development of global capitalism in the nineteenth century was the combination of so many different political, judicial and economic duties in one official. This made the consul not only an efficient state official, but also an effective representative. Until the 1860s the consular institution remained mainly a Western idea, but a growing number of states adopted the institution. Yet the contribution of the consuls to the development of global capitalism has not attracted much interest from scholars. Hopefully the present study will stimulate further research on the history of consuls in Western and non-Western countries.

NOTES

Introduction

1. Also published in F. W. Goding, *A Brief History of the American Consulate General at Guayaquil, Ecuador* (Livermore Falls: The Advertiser Press, 1920).

2. J. O. Kerbey, *An American Consul in Amazonia* (New York: William Edwin Rudge Press, 1911), pp. 179–80.

3. His obituary is published in *Bulletin of the Pan American Union*, 28 (1914), pp. 69–71.

4. Kerbey, *An American Consul in Amazonia*, p. 47.

5. Ibid., p. 79.

6. J. O. Kerbey, *The Land of To-morrow: A Newspaper Exploration up the Amazon and over the Andes to the California of South America* (New York: W. F. Brainard, 1906). Kerbey returned to his beloved Amazonia two more times (in 1898 and 1908), also visiting Peru in 1897.

7. D. Acemoglu and J. A. Robinson, *Why Nations Fail: The Origins of Power, Prosperity, and Poverty* (London: Profile Books, 2012); N. Ferguson, *Civilization: The West and the Rest* (London: Allen Lane, 2011).

8. C. Windler, 'Diplomatic History as a Field for Cultural Analysis: Muslim–Christian Relations in Tunis, 1700–1840', *Historical Journal*, 44:1 (2001), pp. 79–106, on pp. 80–1.

9. A. Greif, 'History Lessons. The Birth of Impersonal Exchange: The Community Responsibility System and Impartial Justice', *Journal of Economic Perspectives*, 20:2 (2006), pp. 221–36.

10. Hibbert discusses the *fonduk*, a building or group of buildings where all merchants from the same commune or city lived, stored their goods and traded while residing in a foreign country. A. B. Hibbert, 'Catalan Consulates in the Thirteenth Century', *Cambridge Historical Journal*, 9:3 (1949), pp. 352–8, on p. 353.

11. Citation of the nineteenth-century specialist on international law, Henry Wheaton (*Elements of International Law*), in R. T. Chang, *The Justice of the Western Consular Courts in Nineteenth-Century Japan* (Westport, CT: Greenwood Press, 1984), p. 40.

12. Ibid.

13. P. R. Teetor, 'England's Earliest Treatise on the Law Merchant: The Essay on Lex Mercatoria from The Little Red Book of Bristol (Circa 1280 AD)', *American Journal of Legal History*, 6:2 (1962), pp. 178–210.

14. S. Shun Liu, *Extraterritoriality: Its Rise and its Decline* (London: P. S. King & Son, Ltd, 1925), pp. 9–47.

15. *The Convention on Rights and Duties of States*, Montevideo, 26 December 1933, at http://www.cfr.org/sovereignty/montevideo-convention-rights-duties-states/p15897 [accessed 1 July 2014].

16. J. F. Coyle, 'The Treaty of Friendship, Commerce, and Navigation in the Modern Era', *Columbia Journal of Transnational Law*, 51 (2013), pp. 302–60, on p. 306.

17. E. Jones, *The European Miracle: Environments, Economies and Geopolitics in the History of Europe and Asia*, 3rd edn (Cambridge: Cambridge University Press, 2003), pp. 104–27.

18. T. Kayaoglu, 'Westphalian Eurocentrism in International Relations Theory', *International Studies Review*, 12 (2010), pp. 193–217.

19. T. Kuran, 'Preface: The Economic Impact of Culture, Religion and the Law', *Journal of Economic Behavior & Organization*, 71 (2009), pp. 589–92; D. Klerman, 'The Emergence of English Commercial Law: Analysis Inspired by the Ottoman Experience', *Journal of Economic Behavior & Organization*, 71 (2009), pp. 638–46; E. Yong-Joong Lee, 'Early Development of Modern International Law in East Asia – With Special Reference to China, Japan and Korea', *Journal of the History of International Law*, 4 (2002), pp. 42–76.

20. B. Bowden, 'The Colonial Origins of International Law: European Expansion and the Classical Standard of Civilization', *Journal of the History of International Law*, 7 (2005), pp. 1–23, on pp. 13–16.

21. For this see H. Bull and A. Watson (eds), *The Expansion of International Society* (Oxford: Clarendon Press, 1984). Philip Curtin reminds us that this expansion did not happen without resistance from non-Western countries. P. D. Curtin, *The World and the West: The European Challenge and the Overseas Response in the Age of Empire* (Cambridge: Cambridge University Press, 2000), pp. 19–37.

22. A. Osiander, 'Before Sovereignty: Society and Politics in Ancien Régime Europe', *Review of International Studies*, 27 (2001) pp. 119–45, on p. 121; A. Osiander, 'Sovereignty, International Relations, and the Westphalian Myth', *International Organization*, 55:2 (2001), pp. 251–87.

23. D. W. Allen, *The Institutional Revolution: Measurement and the Economic Emergence of the Modern World* (Chicago, IL, and London: The University of Chicago Press, 2012), pp. 5–12.

24. A. Watson, *The Evolution of International Society: A Comparative Historical Analysis* (London and New York: Routledge, 2009), p. 275.

25. M. Lang, 'Globalization and its History', *Journal of Modern History*, 78 (2006), pp. 899–931, on pp. 911, 929.

26. C. Chase-Dunn, Y. Kawano and B. D. Brewer, 'Trade Globalization since 1795: Waves of Integration in the World-System', *American Sociological Review*, 65:1 (2000), pp. 77–95.

27. Allen, *The Institutional Revolution*, p. 21.

28. L. Müller and J. Ojala, 'Consular Services of the Nordic Countries during the Eighteenth and Nineteenth Centuries: Did They Really Work?', in G. Boyce and R. Gorski (eds), *Resources and Infrastructures in the Maritime Economy, 1500–2000*, Research in Maritime History Vol. 22, International Maritime Economic History Association (St John's Newfoundland, 2002), pp. 23–43.

29. M. Kandori, 'Social Norms and Community Enforcement', *Review of Economic Studies*, 59:1 (1992), pp. 63–80, on p. 64.

30. A. Greif, 'Reputation and Coalitions in Medieval Trade: Evidence on the Maghribi Traders', *Journal of Economic History*, 49 (1989), pp. 857–82; A. Greif, 'Contract Enforceability and Economic Institutions in Early Trade: The Maghribi Traders' Coalition', *American Economic Review*, 83:3 (1993), pp. 525–48, on pp. 528–31.

31. The *Encyclopædia Britannica* (11th edn, *c.* 1910–22), provides the following definition of a consul: 'a public officer authorized by the state whose commission he bears to manage the commercial affairs of its subjects in a foreign country, and formally permitted by the government of the country wherein he resides to perform the duties which are specified in his commission, or lettre de provision'.

32. J. I. Puente, 'The Nature of the Consular Establishment', *University of Pennsylvania Law Review*, 78 (1929–30), pp. 321–45, on p. 332.

33. I. Stewart, 'Consular Privileges and Immunities under the Treaties of Friendship, Commerce and Consular Rights', *American Journal of International Law*, 21:2 (1927), pp. 257–67.

34. At present the most important international document on consular establishment is the Vienna Convention on Consular Relations (1963).

35. I will use the word 'ambassador' for the diplomats and only occasionally 'minister', to avoid possible confusion with the heads of departments or ministries.

36. Consuls that were not allowed to trade or no longer allowed to trade after the introduction of new regulations could easily appoint someone to take care of their business.

37. House of Lords, Sessional Papers, 1835 (Volume 26), Report from the H. C. Select Committee on Consular establishments; evidence, and appendix, 1–205 (quote 79).

38. A. Broder, 'French Consular Reports', *Business History*, 23:3 (1981), pp. 279–83.

39. United States Department of State, *A Short Account of the Department of State of the United States* (Washington, DC: Government Printing Office, 1922), pp. 32–3.

40. This section is based on F. de Goey, 'The Business of Consuls; Consuls and Businessmen', Paper for the 14th Annual Conference of the EBHA 2010, The Centre for Business History, University of Glasgow, 2010; E. Griffin, *Clippers and Consuls: American Consular and Commercial Relations with Eastern Asia, 1845–1860* (Ann Arbor, MI: Edwards Bros., 1938), pp. 59–60; G. Stuart, *American Diplomatic and Consular Practice* (New York: Appleton-Century-Crofts, 1952), pp. 302–76; C. Lloyd Jones, *The Consular Service of the United States: Its History and Activities* (Philadelphia, PA: The University of Pennsylvania, 1906), pp. 36–58; R. Jones-Bos and M. van Daalen, 'Trends and Developments in Consular Services: The Dutch Experience', *Hague Journal of Diplomacy*, 3 (2008), pp. 87–92.

41. R. Israeli, 'Consul de France in Mid-Nineteenth-Century China', *Modern Asian Studies*, 23:4 (1989), pp. 671–703.

42. *Selections from the Correspondence of Thomas Barclay, Formerly British Consul-General at New York*, ed. G. Lockhart Rives (New York: Harper & Brothers, 1894), pp. 147–8.

43. D. C. M. Platt, 'The Role of the British Consular Service in Overseas Trade, 1825–1914', *Economic History Review*, 15:3 (1963), pp. 494–512.

44. Lloyd Jones, *The Consular Service of the United States*, p. 84.

45. T. C. Smout, 'American Consular Reports on Scotland', *Business History*, 23:3 (1981), pp. 304–9.

46. Lloyd Jones, *The Consular Service of the United States*, p. 74.

47. Griffin, *Clippers and Consuls*, p. 65.

48. Lloyd Jones, *The Consular Service of the United States*, pp. 60–9.

49. D. C. M. Platt, *The Cinderella Service: British Consuls since 1825* (London: Longman, 1971), p. 191.

50. Puente, 'The Nature of the Consular Establishment', p. 322.

51. G. Mattingly, *Renaissance Diplomacy* (Boston, MA: Mifflin, 1955); M. S. Anderson, *The Rise of Modern Diplomacy, 1450–1919* (London: Longman, 1993).

52. Bull and Watson (eds), *The Expansion of International Society*; T. Dunne, 'The English School', in C. Reus-Smith and D. Snidal (eds), *The Oxford Handbook of International Relations* (Oxford: Oxford University Press, 2008), pp. 267–86. Buzan and Little combined international relations and world history (notably I. Wallerstein's world systems theory). B. Buzan and R. Little, *International Systems in World History: Remaking the Study of International Relations* (Oxford: Oxford University Press, 2000).

53. See for instance D. B. Abernethy, *The Dynamics of Global Dominance: European Overseas Empires, 1415–1980* (New Haven, CT, and London: Yale University Press, 2000), pp. 185–202, 225–54.

54. T. Kuran, *The Long Divergence: How Islamic Law Held Back the Middle East* (Princeton, NJ: Princeton University Press, 2010), pp. 254–79.

55. Some examples: L. Müller, *Consuls, Corsairs, and Commerce: The Swedish Consular Service and Long-Distance Shipping, 1720–1815* (Uppsala: Uppsala universitet, 2004); A. Mézin, *Les Consuls de France au Siècle des Lumières (1715–1792)* (Paris: Imprimerie Nationale, 1997); V. Barbour, 'Consular Service in the Reign of Charles II', *American Historical Review*, 33:3 (1928), pp. 553–78.

56. However, the Dutch historian C. B. Wells published his paper on the Dutch Consular Service as a chapter in his dissertation in 1982. C. B. Wells, *Aloofness and Neutrality: Studies on Dutch Foreign Relations and Policy-Making Institutions* (Utrecht: Hes Publishers, 1982), 'The Netherlands Consular Service 1813–1873', pp. 176–201.

57. J. Ulbert and L. Prijac (eds), *Consuls et services consulaires au XIXème siècle – Die Welt der Konsulate im 19. Jahrhundert – Consulship in the Nineteenth Century* (Hamburg: DOBU, Dokumentation & Buch, 2009); J. Ulbert and G. Le Bouëdec (eds), *La fonction consulaire à l'époque moderne. L'Affirmation d'une institution économique et politique (1500–1700)* (Rennes: PUR, 2006).

58. J. Melissen and A. M. Fernández, *Consular Affairs and Diplomacy* (Leiden and Boston, MA: Martinus Nijhof Publishers, 2011).

59. House of Commons Debate, 8 March 1842, vol. 61, cols 220–81, at http://hansard.millbanksystems.com/commons/1842/mar/08/consular-establishment#S3V0061P0_18420308_HOC_12 (272) [accessed 18 June 2014].

60. Labelling this area creates many problems; see M. Lewis and K. E. Wigen, *The Myth of Continents: A Critique of Metageography* (Los Angeles, CA, and London: University of California Press, 1997), pp. 47–73.

61. A valuable repository is the Internet Archive, which contains many digitalized publications: www.archive.org. I also benefitted from digitalized books (ebooks) from Google, Kindle, Apple and other online sources.

62. J. Osterhammel, 'In Search of a Nineteenth Century', *GHI Bulletin*, 32 (Spring 2003), pp. 9–28, on p. 13.

63. G. Jones, *Multinationals and Global Capitalism: From the Nineteenth to the Twenty-First Century* (Oxford: Oxford University Press, 2005), pp. 18–24; G. Jones, *The Evolution of International Business: An Introduction* (London and New York; Routledge, 1996), p. 29.

1 The History of the Consular Institution

1. J. Zourek, 'Consular Intercourse and Immunities', *Yearbook of the International Law Commission*, 2 (1957), pp. 72–7; Liu, *Extraterritoriality*, p. 11.

2. L. Neumann, *Handbuch des Consulatwesens* (Vienna: Von Tendler & Comp., 1854), pp. 1–11.

3. R. S. Lopez, *The Commercial Revolution of the Middle Ages, 950–1350* (Cambridge: Cambridge University Press, 1976); R. Ago, 'The First International Communities in the Mediterranean World', *British Year Book of International Law*, 53:1 (1982), pp. 213–32.

4. Neumann, *Handbuch des Consulatwesens*, pp. 13–5. For the Venetian bailo, see E. Dursteler, 'The Bailo in Constantinople: Crisis and Career in Venice's Early Modern Diplomatic Corps', *Mediterranean Historical Review*, 16:2 (2001), pp. 1–30.

5. C. S. Kennedy, *The American Consul: A History of the United States Consular Service, 1776–1914* (New York: Greenwood Press, 1990), p. 1; D. Abulafia, 'Pisan Commercial Colonies and Consulates in Twelfth-Century Sicily', *English Historical Review*, 93:366 (January 1978), pp. 68–81.

6. H. Spruyt, 'The Origins, Development, and Possible Decline of the Modern State', *Annual Review of Political Science*, 5 (2002), pp. 127–49.

7. Barbour, 'Consular Service', p. 556.

8. O. Yasuaki, 'When was the Law of International Society Born? An Inquiry of the History of International Law from an Intercivilizational Perspective', *Journal of the History of International Law*, 2 (2000), pp. 1–66. See also R. P. Anand's critique, 'Review Article of Onuma Yasuaki's "When was the Law of International Society Born? – An Inquiry of the History of International Law from an Intercivilizational Perspective"', *Journal of the History of International Law*, 6:9 (2004), pp. 1–14.

9. B. Etemad, *Possessing the World: Taking the Measurements of Colonisation from the Eighteenth to the Twentieth Century* (New York and Oxford: Berghann Books, 2007), p. 125.

10. Abernethy, *The Dynamics of Global Dominance*, pp. 81–104.

11. A. W. Ward and G. P. Gooch (eds), *The Cambridge History of British Foreign Policy 1783–1919*, 3 vols (New York: The MacMillan Company, 1923), vol. 3, pp. 620–7.

12. Platt, *The Cinderella Service*, p. 10.

13. Ibid., pp. 10, 14, 54–5.

14. P. Byrd, 'Regional and Functional Specialisation in the British Consular Service', *Journal of Contemporary History*, 7:1/2 (1972), pp. 128–45, on p. 128.

15. Platt, *The Cinderella Service*, p. 130.

16. Byrd, 'Regional and Functional Specialisation', p. 131.

17. Platt, *The Cinderella Service*, p. 21.

18. Ibid., p. 39.

19. Ibid., p. 221.

20. Ibid., pp. 39–41.

21. Ibid., p. 3.

22. House of Commons, Debate 8 March 1842, Consular establishment, at http://hansard.millbanksystems.com/commons/1842/mar/08/consular-establishment#S3V0061P0_18420308_HOC_12, p. 243 [accessed 1 July 2014].

23. Ibid., p. 273.

24. Platt, 'The Role of the British Consular Service'.

25. J. McDermott, 'The British Foreign Office and its German Consuls before 1914', *Journal of Modern History*, 50:1 (March 1978), On Demand Supplement, D1001–D1034 (D1004).

26. Ibid.

27. Byrd, 'Regional and Functional Specialisation', p. 145; C. Larner, 'The Amalgamation of the Diplomatic Service with the Foreign Office', *Journal of Contemporary History*, 7:1/2 (January–April 1972), pp. 107–26.

28. Ulbert and Prijac (eds), *Consuls et services consulaires*, p. 413.

29. A. E. Kersten and B. van der Zwan, 'The Dutch Consular Service in the Nineteenth Century', in Ulbert and Prijac (eds), *Consuls et services consulaires*, pp. 413–22; A. E. Kersten and B. van der Zwan, 'The Dutch Consular Service: In the Interests of a Colonial and Commercial Nation', in Melissen and Fernández (eds), *Consular Affairs and Diplomacy*, pp. 275–302, on p. 277.

30. Wells, *Aloofness and Neutrality*, p. 189; C. A. Tamse, 'The Netherlands Consular Service and the Dutch Consular Reports of the Nineteenth and Twentieth Centuries', *Business History*, 23:3 (1981), pp. 271–7.

31. The oldest regulations concerning consuls date from 24 July 1658. It was issued by the Dutch Republic on behalf of the Dutch consuls not residing in the Levant. Tamse, 'The Netherlands Consular Service', p. 271.

32. Ibid., p. 274.

33. Kersten and Van der Zwan, 'The Dutch Consular Service: In the Interests of a Colonial and Commercial Nation', p. 290.

34. W. H. de Beaufort, 'Twee rapporten over het consulaatwezen', *De Economist*, 52 (1904), pp. 5–21; J. Paulus, 'Ons Consulaatwezen en de Consuls', *De Economist*, 41 (1888), pp. 621–53; W. C. Mees, 'Debat in de Tweede Kamer der Staten-Generaal over onze Consuls', *De Economist*, 45 (1891), pp. 797–802; W. N. van Hamel, 'Ons Consulaat-wezen', *De Economist*, 29 (1876), pp. 1119–28.

35. H. Krabbendam, 'Capital Diplomacy: Consular Activity in Amsterdam and New York, 1800–1940', in G. Harinck and H. Krabbendam (eds), *Amsterdam–New York: Trans-atlantic Relations and Urban Identities since 1653* (Amsterdam: VU University Press, 2005), pp. 167–81; H. Krabbendam, 'Consuls and Citizens: Dutch Diplomatic Representation in American Cities, 1800–1940', in R. P. Swierenga, D. Sinnema and H. Krabbendam (eds), *The Dutch in Urban America* (Holland, MI: Joint Archives of Holland, Hope College, 2004), pp. 59–75.

36. J. F. Matthews, 'Little Favours from my Government: United States Consuls in Mexico, 1821–1865' (PhD dissertation, Texas Christian University, 1993), pp. 2–3.

37. E. Youngquist, 'United States Commercial Treaties: Their Role in Foreign Economic Policy', *Studies in Law and Economic Development*, 2:1 (1967), pp. 72–90.

38. Ibid., p. 76.

39. E. R. Johnson, 'The Early History of the United States Consular Service. 1776–1792', *Political Science Quarterly*, 13:1 (1898), pp. 19–40.

40. The first American consul in Europe was Colonel William Palfrey (1741–80), a former Boston merchant, but the ship *Shillala* that took him to France was lost. P. H. Roberts and R. S. Roberts, *Thomas Barclay (1728–1793): Consul in France, Diplomat in Barbary* (Bethlehem, PA: Associated University Presses, 2008).

41. B. A. Batson, 'American Diplomats in Southeast Asia in the Nineteenth Century: The Case of Siam', *Journal of the Siam Society*, 64 (1978), pp. 39–112, on p. 43.

42. S. MacClintock, 'A Unified Foreign Service', *American Political Science Review*, 16:4 (1922), pp. 600–11.

43. B. E. Powell, 'Jefferson and the Consular Service', *Political Science Quarterly*, 21:4 (1906), pp. 626–38.

44. Kennedy, *The American Consul*, p. 19; W. J. Carr, 'American Consular Service', *American Journal of International Law*, 1 (1907), pp. 891–913, on p. 895.

45. Powell, 'Jefferson', p. 634.

46. G. Bhagat, 'America's Commercial and Consular Relations with India, 1784–1860' (PhD dissertation, Yale University, 1963), pp. 131–41.

47. For the Dutch case see J. C. Westermann, *The Netherlands and the United States: Their Relations in the Beginning of the Nineteenth Century* (Den Haag: Martinus Nijhoff, 1935), pp. 157–90.

48. R. Kark, *American Consuls in the Holy Land 1832–1914* (Jerusalem: The Magnes Press, 1994), p. 51.

49. Daniel Strobel Jr (1768–1839) was US consul in Nantes (1815–16) and Bordeaux (1816–24), when his son George Strobel succeeded him. See http://www.eafsd.org/individuals/93/ [accessed 1 July 2014].

50. *Message from the President of the United States in Relation to the Consular Establishment of the United States, Communicated to the Senate, March 2, 1833* (Washington, DC: F. P. Blair, 1833).

51. R. E. Armstrong Hackler, 'Our Men in the Pacific: A Chronicle of United States Consular Officers at Seven Ports in the Pacific Islands and Australasia during the Nineteenth Century' (PhD dissertation, University of Hawaii, 1978), p. 8.

52. Matthews, 'Little Favours from my Government', pp. 7, 222.

53. C. Strupp, 'Das US-amerikanische Konsularwesen im 19. Jahrhundert', in Ulbert and Prijac (eds), *Consuls et services consulaires*, pp. 218–34. Strupp writes Alexander Hammit, instead of Hammett.

54. Matthews, 'Little Favours from my Government', p. 8.

55. Hackler, 'Our Men in the Pacific', Preface.

56. Matthews, 'Little Favours from my Government', pp. 5–7, 228–30.

57. R. J. Salvucci, 'The Origins and Progress of US–Mexican Trade, 1825–1884: "Hoc opus, hic labor est"', *Hispanic American Historical Review*, 71:4 (1991), pp. 697–735, on p. 703.

58. T. G. Paterson, 'American Businessmen and Consular Service Reform, 1890s to 1906', *Business History Review*, 40:1 (1966), pp. 77–97.

59. Kark, *American Consuls in the Holy Land*, p. 49.

60. Paterson, 'American Businessmen'.

61. D. M. Dozer, 'Secretary of State Elihu Root and Consular Reorganization', *Mississippi Valley Historical Review*, 29:3 (1942), pp. 339–50.

62. Paterson, 'American Businessmen'.

63. For this system see A. Hoogenboom, *Outlawing the Spoils: A History of the Civil Service Reform Movement 1865–1883* (Chicago, IL, and London: University of Illinois Press, 1968).

64. Johnson, 'The Early History', pp. 19–40.

65. Quoted in R. H. Werking, 'The Foreign Service in the 1890s: The Diplomat as Revisionist', *Reviews in American History*, 18:3 (1990), pp. 376–382, on p. 378.

66. Quoted ibid.

67. H. E. Mattox, *The Twilight of Amateur Diplomacy: The American Foreign Service and its Senior Officers in the 1890s* (Kent, OH: Kent State University Press, 1989).

68. T. Roosevelt, 'Six Years of Civil Service Reform', *Scribner's Magazine*, 18 (1895), pp. 238–48; T. Roosevelt, 'The Present Position of Civil Service Reform', *New Princeton Review*, 1:3 (1886), pp. 362–72.

69. 'An Act to Provide for the Reorganization of the Consular Service of the United States', *American Journal of International Law*, 1:3, Supplement: Official Documents (1907), pp. 308–13; Kennedy, *The American Consul*, pp. 209–26.

70. B. Becker, 'The Merchant-Consuls of German States in China, Hong Kong and Macao (1787–1872)', in Ulbert and Prijac (eds), *Consuls et services consulaires*, pp. 329–52.

71. E. S. Fiebig, 'The Consular Service of the Hansa Towns Lübeck, Bremen and Hamburg in the Nineteenth Century', in Ulbert and Prijac (eds), *Consuls et services consulaires*, pp. 248–61; O. Beneke, 'Mordtmann, Andreas David', *Allgemeine Deutsche Biographie*, herausgegeben von der Historischen Kommission bei der Bayerischen Akademie der Wissenschaften, Vol. 22 (1885), p. 219.

72. W. Penkwitt, *Preußen und Brasilien. Zum Aufbau des preußischen Konsularwesens im unabhängigen Kaiserreich (1822–1850)* (Wiesbaden: Franz Steiner Verlag GmbH, 1983), p. 40.

73. I. B. von Berg, *Die Entwicklung des Konsularwesens im Deutschen Reich von 1871–1914 unter besonderer Berücksichtigung der außenhandelsfördernden Funktionen dieses Dienstes* (Cologne: Hundt Druck, 1995), p. 8.

74. Ibid., p. 9.

75. J. Ludwig, 'Zur Geschichte des sächsischen Konsulatswesens (1807–1933)', in Ulbert and Prijac (eds), *Consuls et services consulaires*, pp. 365–79.

76. Von Berg, *Die Entwicklung des Konsularwesens*, p. 51.

77. Ibid., pp. 43–5.

78. Ibid., pp. 34–5.

79. Ibid., p. 53.

80. Ibid., p. 64.

81. Ibid., pp. 58–9.

82. Ibid., pp. 47–9, 86. The main costs of the Consular Service were the career consuls.

83. Ibid., p. 58.

84. Ibid., p. 17.

2 The Middle East and North Africa

1. D. Gofman, 'Negotiating with the Renaissance State: The Ottoman Empire and the New Diplomacy', in V. H. Aksan and D. Gofman (eds), *The Early Modern Ottomans: Remapping the Empire* (New York: Cambridge University Press, 2007), pp. 61–84; C. Emrence, 'Three Waves of Late Ottoman Historiography, 1950–2007', *Middle East Studies Association Bulletin*, 41:2 (2007), pp. 137–51, on p. 144.

2. There is, however, some debate about this. F. Adanir, 'Turkey's Entry into the Concert of Europe', *European Review*, 13:3 (2005), pp. 395–417; H. McKinnon Wood, 'The Treaty of Paris and Turkey's Status in International Law', *American Journal of International Law*, 37:2 (1943), pp. 262–74.

3. For this see D. Rodogno, *Against Massacre: Humanitarian Interventions in the Ottoman Empire 1815–1914* (Princeton, NJ, and London: Princeton University Press, 2012), pp. 1–18, 36–63.

4. S. Faroqhi, *The Ottoman Empire and the World around it* (London: I. B. Taurus, 2004), pp. 2–3, 136–61.

5. T. Ansary, *Destiny Disrupted: A History of the World through Islamic Eyes* (New York: Basic Books, 2009), pp. 178–9.

6. A. H. de Groot, *Nederland en Turkije. Zeshonderd jaar politieke, economische en culturele contacten* (Leiden: Nederlands Instituut voor het Nabije Oosten, 1986), pp. 8–9.

7. R. Fletcher, *The Cross and the Cresent: Christianity and Islam from Muhammad to the Reformation* (New York: Penguin, 2003), pp. 20–1.

8. R. Kasaba, *The Ottoman Empire and the World Economy; The Nineteenth Century* (New York: State University of New York Press, 1988), p. 50.

9. T. Naff, 'The Ottoman Empire and the European States', in Bull and Watson (eds), *The Expansion of International Society*, pp. 143–71.

10. D. L. Jensen, 'The Ottoman Turks in Sixteenth-Century French Diplomacy', *Sixteenth Century Journal*, 16:4 (1985), pp. 451–70, on p. 456.

11. Faroqhi, *The Ottoman Empire*, p. 14.

12. P. Mansel, *Levant: Splendour and Catastrophe on the Mediterranean* (London: John Murray, 2010), pp. 8–9. This later tradition ended only after the Treaty of Belgrade (1739); see Kasaba, *The Ottoman Empire*, p. 32.

13. C. R. Pennell, 'The Origins of the Foreign Jurisdiction Act and the Extension of British Sovereignty', *Historical Research*, 83:221 (2010), pp. 465–86, on p. 469. Naff, 'The Ottoman Empire', p. 147. The term Capitulation derives from the Latin *capitula*, which refers to the chapters or headings of the text.

14. Mansel, *Levant*, p. 8. According to Brown and Hurewitz, the Capitulations were one-sided concessions on the part of the Turks, but Kuran and Alexandrowicz point out that the first known treaties were based on reciprocal rights. P. M. Brown, *Foreigners in Turkey: Their Juridical Status* (Princeton, NJ: Princeton University Press, 1914), p. 12; J. C. Hurewitz, 'Ottoman Diplomacy and the European State System', *Middle East Journal*, 15:2 (1961), pp. 141–52, on p. 145; Kuran, *The Long Divergence*, p. 211; C. H. Alexandrowicz, *The European–African Confrontation: A Study in Treaty Making* (Leiden: Sijthoff, 1973), p. 21.

15. N. Matar, *Turks, Moors and Englishmen in the Age of Discovery* (New York: Columbia University Press, 1999), p. 20.

16. Jensen, 'The Ottoman Turks', p. 458; Hurewitz, 'Ottoman Diplomacy', p. 146; Naff, 'The Ottoman Empire', p. 157.

17. T. Naff, 'Reform and the Conduct of Ottoman Diplomacy in the Reign of Selim III, 1789–1807', *Journal of the American Oriental Society*, 83:3 (1963), pp. 295–315; Hurewitz, 'Ottoman Diplomacy', p. 148.

18. E. A. van Dyck, *Capitulations of the Ottoman Empire: Report of Edward A. van Dyck, Consular Clerk of the United States at Cairo* (Washington, DC: Government Printing Office, 1881), pp. 27–9; Klerman, 'The Emergence of English Commercial Law', pp. 638–46.

19. D. C. North, *Understanding the Process of Economic Change* (Princeton, NJ: Princeton University Press, 1997), pp. 84–5, 119.

20. Mansel, *Levant*, p. 8.

21. Kuran, *The Long Divergence*, p. 209; Ş. Pamuk, 'Institutional Change and the Longevity of the Ottoman Empire, 1500–1800', *Journal of Interdisciplinary History*, 35:2 (2004), pp. 225–47.

22. L. E. Thayer, 'The Capitulations of the Ottoman Empire and the Question of their Abrogation as it Affects the United States', *American Journal of International Law*, 17:2 (1923), pp. 213–14.

23. Pamuk, 'Institutional Change'.

24. Mansel, *Levant*, p. 102.

25. G. R. Berridge, *British Diplomacy in Turkey, 1583 to the Present: A Study in the Evolution of the Resident Embassy* (Leiden: Martinus Nijhoff, 2009), p. 78; G. Iseminger, 'The Old Turkish Hands: The British Levantine Consuls, 1856–1876', *Middle East Journal*, 22 (1968), pp. 297–316, on p. 308.

26. Berridge, *British Diplomacy in Turkey*, p. 87.

27. Iseminger, 'The Old Turkish Hands', p. 308.

28. S. Deringil, '"The Armenian Question is Finally Closed": Mass Conversions of Armenians in Anatolia during the Hamidian Massacres of 1895–1897', *Comparative Studies in Society and History*, 51:2 (2009), pp. 344–71.
29. Liu, *Extraterritoriality*, p. 32.
30. Until Napoleon crowned himself emperor in 1803, he was first consul, and French consuls were called *commissaire* (commissioner). On his way to Egypt in 1803, Drovetti accompanied Mathieu Maximilien Prosper Comte de Lesseps (1771–1832), appointed Deputy-Commissioner of Commercial Relations for Damietta and temporary consul general in Cairo. He was the father of Ferdinand de Lesseps (1805–94).
31. R. T. Ridley, *Napoleon's Proconsul in Egypt: The Life and Times of Bernardino Drovetti* (London: David Brown Book Company, 1998), p. 39.
32. Ibid., p. 23.
33. Ibid., p. 65.
34. E. Rogan, *De Arabieren; een geschiedenis* (Amsterdam: De Bezige Bij, 2010), pp. 91–2.
35. Rodogno, *Against Massacre*, pp. 23 5.
36. Ridley, *Napoleon's Proconsul in Egypt*, p. 30.
37. Mansel, *Levant*, pp. 56–75.
38. Missett relied on the highly experienced consular agent Samuel Briggs (1767–1853) in Alexandria, who was a former agent of the Levant Company and partner in the firm Briggs, Schutz & Walras, later Briggs & Co with Robert Thurburn (1784–1860). F. S. Rodkey, 'The Attempts of Briggs and Company to Guide British Policy in the Levant in the Interest of Mehemet Ali Pasha, 1821–41', *Journal of Modern History*, 5:3 (1933), pp. 324–51.
39. Ridley, *Napoleon's Proconsul in Egypt*, pp. 58–9.
40. Ibid., p. 52.
41. Ibid., p. 50.
42. M. J. Reimer, 'Colonial Bridgehead: Social and Spatial Change in Alexandria, 1850–1882', *International Journal of Middle East Studies*, 20:4 (1988), pp. 531–3.
43. Mansel, *Levant*, p. 59.
44. Ibid., p. 95.
45. Ibid., p. 75–91; Rogan, *De Arabieren*, pp. 107–16.
46. For consuls in the Aegean, see L. P. Gunning, *The British Consular Service in the Aegean and the Collection of Antiquities for the British Museum* (Farnham: Ashgate, 2009).
47. D. Manley and P. Rée, *Henry Salt: Artist, Traveller, Diplomat, Egyptologist* (London: Libri, 2001), p. 130. Several consuls went on explorations and reported on their findings to governments and geographical societies. See for example K. E. Abbott, 'Geographical Notes, Taken during a Journey in Persia in 1849 and 1850', *Journal of the Royal Geographical Society of London*, 25 (1855), pp. 1–78. For French consuls see A. Meyer, 'Service consulaire er archéologie', in Ulbert and Prijac (eds), *Consuls et services consulaires*, pp. 36–45; A. Zambon, 'Louis François Sébastien Fauvel, le consul antiquaire (1753–1838)', in Ulbert and Prijac (eds), *Consuls et services consulaires*, pp. 139–57.
48. Gunning, *The British Consular Service in the Aegean*, p. 137. Collecting antiquities, B. Dolan writes, was increasingly seen as an 'emblem of empire'. Dolan cited in Gunning, *The British Consular Service in the Aegean*, p. 2.
49. G. Annesley, *G. Viscount Valentia's Voyages and Travels to India, Ceylon, The Red Sea, Abyssinia and Egypt* (London: F., C., & J. Rivington, 1811).
50. Manley and Rée, *Henry Salt*, p. 25.
51. Ibid., p. 10.

52. J. J. Halls, *The Life and Correspondence of Henry Salt, Esq., F.R.S. &c. His Britannic Majesty's Late Consul-general in Egypt*, 2 vols (London: Richard Bentley, 1834), vol. 1, pp. 404–5.

53. A Grand Tour included visits to historic and cultural places in continental Europe. It was considered obligatory for the British upper class as part of their education and training.

54. Halls, *The Life and Correspondence of Henry Salt*, vol. 1, p. 445.

55. Manley and Rée, *Henry Salt*, p. 69.

56. Halls, *The Life and Correspondence of Henry Salt*, vol. 1, p. 455.

57. Ibid., p. 469.

58. Besides a personal secretary and an interpreter (dragoman), Salt's household included three horses and caretakers, two Janissaries, one steward, a cook, two footmen and a gardener, one camel to collect water, a mule, and a bull for the mill. Halls, *The Life and Correspondence of Henry Salt*, vol. 1, pp. 403–4, 409, 416, 453.

59. Manley and Rée, *Henry Salt*, p. 74.

60. Ibid.

61. Halls, *The Life and Correspondence of Henry Salt*, vol. 1, p. 484; vol. 2, p. 52.

62. The Rosetta Stone, discovered by Napoleon's army, came in British possession when the British defeated the French troops at Alexandria in 1801. It has been on display in the British Museum since 1802.

63. Manley and Rée, *Henry Salt*, p. 80; Gunning, *The British Consular Service in the Aegean*, pp. 142–5.

64. Gunning, *The British Consular Service in the Aegean*, p. 144.

65. Halls, *The Life and Correspondence of Henry Salt*, vol. 2, pp. 1–31.

66. Ibid., p. 43.

67. Gunning, *The British Consular Service in the Aegean*, p. 143.

68. Manley and Rée, *Henry Salt*, p. 71. For Gliddon see C. Vivian, *Americans in Egypt, 1770–1915: Explorers, Consuls, Travellers, Soldiers, Missionaries, Writers and Scientists* (Jefferson, NC: MacFarland and Company Publishers, 2012), pp. 95–112.

69. Gunning, *The British Consular Service in the Aegean*, pp. 142–5.

70. Halls, *The Life and Correspondence of Henry Salt*, vol. 2, pp. 194–6; Ridley, *Napoleon's Proconsul*, pp. 113–14; Manley and Rée, *Henry Salt*, pp. 19–34.

71. Halls, *The Life and Correspondence of Henry Salt*, vol. 1, p. 502.

72. Ibid., p. 502.

73. Ibid., vol. 2, p. 108.

74. Ibid., p. 202.

75. This refers to the Magistrates' Court located on Bow Street in London.

76. Halls, *The Life and Correspondence of Henry Salt*, vol. 2, p. 236.

77. Ibid., p. 247.

78. Drovetti was not present at Salt's funeral because he was also suffering from bad health and was on leave until January 1828.

79. M. B. Oren, *Power, Faith, and Fantasy: America in the Middle East, 1776 to the Present* (New York: W. W. Norton & Company, 2007), p. 18.

80. A. Hourani, *A History of the Arab Peoples* (New York: Warner Books, 1991), p. 215.

81. Ibid., pp. 228–31.

82. On the Barbary corsairs see A. Tinniswood, *Pirates of Barbary: Corsairs, Conquests, and Captivity in the Seventeenth-Century Mediterranean* (New York: Random House, 2010); D. Panzac, *Barbary Corsairs: The End of a Legend 1800–1820* (Leiden and Boston, MA: Brill, 2005).

83. R. C. Davis, 'Counting European Slaves on the Barbary Coast', *Past & Present*, 172 (2001), pp. 87–124, on p. 118.

84. L. Colley, *Captives: Britain, Empire and the World 1600–1850* (London: Jonathan Cape, 2002); M. A. Bouânani, 'Propaganda for Empire: Barbary Captivity Literature in the US', *Journal of Transatlantic Studies*, 7:4 (2009), pp. 399–412; K. Bekkaoui, *White Women Captives in North Africa: Narratives of Enslavement, 1735–1830* (Basingstoke: Palgrave Macmillan, 2010), pp. 2, 5–6.

85. K. Fleet, *European and Islamic Trade in the Early Ottoman State: The Merchants of Genoa and Turkey* (Cambridge: Cambridge University Press, 1999), p. 44. For the fate of enslaved Muslim women in Christian lands see Bekkaoui, *White Women Captives*, pp. 6–13.

86. Matar, *Turks, Moors and Englishmen*, pp. 19–43.

87. Alexandrowicz, *The European–African Confrontation*, p. 19.

88. Windler, 'Diplomatic History as a Field for Cultural Analysis', p. 81.

89. Panzac, *Barbary Corsairs*, pp. 335–8. The Appendix provides a long list of all treaties concluded between 1605 and 1830. The treaty between Algiers and France was renewed and/or modified twenty-one times between 1628 and 1818; the treaty between England and Algiers nineteen times between 1660 and 1824; the treaty between The Netherlands and Algiers twelve times between 1626 and 1816.

90. C. Windler, 'Tributes and Presents in Franco-Tunisian Diplomacy', *Journal of Early Modern History*, 4 (2000), pp. 168–99.

91. J. Black, *British Diplomats and Diplomacy 1688–1800* (Exeter: University of Exeter Press, 2001), p. 11; C. Windler, 'Representing a State in a Segmentary Society: French Consuls in Tunis from the Ancien Régime to the Restoration', *Journal of Modern History*, 73:2 (2001), pp. 233–74.

92. Windler, 'Diplomatic History as a Field for Cultural Analysis', p. 91.

93. These ceremonies were not very different from those in Europe. Anderson, *The Rise of Modern Diplomacy*, pp. 56–66.

94. R. L. Playfair, *The Scourge of Christendom: Annals of British Relations with Algiers prior to the French Conquest* (London: Smith Elder, 1884), pp. 237–8.

95. Ibid., p. 238.

96. E. Broughton, *Six Years Residence in Algiers* (Edinburgh: H. & J. Pillans, 1839), pp. 11–12.

97. Ibid., p. 12.

98. Kennedy, *The American Consul*, p. 2.

99. In early 1784, Moroccan corsairs captured the Boston brig *Betsey*. The attack was actually intended to force the United States government, recognized by Morocco as early as 1777, to initiate formal diplomatic relations.

100. H. M. Wriston, *Executive Agents in American Foreign Relations* (Baltimore, MD: The Johns Hopkins University Press, 1929), p. 181.

101. See http://avalon.law.yale.edu/18th_century/bar1786t.asp#art20 [accessed 1 July 2014].

102. *State Papers and Publick Documents of the United States*, 10 vols, 2nd edn (Boston, MA: T. B. Wait and Sons, 1817), vol. 10, p. 254.

103. F. Maameri, 'Ottoman Algeria in Western Diplomatic History with Particular Emphasis on Relations with the United States of America, 1776–1816' (PhD dissertation, University of Constantine, Algeria, 2008).

104. C. Sumner, *White Slavery in the Barbary States* (Boston, MA: John P. Jewett and Company, 1853), pp. 79–82.

105. For Cathcart's memoirs see *The Captives: By James Leander Cathcart, Eleven Years a Prisoner in Algiers*, comp. J. B. Newkirk (LaPorte, Herald Print, 1899).

106. P. M. Baepler (ed.), *White Slaves, African Masters: An Anthology of American Barbary Captivity Narratives* (Chicago, IL: University of Chicago Press, 1999), pp. 103–47.

107. *State Papers and Publick Documents* (1817), vol. 10, p. 42.

108. Ibid., p. 45.

109. Ibid., pp. 43–5.

110. Ibid., p. 47.

111. F. E. Ross, 'The Mission of Joseph Donaldson, Jr., to Algiers, 1795–1797', *Journal of Modern History*, 7:4 (1935), pp. 422–33, on p. 425; M. Cantor, 'A Connecticut Yankee in a Barbary Court: Joel Barlow's Algerian Letters to his Wife', *William and Mary Quarterly*, 19:1 (1962), pp. 86–109, on p. 87.

112. For the treaties see http://avalon.law.yale.edu/subject_menus/barmenu.asp [accessed 1 July 2014].

113. M. Cantor, 'Joel Barlow's Mission to Algiers', *Historian*, 25:2 (1963), pp. 172–94.

114. R. Zacks, *The Pirate Coast: Thomas Jefferson, the First Marines, and the Secret Mission of 1805* (New York: Hyperion, 2005), pp. 42–4.

115. C. Prentiss, *The Life of the Late Gen. William Eaton; Several Years an Officer in the United States' Army, Consul at the Regency of Tunis on the Coast of Barbary ... Principally Collected from his Correspondence and Other Manuscripts* (Brookfield: E. Merriam & Co., 1813), p. 54.

116. Ibid., p. 59. The title dey or bey was used for rulers on the Barbary Coast. They were lower in rank than a pasha, who was appointed by the sultan in Istanbul as his replacement.

117. Zacks, *The Pirate Coast*, p. 7.

118. Ibid., pp. 7–8.

119. Prentiss, *The Life of the Late Gen. William Eaton*, p. 85.

120. Ibid., p. 88.

121. *State Papers and Publick Documents* (1817), vol. 5, pp. 392–3.

122. T. Harris, *The Life and Services of Commodore William Bainbridge, United States Navy* (Philadelphia, PA: Carey, Lea & Blanchard, 1837); J. Barnes, *Commodore Bainbridge: From the Gunroom to the Quarter-Deck* (New York: D. Appleton and Company, 1897).

123. D. Abulafia, *The Great Sea: A Human History of the Mediterranean* (London: Oxford University Press, 2011), pp. 532–4.

124. Oren, *Power, Faith, and Fantasy*, pp. 87–8; Lloyd Jones, *The Consular Service of the United States*, pp. 46–8.

125. R. J. Allison, *The Crescent Obscured: The United States and the Muslim World 1776–1815* (Chicago, IL: The University of Chicago Press, 1995), p. 26.

126. M. Kitzen, 'Money Bags or Cannon Balls: The Origins of the Tripolitan War, 1795–1801', *Journal of the Early Republic*, 16:4 (1996), pp. 601–24; Oren, *Power, Faith, and Fantasy*, pp. 17–98.

127. Harris, *The Life and Services of Commodore William Bainbridge*, p. 72.

128. This covert operation is covered extensively in Zacks, *The Pirate Coast*, pp. 103–221; Vivian, *Americans in Egypt*, pp. 39–56.

129. *State Papers and Publick Documents* (1817), vol. 5, p. 395.

130. During the negotiations he benefitted much from the strong support of the Danish consul Nicholas C. Nissen. See Joint Resolution of Congress: Resolution Concerning the Danish Consul at Tripoli, 10 April 1806, at http://avalon.law.yale.edu/19th_century/res004.asp [accessed 1 July 2014].

131. *State Papers and Publick Documents* (1817), vol. 5, p. 439.
132. Abulafia, *The Great Sea*, pp. 532–4.
133. Windler, 'Diplomatic History as a Field for Cultural Analysis', p. 97.
134. *State Papers and Publick Documents of the United States*, 12 vols, 3rd edn (Boston, MA: T. B. Wait and Sons, 1819), vol. 9, pp. 437–8.
135. Treaty of Peace, Signed Algiers 30 June and 3 July 1815, at http://avalon.law.yale.edu/19th_century/bar1815t.asp [accessed 1 July 2014].
136. Abulafia, *The Great Sea*, p. 536.
137. R. F. Nichols, *Advance Agents of American Destiny* (Philadelphia, PA: University of Philadelphia Press, 1956), pp. 108–43.
138. Panzac, *Barbary Corsairs*, pp. 274–92.
139. Windler, 'Diplomatic History as a Field for Cultural Analysis', p. 97.
140. Stuart, *American Diplomatic and Consular Practice*, p. 287.
141. D. Douwes, *The Ottomans in Syria: A History of Justice and Oppression* (London and New York: I. B. Taurus, 2000), pp. 188–211.
142. H. Inalcik and D. Quataert (eds), *An Economic and Social History of the Ottoman Empire, Volume 2: 1600–1914* (Cambridge: Cambridge University Press, 1994), p. 764.
143. A.-K. Rafeq, 'Damascus and the Pilgrim Trade', in L. T. Fawaz and C. A. Bayly (eds), *Modernity and Culture: From the Mediterranean to the Indian Ocean* (New York: Columbia University Press, 2002), pp. 130–44; J. L. Porter, *Five Years in Damascus: Including an Account of the History, Topography, and Antiquities of that City*, 2 vols (London: John Murray, 1855), vol. 1, p. 45.
144. L. Schatkowski Schilcher, 'Review of Ingeborg Huhn, Der Orientalist Johann Gottfried Wetzstein als preussischer Konsul in Damaskus (1849–1861)', *Middle East Studies Association Bulletin*, 27:2 (1993), pp. 266–7.
145. E. Von Mülinen, 'De Nomaden Abschied: Eine Erinnerung an Konsul Dr. Johann Gottfried Wetzstein', *Zeitschrift der Deutschen Morgenländischen Gesellschaft*, 19 (1925), pp. 150–61.
146. J. G. Wetzstein, 'Der Markt in Damascus', *Zeitschrift der Deutschen morgenländischer Gesellschaft*, 11 (1857), pp. 475–525.
147. I. Huhn, *Johann Gottfried Wetzstein, als preußischer Konsul in Damaskus (1849–1861), dargestellt nach seinen hinterlassen Papieren* (Berlin: Klaus Schwarz Verlag, 1989), p. 130.
148. Ibid., p. 132.
149. Ibid., pp. 353–86.
150. Ibid., p. 354.
151. Ibid., p. 361.
152. Ibid., pp. 50–1.
153. J. G. Wetzstein, *Reisebericht über Hauran und die Trachonen* (Berlin: Dietrich Reimer Verlag, 1860), pp. 1–2.
154. The most informative study is L. Tarazi Fawaz, *An Occasion for War: Civil Conflict in Lebanon and Damascus in 1860* (London and New York, I. B. Taurus Publishers, 1994).
155. E. L. Rogan, 'Sectarianism and Social Conflict in Damascus: The 1860 Events Reconsidered', *Arabica*, 51:4 (2004), pp. 493–511; U. Makdisi, 'After 1860: Debating Religion, Reform, and Nationalism in the Ottoman Empire', *International Journal of Middle East Studies*, 34:4 (2002), pp. 601–17.
156. L. T. Fawaz, 'Amīr ʿabd al-Qādir and the Damascus "Incident" in 1860', in B. Marino (ed.), *Études dur les villes du Proche-Orient XVIe–XIXe siècles. Hommage à André Raymond* (Damas: Presses de l'Ifpo, 2001), pp. 263–72.

157. Huhn, *Johann Gottfried Wetzstein*, p. 185.

158. Tarazi Fawaz, *An Occasion for War*, pp. 47–78.

159. Ibid., pp. 101–32.

160. Huhn, *Johann Gottfried Wetzstein*, pp. 181–2.

161. About two thousand Muslims helped Christians; the most famous was the Algerian exile Abd al-Qadir, who was supplied by France with weapons to protect the Western consulates in Damascus. Fawaz, 'Amīr ʿabd al-Qādir'; Tarazi Fawaz, *An Occasion for War*, pp. 88–90, 97–100, 159.

162. In May and June, during the attacks in Mount Lebanon, French and British warships arrived in Beirut and some marines landed to protect Christians and offered transport to safer areas. Rodogno, *Against Massacre*, pp. 91–118.

163. After the Western intervention, an International Committee, composed of delegates of the five participating powers, determined the amount of indemnity to be paid on 150 million piasters, but only 45 million piasters were rewarded. In the end only 35 million piasters were collected. Tarazi Fawaz, *An Occasion for War*, pp. 156–7; Huhn, *Johann Gottfried Wetzstein*, p. 215.

164. S. Baron, 'The Jews and the Syrian Massacres of 1860', *Proceedings of the American Academy for Jewish Research*, 4 (1932–3), pp. 3–31, on p. 7.

165. Ibid., p. 15.

166. N. A. Stillman, *The Jews of Arab Lands: A History and Source Book* (Philadelphia, PA: The Jewish Publication Society of America, 1979), p. 403.

167. On this episode of 1860 see Baron, 'The Jews and the Syrian Massacres'; S. Baron, 'Great Britain and Damascus Jewry in 1860–61 an Archival Study', *Jewish Social Studies*, 2:2 (1940), pp. 179–208.

168. Huhn, *Johann Gottfried Wetzstein*, p. 223.

169. *Reports received from Her Majesty's Consuls Relating to the Condition of Christians in Turkey, 1860* (London, Harrison and Sons, 1861); Iseminger, 'The Old Turkish Hands', pp. 306–7.

170. Rogan, 'Sectarianism', p. 508.

171. Huhn, *Johann Gottfried Wetzstein*, p. 232.

172. P. Heine, 'Das Rohlfs/Wetzstein-Unternehmen in Tunis während des deutsch-französischen Krieges 1870/71', *Die Welt des Islams New Series*, 22:1/4 (1982), pp. 61–6.

173. Abulafia, *The Great Sea*, p. 553; M. E. Fletcher, 'The Suez Canal and World Shipping, 1869–1914', *Journal of Economic History*, 18:4 (1958), pp. 556–73.

174. A. Schölch, 'The "Men on the Spot" and the English Occupation of Egypt in 1882', *Historical Journal*, 19:3 (1976), pp. 773–85.

175. D. Halvorson, 'Prestige, Prudence and Public Opinion in the 1882 British Occupation of Egypt', *Australian Journal of Politics and History*, 56:3 (2010), pp. 423–40.

176. Rafeq, 'Damascus and the Pilgrim Trade', pp. 130–44.

177. K. McPherson, 'Port Cities as Nodal Points of Change: The Indian Ocean, 1890s–1920s', in Fawaz and Bayly (eds), *Modernity and Culture*, pp. 75–95, on p. 88.

178. J. Rabino, 'The Statistical Story of the Suez Canal', *Journal of the Royal Statistical Society*, 50:3 (September 1887), pp. 495–546, on p. 526.

179. Ibid., p. 527.

180. Ansary, *Destiny Disrupted*, pp. 91–2; J. H. Pryor, *Geography, Technology, and War: Studies in the Maritime History of the Mediterranean 649–1571* (Cambridge: Press Syndicate University of Cambridge, 1992), pp. 45, 147–8; E. Tagliacozzo, *The Longest Journey: Southeast Asians and the Pilgrimage to Mecca* (Oxford: Oxford University Press, 2013), pp. 177–203.

181. On the early modern period see M. N. Pearson, *Pious Passengers: The Hajj in Earlier Times* (London: Sterling Publishers, 1994), pp. 37–64.
182. M. Tuchscherer, 'Trade and Port Cities in the Red Sea-Gulf of Aden Region in the Sixteenth and Seventeenth Century', in Fawaz and Bayly (eds), *Modernity and Culture*, pp. 28–46.
183. M. B. Miller, 'Pilgrims' Progress: The Business of the Hajj', *Past & Present*, 191 (2006), pp. 189–229.
184. C. Dubois, 'The Red Sea Ports during the Revolution in Transportation, 1800–1914', in Fawaz and Bayly (eds), *Modernity and Culture*, pp. 58–75.
185. According to Snouck Hurgronje, using statistics from the Jeddah quarantine service, their numbers varied between 36,000 (1899) and 108,000 (1907), and were on average 70,000 between 1880 and 1909. C. Snouck Hurgronje, 'De Hadji-politiek der Indische regeering', *Onze Eeuw*, 9 (1909), pp. 332–61.
186. V. Huber, 'The Unification of the Globe by Disease? The International Sanitary Conferences on Cholera, 1851–1894', *Historical Journal*, 49:2 (2006), pp. 453–76.
187. R. Singha, 'Passport, Ticket, and India-Rubber Stamp: "The Problem of the Pauper Pilgrim" in Colonial India *c.* 1882–1925', in A. Tambe and H. Fischer-Tiné (eds), *The Limits of British Colonial Control in South Asia: Spaces of Disorder in the Indian Ocean Region* (New York: Routledge, 2009), pp. 49–84.
188. M. C. Low, 'Empire and the Hajj: Pilgrims, Plagues, and Pan-Islam under British Surveillance, 1865–1908', *International Journal of Middle East Studies*, 40 (2008), pp. 269–90; Tarazi Fawaz, *An Occasion for War*, p. 104. Whether this attack was related to Pan-Islamism is, however, debatable. The troubles began with a dispute over the registry of the *Irani*: was it a British or a Turkish ship?
189. S. Muhd Khairudin Aljunied, 'Western Images of Meccan Pilgrims in the Dutch East Indies, 1800–1900', *Sari*, 23 (2005), pp. 105–22.
190. Snouck Hurgronje, 'De Hadji-politiek'.
191. Consulaat Djeddah (1871–1904). Dutch National Archives (hereafter NA) 2.05.38, 1398: Stukken betreffende personeel en werkzaamheden Nederlandse consuls in Aziatisch Turkije.
192. M. Witlox, 'Als waakhond en beschermer: het Nederlandse consulaat in Djeddah, 1872–1889', in P. Luykx and A. Manning (eds), *Nederland in de wereld 1870–1950* (Nijmegen: SUN, 1988), pp. 65–85.
193. Quoted in Low, 'Empire and the Hajj', p. 282.
194. Tagliacozzo, *The Longest Journey*, pp. 177–203.
195. Foreign Affairs to Bake, 12 February 1873, NA 2.05.38, 1398: Stukken betreffende personeel en werkzaamheden Nederlandse consuls in Aziatisch Turkije, Consulaat Djeddah (1871–1904).
196. Foreign Affairs to Bake, 30 July 1873, NA 2.05.38, 1398: Stukken betreffende personeel en werkzaamheden Nederlandse consuls in Aziatisch Turkije, Consulaat Djeddah (1871–1904); P. C. Molhuysen and P. J. Blok (eds), 'Bake, Mr. Rudolph Willem Johan Cornelis de Menthon', *Nieuw Nederlandsch biografisch woordenboek. Deel 8* (Leiden: A. W. Sijthoff, 1930). After his return a lengthy correspondence with the Ministry of Foreign Affairs started to reclaim the money De Menthon Bake had collected illegally from the pilgrims, and had obtained from his other business activities.
197. Ministerie van Buitenlandsche Zaken, *Verzameling van consulaire en andere berigten en verslagen over nijverheid, handel en scheepvaart* (Den Haag: Van Weelden en Mingelen, 1874), pp. 515–26 (report W. Hanegraaff). Willem Hanegraaff died in Alexandria in

the Hospital Allemand des Diaconnesses. Acte de Decis, 22 June 1878, NA 2.05.38, 1398: Stukken betreffende personeel en werkzaamheden Nederlandse consuls in Aziatisch Turkije, Consulaat Djeddah (1871–1904).

198. Ministerie van Buitenlandsche Zaken, *Verzameling van consulaire en andere berigten*, pp. 515–26 (report W. Hanegraaff).

199. Ibid.

200. Ibid.

201. Kruyt to Foreign Affairs, 18 October 1878, NA 2.05.38 BuZa B dossiers, 1398: Stukken betreffende personeel en werkzaamheden Nederlandse consuls in Aziatisch Turkije, Consulaat Djeddah (1871–1904).

202. Ministerie van Buitenlandsche Zaken, *Verzameling van consulaire en andere berigten en verslagen over nijverheid, handel en scheepvaart* (Den Haag: Gebroeders Van Cleef, 1884), pp. 28–31 (Report consul J. A. Kruijt).

203. The Ocean Steamship Company, established in 1865 by Alfred and Philip Holt from Liverpool, operated a shipping business between India and China, but after the opening of the Suez Canal extended its service to England.

204. Miller, 'Pilgrims' Progress', p. 209.

3 The Far East

1. For the Sino-centric system I relied on J. Waley-Cohen, *The Sextants of Beijing: Global Currents in Chinese History* (New York and London: W. W. Norton & Company, 1999), pp. 11–17; G. Deng, *Maritime Sector, Institutions, and Sea Power of Premodern China* (Westport, CT: Greenwood Press, 1999), pp. 147–54; D. C. Kang, *East Asia before the West: Five Centuries of Trade and Tribute* (New York: Columbia University Press, 2010); T. Hamashita, *China, East Asia and the Global Economy: Regional and Historical Perspectives* (New York: Routledge, 2008); G. Arrighi, T. Hamashita and M. Selden (eds), *The Resurgence of East Asia: 500, 150 and 50 year Perspectives* (London and New York: Routledge, 2003).

2. K. R. Hall, 'Sojourning Communities, Ports-of-Trade, and Commercial Networking in Southeast Asia's Eastern Regions, *c.* 1000–1400', in M. A. Aung-Thwin and K. R. Hall, *New Perspectives on the History and Historiography of Southeast Asia: Continuing Explorations* (London and New York: Routledge, 2011), pp. 56–74.

3. D. P. Chandler, 'Cambodja's Relations with Siam in the Early Bangkok Period: The Politics of a Tributary State', *Journal of the Siam Society*, 60:1 (1972), pp. 153–70; R. Ptak, 'Ming Maritime Trade to Southeast Asia, 1368–1567: Visions of a "System"', in C. Guillot et al. (eds), *From the Mediterranean to the China Sea: Miscellaneous Notes* (Wiesbaden: Otto Harrassowitz, 1998), pp. 157–92.

4. T. Hamashita, 'Tribute and Treaties: East Asian Treaty Ports Networks in the Era of Negotiation, 1834–1894', *European Journal of East Asian Studies*, 1:1 (2002), pp. 59–87; T. Hamashita, 'Tribute and Treaties: Maritime Asia and Treaty Port Networks in the Era of Negotiations, 1800–1900', in Arrighi, Hamashita and Selden (eds), *The Resurgence of East Asia*, pp. 17–50.

5. F. Broeze (ed.), *Brides of the Sea: Port Cities of Asia from the Sixteenth–Twentieth Centuries* (Kensington: New South Wales University Press, 1989); H. Masashi (ed.), *Asian Port Cities, 1600–1800: Local and Foreign Cultural Interactions* (Singapore and Kyoto: NUS Press in Association with Kyoto University Press, 2009).

6. J. K. Fairbank, *Trade and Diplomacy on the China Coast: The Opening of the Treaty Ports, 1842–1854* (Stanford, CA: Stanford University Press, 1969), p. 161.

7. T. Chang, 'Malacca and the Failure of the First Portuguese Embassy to Peking', *Journal of Southeast Asian History*, 3:2 (1962), pp. 50–3.
8. A. Ljungstedt, *An Historical Sketch of the Portuguese Settlements in China* (London: J. Munroe, 1836), pp. 75–8; L. Chen, 'Universalism and Equal Sovereignty as Contested Myths of International Law in the Sino-Western Encounter', *Journal of the History of International Law*, 13 (2011), pp. 75–116. The Portuguese paid tribute for Macao until 1849 when they declared it a Portuguese possession. This was not officially the case until the treaty with China in 1887. Yen Ching-hwang, *Coolies and Mandarins: China's Protection of Overseas Chinese during the Late Ch'ing Period (1851–1911)* (Singapore: Singapore University Press, 1985), pp. 52–3.
9. For the Canton system see V. M. Garrett, *Heaven is High, the Emperor is Far Away: Merchants and Mandarins in Old Canton* (New York: Oxford University Press, 2002); L. Blussé, *Visible Cities: Canton, Nagasaki, and Batavia and the Coming of the Americans* (Cambridge, MA: Harvard University Press, 2008), pp. 50–4.
10. I. C. Y. Hsu, *The Rise of Modern China* (Oxford: Oxford University Press, 1999), p. 201.
11. Fairbank, *Trade and Diplomacy*, p. 213.
12. Israeli, 'Consul de France in Mid-Nineteenth-Century China'; R. Israeli, 'Diplomacy of Contempt: The French Consuls and the Mandarins in Nineteenth-Century China', *Modern Asian Studies*, 26:2 (1992), pp. 363–94.
13. Fairbank, *Trade and Diplomacy*, p. 213.
14. Ibid., p. 173.
15. Platt, *The Cinderella Service*, pp. 206–7.
16. Hamel to Foreign Affairs, 10 November 1880, NA 2.05.38 BuZa/B-dossiers, 1.2.2.7 Siam (Thailand), Inv. no. 1389 Siam 1880–1893.
17. Hamel to Foreign Affairs, 25 September 1882, 31 December 1883, NA 2.05.38 BuZa/B-dossiers, 1.2.2.7 Siam (Thailand), Inv. no. 1389 Siam 1880–1893.
18. Platt, *The Cinderella Service*, p. 196; Fairbank, *Trade and Diplomacy*, pp. 167–8.
19. M. Paske-Smith, *Western Barbarians in Japan and Formosa in Tokugawa Days, 1603–1868* (Kobe: J. L. Thompson, 1930), pp. 238–9.
20. Paske-Smith notes that he resigned in 1861 when his chances to succeed Alcock were blocked. Ibid., p. 238.
21. Y. A. Honjo, *Japan's Early Experience of Contract Management in the Treaty Ports* (London: Japan Library, 2003), pp. 25–52, on p. 26.
22. M. Keliher, 'Anglo-American Rivalry and the Origins of US China Policy', *Diplomatic History*, 32:2 (2007), pp. 227–58; D. D. Johnson with G. D. Best, *The United States in the Pacific: Private Interests and Public Policies, 1784–1899* (Westport, CT: Praeger, 1995), pp. xvi–xvii.
23. J. R. Fichter, *So Great a Profit: How the East Indies Trade Transformed Anglo-American Capitalism* (Cambridge, MA: Harvard University Press, 2010).
24. For this journey see E. J. Dolin, *When America First Met China* (New York and London: Liveright, 2012).
25. A. O. Aldridge, *The Dragon and the Eagle: The Presence of China in the American Enlightenment* (Detroit, MI: Wayne State University Press, 1993), pp. 120–44.
26. Ibid., p. 100; see also K. Akemi Yokota, *Unbecoming British: How Revolutionary America Became a Postcolonial Nation* (Oxford: Oxford University Press 2011), pp. 117–20.
27. *The Journals of Major Samuel Shaw, the First American Consul at Canton, with a Life of the Author*, ed. J. Quincy (Boston, MA: Wm. Crosby and H. P. Nichols, 1847), p. 164.

4156 - PB - 13mm - 0 - 1858426-6 - 1 - 9780367669126 - 2UP-450mm-Web-TECNAU 2025/05/01 13:10:50

28. On Vieillard see H. Cordier, 'Américains et Français à Canton au XVIIIe siècle', *Journal de la Société des Américanistes*, 2 (1898), pp. 1–13.

29. *The Journals of Major Samuel Shaw*, p. 183.

30. Ibid., p. 169.

31. Ibid., p. 242.

32. Aldridge, *The Dragon and the Eagle*, pp. 122–4.

33. *The Journals of Major Samuel Shaw*, p. 186.

34. E. P. Scully, *Bargaining with the State from Afar: American Citizenship in Treaty Port China 1844–1942* (New York: Columbia University Press, 2001), p. 35.

35. In 1773 the Englishman Francis Scott was handed over to the Chinese by the Portuguese vicar-general of Macao after killing a Chinese. Scott was found guilty and strangled to death. The demand for the protection of Western traders became even more evident during the Terranova Case of 1821. J. B. Askew, 'Re-Visiting New Territory: The Terranova Incident Re-Examined', *Asian Studies Review*, 28 (2004), pp. 351–71; Scully, *Bargaining with the State from Afar*, pp. 36–8.

36. *The Journals of Major Samuel Shaw*, p. 189.

37. Dolin, *When America First Met China*, p. 90; T. Dennett, *Americans in Eastern Asia: A Critical Study of the Policy of the United States with Reference to China, Japan and Korea in the Nineteenth Century* (New York: Octagon Books, 1979), p. 45.

38. D. Ramsay, Chairman of Congress, on behalf of John Hancock President, to Samuel Shaw Esq., 27 January 1786, at http://wwwapp.cc.columbia.edu/ldpd/jay/image?key=columbia.jay.01858&p=2&level=2 [accessed 18 April 2012].

39. Letter Jay to Shaw, 30 January 1786, The Papers of John Jay, Columbia University Libraries, at http://wwwapp.cc.columbia.edu/ldpd/jay/item?mode=item&key=columbia.jay.01858 [accessed 18 June 2014]; Dennett, *Americans in Eastern Asia*, p. 62.

40. Letter Jay to Shaw, 30 January 1786 and Reply of Shaw to Jay, 30 January 1786. The Papers of John Jay, Columbia University Libraries, at http://wwwapp.cc.columbia.edu/ldpd/jay/item?mode=item&key=columbia.jay.01861 [accessed 18 June 2014].

41. *The Journals of Major Samuel Shaw*, p. 233.

42. K. S. Latourette, 'The History of Early Relations between the US and China, 1784–1844', *Transactions of the Connecticut Academy Arts and Sciences* (New Haven, CT: Yale University Press, 1917–1918), vol. 22, pp. 1–209, on p. 60.

43. Scully, *Bargaining with the State from Afar*, p. 32.

44. *The Journals of Major Samuel Shaw*, p. 180.

45. A. Delano, *A Narrative of Voyages and Travels in the Northern and Southern Hemispheres: Comprising Three Voyages Round the World; Together with a Voyage of Survey and Discovery in the Pacific Ocean and Oriental Islands* (Boston, MA: E. G., House, 1817). For Delano, see H. Hughes, 'Seeing Unseeing: The Historical Amasa Delano and his Voyages', Drew Archival Library of Massachusetts, March 2010, at http://drewarchives.files.wordpress.com/2010/03/henryhughespaper.pdf. [accessed 19 June 2012].

46. The firm Shaw & Randall also fitted out the *Columbia* and *Lady Washington* that sailed to the north-west coast via Cape Horn to buy furs that could be sold in China. After the death of Shaw the firm was dissolved. Dennett, *Americans in Eastern Asia*, p. 71.

47. Aldridge, *The Dragon and the Eagle*, p. 103.

48. Delano, *A Narrative of Voyages*, p. 35.

49. Ibid., pp. 22–3.

50. *The Journals of Major Samuel Shaw*, p. 63. In May 1798, Shaw was replaced by Samuel Snow (1758–1838) from Providence, partner in the firm Munro, Snow & Munro, who

remained in Canton until 1804 to be succeeded by Edward Carrington (1775–1843), consul until 1814. J. M. Downs, 'A Study in Failure – Hon Samuel Snow', *Rhode Island History*, 25:1 (1966), pp. 1–9.

51. Dennett, *Americans in Eastern Asia*, p. 75.

52. Ibid., pp. 76–80.

53. P. A. Varg, 'The Myth of the China Market, 1890–1914', *American Historical Review*, 73:3 (1968), pp. 742–58; J. K. Fairbank, 'Introduction: Patterns and Problems', in E. R. May and J. K. Fairbank (eds), *America's China Trade in Historical Perspective: The Chinese and American Performance* (Cambridge, MA: Harvard University Press, 1986), pp. 1–11, on p. 2; Y. Hao, 'Chinese Teas to America – A Synopsis', in E. R. May and J. K. Fairbank (eds), *America's China Trade in Historical Perspective: The Chinese and American Performance* (Cambridge, MA: Harvard University Press, 1986), pp. 11–33, on p. 31.

54. M. Rajo Sathian, 'Suzerain–Tributary Relations: An Aspect of Traditional Siamese Statecraft (*c.* 19th century)', *JATI – Journal of Southeast Asian Studies*, 11:1 (2006), pp. 108–25.

55. Y. Ishhi, 'Seventeenth-Century Japanese Documents about Siam', *Journal of the Siam Society*, 59:2 (1971), pp. 161–74.

56. O. Farouk Shaeik Ahmad, 'Muslims in the Kingdom of Ayutthaya', *Jebat: Malaysian Journal of History, Politics and Strategic Studies*, 10 (1980), pp. 206–14.

57. H. R. H. Prince Damrong Rajanubhab, 'The Introduction of Western Culture in Siam', *Journal of the Siam Society*, 20:2 (1926–7), pp. 89–101; B. Ruangsilp, 'Dutch East India Company Merchants at the Court of Ayutthaya: Dutch Perceptions of the Thai Kingdom, *c.* 1604–1765' (PhD dissertation, Leiden University, 2007); V. Lieberman, *Strange Parallels: Southeast Asia in Global Context, c. 800–1830. Volume 1, Integration on the Mainland* (New York: Cambridge University Press, 2003), p. 287.

58. H. de Mendonha e Cunha, 'The 1820 Land Concession to the Portuguese', *Journal of the Siam Society*, 59:2 (1971), pp. 145–50; Rajanubhab, 'The Introduction', p. 93.

59. De Mendonha e Cunha, 'The 1820 Land Concession', p. 149.

60. *Two Yankee Diplomats in 1830s Siam by Edmund Roberts and W. S. W. Ruschenberger M.D.*, ed. and intro. M. Smithies (Bangkok: Orchid Press, 2002), p. 11.

61. R. H. Miller, *The United States and Vietnam 1787–1941* (Washington, DC: National Defense University Press, 1990), pp. 19–41. For his mission to Cochin China he was provided with several sheep as presents, as the ruler had previously indicated. Wriston, *Executive Agents*, p. 339.

62. E. Tagliacozzo, 'Ambiguous Commodities, Unstable Frontiers: The Case of Burma, Siam, and Imperial Britain, 1800–1900', *Comparative Studies in Society and History*, 46:2 (2004), pp. 354–77, on p. 357.

63. Miller, *The United States and Vietnam*, pp. 41–57. Balestier, US consul for Rhio (Island of Bintang, 1834–6) and Singapore (1836–49), was appointed Special Commissioner of the United States to Cochin China and instructed to negotiate a commercial treaty with Siam. *The Complete Journal of Townsend Harris: First American Consul and Minister to Japan*, ed. M. E. Cosenza, rev. edn (Rutland: Charles E. Tuttle Company, 1959), n. on pp. 11, 25–6; Wriston, *Executive Agents*, pp. 344–6.

64. Rajanubhab, 'The Introduction', p. 96.

65. A. Webster, *Gentlemen Capitalists: British Imperialism in South East Asia 1770–1890* (London: I. B. Taurus, 1998), p. 240.

66. M. R. Auslin, *Negotiating with Imperialism: The Unequal Treaties and the Culture of Japanese Diplomacy* (Cambridge, MA: Harvard University Press, 2004), p. 23.

67. Damrong Rajanubhab notes that after 1855 Siam sent ambassadors to Europe after an interval of two centuries. It is not known whether they had consuls in Europe. Rajanubhab, 'The Introduction', p. 98.
68. Tagliacozzo, 'Ambiguous Commodities', p. 359.
69. Auslin, *Negotiating with Imperialism*, pp. 22–5.
70. Tagliacozzo, 'Ambiguous Commodities', p. 354.
71. Ibid., pp. 359–60.
72. Webster, *Gentlemen Capitalists*, p. 241.
73. Pickenpack to Foreign Affairs, Bangkok, 20 April 1858, NA Buitenlandse Zaken, 2.05.01, Inv. no. 3065, Siam, 1858–1868. Unfortunately, few documents have been preserved and those that have been are mostly damaged. Pickenpack seemed to have functioned rather well most of the time. In Hamburg he continued his relationship with Siam: he became consul general for Siam and in 1900 established the *Ostasiatischen Verein*.
74. K. S. Nasution, *More than Merchants: A History of the German-Speaking Community in Penang, 1800s–1940s* (Penang: Areca Books, 2006), pp. 47–8.
75. Acting consul (Vincent Pickenpack) to Foreign Affairs, Bangkok, 15 January 1872, NA 2.05.38 BuZa/B-dossiers, 1.2.2.7 Siam (Thailand), 1388 Siam 1871–1879.
76. Senn van Basel to Foreign Affairs, 7 September 1874, NA 2.05.38 BuZa/B-dossiers, 1.2.2.7 Siam (Thailand), 1388 Siam 1871–1879; Cabinet of the King to Foreign Affairs, 1 February 1875; Royal Commission (KB) Van Basel, 18 February 1875.
77. Senn van Basel to Foreign Affairs, 14 June 1875, NA 2.05.38 BuZa/B-dossiers, 1.2.2.7 Siam (Thailand), 1388 Siam 1871–1879.
78. G. Kiauw Nio Liem, 'De rechtspositie der Chinezen in Nederlands-Indië 1848–1942, Wetgevingsbeleid tussen beginsel en belang' (PhD dissertation, Leiden University, 2009), pp. 437–43.
79. Note to Foreign Affairs on complaints against Senn van Basel (Nota voor ZExc. Klagten tegen den Consul te Bangkok, Senn van Basel), NA 2.05.38 BuZa/B-dossiers, 1.2.2.7 Siam (Thailand), 1388 Siam, 1871–1879.
80. Consul General Singapore to Foreign Affairs, 27 March 1878; copy letter J. U. Torrey to Read, Bangkok, 22 March 1878, NA 2.05.38 BuZa/B-dossiers, 1.2.2.7 Siam (Thailand), 1388 Siam, 1871–1879.
81. Consul Salmon to Foreign Affairs, 26 July 1878, NA 2.05.38 BuZa/B-dossiers, 1.2.2.7 Siam (Thailand), 1388 Siam, 1871–1879.
82. Consul Salmon Foreign Affairs, Bangkok, 19 September 1878, NA 2.05.38 BuZa/B-dossiers, 1.2.2.7 Siam (Thailand), 1388 Siam, 1871–1879.
83. Consul Salmon Foreign Affairs, 20 October 1878, NA 2.05.38 BuZa/B-dossiers, 1.2.2.7 Siam (Thailand), 1388 Siam, 1871–1879.
84. Colonies to Foreign Affairs, 1 November 1878, NA 2.05.38 BuZa/B-dossiers, 1.2.2.7 Siam (Thailand), 1388 Siam, 1871–1879.
85. Consul Salmon to Foreign Affairs, Bangkok, 28 February 1879; Consul Salmon to Foreign Affairs, Bangkok, 18 October 1879; Medical Attendant (G Bensonsmith?), 19 October 1879, NA 2.05.38 BuZa/B-dossiers, 1.2.2.7 Siam (Thailand), 1388 Siam, 1871–1879.
86. Hamel to Foreign Affairs, 8 October 1880 (Globe Hotel, Bangkok), NA 2.05.38 BuZa/B-dossiers, 1.2.2.7 Siam (Thailand), 1389 Siam, 1880–1893.
87. Hamel to Foreign Affairs, 10 November 1880, NA 2.05.38 BuZa/B-dossiers, 1.2.2.7 Siam (Thailand), 1389 Siam, 1880–1893.

88. Hamel to Foreign Affairs, 1 December 1880, 2.05.38 BuZa/B-dossiers, 1.2.2.7 Siam (Thailand), 1389 Siam, 1880–1893.

89. Hamel to Foreign Affairs, 10 November 1880, NA 2.05.38 BuZa/B-dossiers, 1.2.2.7 Siam (Thailand), 1389 Siam, 1880–1893.

90. Hamel to Foreign Affairs, 10 November 1880, NA 2.05.38 BuZa/B-dossiers, 1.2.2.7 Siam (Thailand), 1389 Siam, 1880–1893.

91. Hamel to Foreign Affairs, 23 November 1880, NA 2.05.38 BuZa/B-dossiers, 1.2.2.7 Siam (Thailand), 1389 Siam, 1880–1893.

92. Hamel to Foreign Affairs, 4 April 1881, NA 2.05.38 BuZa/B-dossiers, 1.2.2.7 Siam (Thailand), 1389 Siam, 1880–1893.

93. By Royal Commission (KB) of 18 February 1890, P.S. Hamel became consul general of the Netherlands for the South China ports. See p. 84.

94. Foreign Affairs, 3 September 1886, NA 2.05.38 BuZa/B-dossiers, 1.2.2.7 Siam (Thailand), 1389 Siam, 1880–1893.

95. For Japan I relied on A. Gordon, *A Modern History of Japan: From Tokugawa Times to the Present*, 2nd edn (New York and Oxford: Routledge, 2009); J. L. McClain, *Japan: A Modern History* (New York: W. W. Norton & Company, 2002); L. M. Cullen, *A History of Japan, 1582–1941: Internal and External Worlds* (Cambridge: Cambridge University Press, 2003). For Japan's international relations see S. Suzuki, *Civilization and Empire: China and Japan's Encounter with European International Society* (London and New York: Routledge, 2009). For Japan's relations with China see J. A. Fogel, *Articulating the Sinosphere: Sino-Japanese Relations in Space and Time* (Cambridge, MA: Harvard University Press 2009); M. B. Jansen, *China in the Tokugawa World* (Cambridge, MA, and London: Harvard University Press, 1992).

96. For the Dutch in Japan see A. Clulow, *The Company and the Shogun: The Dutch Encounter with the Tokugawa in Japan* (New York: Columbia University Press, 2014).

97. W. McOmie, *The Opening of Japan 1853–1855: A Comparative Study of the American, British, Dutch and Russian Naval Expeditions to Compel the Tokugawa Shogunate to Conclude Treaties and Open Ports to their Ships* (Kent: Global Oriental, 2006); G. Feifer, *Breaking Open Japan: Commodore Perry, Lord Abe, and American Imperialism in 1853* (New York: Harper Collins, 2006). For Japanese perspectives see H. Mitani, *Escape from Impasse: The Decision to Open Japan* (Tokyo: I-House Press, 2006) and M. Itoh, *Globalization of Japan: Japanese Sakuko Mentality and US Efforts to Open Japan* (New York: St Martin's Press, 1998).

98. 'If there be any other sort of goods wanted or any business which shall require to be arranged, there shall be careful deliberation between the particles in order to settle such matters.' W. G. Beasley, *Select Documents on Japanese Foreign Policy, 1853–1868* (London: Oxford University Press, 1967, reprint), pp. 119–28, on p. 121.

99. Kennedy, *The American Consul*, pp. 117–26.

100. J. L. Hammersmith, *Spoilsmen in a 'Flowery Fairyland': The Development of the US Legation in Japan, 1859–1906* (Kent, OH: Kent State University Press, 1998), p. 3.

101. *The Complete Journal of Townsend Harris*, pp. 6–7.

102. His journal is available in an English translation: H. Heusken, *Japan Journal 1855–1861*, trans. and ed. J. C. van der Corput and R. A. Wilson (New Brunswick, NJ: Rutgers University Press, 1964).

103. *The Complete Journal of Townsend Harris*, p. 293.

104. Ibid., p. 374.

105. For life in the settlements see J. E. Hoare, *Japan's Treaty Ports and Foreign Settlements: The Uninvited Guests, 1858–1899* (Sandgate: Japan Library, 1994).
106. He published his memoirs in M. A. S. Von Brandt, *Dreiunddriessig Jahre in Ost-Asien. Erinerungen eines deutschen Diplomaten* (Leipzig: Georg Wigand Verlag, 1901).
107. Besides Prussia, the Hanseatic cities of Hamburg, Bremen and Lübeck, the states of the Zollverein and Mecklenburg also participated in the mission. B. Eberstein, *Preußen und China. Eine Geschichte schwieriger Beziehungen* (Berlin: Duncker & Humblot, 2007), p. 175.
108. The mission was additionally instructed to found a German colony on one of the Pacific Islands or in South America. Von Eulenburg settled for Formosa (Taiwan), but the plan was not executed. H. Stoecker, *Deutschland und China im 19. Jahrhundert. Das Eindringen des deutschen Kapitalismus* (Berlin: Rütten & Loening, 1958), pp. 55–61, 69–85; Eberstein, *Preußen und China*, pp. 200–3.
109. R. Wippich, *"Strich mit Mütze". Max von Brandt und Japan – Diplomat, Publizist, Propagandist* (Tokyo: OAG, 1995), p. 11.
110. M. Miyake, 'German Cultural and Political Influence on Japan, 1870–1914', in J. A. Moses and P. M. Kennedy (eds), *Germany in the Pacific and Far East, 1870–1914* (St Lucia: University of Queensland Press, 1977), pp. 156–85.
111. Wippich, *"Strich mit Mütze"*, p. 24.
112. H. Stahncke, *Die diplomatische Beziehungen zwischen Deutschland und Japan 1854–1868* (Stuttgart: Franz Steiner Verlag, 1987), p. 174; Wippich, *"Strich mit Mütze"*, p. 40.
113. The well-known British diplomat Satow hardly mentions Von Brandt in his recollections. E. M. Satow, *A Diplomat in Japan* (London: Seeley, Service & Co. Ltd., 1921), pp. 67, 173, 325.
114. Stahncke, *Die diplomatische Beziehungen*, pp. 167–9, 195–7.
115. For a discussion of Germans in Japan in the 1860s and 1870s see K. Meissner, *Deutsche in Japan* (Wiesbaden and Tokyo: Kommissionsverlag Otto Harrassowitz, 1961).
116. Stahncke, *Die diplomatische Beziehungen*, pp. 128–9 (n. 32), 150–1 (n. 124); E. Zielke, 'Konsul Louis Kniffler – Der Pionier des deutschen Japanhandels. 1859 Gründete er das erste deutschen Unternehmen in Japan', *Zeitschrift für Unternehmensgeschichte*, 25:1 (1980), pp. 1–11.
117. M. H. Gildemeister, *Ein Hanseat in Japan 1859–1868, bearb. von Maria Möring* (Hamburg: Verlag Hanseatischer Merkur, 1993).
118. Stahncke, *Die diplomatische Beziehungen*, p. 176.
119. Wippich, *"Strich mit Mütze"*, p. 47.
120. Eberstein, *Preußen und China*.
121. Wippich, *"Strich mit Mütze"*, pp. 73–4.
122. Stahncke, *Die diplomatische Beziehungen*, pp. 222–3.
123. Wippich, *"Strich mit Mütze"*, pp. 64–9.
124. For the role of Von Brandt in China see R. F. Szipple, 'Max von Brandt and German Imperialism in East Asia in the Late Nineteenth Century' (PhD dissertation, University of Notre Dame, 1989); H. Stoecker, 'Germany and China, 1861–94', in Moses and Kennedy (eds), *Germany in the Pacific and Far East, 1870–1914*, pp. 26–40; J. E. Schrecker, 'Kiautschou and the Problems of German Colonialism', in Moses and Kennedy (eds), *Germany in the Pacific and Far East, 1870–1914*, pp. 185–209.
125. Wippich, *"Strich mit Mütze"*, pp. 121–32.
126. S. Takao, 'Murder of Ludwig Haber, German Consul at Hakodate', *Journal of Konan University: Research Institute*, 95 (January 2008), pp. 113–48. See also L. Haber, 'The

Consul and the Samurai: The Murder of Ludwig Haber at Hakodate in 1874. P. Fraenkel', at http://ludwighaber.blogspot.nl/2007_03_01_archive.html [accessed 11 June 2014].

127. Y. Zhang, 'System, Empire and State in Chinese International Relations', *Review of International Studies*, 27 (2001), pp. 43–63.

128. For Dutch–Chinese relations in the nineteenth century see F. P. van der Putten, 'Small Powers and Imperialism: The Netherlands in China, 1886–1905', *Itinerario*, 20 (1996), pp. 115–31; C. Hongsheng and L. Blussé (eds), *Sailing to the Pearl River: Dutch Enterprise in South China 1600–2000* (Guangzhou: Guangzhou Publishing House, 2004); L. Blussé and F. van Luyn, *China en de Nederlanders. Geschiedenis van de Nederlands-Chinese betrekkingen 1600–2007* (Zutphen: Walburg Pers, 2008); F. van Dongen, *Tussen Neutraliteit en Imperialisme: De Nederlands-Chinese Betrekkingen van 1863 tot 1901* (Groningen: Wolters, 1966).

129. This meant that he did not receive the salary of a *Chargé d'Affaires*.

130. Between 1865 and 1870, the *Surinaamsche Immigratie Maatschappij* (Surinam Immigration Company, established in 1865) contracted about two thousand Chinese labourers. When Ferguson met the directors of the Surinam Immigration Company it was in the process of being liquidated, because the costs of contracting Chinese were too expensive.

131. For this company see *Deli Maatschappij 1869–1919* (Amsterdam: Vereenigde Drukkerijen Roeloffzen-Hübner & Van Santen en Gebroeders Binger, 1919).

132. W. Look Lai, 'Asian Contract and Free Migrations to the Americas', in D. Eltis (ed.), *Coerced and Free Migration: Global Perspectives* (Stanford, CA: Stanford University Press, 2002), pp. 229–59.

133. J. Breman, *Taming the Coolie Beast: Plantation Society and the Colonial Order in Southeast Asia* (Delhi: Oxford University Press, 1989), p. 35.

134. F. van Dongen, 'The Cautious Imperialists', in J. W. Schulte Nordholt and D. van Arkel (eds), *Acta Historiae Neerlandica*, 4 (Leiden: Brill, 1970), pp. 146–70, on p. 154.

135. Report of Ferguson on China (Verslag van den Staatkundigen Toestand van China, ingezonden bij Missive van den Consul-Generaal en Zaakgelastigde), 28 December 1874, NA 2.05.38 BuZa B-dossiers, inv no. 1326 China consuls.

136. Breman, *Taming the Coolie Beast*, pp. 37–45.

137. Yen, *Coolies and Mandarins*, p. 161. However, Reid points out discrepancies between the official Chinese report and the information supplied by the delegation to the British authorities in Singapore after their visit to Deli. A. Reid, 'Early Chinese Migration into North Sumatra', in J. Ch'en and N. Tarling (eds), *Studies in the Social History of China and South-East Asia: Essays in Memory of Victor Purcell* (Cambridge: Cambridge University Press, 1970), p. 311 (here n. 4).

138. Yen, *Coolies and Mandarins*, ch. 4, pp. 135–204.

139. 'Levensbericht van Prof. Dr. J. J. M. de Groot', *Handelingen en mededeelingen van de Maatschappij der Nederlandsche Letterkunde te Leiden, over het jaar 1921–1922* (Leiden: E. J. Brill, 1922), pp. 1–17.

140. R. J. Zwi Werblowsky, *The Beaten Track of Science: The Life and Work of J. J. M. de Groot*, ed. H. Walravens (Wiesbaden: Harrassowitz Verlag, 2002), pp. 37–53.

141. Ibid., p. 44.

142. Van den Honert to Foreign Affairs, 5 August 1888, NA 2.05.03 BuZa, A-Dossiers, 244 Koeliehandel 1866–1889.

143. Ferguson to Foreign Affairs, 9 October 1888, NA 2.05.03 BuZa, A-Dossiers, 244 Koeliehandel 1866–1889.

144. Consul General of the Netherlands in the Straits Settlements to Governeur General in the Dutch East Indies, 13 April 1889, NA 2.05.03 BuZa, A-Dossiers, 244 Koeliehandel 1866–1889.

145. Previously, Ferguson published books on the Red Cross and a *Manual of International Law, for the Use of Navies, Colonies and Consulates*. He wrote the last book because consuls had little knowledge of international law, particularly with respect to non-Western societies like China. J. P. A. François, 'Twee Nederlandse volkenrechtschrijvers uit de 19e eeuw', *Netherlands International Law Review*, 13:1 (1966), pp. 29–33.

146. Blussé and Van Luyn, *China en de Nederlanders*, p. 163. More recently Blussé reiterated this, calling Ferguson 'an avowed apponent of contract labor'. L. Blussé, 'Sinologists (1854–1911)', in W. I. Idema (ed.), *Chinese Studies in the Netherlands: Past, Present and Future* (Leiden: Brill, 2014), pp. 27–69, on p. 61.

147. P. Crawford Campbell, *Chinese Coolie Emigration to Countries within the British Empire* (1923; London: King Publication, 1971), pp. 10, 16–8.

148. Ferguson to Foreign Affairs, 21 December 1889, NA 2.05.03 BuZa/A-dossiers, 244 Koeliehandel, Emigratie van Chinezen 1866–1889.

149. Cremer to Foreign Affairs, 7 January 1890, NA 2.05.03 BuZa/A-dossiers, 244 Koeliehandel, Emigratie van Chinezen 1866–1889. Cremer would become Minister of Colonial Affairs in 1897–1901 and president of the NHM between 1907 and 1913. C. J. K. van Aalst, 'Levensbericht van Jacob Theodoor Cremer, 30 Juni 1847–14 Augustus 1923', *Jaarboek van de Maatschappij der Nederlandse Letterkunde* (1924), pp. 48–62.

150. M. van Klaveren, 'Death among Coolies: Mortality of Chinese and Javanese Labourers on Sumatra in the Early Years of Recruitment, 1882–1909', *Itinerario*, 21 (1997), pp. 111–25, on p. 112.

151. Hamel to Th. Delprat, Hoofdingenieur, Chef van den Dienst der Kolenontginning ter Sumatra's Westkust, 29 september 1900, NA 2.05.03 BuZa/A-dossiers, 245 Koeliehandel Emigratie Chinezen 1890–1904.

152. Yen, *Coolies and Mandarins*, p. 177.

153. Van der Putten, 'Small Powers', p. 122.

4 North and South America

1. Ferguson, *Civilization*, pp. 96–115.

2. W. McDougall, *Promised Land, Crusader State: The American Encounter with the World since 1776* (New York: Houghton Mifflin Harcourt, 1997), pp. 77–8.

3. L. J. Sadosky, 'Revolutionary Negotiations: A History of American Diplomacy with Europe and Native America in the Age of Jefferson' (PhD dissertation, University of Virginia, 2003), p. 105.

4. For the treaties see http://avalon.law.yale.edu/18th_century/fr1788-1.asp#art2 [accessed 18 June 2014].

5. Convention Defining and Establishing the Functions and Privileges of Consuls and Vice Consuls, signed at Versailles 14 November 1788, at http://avalon.law.yale.edu/18th_century/fr-1788.asp [accessed 18 June 2014].

6. *The Diplomatic Correspondence of the United States from the Signing of the Definitive Treaty of Peace, 10 September, 1783, to the Adoption of the Constitution, March 4, 1789*, 3 vols (New York: Blair & Rives, 1837), vol. 3, p. 93 (John Temple to John Jay, New York, 23 November 1785).

7. Ibid., p. 94 (John Jay to the President of Congress, 24 November 1785).

8. J. L. Neel, *Phineas Bond: A Study in Anglo-American Relations, 1786–1812* (Philadelphia, PA: University of Pennsylvania Press, 1968), p. 35.
9. *The Diplomatic Correspondence of the United States*, vol. 3, p. 105 (From John Jay to the President of Congress, 8 December 1786).
10. Ibid., pp. 105–8 (Report of John Jay on the preceding latter, 28 March 1786).
11. 'Letters of Phineas Bond, British Consul at Philadelphia, to the Foreign Office of Great Britain, 1787, 1788, 1789', *Annual Report of the American Historical Association for the Year 1896 in Two Volumes. Report of the Historical Manuscripts Commission of the American Historical Association* (Washington, DC: Government Printing Office, 1897), pp. 532–4 (Bond to Carmarthen, 16 May 1787).
12. R. Agstner, 'From Apalachicola to Wilkes-Barre: Austria(-Hungary) and its Consulates in the United States of America, 1820–1917', *Austrian History Yearbook*, 37 (2006), pp. 163–81, on p. 165.
13. L. A. White, 'The South in the 1850s as Seen by British Consuls', *Journal of Southern History*, 1:1 (1935), pp. 33–48, on p. 33.
14. L. A. White, 'The United States in the 1850s as Seen by British Consuls', *Mississippi Valley Historical Review*, 19:4 (1933), pp. 509–36.
15. P. Evans and T. P. Govan, 'A Belgian Consul on Conditions in the South in 1860 and 1862', *Journal of Southern History*, 3:4 (1937), pp. 478–91, on p. 481.
16. White, 'The United States in the 1850s', p. 519.
17. J. M. Viana Pedreira, 'From Growth to Collapse: Portugal, Brazil, and the Breakdown of the Old Colonial System (1750–1830)', *Hispanic American Historical Review*, 80:4 (2000), pp. 839–64.
18. B. Fausto, *A Concise History of Brazil* (Cambridge: Cambridge University Press, 1999), p. 21.
19. For this specific institution see R. S. Smith, 'A Research Report on Consulado History', *Journal of Inter-American Studies*, 3:1 (1961), pp. 41–52; R. S. Smith, 'The Institution of the Consulado in New Spain', *Hispanic American Historical Review*, 24:1 (1944), pp. 61–83.
20. F. L. Paxson, *The Independence of the South Republics: A Study in Recognition and Foreign Policy*, 2nd edn (Philadelphia, PA: Ferris & Leach, 1916), p. 56.
21. G. R. Andrews, 'Spanish American Independence: A Structural Analysis', *Latin American Perspectives*, 12:1 (1985), pp. 105–32.
22. R. F. Nichols, 'Trade Relations and the Establishment of the United States Consulates in Spanish America, 1779–1809', *Hispanic American Historical Review*, 13:3 (1933), pp. 289–313.
23. M. T. Gilderhus, 'The Monroe Doctrine: Meanings and Implications', *Presidential Studies Quarterly*, 36:1 (2006), pp. 5–16.
24. Ibid., p. 8.
25. W. S. Robertson, 'The Recognition of the Hispanic American Nations by the United States', *Hispanic American Historical Review*, 1:3 (1918), pp. 239–69.
26. E. J. Ferguson, 'Business, Government, and Congressional Investigation in the Revolution', *William and Mary Quarterly*, 16:3 (1959), pp. 293–318; Wriston, *Executive Agents*, pp. 3–5.
27. Wriston, *Executive Agents*, pp. 104–7.
28. Nichols, *Advance Agents*, pp. 11–12.
29. Wriston, *Executive Agents*, p. 179.

30. J. J. Johnson, *A Hemisphere Apart: The Foundations of United States Policy toward Latin America* (Baltimore, MD, and London: The Johns Hopkins University Press, 1990), p. 115.
31. W. S. Robertson, 'The First Legations of the United States in Latin America', *Mississippi Valley Historical Review*, 2:2 (1915), pp. 183–212, on p. 184; Paxson, *The Independence*, p. 114; W. R. Manning, *Diplomatic Correspondence of the United States concerning the Independence of the Latin-American Nations*, 3 vols (New York: Oxford University Press, 1925), vol. 1, p. 87.
32. Robertson, 'The Recognition of the Hispanic American Nations by the United States'.
33. W. Shaler, 'Journal of a Voyage between China and the North-Western Coast of America, Made in 1804', *American Register*, Volume 3, Part 1 (Philadelphia, PA: C. & A. Conrad, 1808), pp. 137–75.
34. M. Smith, 'The Myth of American Isolationism: Commerce, Diplomacy, and Military Affairs in the Early Republic', Special report from the B. Kenneth Simon Center for Principles and Politics, 134 (2013), pp. 5–47, on p. 5.
35. J. C. A. Stagg, 'The Political Essays of William Shaler', *William and Mary Quarterly*, 59:2 (2002), pp. 449–80, at http://oieahc.wm.edu/wmq/Apr02/stagg.pdf [accessed 18 June 2014].
36. Nichols, *Advance Agents*, pp. 84–5.
37. Stagg, 'The Political Essays of William Shaler', Essay 1 'No. 1 Essays on the Revolution in So. America'. The essays have no page numbers.
38. Ibid., Essay 3 'Untitled'.
39. D. R. Murray, *Odious Commerce: Britain, Spain and the Abolition of the Cuban Slave Trade* (Cambridge: Cambridge University Press, 2002), p. 33.
40. Stagg, 'The Political Essays of William Shaler', Essay 3 'Untitled', Essay 4 'Notes on Manners and Society in Havana Cuba'.
41. I. J. Cox, 'Monroe and the Early Mexican Revolutionary Agents', *American Historical Association Annual Register*, 1 (1911), pp. 199–215.
42. Stagg, 'The Political Essays of William Shaler', Essay 1 'No. 1 Essays on the Revolution in So. America'.
43. Ibid., Essay 6 'Untitled'.
44. Nichols, *Advance Agents*, pp. 103–43.
45. Ibid., pp. 143–57.
46. C. J. Stillé, *The Life and Services of Joel R. Poinsett, the Confidential Agent in South Carolina of President Jackson during the Nullification Troubles of 1832* (Philadelphia, PA: The Pennsylvania Magazine of History and Biography, 1888); D. M. Parton, *The Diplomatic Career of Joel Roberts Poinsett* (Washington, DC: The Catholic University of America, 1934); C. L. Chandler, 'The Life of Joel Roberts Poinsett', *Pennsylvania Magazine of History and Biography*, 59:1 (1935), pp. 1–32; H. F. Peterson, *Argentina and the United States: 1810–1960* (New York: University Publishers Inc., 1964), pp. 15–9; Paxson, *The Independence*, pp. 109–15.
47. Paxson, *The Independence*, p. 110.
48. Chandler, 'The Life of Joel Roberts Poinsett', p. 6.
49. G. B. Dyer and C. L. Dyer, 'A Century of Strategic Intelligence Reporting: Mexico, 1822–1919', *Geographical Review*, 44:1 (1954), pp. 49–69.
50. L. Mangiafico, 'Joel R. Poinsett: First US Envoy in Latin America', *Foreign Service Journal* (2012), pp. 46–9.
51. Manning, *Diplomatic Correspondence*, vol. 1, pp. 6–7; Paxson, *The Independence*, p. 111.

52. Paxson, *The Independence*, p. 112.
53. C. L. Chandler, 'United States Shipping in the La Plata Region, 1809–1810', *Hispanic American Historical Review*, 3:2 (1920), pp. 159–76; C. L. Chandler, 'United States Merchant Ships in the Rio de La Plata (1801–1808), as shown by Early Newspapers', *Hispanic American Historical Review*, 2:1 (1919), pp. 26–54.
54. Chandler, 'The Life of Joel Roberts Poinsett', p. 22.
55. Parton, *The Diplomatic Career of Joel Roberts Poinsett*, p. 6.
56. Chandler, 'The Life of Joel Roberts Poinsett', p. 26.
57. Ibid., p. 28.
58. Paxson, *The Independence*, p. 113.
59. W. S. Robertson, 'Documents Concerning the Consular Service of the United States in Latin America, with Introductory Note', *Mississippi Valley Historical Review*, 2:4 (1916), pp. 561–8, on p. 563.
60. Paxson, *The Independence*, p. 113. During his consulate, Halsey remained an active businessman and frequently interfered in domestic politics. He is still remembered for introducing new breeds of sheep in Argentine. He was on bad terms with other local American businessmen, including David Curtis De Forest (1774–1825), a Yankee merchant and privateer.
61. Parton, *The Diplomatic Career of Joel Roberts Poinsett*, p. 17.
62. Ibid., p. 42.
63. Stillé, *The Life and Services of Joel R. Poinsett*, p. 28; C. I. Bevans (comp.), *Treaties and other International Agreements of the United States, 1776–1949*, 13 vols (Washington, DC: Department of State Publication, 1968–76), vol. 5. The first US–Argentine commercial treaty dates from 1853 (pp. 61–7).
64. W. L. Neumann, 'United States Aid to the Chilean Wars of Independence', *Hispanic American Historical Review*, 27:2 (1947), pp. 204–19.
65. Stillé, *The Life and Services of Joel R. Poinsett*, p. 28.
66. Wriston, *Executive Agents*, p. 414.
67. Ibid., p. 415.
68. J. C. Pine, 'William G. D. Worthington: United States Special Agent, 1817–1819', *Arkansas Academy of Science Proceedings*, 12 (1958), pp. 46–7; Peterson, *Argentina and the United States*, pp. 32–4.
69. Wriston, *Executive Agents*, p. 421.
70. Pine, 'William G. D. Worthington', p. 46.
71. H. B. Cox, 'Reasons for Joel R. Poinsett's Refusal of a Second Mission to South America', *Hispanic American Historical Review*, 43:3 (1963), pp. 405–8; Paxson, *The Independence*, p. 123; Manning, *Diplomatic Correspondence*, vol. 1, pp. 39–40.
72. Manning, *Diplomatic Correspondence*, vol. 1, pp. 146–9.
73. Ibid., pp. 160–1.
74. Ibid., pp. 185–6.
75. W. R. Manning, 'Poinsett's Mission to Mexico', *American Journal of International Law* (1913), pp. 781–823.
76. Salvucci, 'The Origins and Progress'.
77. K. Schultz, 'The Transfer of the Portuguese Court and Ideas of Empire', *Portuguese Studies Review*, 15:1–2 (2007), pp. 367–91.
78. L. Bethell, 'The Independence of Brazil and the Abolition of the Brazilian Slave Trade: Anglo-Brazilian Relations, 1822–1826', *Journal of Latin American Studies*, 1:2 (1969), pp. 115–47. More extensively treated in L. Bethell, *The Abolition of the Brazilian Slave*

Trade: Britain, Brazil and the Slave Trade Question 1807–1869 (Cambridge: Cambridge University Press, 1970).

79. Fausto, *A Concise History of Brazil*, p. 64.
80. P. E. Schramm, *Deutschland und Übersee. Der deutsche Handel mit den andere Kontinenten, insbesondere Afrika, von Karl V. bis zu Bismarck* (Braunschweig: Georg Westermann Verlag, 1950), pp. 68–73.
81. This case is primarily based on Penkwitt, *Preußen und Brasilien*.
82. G. Ferrez, *Saudades do Rio de Janeiro* (Rio de Janeiro: Co. Ed. Nacional, 1957).
83. Besides his consulate, Theremin was and is still known as a respected painter of Brazilian landscapes.
84. Penkwitt, *Preußen und Brasilien*, p. 36, n. 2; Schramm, *Deutschland und Übersee*, pp. 68–9.
85. Penkwitt, *Preußen und Brasilien*, p. 83.
86. Oriolla was the son of a Brazilian living in Berlin. He was appointed Prussian ambassador in Rio in 1850. During their stay they were received by Consul Leon Theremin. 'Rio is his second maternal city; he has spent here the greater part of his youth, and now, grown up to manhood, he has succeeded his father in the Consulate'. Prince Adalbert, *Travels in the South of Europe and in Brazil: With a Voyage up the Amazon and the Xingu by His Royal Highness Prince Adalbert of Prussia* (London: David Bogue Publisher, 1849), p. 218.
87. According to the journal *Der Deutsche Pionier* (the German Pioneer) he migrated in 1845. *Der Deutsche Pionier* (published by Der Deutsche Pionier-Verein von Cincinnati (DPVC), 1868–1961) des 16. Jahrgangs (1884–5), pp. 206–7, at http://www.nausa.uni-oldenburg.de/pionier/frame.html [accessed 18 June 2014].
88. E. R. Carhart, 'The New York Produce Exchange', *Annals of the American Academy of Political and Social Science*, 38:2 (1911), pp. 206–21.
89. 'Obituary Rudolph C. Burlage', *New York Times*, 29 June 1883; *Der Deutsche Pionier*, pp. 206–7, at http://www.nausa.uni-oldenburg.de/pionier/frame.html [accessed 18 June 2014].
90. A. J. Veenendaal, *Slow Train to Paradise: How Dutch Investments Helped Build American Railroads* (Stanford, CA: Stanford University Press, 1995), p. 74.
91. NA 2.05.13 BuZa, Gezantschap VS/Legatie Washington, Inv. no. 59 (1853–1855).
92. E. H. Berwanger, *The British Foreign Service and the American Civil War* (Lexington, KY: The University Press of Kentucky, 1994) p. 13; M. L. Bonham Jr, *The British Consuls in the Confederacy* (New York: Columbia University, 1911).
93. *Correspondence of the Department of State in Relation to the British Consuls Resident in the Confederate States* (Richmond: Sentinel Office, 1863), p. 7.
94. On this King Cotton Diplomacy: Berwanger, *The British Foreign Service*, pp. 19–20.
95. Ibid., p. 95.
96. Burlage to Roest van Limburg, 5 August 1862, NA 2.05.13 BuZa, Gezantschap VS/Legatie Washington, Inv. no. 61 (1859–1862).
97. Berwanger, *The British Foreign Service*, p. 145.
98. Burlage to Roest van Limburg, 17 May 1862, NA 2.05.13 BuZa, Gezantschap VS/Legatie Washington, Inv. no. 61 (1859–1862).
99. R. L. Cohn, 'The Transition from Sail to Steam in Immigration to the United States', *Journal of Economic History*, 65:2 (2005), pp. 469–95, on p. 475, table 2.

100. A. A. Keeling, 'The Business of Transatlantic Migration between Europe and the United States of America, 1900–1914' (PhD dissertation, University of California, 2005), pp. 23, 330.

101. T. Feys, 'The Battle for the Migrants: The Evolution from Port to Company Competition, 1840–1914', in T. Feys et al. (eds), *Maritime Transport and Migration: The Connections between Maritime and Migration Networks* (St John's: International Maritime Economic History Association, 2007), pp. 27–49, on p. 40.

102. Burlage to Van Pestel, 3 May 1878 and 7 May 1878, NA 2.05.13 BuZa, Gezantschap VS/Legatie Washington, Inv. no. 70 (1878, 1879, 1880, 1881).

103. Burlage to Mazel, 11 June 1867, NA 2.05.13 BuZa, Gezantschap VS/Legatie Washington, Inv. no. 63 (1866–1868).

104. Burlage to Roest van Limburg, 17 November 1864, NA 2.05.13 BuZa, Gezantschap VS/Legatie Washington, Inv. no. 62 (1863–1865).

105. Ministerie van Buitenlandsche Zaken, *Verzameling van consulaire en andere berigten en verslagen over nijverheid, handel en scheepvaart* (R. C. Burlage, Consul Generaal New York, Verslag over 1882, 23 mei 1883).

106. Planten was born in Amsterdam but migrated to the United States with his family in 1845. His father established the firm H. Planten & Son in New York, producing gelatine capsules. Jan Rutger continued the business until 1908. In March 1874 he became vice-consul to New York, assisting Burlage. He was a very wealthy citizen and generously supported Dutch immigrants in New York. H. J. Kiewiet de Jonge, 'Levensbericht van J. R. Planten', *Jaarboek van de Maatschappij der Nederlandse Letterkunde* (Leiden: E. J. Brill, 1914), pp. 152–4.

107. Bevans (comp.), *Treaties*, vol. 10 (Nepal–Peru), pp. 6–19.

108. Westermann, *The Netherlands and the United States*, pp. 191–224.

109. Bevans, *Treaties*, vol. 10, p. 23.

110. W. B. Smith, *America's Diplomats and Consuls of 1776–1865: A Geographic and Biographic Directory of the Foreign Service from the Declaration of Independence to the End of the Civil War* (Washington, DC: US Department of State, 1987).

111. K. Fatah-Black, 'The Patriot coup d'état in Curaçao, 1796', in W. Klooster and G. Oostindie (eds), *Curaçao in the Age of Revolutions, 1795–1800* (Leiden: KITLV Press, 2011), pp. 123–41; H. Jordaan, 'Patriots, Privateers and International Politics: The Myth of the Conspiracy of Jean Baptiste Tierce Cadet', in Klooster and Oostindie (eds), *Curaçao in the Age of Revolutions, 1795–1800*, pp. 141–71.

112. Westermann, *The Netherlands and the United States*, p. 217; C. C. Goslinga, *The Dutch in the Caribbean and in Surinam 1791/5–1942* (Assen: Van Gorcum, 1990).

113. Bevans, *Treaties*, vol. 10, p. 28.

114. The first Sephardic Jews from the Netherlands, including the families of Alvares Correa, Henriquez, Jessurun, Levy Maduro, Marchena, Henriquez Moron, Namias de Crasto and Pardo, arrived on Curaçao in 1659 and by the mid-nineteenth century they were the wealthiest merchants on the island. See http://www.dutchjewry.org/drieluik/curacao/curacao.htm [accessed 18 June 2014].

115. For this conflict see W. L. Harris, 'The Reluctant Diplomacy of Jose Maria Rojas, 1873–1883' (PhD dissertation, University of Florida, 1973), pp. 77–131.

116. A. T. Brusse, *Curaçao en zijne bewoners* (Curaçao: Internationale Drukkerij, 1882), pp. 139–44.

117. Rojas tried to influence Dutch public opinion by arranging the publication of pamphlets and booklets to represent the Venezuelan case. Amigo de las Antillas (pseud. Willem Sassen), *Het Nederlandsch Venezuelaansch incident 1875* (Typographia Belgica, 1875).

118. R. van Vuurde, *Nederland en de Monroeleer, 1895–1914: Europese belangenbehartiging in de Amerikaanse invloedssfeer* (Amsterdam: De Bataafsche Leeuw, 1998).

119. G. C. Herring, *From Colony to Superpower: US Foreign Relations since 1776* (New York: Oxford University Press, 2008), pp. 153–5.

120. Roosevelt Study Center (RSC), Middelburg, The Netherlands, M77 Diplomatic Instructions of the Department of State, Roll 124, Dispatch no. 3, 13 March 1876.

121. L. D. Langley, *Struggle for the American Mediterranean: United States–European Rivalry in the Gulf-Caribbean, 1776–1904* (Athens, GA: The University of Georgia Press, 1976).

122. This case is based primarily on J. Hartog, *US Consul in Nineteenth-Century Curaçao: The Life and Works of Leonard Burlington Smith*, 2nd edn (Aruba: VAD, 1971).

123. Ibid., p. 38.

124. This company was established by the *KWIM* and renamed *Curaçaose Handelmaatschappij* in 1911.

125. The company was taken over in 1912 by the Amsterdam-based shipping company *Koninklijke Nederlandse Stoomvaart Maatschappij* (KNSM; Royal Netherlands Steamship Company).

126. Hartog, *US Consul in Nineteenth-Century Curaçao*, p. 57.

127. M. E. Stansfield, *Red Rubber, Bleeding Trees: Violence, Slavery, and Empire in Northwest Amazonia, 1850–1933* (Albuquerque, NM: University of New Mexico Press, 1998); B. Weinstein, *The Amazon Rubber Boom, 1850–1920* (Stanford, CA: Stanford University Press, 1983).

128. J. P. Rodriguez, *Slavery in the Modern World: A History of Political, Social, and Economic Oppression* (Santa Barbara, CA: ABC Clio, 2011), pp. 116–19. Until 1908 the name was Peruvian Amazon Rubber Company.

129. *Correspondence Respecting the Treatment of British Colonial Subjects and Native Indians Employed in the Collection of Rubber in the Putumayo District, Presented to both Houses of Parliament by Command of His Majesty, July 1912* (London: Harrison and Sons, 1912), pp. 7, 53–4.

130. Ibid., pp. 10–11.

131. His reports are included in United States Department of State, *Slavery in Peru: Message from the President of the United States, Transmitting Report of the Secretary of State, with Accompanying Papers, Concerning the Alleged Existence of Slavery in Peru* (Washington, DC: Government Printing Office, 1913). The first report appears on pp. 100–11, the second report on pp. 111–18.

132. United States Department of State, *Slavery in Peru*, pp. 114–15.

133. Stansfield, *Red Rubber*, pp. 134–6.

134. Ibid., pp. 126–34.

135. He published his experiences in W. E. Hardenburg, *The Putumayo, the Devil's Paradise; Travels in the Peruvian Amazon Region and an Account of the Atrocities Committed upon the Indians Therein* (London: T. F. Unwin, 1912).

136. J. Tully, *The Devil's Milk: A Social History of Rubber* (New York: Monthly Review Press, 2011), pp. 90–2.

137. Formed in 1909 through the amalgamation of British and Foreign Anti-Slavery Society (1835) and the Aborigines' Protection Society (1837).

138. House of Commons Debate, 3 March 1910, Written answers, at http://hansard. millbanksystems.com/written_answers/1910/mar/03/peruvian-amazon-company [accessed 18 June 2014].

139. United States Department of State, *Slavery in Peru*, pp. 117–18.

140. House of Commons Debate, 13 June 1910, Oral answers to questions, at http://hansard. millbanksystems.com/commons/1910/jun/13/putumayo-valley-peruvian-amazon-company [accessed 18 June 2014].

141. There are many biographies on Casement. The most detailed on his consular work is S. Ó Siocháin, *Roger Casement: Imperialist, Rebel, Revolutionary* (Dublin: The Lilliput Press, 2008). Casement has inspired M. Vargas Llosa to write a historical novel: *El sueño del celta* (Madrid: Alfaguara, 2010), which has been translated into English as *The Dream of the Celt* (London: Faber, 2012).

142. J. Goodman, *The Devil and Mr Casement: One Man's Struggle for Human Rights in South America's Heart of Darkness* (London: Verso, 2009). The diaries controversy is discussed in A. Mitchell, *The Amazon Journal of Roger Casement* (Dublin: Anaconda Editions, 1997). In contrast to Mitchell, R. Sawyer is convinced that they are authentic. R. Sawyer (ed.), *Roger Casement's Diaries – 1910: The Black and the White* (London: Pimlico, 1997).

143. *Correspondence Respecting the Treatment of British Colonial Subjects*.

144. Ó Siocháin, *Roger Casement*, p. 273.

145. Ibid., pp. 278–95.

146. Mitchell, *The Amazon Journal*, p. 128.

147. Ibid., p. 424.

148. *Correspondence Respecting the Treatment of British Colonial Subjects*; M. Taussig, 'Culture of Terror – Space of Death: Roger Casement's Putumayo Report and the Explanation of Torture', *Comparative Studies in Society and History*, 26:3 (1984), pp. 467–97.

149. Ó Siocháin, *Roger Casement*, pp. 300–16.

150. P. F. Martin, *Peru of the Twentieth Century* (London: Edward Arnold, 1911), pp. 311–12.

151. Ibid., p. 314.

152. United States Department of State, *Slavery in Peru*, p. 121.

153. Ó Siocháin, *Roger Casement*, pp. 315–21.

154. Ibid., p. 323.

155. *Correspondence Respecting the Treatment of British Colonial Subjects*, pp. 154–60; United States Department of State, *Slavery in Peru*, p. 133.

156. Stansfield, *Red Rubber*, pp. 165–7.

157. United States Department of State, *Slavery in Peru*, p. 125.

158. *Correspondence Respecting the Treatment of British Colonial Subjects*, p. 161.

159. United States Department of State, *Slavery in Peru*, pp. 5–7.

160. Ibid., p. 49.

161. Ibid., p. 46.

162. Ibid., p. 52.

163. Ó Siocháin, *Roger Casement*, pp. 344–8.

164. *Report and Special Report from the Select Committee on Putumayo, together with the Proceedings of the Committee, Minutes of Evidence and Appendices* (London: Wyman and Sons, 1913) (Parliament, 1913. House of Commons Reports and papers. no. 148.)

165. Ó Siocháin, *Roger Casement*, pp. 357–8.

166. A. Porter, 'Sir Roger Casement and the International Humanitarian Movement', *Journal of Imperial and Commonwealth History*, 29:2 (2001), pp. 59–74.

5 Sub-Saharan Africa

1. G. W. Irwin, 'Precolonial African Diplomacy: The Example of Asante', *International Journal of African Historical Studies*, 8:1 (1975), pp. 81–96, on p. 83.

2. N. Lante Wallace-Bruce, 'Africa and International Law – The Emergence to Statehood', *Journal of Modern African Studies*, 23:4 (1985), pp. 575–602, on p. 583.

3. A. Southall, 'State Formation in Africa', *Annual Review of Anthropology*, 4 (1974), pp. 153–65; A. Southall, 'The Segmentary State in Africa and Asia', *Comparative Studies in Society and History*, 30:1 (1988), pp. 52–82.

4. R. Smith, 'Peace and Palaver: International Relations in Pre-Colonial West Africa', *Journal of African History*, 14:4 (1973), pp. 599–621, on pp. 600–11.

5. R. Law, 'Madiki Lemon, the "English Captain" at Ouidah, 1843–1852: An Exploration in Biography', *History in Africa*, 37 (2010), pp. 107–23; R. Law, *Ouidah: The Social History of a West African Slaving 'Port', 1727–1892* (Athens, OH: Ohio University Press, 2004), pp. 162–3.

6. Smith, 'Peace and Palaver', pp. 603, 618.

7. R. Law, 'Central and Eastern Wangara: An Indigenous West African Perception of the Political and Economic Geography of the Slave Coast as Recorded by Joseph Dupuis in Kumasi, 1820', *History in Africa*, 22 (1995), pp. 281–305.

8. Smith, 'Peace and Palaver', p. 606.

9. J. Thornton, 'Early Kongo–Portuguese Relations: A New Interpretation', *History in Africa*, 8 (1981), pp. 183–204.

10. J. Thornton, *Africa's Discovery of Europe, 1450–1850* (New York: Oxford University Press, 2002), p. 19.

11. J. A. D. Alie, *A New History of Sierra Leone* (New York: St Martin's Press, 1990), pp. 33–5.

12. Smith, 'Peace and Palaver', p. 617.

13. J. E. Inikori, 'Africa and the Trans-Atlantic Slave Trade', in T. Falola (ed.), *Africa*, 2 vols (Durham, NC: Carolina Academic Press, 2003), vol. 1 (African History before 1885), pp. 393–5.

14. C. W. Newbury, 'General Introduction', in C. W. Newbury, *British Policy towards West Africa: Select Documents 1786–1874*, 2 vols (Oxford: Clarendon Press, 1965), vol. 1, pp. 3–44, on p. 25.

15. Ibid., p. 21.

16. F. Shaikh, 'Judicial Diplomacy: British Officials and the Mixed Commission Courts', in K. Hamilton and P. Salmon (eds), *Slavery, Diplomacy and Empire: Britain and the Suppression of the Slave Trade, 1807–1975* (Brighton: Sussex Academic Press, 2009), pp. 42–65, on p. 49.

17. F. H. Rankin, *The White Man's Grave: A Visit to Sierra Leone in 1834* (London: Richard Bentley, 1836), p. viii; W. W. Shreeve, *Sierra Leone: The Principal British Colony on the Western Coast of Africa* (London: Simmonds & Co., 1848), p. 101. Another notoriously unhealthy place was the island Fernando Po, called the 'Foreign Office Grave'. To this place was sent the British explorer, soldier and orientalist Richard Burton, who became British consul in 1861. W. P. Dodge, *The Real Richard Burton* (London: T. Fisher Unwin, 1907), p. 139.

18. Alie, *A New History*, p. 54.

19. L. Bethell, 'The Mixed Commissions for the Suppression of the Transatlantic Slave Trade in the Nineteenth Century', *Journal of African History*, 7:1 (1966), pp. 79–93; Shaikh,

'Judicial Diplomacy', pp. 48–9. The captured black slaves on the ships, about 65,000 to 80,000 in total, were set free. A. M. Howard, 'Nineteenth-Century Coastal Slave Trading and the British Abolition Campaign in Sierra Leone', *Slavery & Abolition: A Journal of Slave and Post-Slave Studies*, 27:1 (2006), pp. 23–49.

20. D. Northrup, 'The Compatibility of the Slave and Palm Oil Trades in the Bight of Biafra', *Journal of African History*, 17:3 (1976), pp. 353–64.

21. Schramm, *Deutschland und Übersee*, pp. 205–16, 558–60.

22. B. D. Naranch, 'Between Cosmopolitanism and German Colonialism: Nineteenth-Century Hanseatic Networks in Emerging Tropical Markets', in A. Gestrich and M. Schulte Beerbühl (eds), *Cosmopolitan Networks in Commerce and Society 1660–1914* (London: German Historical Institute, 2011), pp. 99–133.

23. Schramm, *Deutschland und Übersee*, p. 208.

24. Ibid., p. 210.

25. 'Obituary: The Chevalier de Colquhoun', *Gentleman's Magazine*, 199 (London: John Bowyer Nichols & Sons, October 1855), p. 435.

26. Schramm, *Deutschland und Übersee*, p. 215.

27. Shreeve, *Sierra Leone*, p. 82.

28. The appointment was made by the commander-in-chief of the US Naval Forces in the Mediterranean and off the West Coast of Africa, Isaac Mayo. D. L. Canney, *Africa Squadron: The US Navy and the Slave Trade, 1842–1861* (Washington, DC: Potomac Books Inc., 2006), pp. 157–73. Mayo did not act on instructions from his government. G. E. Brooks Jr, *Yankee Traders, Old Coasters and African Middlemen: A History of American Legitimate Trade with West Africa in the Nineteenth Century* (Boston, MA: Boston University Press, 1970), p. 120.

29. I. Kargbo, 'The US Consulate and the Promotion of Trade in Sierra Leone, 1859–1880', in A. Jalloh and T. Falola (eds), *The United States and West Africa: Interactions and Relations* (Rochester: University of Rochester Press, 2008), pp. 38–61.

30. Compare Brooks Jr, *Yankee Traders*, pp. 130–1.

31. Mayo–Taylor, 7 February 1855, Despatches from United States Consuls in Sierra Leone, 1858–1906 (22 February 1858–28 March 1881), The National Archives and Record Service (Washington 1960).

32. US Merchants Petition, September 1857, West Coast of Africa, Sierra Leone, Despatches from United States Consuls in Sierra Leone, 1858–1906 (22 February 1858–28 March 1881), The National Archives and Record Service (Washington 1960).

33. Taylor–Department of State, 22 February 1858, Despatches from United States Consuls in Sierra Leone, 1858–1906 (22 February 1858–28 March 1881), The National Archives and Record Service (Washington 1960).

34. Brooks Jr, *Yankee Traders*, p. 131.

35. Report Taylor, 22 February 1859, Despatches from United States Consuls in Sierra Leone, 1858–1906 (22 February 1858–28 March 1881), The National Archives and Record Service (Washington 1960).

36. Kargbo, 'The US Consulate', p. 41.

37. Ibid., p. 42.

38. According to Kargbo, Taylor remained Acting Consul until 1866, but the Annual Report of 1861 and all subsequent correspondence until 1870 was signed by Henry Rider, a merchant from Salem, Massachusetts appointed US consular agent, not acting consul, in September 1860. Kargbo, 'The US Consulate'. In one of his letters (22 March 1866) to the Department of State, Rider recalls his arrival in Sierra Leone in April 1859

and the death of Taylor later that year. Rider–Secretary of State, 22 March 1866, Despatches from United States Consuls in Sierra Leone, 1858–1906 (22 February 1858–28 March 1881), The National Archives and Record Service (Washington 1960).

39. C. Fyfe, *A History of Sierra Leone* (Oxford: Oxford University Press, 1962), p. 296.
40. Brooks Jr, *Yankee Traders*, p. 219.
41. Ibid., p. 126.
42. Kargbo, 'The US Consulate', p. 41.
43. Ibid., p. 45.
44. Brooks Jr, *Yankee Traders*, p. 219.
45. Lewis to Washington, 12 March 1880, Despatches from United States Consuls in Sierra Leone, 1858–1906 (22 February 1858–28 March 1881), The National Archives and Record Service (Washington 1960).
46. Brooks Jr, *Yankee Traders*, pp. 305–9.
47. Ibid., pp. 5–6.
48. Ibid., p. 7.
49. J. Bandinel, *Some Account of the Trade in Slaves from Africa as Connected with Europe and America* (London: Longman, Brown & Co., 1842), p. 101.
50. K. Hamilton and F. Shaikh, 'Introduction', in Hamilton and Salmon (eds), *Slavery, Diplomacy and Empire*, pp. 1–20. Even British traders did not immediately give up the trade, for this see M. Sherwood, 'Perfidious Albion: Britain, the USA, and Slavery in the 1840s and 1860s', *Contributions in Black Studies*, 13/14 (1995), pp. 174–200.
51. H. H. Wilson, 'Some Principal Aspects of British Efforts to Crush the African Slave Trade, 1807–1929', *American Journal of International Law*, 44:3 (1950), pp. 505–27; K. O. Dike, *Trade and Politics in the Niger Delta 1830–1885: An Introduction to the Economic and Political History of Nigeria* (Westport, CT: Greenwood Press, 1956), p. 83.
52. K. Mann, *Slavery and the Birth of an African City; Lagos 1760–1900* (Bloomington, IL, and Indianapolis, IN: Indiana University Press, 2007), pp. 34, 43.
53. Ibid., p. 91.
54. Dike, *Trade and Politics*, pp. 86–7.
55. J. S. Martinez, *The Slave Trade and the Origins of International Human Rights Law* (Oxford: Oxford University Press, 2012), p. 146.
56. A. Lambert, 'Slavery, Free Trade and Naval Strategy, 1840–1860', in Hamilton and Salmon (eds), *Slavery, Diplomacy and Empire*, pp. 65–81, on p. 78.
57. M. Lynn, *Commerce and Economic Change in West Africa: The Palm Oil Trade in the Nineteenth Century* (Cambridge: Cambridge University Press, 1997).
58. Ibid., p. 3.
59. Ibid., pp. 133–7.
60. K. O. Dike, 'John Beecroft, 1790–1854. Her Britannic Majesty's Consul to the Bights of Benin and Biafra 1849–1854', *Journal of the Historical Society of Nigeria*, 1:1 (1956), pp. 5–15.
61. For the history of Fernando Po see I. K. Sundiata, *From Slaving to Neoslavery: The Bight of Biafra and Fernando Po in the Era of Abolition, 1827–1930* (Madison, WI: The University of Wisconsin Press, 1996).
62. J. Holan, *Travels in Madeira Sierra Leone, Teneriffe, St. Jago, Cape Coast, Fernando Po, Princes Island, etc. etc.*, 2nd edn (London: George Routledge, 1840), pp. 242–3.
63. W. N. M. Geary, *Nigeria under British Rule* (London: Frank Cass & Co Ltd, 1965), p. 74. The buildings were sold to Dillon, Tennant & Co., but the firm failed in 1837 and they were taken over by the West African Company (in 1842 it was handed over to the

Baptist Missionary Society). H. Roe, *West African Scenes: Descriptions of Fernando Po* (London: Elliot Stock, 1874), p. 6.

64. Dike, 'John Beecroft', p. 9.
65. R. Jamieson, *Commerce with Africa, with Suggestions for the Development of the Commercial Resources of Western Central Africa* (London: Effingham Wilson, 1859). In this publication Jamieson argued that 'the theory on which those treaties is based, namely, that lawful commerce cannot co-exist with Slave trade, is fallacious' (p. 20).
66. Dike, *Trade and Politics in the Niger Delta*, p. 77; Dike, 'John Beecroft', pp. 5–15.
67. Geary, *Nigeria under British Rule*, p. 78.
68. W. D. McIntyre, 'Commander Glover and the Colony of Lagos, 1861–73', *Journal of African History*, 4:1 (1963), pp. 57–79.
69. S. E. Slater, 'The British Consulate at Fernando Po: 1854–1879' (MA Thesis, University of Calgary, 1983), p. 34.
70. Ibid., pp. 6–7.
71. Newbury, *British Policy towards West Africa*, vol. 1, p. 385.
72. Ibid.
73. With Dahomey, in possession of the port Whydah since 1727, it was able to conclude a treaty of amity and commerce in December 1847, but this did not include the slave trade.
74. B. Beolens, M. Watkins and M. Grayson, *The Eponym Dictionary of Reptiles* (Baltimore, MD: The Johns Hopkins University Press, 2011), p. 94. For Campbell see R. S. Smith, *The Lagos Consulate 1851–1861* (London: The Macmillan Press, 1978), pp. 49–99.
75. Dike, *Trade and Politics in the Niger Delta*, p. 130; Newbury, *British Policy towards West Africa*, vol. 1, p. 348.
76. Beecroft quoted in Mann, *Slavery and the Birth of an African City*, p. 95.
77. Ibid., p. 96.
78. A. D. Nzemeke, 'Local Patronage and Commercial Enterprise in Lagos 1850–1861', *Africa: Rivista trimestrale di studi e documentazione dell'Istituto italiano per l'Africae l'Oriente*, 47:1 (1992), pp. 105–14.
79. Newbury, *British Policy towards West Africa*, vol. 1, p. 375.
80. C. Anyangwe, *The Secrets of an Aborted Decolonisation: The Declassified British Secret Files on the Southern Cameroons* (Langaa: Bamenda, 2010), pp. 17–18.
81. Slater, 'The British Consulate at Fernando Po', pp. 50–1.
82. Ibid., p. 54. There are many biographies on Burton. The most recent, which includes a discussion of his consular period, is J. R. Godsall, *The Tangled Web: A Life of Sir Richard Burton* (De Montfort Mews: Troubador Publishing Ltd, 2008). J. L. Newman's volume that focuses on Africa is *Paths without Glory: Richard Francis Burton in Africa* (Washington, DC: Potomac Books, 2010).
83. Slater, 'The British Consulate at Fernando Po', p. 190. He was the younger brother of David Livingstone (1813–73).
84. P. P. Ekeh (ed.), *Warri City: And British Colonial Rule in Western Niger Delta* (Buffalo, NY: Urhobo Historical Society, 2004), pp. 45–8.
85. E. Roberts, *Embassy to the Eastern Courts of Cochin-China, Siam, and Muscat: in the US Sloop-of-War Peacock, David Geisinger, Commander, during the years 1832-3-4* (New York: Harper & Bros., 1837).
86. Bevans (comp.), *Treaties*, vol. 9, pp. 1291–4: Treaty of Amity and Commerce between the USA and Muscat (21 September 1833).
87. J. Woodfork, 'The Omani Empire', in Falola (ed.), *Africa*, vol. 1 (African History before 1885), pp. 321–35, on p. 326.

88. She married the German merchant Rudolph Heinrich Ruete (1839–70), agent of the firm Hansing & Co., in 1867 and changed her name to Emily Ruete. See her published memoirs in E. Ruete, née Princess of Oman and Zanzibar, *Memoirs of an Arabian Princess: An Autobiography* (New York: D. Appleton and Company, 1888). A new and extended translation appeared in 1993: *An Arabian Princess between Two Worlds: Memoirs, Letters Home, Sequels to the Memoirs Syrian Customs and Usages by Sayyida Salme/ Emily Ruete*, ed. and intro. E. van Donzel (Leiden: E. J. Brill, 1993), pp. 222, 327–34.

89. Quoted in M. R. Bhacker, *Trade and Empire in Muscat and Zanzibar: Roots of British Domination* (London and New York: Routledge, 1992), p. 132.

90. Sir Fairfax Moresby (1786–1877) was a senior officer at Mauritius whose duties included the suppression of the slave trade.

91. Bhacker, *Trade and Empire*, pp. 164–79.

92. R. L. Pouwels, 'Eastern Africa and the Indian Ocean to 1800: Reviewing Relations in Historical Perspective', *International Journal of African Historical Studies*, 35:2/3 (2002), pp. 385–425.

93. Bhacker, *Trade and Empire*, p. 120.

94. According to the British consul John Kirk (1832–1922), who from 1873 became consul general, in 1870 there were 3,657 Indians on Zanzibar. C. G. Bhatt, 'India and Africa Unique Historical Bonds and Present Prospects, with Special Reference to Kutchis in Zanzibar', Working Paper: No. 5, University of Mumbai, Centre for African Studies (2008).

95. Many Banyans (also known as Bhatias) belonged to Indian families that had come to East Africa, including Zanzibar, several generations before. Their number on Zanzibar increased from *c.* 1,000 in 1840 to 5,000–6,000 in 1860, but apparently declined thereafter. C. Goswami, *The Call of the Sea: Kachchhi Traders in Muscat and Zanzibar, c. 1800–1880* (Hyderabad: Orient BlackSwan, 2011).

96. According to William Ruschenberger (1807–95), the surgeon accompanying Roberts, thirty-two vessels of the forty-one (or 5,497 tons a total of 7,559 tons) in the port of Zanzibar between 16 September 1832 and 26 May 1834 came from the United States and only seven came from Great Britain. W. S. W. Ruschenberger, *Narrative of a Voyage Round the World during the Years 1835–36–37, Including a Narrative of an Embassy to the Sultan of Muscat and the King of Siam* (Philadelphia, PA: Carby, Lea, & Blanchard, 1838), p. 47.

97. R. Coupland, *East Africa and its Invaders: From the Earliest Times to the Death of Seyyid Said in 1856* (Oxford: Clarendon Press, 1938), pp. 361–87, 421–59.

98. Rev. Dr J. L. Krapf, *Travels Researches and Missionary Labours during an Eighteen Years Residence in Eastern Africa* (Boston, MA: Ticknor and Fields, 1860), pp. 102–3.

99. M. D. E. Nwulia, *Britain and Slavery in East Africa* (Washington, DC: Three Continents Press, 1952), p. 99.

100. N. R. Bennett and G. E. Brooks (eds), *New England Merchants in Africa: A History through Documents 1802–1865* (Boston, MA: Boston University Press, 1965), p. 192.

101. Ruete, *An Arabian Princess* (1993), p. 329.

102. G. J. Pierson, 'US Consuls in Zanzibar and the Slave Trade, 1870–1890', *Historian*, 55 (Autumn 1992), pp. 53–68; P. Duignan and L. H. Gann, *The United States and Africa: A History* (Cambridge: Cambridge University Press, 1987), pp. 140–4.

103. Goswami, *The Call of the Sea*, p. 141.

104. Bennett and Brooks (eds), *New England Merchants in Africa*, p. 197.

105. J. R. Browne, *Etchings of a Whaling Cruise, with Notes of a Sojourn on the Island Zanzibar to which is Appended a Brief History of Whale Fishery, its Past and Present Condition* (New York: Harper & Brothers Publishers, 1846).

106. Bennett and Brooks (eds), *New England Merchants in Africa*, p. 206.

107. Browne, *Etchings of a Whaling Cruise*, pp. 374–5.

108. For the history of his trading activities see Goswami, *The Call of the Sea*, pp. 191–239.

109. J. B. F. Osgood, *Notes of Travel; or, Recollections of Majunga, Zanzibar, Muscat, Aden, Mocha, and Other Eastern Ports* (Salem: G. Creamer, 1854), p. 54; R. F. Burton, *Zanzibar: City, Island and Coast*, 2 vols (London: Tinsley Brothers, 1872), vol. 1, p. 271. Jairam Shivji collected the customs from 1834 to 1854.

110. Bennett and Brooks (eds), *New England Merchants in Africa*, p. 216.

111. Bevans (comp.), *Treaties*, vol. 9, pp. 1291–4: Treaty of Amity and Commerce between the USA and Muscat (21 September 1833).

112. Bhacker, *Trade and Empire*, pp. 158–60.

113. Bennett and Brooks (eds), *New England Merchants in Africa*, pp. 203–4.

114. Ibid., pp. 239–41; M. V. Jackson Haight, *European Powers and South-East Africa. A Study of International Relations on the South-East Coast of Africa 1796–1856* (New York: Frederick A. Praeger, 1967), p. 102.

115. Goswami, *The Call of the Sea*, p. 205.

116. W. Gilbert, 'Our Man in Zanzibar: Richard Waters, American Consul (1837–1845)' (BA dissertation, Wesleyan University, 2011), p. 55; Bennett and Brooks (eds), *New England Merchants in Africa*, pp. 210, 224–5, 226.

117. Bhacker, *Trade and Empire*, p. 159.

118. From 1841 to *c.* 1846 there was also the firm of Robert Cogan & Company on Zanzibar. Robert Cogan, an ex-officer of the Indian Navy, had negotiated the commercial treaty with Said bin Sultan in 1839. Coupland, *East Africa and its Invaders*, pp. 480, 488–9.

119. Norsworthy was dismissed by Newman, Hunt and Christopher in 1837 and replaced by John Studdy Leigh. J. S. Leigh and J. S. Kirkman, 'The Zanzibar Diary of John Studdy Leigh', *International Journal of African Historical Studies*, 13:2 (1980), pp. 281–312 (Part 1); J. S. Leigh and J. S. Kirkman, 'The Zanzibar Diary of John Studdy Leigh', *International Journal of African Historical Studies*, 13:3 (1980), pp. 492–507 (Part 2); H. G. Marcus and M. E. Page, 'John Studdy Leigh: First Footsteps in East Africa?', *International Journal of African Historical Studies*, 5:3 (1972), pp. 470–8.

120. Coupland, *East Africa and its Invaders*, p. 493.

121. A. Sheriff, *Slaves, Spices, and Ivory in Zanzibar: Integration of an East African Commercial Empire into the World Economy, 1770–1873* (Athens, OH: Ohio University Press, 1987), pp. 98–9.

122. Duignan and Gann, *The United States and Africa*, pp. 140–4.

123. For the Zanzibar mission see J. Martineau, *The Life and Correspondence of the Right Hon. Sir Bartle Frere, Bart., G.C.B., F.R.S., etc.*, 2 vols (London: John Murray, 1895), vol. 2, pp. 65–125.

124. B. S. Cave, 'The End of Slavery in Zanzibar and British East Africa', *Journal of the Royal African Society*, 9:33 (1909), pp. 20–33.

125. Martineau, *The Life and Correspondence*, vol. 2, p. 95.

126. B. Dubins, 'Nineteenth-Century Travel Literature on the Comoro Islands: A Bibliographical Essay', *African Studies Bulletin*, 12:2 (1969), pp. 138–46; E. A. Alpers, 'A Complex Relationship: Mozambique and the Comoro Islands in the Nineteenth and Twentieth Centuries (Une relation complexe: le Mozambique et les Comores aux 19e et 20e siècles)', *Cahiers d'Études Africaines*, 41:161 (2001), pp. 73–95.

127. G. Campbell, 'Madagascar and the Slave Trade, 1810–1895', *Journal of African History*, 22:2 (1981), pp. 203–27; G. Campbell, 'Labour and the Transport Problem in Imperial Madagascar, 1810–1895', *Journal of African History*, 21:3 (1980), pp. 341–56.

128. Dubins, 'Nineteenth-Century Travel Literature'.

129. P. Colomb, *Slave Catching in the Indian Ocean* (London: Longmans, Green & Company, 1873), p. 490. This is based on a letter from Colonel Pelly in Cape Town written for the Foreign Office in October 1861 on Sunley's operations.

130. G. W. Clendennen and P. W. Nottingham, *William Sunley and David Livingstone: A Tale of Two Consuls* (Madison, WI: African Studies Program, University of Wisconsin-Madison, 2000), p. 83.

131. Ibid.

132. According to Coupland it was 6,000 acres; in 1873, however, Coupland quotes C. H. Hill, a member of the Frere Mission to Zanzibar, saying it was 700 acres. R. Coupland, *The Exploitation of East Africa, 1856–1890: The Slave Trade and the Scramble* (London: Faber and Faber, 1839), pp. 175, 177.

133. Colomb, *Slave Catching*, p. 491.

134. Clendennen and Nottingham, *William Sunley*, p. 33.

135. A. de Horsey, 'On the Comoro Islands', *Journal of the Royal Geographical Society of London*, 34 (1864), pp. 258–63.

136. Clendennen and Nottingham, *William Sunley*, pp. 54–5.

137. Sunley to Russell quoted in Coupland, *The Exploitation of East Africa*, p. 175.

138. House of Commons Debate, 15 May 1862, vol. 166, cols 1744–7, at http://hansard.millbanksystems.com/commons/1862/may/15/the-slave-trade-question#S3V0166P0_18620515_HOC_3 [accessed 18 June 2014].

139. Ibid.

140. Colomb, *Slave Catching*, p. 492.

141. Ibid., p. 493.

142. Dubins, 'Nineteenth-Century Travel Literature', p. 146; M. C. M., 'The Island Johanna', *Leisure Hour* (1876), pp. 52–5.

143. Wylde quoted in Coupland, *The Exploitation of East Africa*, pp. 177–8 (n. 2).

144. Clendennen and Nottingham, *William Sunley*, p. 56.

145. After 1844 the name Polak was changed in Kerdijk. On Lodewijk Pincoffs see B. Oosterwijk, *Ik verlang geen dank. Lodewijk Pincoffs (1827–1911)* (Rotterdam: Uitgeverij Douane, 2011).

146. Simon married Matilda da Costa (1818–91) in 1841 in the British Chaplaincy Baden-Baden (Germany). They had five children. See http://www.varrall.net/wc25/wc25_440.htm [accessed 2 February 2012]. Simon died on 5 June 1902 in Minehead, Somerset, in Great Britain.

147. C. Reinhardt and A. S. Travis, *Heinrich Caro and the Creation of Modern Chemical Industry* (Dordrecht: Kluwer Academic Publishers, 2000), p. 46.

148. *London Gazette*, January 1852.

149. H. Muller, *Muller. Een Rotterdams zeehandelaar Hendrik Muller Szn (1819–1898)* (Schiedam: Interbook International BV, 1977).

150. The firm was previously known as Victor et Louis Régis. Lynn, *Commerce and Economic Change*, pp. 141–2. Victor Régis (1803–81) and Louis Régis (1812–89) from Marseilles were traders in gum, palm oil and slaves in Gabon and on the Ivory Coast. In 1857 or 1858 the company signed a contract with the French government to transport 14,000 Africans (or 30,000, according to the *New York Times*) to the French West Indies. J. Suret-Canale,

Essays on African History: From the Slave Trade to Neo-Colonialism (London: C. Hurst & Co., London, 1988), pp. 72–3; 'The African Slave Trade; Letter from on Board the Niagara. The French Emigrant System The English "Apprentices" The Immense Profits of the Slave-trade The Slaver Erie, &c.', *New York Times*, 24 December 1860.

151. Lynn, *Commerce and Economic Change*, p. 142.

152. He additionally was able to collect African curios and some were sold to private persons, while others were given to Dutch museums. The zoo in Rotterdam (*Diergaarde Blijdorp*) received a complete West African hut in early 1861. For more on this trade see R. J. Willink, *Stages in Civilisation: Dutch Museums in Quest of West Central African Collections (1856–1889)* (Leiden: CNWS Publications, 2007).

153. Original Commission King Willem III, 10 October 1859 and Exequatur Dom Pedro of Portugal for L. P. Kerdijk, 18 November 1859, NA 2.05.01, Inv. no. 3061.

154. Copy letter Kerdijk & Pincoffs, June 1858, NA 2.05.10.12 Legatie Portugal, Inv. no. 88.

155. Investigations in 1876 by the Dutch Ministry of Foreign Affairs and the British Foreign Office revealed that no such treaty was ever signed between Great Britain and Portugal. C. B. Wells, *Bescheiden betreffende de Buitenlandse Politiek van Nederland 1848–1919* (Den Haag: Martinus Nijhoff, 1972). Tweede periode 1871–1898, tweede deel 1874–1880, pp. 334–8, 339–43, 347–51, 355–8.

156. Copy of letter Kerdijk & Pincoffs to Minister of Foreign Affairs, June 1858, NA 2.05.10.12 Legatie Portugal, Inv. no. 88.

157. Copy of letter of Minister of Foreign Affairs to Kerdijk & Pincoffs, The Hague 21 June 1858, NA 2.05.10.12 Legatie Portugal, Inv. no. 88. Negotiations between both governments took place between 1845 and 1849 and again in the mid-1850s. The Netherlands and Portugal finally signed a consular convention (3 June 1856), but only much later concluded a treaty of commerce and navigation (9 January 1875). Consular Convention of the Netherlands en Portugal, 3 June 1856 (Staatsblad 1857, no. 110).

158. Copy of letter of Kerdijk & Pincoffs to Minister of Foreign Affairs, Rotterdam, 29 September 1858, NA 2.05.10.12 Legatie Portugal, Inv. no. 88.

159. B. van Goldstein, Legatie NL te Lissabon, 22 January 1859, NA 2.05.10.12 Legatie Portugal, Inv. no. 88.

160. Netherlands Legation Lisbon to Minister of Foreign Affairs, 22 January 1859, NA 2.05.10.12 Legatie Portugal, Inv. no. 88.

161. Kerdijk & Pincoffs – BZ, 7 maart 1859, NA 2.05.01, Inv. no. 3061.

162. Min van BZ aan Jhr Heldewier, zaakgelastigde te Lissabon, 10 maart 1859, NA 2.05.10.12 Legatie Portugal, Inv. no. 88.

163. Bernardo de Sá Nogueira de Figueiredo, *Facts and Statements concerning the Right of the Crown of Portugal to the Territories of Molembo, Cabinda, Ambriz, and Other Places on the West Coast of Africa, Situated between the Fifth Degree Twelve Minutes, and the Eighth Degree of South Latitude by the Viscount de Sa da Bandeira, Lisbon 1855* (Lisbon: Herbert J. Fitch, 1877), pp. 59–73; L. Cordeiro, *Portugal and the Congo: A Statement Prepared by the African Committee of the Lisbon Geographical Society* (London: Edward Stanford, 1883), pp. 60–1.

164. See 10 april 1859, P. D. Mouchet to Legatie Lissabon, NA 2.05.10.12 Legatie Portugal, Inv. no. 88; Legatie Lissabon to Foreign Affairs, 12 April 1859, NA 2.05.01, Inv. no. 3061.

165. Copy Royal Commission (KB), 5 October 1859, appointment L. P. Kerdijk to Ambriz, Consul der Nederlanden in de Portugesche bezittingen ter Zuidwestkust van Afrika en zulks buiten kosten of bezwaar van het Rijk, NA 2.05.10.12 Legatie Portugal, Inv. no.

88; 12 October 1859, Foreign Affairs to Legatie Lissabon, NA 2.05.10.12 Legatie Portugal, Inv. no. 88; 9 december 1859, Legatie Lissabon to Kerdijk, NA 2.05.10.12 Legatie Portugal, Inv. no. 88.

166. Kerdijk to Foreign Affairs, 2 May 1860, NA 2.05.01, Inv. no. 3061.

167. Kerdijk to Foreign Affairs, 4 August 1860, NA 2.05.01, Inv. no. 3061.

168. Huntley to Kerdijk, copy 3 August 1860, NA 2.05.01, Inv. no. 3061.

169. Foreign Affairs to Kerdijk & Pincoffs, 25 September 1860, NA 2.05.01, Inv. no. 3061.

170. Kerdijk & Pincoffs to Foreign Affairs, 28 September 1860, NA 2.05.01, Inv. no. 3061.

171. Foreign Affairs to Dutch King, 5 October 1860; Honorable discharge H. P. Kerdijk; Foreign Affairs to Kerdijk, 9 October 1860, NA 2.05.01, Inv. no. 3061.

172. *AHV* to Foreign Affairs, 4 February 1870, NA 2.05.01, Inv. no. 3061.

173. Foreign Affairs to *AHV*, 11 February 1870; *AHV* to Foreign Affairs, 12 February 1870, NA 2.05.01, Inv. no. 3061.

174. R. F. Burton, *Two Trips to Gorilla Land and the Cataracts of the Congo*, 2 vols (London: Sampson Low, Marston, Low, and Searle, 1876), vol. 1, pp. 64–5.

175. Ibid., vol. 2, pp. 85–96.

176. From 1869 until 1875 the chief agent of the *AHV* was A. d'Angremond, who also acted as Dutch consul. The chief agent of the *AHV* between 1875 and 1878, A. F. H. Pape, was also the Dutch consul. In 1886, the chief agent of the successor of the *AHV*, the New African Trading Company (*NAHV*), Frederik de la Fontaine Verwey (*c.* 1856–1940), was appointed Dutch consul for the Congo Free State and received his exequatur not from Lisbon, but from Brussels.

177. The claims were based on the discovery in 1584 by Diogo Cão. Cordeiro, *Portugal and the Congo*, p. 65.

178. *Correspondence Relating to Negotiations between the Governments of Great Britain and Portugal for conclusion of the Congo Treaty: 1882–84* (London: Harrison and Sons, 1884). James F. Hutton, whose firm was very active in South-West Africa, was chairman of the Chamber of Commerce in Manchester. He wrote to the British government: 'There is not an African merchant, whether British, French, German, or Dutch, who is not strongly opposed to the annexation of the Congo and adjacent neutral territory by Portugal'. Printed leaflet of petition of the Chamber of Commerce (James F. Hutton!) in Manchester, Congo Treaty, 5 March 1884, NA 2.05.03, Inv. no. 204.

179. V. Viaene, 'King Leopold's Imperialism and the Origins of the Belgian Colonial Party, 1860–1905', *Journal of Modern History*, 80:4 (December 2008), pp. 741–90; G. Vanthemsch, *Belgium and the Congo, 1885–1980* (New York: Cambridge University Press, 2012).

180. Louis points out that Casement claimed to have planned the trip a year before and it was only accidental that it followed soon after the House of Commons debate. In fact, he received his orders for the investigation on 4 June 1903. W. R. Louis, 'Roger Casement and the Congo', *Journal of African History*, 5:1 (1964), pp. 99–120, on p. 102 (n. 31).

181. E. D. Morel, *Red Rubber: The Story of the Rubber Slave Trade which Flourished on the Congo for Twenty Years, 1890–1910*, rev. edn (1906; Manchester: National Labour Press, 1919).

182. *The Congo: A Report of the Commission of Enquiry Appointed by the Congo Free State Government. A Translation* (New York and London: G. P. Putnam's Sons, 1906).

183. R. Anstey, 'The Congo Rubber Atrocities – A Case Study', *African Historical Studies*, 4: 1 (1971), pp. 59–76, on p. 62.

184. Porter, 'Sir Roger Casement'.

WORKS CITED

Primary Sources

National Archive (NA), The Hague, The Netherlands

Ministerie van Buitenlandse Zaken: A-Dossiers, 1815–1940, nummer toegang 2.05.0, 244, Koeliehandel, 1866–1889.

Ministerie van Buitenlandse Zaken: A-Dossiers, 1815–1940, nummer toegang 2.05.0, 245, Koeliehandel Emigratie Chinezen, 1890–1904.

Ministerie van Buitenlandse Zaken, 1813–1870, nummer toegang 2.05.01, 3061, Portugese bezittingen in Afrika, 1859–1870.

Ministerie van Buitenlandse Zaken, 1813–1870, nummer toegang 2.05.01, 3065, Siam (Thailand), 1858–1868.

Ministerie van Buitenlandse Zaken: A-Dossiers, 1815–1940, nummer toegang 2.05.03, 204, A.106: Congo-aangelegenheden, 1884–1890.

Nederlands Gezantschap in Portugal (1789) 1823–1898, nummer toegang 2.05.10.12, 88, Ingekomen en minuten van uitgaande brieven betreffende de bescherming van de Nederlandse handel op de Portugese bezittingen ter Zuid-West kast van Afrika, met name in Ambris, 1858–1860, 1864.

Gezantschap in de Verenigde Staten van Amerika, 1814–1940 (1946), nummer toegang 2.05.13, 59 (1853–1855).

Gezantschap in de Verenigde Staten van Amerika, 1814–1940 (1946), nummer toegang 2.05.13, 61 (1859–1862).

Gezantschap in de Verenigde Staten van Amerika, 1814–1940 (1946), nummer toegang 2.05.13, 63 (1866–1868).

Gezantschap in de Verenigde Staten van Amerika, 1814–1940 (1946), nummer toegang 2.05.13, 62 (1863–1865).

Gezantschap in de Verenigde Staten van Amerika, 1814–1940 (1946), nummer toegang 2.05.13, 70 (1878, 1879, 1880, 1881).

Ministerie van Buitenlandse Zaken: B-dossiers, nummer toegang 2.05.38, 1.2.2.7 Siam (Thailand), 1388, Siam, 1871–1879.

Ministerie van Buitenlandse Zaken: B-dossiers, nummer toegang 2.05.38, 1.2.2.7 Siam (Thailand), 1389, Siam, 1880–1893.

Ministerie van Buitenlandse Zaken: B-dossiers, nummer toegang 2.05.38, 1326, China consuls.

The National Archives and Record Service

Despatches from United States Consuls in Sierra Leone, 1858–1906 (22 February 1858–28 March 1881) (Washington 1960), at https://archive.org/details/768331_1 [accessed 10 August 2013].

Roosevelt Study Center (RSC), Middelburg, The Netherlands

M77 Diplomatic Instructions of the Department of State, Roll 124, Dispatch no. 3, 13 March 1876.

Internet Sources

[Anon.], 'The African Slave Trade; Letter from on Board the Niagara. The French Emigrant System The English "Apprentices" The Immense Profits of the Slave-trade The Slaver Erie, &c.', *New York Times*, 24 December 1860, at http://www.nytimes.com/1860/12/24/news/african-slave-trade-letter-board-niagara-french-emigrant-system-english.html [accessed 18 July 2013].

[Anon.], 'Obituary: Rudolph C. Burlage', *New York Times*, 29 June 1883, at http://query.nytimes.com/gst/abstract.html?res=F5061EF93E5910738DDDA00A94DE405B838 4F0D3 [accessed 10 May 2013].

The Avalon Project, Documents in Law, History and Diplomacy, at http://avalon.law.yale.edu/default.asp [accessed 5 March 2012].

The Convention on Rights and Duties of States, Montevideo, 26 December 1933, at http://www.cfr.org/sovereignty/montevideo-convention-rights-duties-states/p15897 [accessed 22 February 2012].

Der Deutsche Pionier (published by Der Deutsche Pionier-Verein von Cincinnati (DPVC), 1868–1961) des 16. Jahrgangs (1884–5), pp. 206–7, at http://www.nausa.uni-oldenburg.de/pionier/frame.html [accessed 18 June 2014].

Haber, L. 'The Consul And The Samurai. The Murder of Ludwig Haber at Hakodate in 1874. P. Fraenkel', at http://ludwighaber.blogspot.nl/2007_03_01_archive.html [accessed 11 June 2014].

House of Commons Debate, 8 March 1842, Consular establishment, at

http://hansard.millbanksystems.com/commons/1842/mar/08/consular-establishment#S3 V0061P0_18420308_HOC_12 [accessed 18 June 2014].

House of Commons Debate, 15 May 1862, vol. 166, cols 1744–7, at http://hansard.millbanksystems.com/commons/1862/may/15/the-slave-trade-question# S3V0166P0_18620515_HOC_3 [accessed 18 June 2014].

House of Commons Debate, 15 May 1862, vol. 166, cols 1744–7, at http://hansard.millbanksystems.com/commons/1862/may/15/the-slave-trade-question# S3V0166P0_18620515_HOC_3 [accessed 18 June 2014].

House of Commons Debate, 3 March 1910, Written answers, at http://hansard.millbanksystems.com/written_answers/1910/mar/03/peruvian-amazon-company [accessed 18 June 2014].

House of Commons Debate, 13 June 1910, Oral answers to questions, at http://hansard. millbanksystems.com/commons/1910/jun/13/putumayo-valley-peruvian-amazon-company [accessed 18 June 2014].

Hughes, H., 'Seeing Unseeing: The Historical Amasa Delano and his Voyages', Drew Archival Library of Massachusetts, March 2010, at http://drewarchives.files.wordpress. com/2010/03/henryhughespaper.pdf [accessed 18 June 2014].

John, J., Letter Jay to Shaw, 30 January 1786, The Papers of John Jay, Columbia University Libraries, at http://wwwapp.cc.columbia.edu/ldpd/jay/item?mode=item&key=columbia. jay.01858 [accessed 18 June 2014].

—, Letter Jay to Shaw, 30 January 1786 and Reply of Shaw to Jay, 30 January 1786, The Papers of John Jay, Columbia University Libraries, at http://wwwapp.cc.columbia.edu/ldpd/ jay/item?mode=item&key=columbia.jay.01861 [accessed 18 June 2014].

London Gazette (January 1852).

Ramsay, D., Chairman of Congress, on behalf of John Hancock President, to Samuel Shaw Esq., 27 January 1786, at http://wwwapp.cc.columbia.edu/ldpd/jay/image?key=columbia. jay.01858&p=2&level=2 [accessed 18 April 2012].

Stagg, J. C. A., 'The Political Essays of William Shaler', *William and Mary Quarterly* 59:2 (2002), pp. 449–80, at http://oieahc.wm.edu/wmq/Apr02/stagg.pdf [accessed 18 June 2014].

Secondary Sources

Aalst, C. J. K. van, 'Levensbericht van Jacob Theodoor Cremer, 30 Juni 1847–14 Augustus 1923', *Jaarboek van de Maatschappij der Nederlandse Letterkunde* (1924), pp. 48–62.

Abbott, K. E., 'Geographical Notes, Taken during a Journey in Persia in 1849 and 1850', *Journal of the Royal Geographical Society of London*, 25 (1855), pp. 1–78.

Abernethy, D. B., *The Dynamics of Global Dominance: European Overseas Empires, 1415–1980* (New Haven, CT, and London: Yale University Press, 2000).

Abulafia, D., 'Pisan Commercial Colonies and Consulates in Twelfth-Century Sicily', *English Historical Review*, 93:366 (January 1978), pp. 68–81.

—, *The Great Sea: A Human History of the Mediterranean* (London: Oxford University Press, 2011).

Acemoglu, D. and J. A. Robinson, *Why Nations Fail: The Origins of Power, Prosperity, and Poverty* (London: Profile Books, 2012).

Adalbert, Prince, *Travels in the South of Europe and in Brazil: With a Voyage up the Amazon and the Xingu by His Royal Highness Prince Adalbert of Prussia* (London: David Bogue Publisher, 1849).

Adanir, F., 'Turkey's Entry into the Concert of Europe', *European Review*, 13:3 (2005), pp. 395–417.

Agstner, R., 'From Apalachicola to Wilkes-Barre: Austria(-Hungary) and its Consulates in the United States of America, 1820–1917', *Austrian History Yearbook*, 37 (2006), pp. 163–81.

Ago, R., 'The First International Communities in the Mediterranean World', *British Year Book of International Law*, 53:1 (1982), pp. 213–32.

Aldridge, A. O., *The Dragon and the Eagle: The Presence of China in the American Enlightenment* (Detroit, MI: Wayne State University Press, 1993).

Alexandrowicz, C. H., *The European–African Confrontation: A Study in Treaty Making* (Leiden: Sijthoff, 1973).

Alie, J. A. D., *A New History of Sierra Leone* (New York: St Martin's Press, 1990).

Allen, D. W., *The Institutional Revolution: Measurement and the Economic Emergence of the Modern World* (Chicago, IL, and London: The University of Chicago Press, 2012).

Allison, R. J., *The Crescent Obscured: The United States and the Muslim World 1776–1815* (Chicago, IL: The University of Chicago Press, 1995).

Alpers, E. A., 'A Complex Relationship: Mozambique and the Comoro Islands in the Nineteenth and Twentieth Centuries (Une relation complexe: le Mozambique et les Comores aux 19e et 20e siècles)', *Cahiers d'Études Africaines*, 41:161 (2001), pp. 73–95.

Amigo de las Antillas (pseud. Willem Sassen), *Het Nederlandsch Venezuelaansch incident 1875* (Typographia Belgica, 1875).

Anand, R. P., 'Review Article of Onuma Yasuaki's "When was the Law of International Society Born? – An Inquiry of the History of International Law from an Intercivilizational Perspective"', *Journal of the History of International Law*, 6:9 (2004), pp. 1–14.

Anderson, M. S., *The Rise of Modern Diplomacy, 1450–1919* (London: Longman, 1993).

Andrews, G. R., 'Spanish American Independence: A Structural Analysis', *Latin American Perspectives*, 12:1 (1985), pp. 105–32.

Annesley, G., *G. Viscount Valentia's Voyages and Travels to India, Ceylon, The Red Sea, Abyssinia and Egypt* (London: F., C., & J. Rivington, 1811).

[Anon.], 'An Act to Provide for the Reorganization of the Consular Service of the United States', *American Journal of International Law*, 1:3, Supplement: Official Documents (1907), pp. 308–13.

[Anon.], 'Obituary: The Chevalier de Colquhoun', *Gentleman's Magazine*, 199 (London: John Bowyer Nichols & Sons, October 1855), p. 435.

[Anon.], 'Obituary: J. O. Kerbey', *Bulletin of the Pan American Union*, 28 (1914), pp. 69–71.

Ansary, T., *Destiny Disrupted: A History of the World through Islamic Eyes* (New York: Basic Books, 2009).

Anstey, R., 'The Congo Rubber Atrocities – A Case Study', *African Historical Studies*, 4: 1 (1971), pp. 59–76.

Anyangwe, C., *The Secrets of an Aborted Decolonisation: The Declassified British Secret Files on the Southern Cameroons* (Langaa: Bamenda, 2010).

Armstrong Hackler, R. E., 'Our Men in the Pacific: A Chronicle of United States Consular Officers at Seven Ports in the Pacific Islands and Australasia during the Nineteenth Century' (PhD dissertation, University of Hawaii, 1978).

Arrighi, G., T. Hamashita and M. Selden (eds), *The Resurgence of East Asia: 500, 150 and 50 year Perspectives* (London and New York: Routledge, 2003).

Askew, J. B., 'Re-Visiting New Territory: The Terranova Incident Re-Examined', *Asian Studies Review*, 28 (2004), pp. 351–71.

Auslin, M. R., *Negotiating with Imperialism: The Unequal Treaties and the Culture of Japanese Diplomacy* (Cambridge, MA: Harvard University Press, 2004).

Baepler, P. M. (ed.), *White Slaves, African Masters: An Anthology of American Barbary Captivity Narratives* (Chicago, IL: University of Chicago Press, 1999).

Bandinel, J., *Some Account of the Trade in Slaves from Africa as Connected with Europe and America* (London: Longman, Brown & Co., 1842).

Barbour, V., 'Consular Service in the Reign of Charles II', *American Historical Review*, 33:3 (1928), pp. 553–78.

Barclay, T., *Selections from the Correspondence of Thomas Barclay, Formerly British Consul-General at New York*, ed. G. Lockhart Rives (New York: Harper & Brothers, 1894).

Barnes, J., *Commodore Bainbridge: From the Gunroom to the Quarter-Deck* (New York: D. Appleton and Company, 1897).

Baron, S., 'The Jews and the Syrian Massacres of 1860', *Proceedings of the American Academy for Jewish Research*, 4 (1932–3), pp. 3–31.

—, 'Great Britain and Damascus Jewry in 1860–61 an Archival Study', *Jewish Social Studies*, 2:2 (1940), pp. 179–208.

Batson, B. A., 'American Diplomats in Southeast Asia in the Nineteenth Century: The Case of Siam', *Journal of the Siam Society*, 64 (1978), pp. 39–112.

Beasley, W. G., *Select Documents on Japanese Foreign Policy, 1853–1868* (London: Oxford University Press, 1967, reprint).

Beaufort, W. H. de, 'Twee rapporten over het consulaatwezen', *De Economist*, 52 (1904), pp. 5–21.

Becker, B., 'The Merchant-Consuls of German States in China, Hong Kong and Macao (1787–1872)', in J. Ulbert and L. Prijac (eds), *Consuls et services consulaires au XIXème siècle – Die Welt der Konsulate im 19. Jahrhundert – Consulship in the Nineteenth Century* (Hamburg: DOBU, Dokumentation & Buch, 2009), pp. 329–52.

Bekkaoui, K., *White Women Captives in North Africa: Narratives of Enslavement, 1735–1830* (Basingstoke: Palgrave Macmillan, 2010).

Beneke, O., 'Mordtmann, Andreas David', *Allgemeine Deutsche Biographie*, herausgegeben von der Historischen Kommission bei der Bayerischen Akademie der Wissenschaften, Vol. 22 (1885), p. 219.

Bennett, N. R. and G. E. Brooks (eds), *New England Merchants in Africa: A History through Documents 1802–1865* (Boston, MA: Boston University Press, 1965).

Beolens, B., M. Watkins and M. Grayson, *The Eponym Dictionary of Reptiles* (Baltimore, MD: The Johns Hopkins University Press, 2011).

Berg, I. B. von, *Die Entwicklung des Konsularwesens im Deutschen Reich von 1871–1914 unter besonderen Berücksichtigung der außenhandelsfördernden Funktionen dieses Dienstes* (Cologne: Hundt Druck, 1995).

Berridge, G. R., *British Diplomacy in Turkey, 1583 to the Present: A Study in the Evolution of the Resident Embassy* (Leiden: Martinus Nijhoff, 2009).

Berwanger, E. H., *The British Foreign Service and the American Civil War* (Lexington, KY: The University Press of Kentucky, 1994).

Bethell, L., 'The Mixed Commissions for the Suppression of the Transatlantic Slave Trade in the Nineteenth Century', *Journal of African History*, 7:1 (1966), pp. 79–93.

—, 'The Independence of Brazil and the Abolition of the Brazilian Slave Trade: Anglo-Brazilian Relations, 1822–1826', *Journal of Latin American Studies*, 1:2 (1969), pp. 115–47.

—, *The Abolition of the Brazilian Slave Trade: Britain, Brazil and the Slave Trade Question 1807–1869* (Cambridge: Cambridge University Press, 1970).

Bevans, C. I. (comp.), *Treaties and other International Agreements of the United States, 1776–1949*, 13 vols (Washington, DC: Department of State Publication, 1968–76).

Bhacker, M. R., *Trade and Empire in Muscat and Zanzibar: Roots of British Domination* (London and New York: Routledge, 1992).

Bhagat, G., 'America's Commercial and Consular Relations with India, 1784–1860' (PhD dissertation, Yale University, 1963).

Bhatt, C. G., 'India and Africa Unique Historical Bonds and Present Prospects, with Special Reference to Kutchis in Zanzibar', Working Paper: No. 5, University of Mumbai, Centre for African Studies (2008).

Black, J., *British Diplomats and Diplomacy 1688–1800* (Exeter: University of Exeter Press, 2001).

Blussé, L., *Visible Cities: Canton, Nagasaki, and Batavia and the Coming of the Americans* (Cambridge, MA: Harvard University Press, 2008).

—, 'Sinologists (1854–1911)', in W. I. Idema (ed.), *Chinese Studies in the Netherlands: Past, Present and Future* (Leiden: Brill, 2014), pp. 27–69.

Blussé, L. and F. van Luyn, *China en de Nederlanders. Geschiedenis van de Nederlands-Chinese betrekkingen 1600–2007* (Zutphen: Walburg Pers, 2008).

Bond, P., 'Letters of Phineas Bond, British Consul at Philadelphia, to the Foreign Office of Great Britain, 1787, 1788, 1789', *Annual Report of the American Historical Association for the Year 1896 in Two Volumes. Report of the Historical Manuscripts Commission of the American Historical Association* (Washington, DC: Government Printing Office, 1897), pp. 532–4.

Bonham Jr, M. L., *The British Consuls in the Confederacy* (New York: Columbia University, 1911).

Bouânani, M. A., 'Propaganda for Empire: Barbary Captivity Literature in the US', *Journal of Transatlantic Studies*, 7:4 (2009), pp. 399–412.

Bowden, B., 'The Colonial Origins of International Law: European Expansion and the Classical Standard of Civilization', *Journal of the History of International Law*, 7 (2005), pp. 1–23.

Breman, J., *Taming the Coolie Beast: Plantation Society and the Colonial Order in Southeast Asia* (Delhi: Oxford University Press, 1989).

Broder, A., 'French Consular Reports', *Business History*, 23:3 (1981), pp. 279–83.

Broeze, F. (ed.), *Brides of the Sea: Port Cities of Asia from the Sixteenth–Twentieth Centuries* (Kensington: New South Wales University Press, 1989).

Brooks Jr, G. E., *Yankee Traders, Old Coasters and African Middlemen: A History of American Legitimate Trade with West Africa in the Nineteenth Century* (Boston, MA: Boston University Press, 1970).

Broughton, E., *Six Years Residence in Algiers* (Edinburgh: H. & J. Pillans, 1839).

Brown, P. M., *Foreigners in Turkey: Their Juridical Status* (Princeton, NJ: Princeton University Press, 1914).

Browne, J. R., *Etchings of a Whaling Cruise, with Notes of a Sojourn on the Island Zanzibar to which is Appended a Brief History of Whale Fishery, its Past and Present Condition* (New York: Harper & Brothers Publishers, 1846).

Brusse, A. T., *Curaçao en zijne bewoners* (Curaçao: Internationale Drukkerij, 1882), pp. 139–44.

Bull, H. and A. Watson (eds), *The Expansion of International Society* (Oxford: Clarendon Press, 1984).

Burton, R. F., *Zanzibar: City, Island and Coast*, 2 vols (London: Tinsley Brothers, 1872).

—, *Two Trips to Gorilla Land and the Cataracts of the Congo*, 2 vols (London: Sampson Low, Marston, Low, and Searle, 1876).

Buzan, B. and R. Little, *International Systems in World History: Remaking the Study of International Relations* (Oxford: Oxford University Press, 2000).

Byrd, P., 'Regional and Functional Specialisation in the British Consular Service', *Journal of Contemporary History*, 7:1/2 (1972), pp. 128–45.

Campbell, G., 'Labour and the Transport Problem in Imperial Madagascar, 1810–1895', *Journal of African History*, 21:3 (1980), pp. 341–56.

—, 'Madagascar and the Slave Trade, 1810–1895', *Journal of African History*, 22:2 (1981), pp. 203–27.

Canney, D. L., *Africa Squadron: The US Navy and the Slave Trade, 1842–1861* (Washington, DC: Potomac Books Inc., 2006).

Cantor, M., 'A Connecticut Yankee in a Barbary Court: Joel Barlow's Algerian Letters to his Wife', *William and Mary Quarterly*, 19:1 (1962), pp. 86–109.

—, 'Joel Barlow's Mission to Algiers', *Historian*, 25:2 (1963), pp. 172–94.

Carhart, E. R., 'The New York Produce Exchange', *Annals of the American Academy of Political and Social Science*, 38:2 (1911), pp. 206–21.

Carr, W. J., 'American Consular Service', *American Journal of International Law*, 1 (1907), pp. 891–913, on p. 895.

Cathcart, J. L., *The Captives: By James Leander Cathcart, Eleven Years a Prisoner in Algiers*, comp. J. B. Newkirk (LaPorte, Herald Print, 1899).

Cave, B. S., 'The End of Slavery in Zanzibar and British East Africa', *Journal of the Royal African Society*, 9:33 (1909), pp. 20–33.

Chandler, C. L., 'United States Merchant Ships in the Rio de La Plata (1801–1808), as shown by Early Newspapers', *Hispanic American Historical Review*, 2:1 (1919), pp. 26–54.

—, 'United States Shipping in the La Plata Region, 1809–1810', *Hispanic American Historical Review*, 3:2 (1920), pp. 159–76.

—, 'The Life of Joel Roberts Poinsett', *Pennsylvania Magazine of History and Biography*, 59:1 (1935), pp. 1–32.

Chandler, D. P., 'Cambodja's Relations with Siam in the Early Bangkok Period: The Politics of a Tributary State', *Journal of the Siam Society*, 60:1 (1972), pp. 153–70.

Chang, R. T., *The Justice of the Western Consular Courts in Nineteenth-Century Japan* (Westport, CT: Greenwood Press, 1984).

Chang, T., 'Malacca and the Failure of the First Portuguese Embassy to Peking', *Journal of Southeast Asian History*, 3:2 (1962), pp. 50–3.

Chase-Dunn, C., Y. Kawano and B. D. Brewer, 'Trade Globalization since 1795: Waves of Integration in the World-System', *American Sociological Review*, 65:1 (2000), pp. 77–95.

Chen, L., 'Universalism and Equal Sovereignty as Contested Myths of International Law in the Sino-Western Encounter', *Journal of the History of International Law*, 13 (2011), pp. 75–116.

Clendennen, G. W. and P. W. Nottingham, *William Sunley and David Livingstone: A Tale of Two Consuls* (Madison, WI: African Studies Program, University of Wisconsin-Madison, 2000).

Clulow, A., *The Company and the Shogun: The Dutch Encounter with the Tokugawa in Japan* (New York: Columbia University Press, 2014).

Cohn, R. L., 'The Transition from Sail to Steam in Immigration to the United States', *Journal of Economic History*, 65:2 (2005), pp. 469–95.

Colley, L., *Captives: Britain, Empire and the World 1600–1850* (London: Jonathan Cape, 2002).

Colomb, P., *Slave Catching in the Indian Ocean* (London: Longmans, Green & Company, 1873).

The Congo: A Report of the Commission of Enquiry Appointed by the Congo Free State Government: A Translation (New York and London: G. P. Putnam's Sons, 1906).

Cordeiro, L., *Portugal and the Congo: A Statement Prepared by the African Committee of the Lisbon Geographical Society* (London: Edward Stanford, 1883).

Cordier, H., 'Américains et Français à Canton au XVIIIe siècle', *Journal de la Société des Américanistes*, 2 (1898), pp. 1–13.

Correspondence of the Department of State in Relation to the British Consuls Resident in the Confederate States (Richmond: Sentinel Office, 1863).

Correspondence Relating to Negotiations between the Governments of Great Britain and Portugal for Conclusion of the Congo Treaty: 1882–84 (London: Harrison and Sons, 1884).

Correspondence Respecting the Treatment of British Colonial Subjects and Native Indians Employed in the Collection of Rubber in the Putumayo District, Presented to both Houses of Parliament by Command of His Majesty, July 1912 (London: Harrison and Sons, 1912).

Coupland, R., *The Exploitation of East Africa 1856–1890: The Slave Trade and the Scramble* (London: Faber and Faber, 1839).

—, *East Africa and its Invaders: From the Earliest Times to the Death of Seyyid Said in 1856* (Oxford: Clarendon Press, 1938).

Cox, H. B., 'Reasons for Joel R. Poinsett's Refusal of a Second Mission to South America', *Hispanic American Historical Review*, 43:3 (1963), pp. 405–8.

Cox, I. J., 'Monroe and the Early Mexican Revolutionary Agents', *American Historical Association Annual Register*, 1 (1911), pp. 199–215.

Coyle, J. F., 'The Treaty of Friendship, Commerce, and Navigation in the Modern Era', *Columbia Journal of Transnational Law*, 51 (2013), pp. 302–60.

Crawford Campbell, P., *Chinese Coolie Emigration to Countries within the British Empire* (1923; London: King Publication, 1971).

Cullen, L. M., *A History of Japan, 1582–1941: Internal and External Worlds* (Cambridge: Cambridge University Press, 2003).

Cunha, H. De Mendonha e, 'The 1820 Land Concession to the Portuguese', *Journal of the Siam Society*, 59:2 (1971), pp. 145–50.

Curtin, P. D., *The World and the West: The European Challenge and the Overseas Response in the Age of Empire* (Cambridge: Cambridge University Press, 2000), pp. 19–37.

Davis, R. C., 'Counting European Slaves on the Barbary Coast', *Past & Present*, 172 (2001), pp. 87–124.

Delano, A., *A Narrative of Voyages and Travels in the Northern and Southern Hemispheres: Comprising Three Voyages Round the World; Together with a Voyage of Survey and Discovery in the Pacific Ocean and Oriental Islands* (Boston, MA: E. G., House, 1817).

Deng, G., *Maritime Sector, Institutions, and Sea Power of Premodern China* (Westport, CT: Greenwood Press, 1999).

Dennett, T., *Americans in Eastern Asia: A Critical Study of the Policy of the United States with Reference to China, Japan and Korea in the Nineteenth Century* (New York: Octagon Books, 1979).

Deringil, S., '"The Armenian Question is Finally Closed": Mass Conversions of Armenians in Anatolia during the Hamidian Massacres of 1895–1897', *Comparative Studies in Society and History*, 51:2 (2009), pp. 344–71.

Dike, K. O., 'John Beecroft, 1790–1854. Her Britannic Majesty's Consul to the Bights of Benin and Biafra 1849–1854', *Journal of the Historical Society of Nigeria*, 1:1 (1956), pp. 5–15.

—, *Trade and Politics in the Niger Delta 1830–1885: An Introduction to the Economic and Political History of Nigeria* (Westport, CT: Greenwood Press, 1956).

The Diplomatic Correspondence of the United States from the Signing of the Definitive Treaty of Peace, 10 September, 1783, to the Adoption of the Constitution, March 4, 1789, 3 vols (New York: Blair & Rives, 1837).

Dodge, W. P., *The Real Richard Burton* (London: T. Fisher Unwin, 1907).

Dolin, E. J., *When America First Met China* (New York and London: Liveright, 2012).

Dongen, F. van, *Tussen Neutraliteit en Imperialisme: De Nederlands-Chinese Betrekkingen van 1863 tot 1901* (Groningen: Wolters, 1966).

—, 'The Cautious Imperialists', in J. W. Schulte Nordholt and D. van Arkel (eds), *Acta Historiae Neerlandica*, 4 (Leiden: Brill, 1970), p. 146–70.

Douwes, D., *The Ottomans in Syria: A History of Justice and Oppression* (London and New York: I. B. Taurus, 2000).

Downs, J. M., 'A Study in Failure – Hon Samuel Snow', *Rhode Island History*, 25:1 (1966), pp. 1–9.

Dozer, D. M., 'Secretary of State Elihu Root and Consular Reorganization', *Mississippi Valley Historical Review*, 29:3 (1942), pp. 339–50.

Dubins, B., 'Nineteenth-Century Travel Literature on the Comoro Islands: A Bibliographical Essay', *African Studies Bulletin*, 12:2 (1969), pp. 138–46.

Dubois, C., 'The Red Sea Ports during the Revolution in Transportation, 1800–1914', in L. T. Fawaz and C. A. Bayly (eds), *Modernity and Culture: From the Mediterranean to the Indian Ocean* (New York: Columbia University Press, 2002), pp. 58–75.

Duignan, P. and L. H. Gann, *The United States and Africa: A History* (Cambridge: Cambridge University Press, 1987).

Dunne, T., 'The English School', in C. Reus-Smith and D. Snidal (eds), *The Oxford Handbook of International Relations* (Oxford: Oxford University Press, 2008), pp. 267–86.

Dursteler, E., 'The Bailo in Constantinople: Crisis and Career in Venice's Early Modern Diplomatic Corps', *Mediterranean Historical Review*, 16:2 (2001), pp. 1–30.

Dyck, E. A. van, *Capitulations of the Ottoman Empire: Report of Edward A. van Dyck, Consular Clerk of the United States at Cairo* (Washington, DC: Government Printing Office, 1881).

Dyer, G. B. and C. L. Dyer, 'A Century of Strategic Intelligence Reporting: Mexico, 1822–1919', *Geographical Review*, 44:1 (1954), pp. 49–69.

Eberstein, B., *Preußen und China. Eine Geschichte schwieriger Beziehungen* (Berlin: Duncker & Humblot, 2007).

Ekeh, P. P. (ed.), *Warri City: And British Colonial Rule in Western Niger Delta* (Buffalo, NY: Urhobo Historical Society, 2004).

Emrence, C., 'Three Waves of Late Ottoman Historiography, 1950–2007', *Middle East Studies Association Bulletin*, 41:2 (2007), pp. 137–51.

Etemad, B., *Possessing the World: Taking the Measurements of Colonisation from the Eighteenth to the Twentieth Century* (New York and Oxford: Berghahn Books, 2007).

Evans, P. and T. P. Govan, 'A Belgian Consul on Conditions in the South in 1860 and 1862', *Journal of Southern History*, 3:4 (1937), pp. 478–91.

Fairbank, J. K., *Trade and Diplomacy on the China Coast: The Opening of the Treaty Ports, 1842–1854* (Stanford, CA: Stanford University Press, 1969).

—, 'Introduction: Patterns and Problems', in E. R. May and J. K. Fairbank (eds), *America's China Trade in Historical Perspective: The Chinese and American Performance* (Cambridge, MA: Harvard University Press, 1986), pp. 1–11.

Faroqhi, S., *The Ottoman Empire and the World around it* (London: I. B. Taurus, 2004).

Farouk Shaeik Ahmad, O., 'Muslims in the Kingdom of Ayutthaya', *Jebat: Malaysian Journal of History, Politics and Strategic Studies*, 10 (1980), pp. 206–14.

Fatah-Black, K., 'The Patriot coup d'état in Curaçao, 1796', in W. Klooster and G. Oostindie (eds), *Curaçao in the Age of Revolutions, 1795–1800* (Leiden: KITLV Press, 2011), pp. 123–41.

Fausto, B., *A Concise History of Brazil* (Cambridge: Cambridge University Press, 1999).

Fawaz, L., 'Amīr 'abd al-Qādir and the Damascus "Incident" in 1860', in B. Marino (ed.), *Études dur les villes du Proche-Orient XVIe–XIXe siècles. Hommage à André Raymond* (Damas: Presses de l'Ifpo, 2001), pp. 263–72.

Fiebig, E. S., 'The Consular Service of the Hansa Towns Lübeck, Bremen and Hamburg in the Nineteenth Century', in Ulbert and Prijac (eds), *Consuls et services consulaires*, pp. 248–61.

Figueiredo, B. de Sá Nogueira de, *Facts and Statements concerning the Right of the Crown of Portugal to the Territories of Molembo, Cabinda, Ambriz, and Other Places on the West Coast of Africa, Situated between the Fifth Degree Twelve Minutes, and the Eighth Degree of South Latitude by the Viscount de Sa da Bandeira, Lisbon 1855* (Lisbon: Herbert J. Fitch, 1877).

Feifer, G., *Breaking Open Japan: Commodore Perry, Lord Abe, and American Imperialism in 1853* (New York: Harper Collins, 2006).

Ferguson, E. J., 'Business, Government, and Congressional Investigation in the Revolution', *William and Mary Quarterly*, 16:3 (1959), pp. 293–318.

Ferguson, J. H., *A Philosophy of Civilizations: A Sociological Study* (London: W. B. Whittingham & Co., 1889).

Ferguson, N., *Civilization: The West and the Rest* (London: Allen Lane, 2011).

Ferrez, G., *Saudades do Rio de Janeiro* (Rio de Janeiro: Co. Ed. Nacional, 1957).

Feys, T., 'The Battle for the Migrants: The Evolution from Port to Company Competition, 1840–1914', in T. Feys et al. (eds), *Maritime Transport and Migration: The Connections between Maritime and Migration Networks* (St John's: International Maritime Economic History Association, 2007), pp. 27–49.

Fichter, J. R., *So Great a Profit: How the East Indies Trade Transformed Anglo-American Capitalism* (Cambridge, MA: Harvard University Press, 2010).

Fleet, K., *European and Islamic Trade in the Early Ottoman State: The Merchants of Genoa and Turkey* (Cambridge: Cambridge University Press, 1999).

Fletcher, M. E., 'The Suez Canal and World Shipping, 1869–1914', *Journal of Economic History*, 18:4 (1958), pp. 556–73.

Fletcher, R., *The Cross and the Cresent: Christianity and Islam from Muhammad to the Reformation* (New York: Penguin, 2003).

Fogel, J. A., *Articulating the Sinosphere: Sino-Japanese Relations in Space and Time* (Cambridge, MA: Harvard University Press 2009).

François, J. P. A., 'Twee Nederlandse volkenrechtschrijvers uit de 19e eeuw', *Netherlands International Law Review*, 13:1 (1966), pp. 29–33.

Fyfe, C., *A History of Sierra Leone* (Oxford: Oxford University Press, 1962).

Garrett, V. M., *Heaven is High, the Emperor is Far Away: Merchants and Mandarins in Old Canton* (New York: Oxford University Press, 2002).

Geary, W. N. M., *Nigeria under British Rule* (London: Frank Cass & Co Ltd, 1965).

Gilbert, W., 'Our Man in Zanzibar: Richard Waters, American Consul (1837–1845)' (BA dissertation, Wesleyan University, 2011).

Gildemeister, M. H., *Ein Hanseat in Japan 1859–1868, bearb. von Maria Möring* (Hamburg: Verlag Hanseatischer Merkur, 1993).

Gilderhus, M. T., 'The Monroe Doctrine: Meanings and Implications', *Presidential Studies Quarterly*, 36:1 (2006), pp. 5–16.

Goding, F. W., *A Brief History of the American Consulate General at Guayaquil, Ecuador* (Livermore Falls: The Advertiser Press, 1920).

Godsall, J. R., *The Tangled Web: A Life of Sir Richard Burton* (De Montfort Mews: Troubador Publishing Ltd, 2008).

Goey, F. de, 'The Business of Consuls; Consuls and Businessmen', Paper for the 14th Annual Conference of the EBHA 2010, The Centre for Business History, University of Glasgow, 2010.

Gofman, D., 'Negotiating with the Renaissance State: The Ottoman Empire and the New Diplomacy', in V. H. Aksan and D. Gofman (eds), *The Early Modern Ottomans: Remapping the Empire* (New York: Cambridge University Press, 2007), pp. 61–84.

Goodman, J., *The Devil and Mr Casement: One Man's Struggle for Human Rights in South America's Heart of Darkness* (London: Verso, 2009).

Gordon, A., *A Modern History of Japan: From Tokugawa Times to the Present*, 2nd edn (New York and Oxford: Routledge, 2009).

Goslinga, C. C., *The Dutch in the Caribbean and in Surinam 1791/5–1942* (Assen: Van Gorcum, 1990).

Goswami, C., *The Call of the Sea: Kachchhi Traders in Muscat and Zanzibar, c. 1800–1880* (Hyderabad: Orient BlackSwan, 2011).

Greif, A., 'Reputation and Coalitions in Medieval Trade: Evidence on the Maghribi Traders', *Journal of Economic History*, 49 (1989), pp. 857–82.

—, 'Contract Enforceability and Economic Institutions in Early Trade: The Maghribi Traders' Coalition', *American Economic Review*, 83:3 (1993), pp. 525–48

—, 'History Lessons. The Birth of Impersonal Exchange: The Community Responsibility System and Impartial Justice', *Journal of Economic Perspectives*, 20:2 (2006), pp. 221–36.

Griffin, E., *Clippers and Consuls: American Consular and Commercial Relations with Eastern Asia, 1845–1860* (Ann Arbor, MI: Edwards Bros., 1938).

Groot, A. H. de, *Nederland en Turkije. Zeshonderd jaar politieke, economische en culturele contacten* (Leiden: Nederlands Instituut voor het Nabije Oosten, 1986).

Groot, J. J. M. de, 'Levensbericht van Prof. Dr. J. J. M. de Groot', *Handelingen en mededeelingen van de Maatschappij der Nederlandsche Letterkunde te Leiden, over het jaar 1921–1922* (Leiden: E. J. Brill, 1922), pp. 1–17.

Gunning, L. P., *The British Consular Service in the Aegean and the Collection of Antiquities for the British Museum* (Farnham: Ashgate, 2009).

Hall, K. R., 'Sojourning Communities, Ports-of-Trade, and Commercial Networking in Southeast Asia's Eastern Regions, c. 1000–1400', in M. A. Aung-Thwin and K. R. Hall,

New Perspectives on the History and Historiography of Southeast Asia: Continuing Explorations (London and New York: Routledge, 2011), pp. 56–74.

Halls, J. J., *The Life and Correspondence of Henry Salt, Esq., F.R.S. &c. His Britannic Majesty's Late Consul-General in Egypt*, 2 vols (London: Richard Bentley, 1834).

Halvorson, D., 'Prestige, Prudence and Public Opinion in the 1882 British Occupation of Egypt', *Australian Journal of Politics and History*, 56:3 (2010), pp. 423–40.

Hamashita, T., 'Tribute and Treaties: East Asian Treaty Ports Networks in the Era of Negotiation, 1834–1894', *European Journal of East Asian Studies*, 1:1 (2002), pp. 59–87.

—, 'Tribute and Treaties: Maritime Asia and Treaty Port Networks in the Era of Negotiations, 1800–1900', in G. Arrighi, T. Hamashita and M. Selden (eds), *The Resurgence of East Asia: 500, 150 and 50 Year Perspectives* (London and New York: Routledge, 2003), pp. 17–50.

—, *China, East Asia and the Global Economy: Regional and Historical Perspectives* (New York: Routledge, 2008).

Hamel, W. N. van, 'Ons Consulaat-wezen', *De Economist*, 29 (1876), pp. 1119–28.

Hammersmith, J. L., *Spoilsmen in a 'Flowery Fairyland': The Development of the US Legation in Japan, 1859–1906* (Kent, OH: Kent State University Press, 1998).

Hao, Y., 'Chinese Teas to America – A Synopsis', in E. R. May and J. K. Fairbank (eds), *America's China Trade in Historical Perspective: The Chinese and American Performance* (Cambridge, MA: Harvard University Press, 1986), pp. 11–33.

Hardenburg, W. E., *The Putumayo, the Devil's Paradise; Travels in the Peruvian Amazon Region and an Account of the Atrocities Committed upon the Indians Therein* (London: T. F. Unwin, 1912).

Harris, T., *The Life and Services of Commodore William Bainbridge, United States Navy* (Philadelphia, PA: Carey, Lea & Blanchard, 1837).

Harris, T., *The Complete Journal of Townsend Harris: First American Consul and Minister to Japan*, ed. M. E. Cosenza, rev. edn (Rutland: Charles E. Tuttle Company, 1959).

Harris, W. L., 'The Reluctant Diplomacy of Jose Maria Rojas, 1873–1883' (PhD dissertation, University of Florida, 1973).

Hartog, J., *US Consul in Nineteenth-Century Curaçao: The Life and Works of Leonard Burlington Smith*, 2nd edn (Aruba: VAD, 1971).

Heine, P., 'Das Rohlfs/Wetzstein-Unternehmen in Tunis während des deutsch-französischen Krieges 1870/71', *Die Welt des Islams New Series*, 22:1/4 (1982), pp. 61–6.

Herring, G. C., *From Colony to Superpower: US Foreign Relations since 1776* (New York: Oxford University Press, 2008), pp. 153–5.

Heusken, H., *Japan Journal 1855–1861*, trans. and ed. J. C. van der Corput and R. A. Wilson (New Brunswick, NJ: Rutgers University Press, 1964).

Hibbert, A. B., 'Catalan Consulates in the Thirteenth Century', *Cambridge Historical Journal*, 9:3 (1949), pp. 352–8.

Hoare, J. E., *Japan's Treaty Ports and Foreign Settlements: The Uninvited Guests, 1858–1899* (Sandgate: Japan Library, 1994).

Holan, J., *Travels in Madeira Sierra Leone, Teneriffe, St. Jago, Cape Coast, Fernando Po, Princes Island, etc. etc.*, 2nd edn (London: George Routledge, 1840).

Hongsheng, C. and L. Blussé (eds), *Sailing to the Pearl River: Dutch Enterprise in South China 1600–2000* (Guangzhou: Guangzhou Publishing House, 2004).

Honjo, Y. A., *Japan's Early Experience of Contract Management in the Treaty Ports* (London: Japan Library, 2003).

Hoogenboom, A., *Outlawing the Spoils: A History of the Civil Service Reform Movement 1865–1883* (Chicago, IL, and London: University of Illinois Press, 1968).

Horsey, A. de, 'On the Comoro Islands', *Journal of the Royal Geographical Society of London*, 34 (1864), pp. 258–63.

Hourani, A., *A History of the Arab Peoples* (New York: Warner Books, 1991).

Howard, A. M., 'Nineteenth-Century Coastal Slave Trading and the British Abolition Campaign in Sierra Leone', *Slavery & Abolition: A Journal of Slave and Post-Slave Studies*, 27:1 (2006), pp. 23–49.

Hsu, I. C. Y., *The Rise of Modern China* (Oxford: Oxford University Press, 1999).

Huber, V., 'The Unification of the Globe by Disease? The International Sanitary Conferences on Cholera, 1851–1894', *Historical Journal*, 49:2 (2006), pp. 453–76.

Huhn, I., *Johann Gottfried Wetzstein, als preußischer Konsul in Damaskus (1849–1861), dargestellt nach seinen hinterlassen Papieren* (Berlin: Klaus Schwarz Verlag, 1989).

Hurewitz, J. C., 'Ottoman Diplomacy and the European State System', *Middle East Journal*, 15:2 (1961), pp. 141–52.

Inalcik, H. and D. Quataert (eds), *An Economic and Social History of the Ottoman Empire, Volume 2: 1600–1914* (Cambridge: Cambridge University Press, 1994).

Inikori, J. E., 'Africa and the Trans-Atlantic Slave Trade', in T. Falola (ed.), *Africa*, 2 vols (Durham, NC: Carolina Academic Press, 2003).

Irwin, G. W., 'Precolonial African Diplomacy: The Example of Asante', *International Journal of African Historical Studies*, 8:1 (1975), pp. 81–96.

Iseminger, G., 'The Old Turkish Hands: The British Levantine Consuls, 1856–1876', *Middle East Journal*, 22 (1968), pp. 297–316.

Ishhi, Y., 'Seventeenth-Century Japanese Documents about Siam', *Journal of the Siam Society*, 59:2 (1971), pp. 161–74.

Israeli, R., 'Consul de France in Mid-Nineteenth-Century China', *Modern Asian Studies*, 23:4 (1989), pp. 671–703.

—, 'Diplomacy of Contempt: The French Consuls and the Mandarins in Nineteenth-Century China', *Modern Asian Studies*, 26:2 (1992), pp. 363–94.

Itoh, M., *Globalization of Japan: Japanese Sakuko Mentality and US Efforts to Open Japan* (New York: St Martin's Press, 1998).

Jackson Haight, M. V., *European Powers and South-East Africa. A Study of International Relations on the South-East Coast of Africa 1796–1856* (New York: Frederick A. Praeger, 1967).

Jamieson, R., *Commerce with Africa, with Suggestions for the Development of the Commercial Resources of Western Central Africa* (London: Effingham Wilson, 1859).

Jansen, M. B., *China in the Tokugawa World* (Cambridge, MA, and London: Harvard University Press, 1992).

Jensen, D. L., 'The Ottoman Turks in Sixteenth-Century French Diplomacy', *Sixteenth Century Journal*, 16:4 (1985), pp. 451–70.

Johnson, D. D. with G. D. Best, *The United States in the Pacific: Private Interests and Public Policies, 1784–1899* (Westport, CT: Praeger, 1995).

Johnson, E. R., 'The Early History of the United States Consular Service. 1776–1792', *Political Science Quarterly*, 13:1 (1898), pp. 19–40.

Johnson, J. J., *A Hemisphere Apart: The Foundations of United States Policy toward Latin America* (Baltimore, MD, and London: The Johns Hopkins University Press, 1990).

Jones, E., *The European Miracle: Environments, Economies and Geopolitics in the History of Europe and Asia*, 3rd edn (Cambridge: Cambridge University Press, 2003).

Jones, G., *The Evolution of International Business: An Introduction* (London and New York; Routledge, 1996).

—, *Multinationals and Global Capitalism: From the Nineteenth to the Twenty-First Century* (Oxford: Oxford University Press, 2005).

Jones-Bos, R. and M. van Daalen, 'Trends and Developments in Consular Services: The Dutch Experience', *Hague Journal of Diplomacy*, 3 (2008), pp. 87–92.

Jordaan, H., 'Patriots, Privateers and International Politics: The Myth of the Conspiracy of Jean Baptiste Tierce Cadet', in Klooster and Oostindie (eds), *Curaçao in the Age of Revolutions, 1795–1800*, pp. 141–71.

Kandori, M., 'Social Norms and Community Enforcement', *Review of Economic Studies*, 59:1 (1992), pp. 63–80.

Kang, D. C., *East Asia before the West: Five Centuries of Trade and Tribute* (New York: Columbia University Press, 2010).

Kargbo, I., 'The US Consulate and the Promotion of Trade in Sierra Leone, 1859–1880', in A. Jalloh and T. Falola (eds), *The United States and West Africa: Interactions and Relations* (Rochester, NY: University of Rochester Press, 2008), pp. 38–61.

Kark, R., *American Consuls in the Holy Land 1832–1914* (Jerusalem: The Magnes Press, 1994).

Kasaba, R., *The Ottoman Empire and the World Economy; The Nineteenth Century* (New York: State University of New York Press, 1988).

Kayaoglu, T., 'Westphalian Eurocentrism in International Relations Theory', *International Studies Review*, 12 (2010), pp. 193–217.

Keeling, A. A., 'The Business of Transatlantic Migration between Europe and the United States of America, 1900–1914' (PhD dissertation, University of California, 2005).

Keliher, M., 'Anglo-American Rivalry and the Origins of US China Policy', *Diplomatic History*, 32:2 (2007), pp. 227–58.

Kennedy, C. S., *The American Consul: A History of the United States Consular Service, 1776–1914* (New York: Greenwood Press, 1990).

Kerbey, J. O., *The Land of To-morrow: A Newspaper Exploration up the Amazon and over the Andes to the California of South America* (New York: W. F. Brainard, 1906).

—, *An American Consul in Amazonia* (New York: William Edwin Rudge Press, 1911).

Kersten, A. E. and B. van der Zwan, 'The Dutch Consular Service in the Nineteenth Century', in Ulbert and Prijac (eds), *Consuls et services consulaires*, pp. 413–22.

—, 'The Dutch Consular Service: In the Interests of a Colonial and Commercial Nation', in J. Melissen and A. M. Fernández (eds), *Consular Affairs and Diplomacy* (Leiden and Boston, MA: Martinus Nijhoff Publishers, 2011), pp. 275–302.

Kiewiet de Jonge, H. J., 'Levensbericht van J. R. Planten', *Jaarboek van de Maatschappij der Nederlandse Letterkunde* (Leiden: E. J. Brill, 1914), pp. 152–4.

Kitzen, M., 'Money Bags or Cannon Balls: The Origins of the Tripolitan War, 1795–1801', *Journal of the Early Republic*, 16:4 (1996), pp. 601–24.

Klaveren, M. van, 'Death among Coolies: Mortality of Chinese and Javanese Labourers on Sumatra in the Early Years of Recruitment, 1882–1909', *Itinerario*, 21 (1997), pp. 111–25.

Klerman, D., 'The Emergence of English Commercial Law: Analysis Inspired by the Ottoman Experience', *Journal of Economic Behavior & Organization*, 71 (2009), pp. 638–46.

Krabbendam, H., 'Consuls and Citizens: Dutch Diplomatic Representation in American Cities, 1800–1940', in R. P. Swierenga, D. Sinnema and H. Krabbendam (eds), *The Dutch in Urban America* (Holland, MI: Joint Archives of Holland, Hope College, 2004), pp. 59–75.

—, 'Capital Diplomacy: Consular Activity in Amsterdam and New York, 1800–1940', in G. Harinck and H. Krabbendam (eds), *Amsterdam–New York: Transatlantic Relations and Urban Identities since 1653* (Amsterdam: VU University Press, 2005), pp. 167–81.

Krapf, Rev. Dr J. L., *Travels Researches and Missionary Labours during an Eighteen Years Residence in Eastern Africa* (Boston, MA: Ticknor and Fields, 1860).

Kuran, T., 'Preface: The Economic Impact of Culture, Religion and the Law', *Journal of Economic Behavior & Organization*, 71 (2009), pp. 589–92.

—, *The Long Divergence: How Islamic Law Held Back the Middle East* (Princeton, NJ: Princeton University Press, 2010).

Lambert, A., 'Slavery, Free Trade and Naval Strategy, 1840–1860', in K. Hamilton and P. Salmon (eds), *Slavery, Diplomacy and Empire: Britain and the Suppression of the Slave Trade, 1807–1975* (Brighton: Sussex Academic Press, 2009), pp. 65–81.

Lang, M., 'Globalization and its History', *Journal of Modern History*, 78 (2006), pp. 899–931.

Langley, L. D., *Struggle for the American Mediterranean: United States–European Rivalry in the Gulf-Caribbean, 1776–1904* (Athens, GA: The University of Georgia Press, 1976).

Lante Wallace-Bruce, N., 'Africa and International Law – The Emergence to Statehood', *Journal of Modern African Studies*, 23:4 (1985), pp. 575–602.

Larner, C., 'The Amalgamation of the Diplomatic Service with the Foreign Office', *Journal of Contemporary History*, 7:1/2 (January–April 1972), pp. 107–26.

Latourette, K. S., 'The History of Early Relations between the US and China, 1784–1844', *Transactions of the Connecticut Academy Arts and Sciences* (New Haven, CT: Yale University Press, 1917–1918), vol. 22, pp. 1–209.

Law, R., 'Central and Eastern Wangara: An Indigenous West African Perception of the Political and Economic Geography of the Slave Coast as Recorded by Joseph Dupuis in Kumasi, 1820', *History in Africa*, 22 (1995), pp. 281–305.

—, *Ouidah: The Social History of a West African Slaving 'Port', 1727–1892* (Athens, OH: Ohio University Press, 2004).

—, 'Madiki Lemon, the "English Captain" at Ouidah, 1843–1852: An Exploration in Biography', *History in Africa*, 37 (2010), pp. 107–23.

Lee, E. Yong-Joong, 'Early Development of Modern International Law in East Asia – With Special Reference to China, Japan and Korea', *Journal of the History of International Law*, 4 (2002), pp. 42–76.

Leigh J. S. and J. S. Kirkman, 'The Zanzibar Diary of John Studdy Leigh', *International Journal of African Historical Studies*, 13:2 (1980), pp. 281–312 (Part 1).

—, 'The Zanzibar Diary of John Studdy Leigh', *International Journal of African Historical Studies*, 13:3 (1980), pp. 492–507 (Part 2).

Lewis, M. and K. E. Wigen, *The Myth of Continents: A Critique of Metageography* (Los Angeles, CA, and London: University of California Press, 1997).

Lieberman, V., *Strange Parallels: Southeast Asia in Global Context, c. 800–1830. Volume 1, Integration on the Mainland* (New York: Cambridge University Press, 2003).

Ljungstedt, A., *An Historical Sketch of the Portuguese Settlements in China* (London: J. Munroe, 1836).

Lloyd Jones, C., *The Consular Service of the United States: Its History and Activities* (Philadelphia, PA: The University of Pennsylvania, 1906).

Look Lai, W., 'Asian Contract and Free Migrations to the Americas', in D. Eltis (ed.), *Coerced and Free Migration: Global Perspectives* (Stanford, CA: Stanford University Press, 2002), pp. 229–59.

Lopez, R. S., *The Commercial Revolution of the Middle Ages, 950–1350* (Cambridge: Cambridge University Press, 1976).

Louis, W. R., 'Roger Casement and the Congo', *Journal of African History*, 5:1 (1964), pp. 99–120.

Low, M. C., 'Empire and the Hajj: Pilgrims, Plagues, and Pan-Islam under British Surveillance, 1865–1908', *International Journal of Middle East Studies*, 40 (2008), pp. 269–90.

Ludwig, J., 'Zur Geschichte des sächsischen Konsulatswesens (1807–1933)', in Ulbert and Prijac (eds), *Consuls et services consulaires*, pp. 365–79.

Lynn, M., *Commerce and Economic Change in West Africa: The Palm Oil Trade in the Nineteenth Century* (Cambridge: Cambridge University Press, 1997).

M. C. M., 'The Island Johanna', *Leisure Hour* (1876), pp. 52–5.

Maameri, F., 'Ottoman Algeria in Western Diplomatic History with Particular Emphasis on Relations with the United States of America, 1776–1816' (PhD dissertation, University of Constantine, Algeria, 2008).

McClain, J. L., *Japan: A Modern History* (New York: W. W. Norton & Company, 2002).

MacClintock, S., 'A Unified Foreign Service', *American Political Science Review*, 16:4 (1922), pp. 600–11.

McDermott, J., 'The British Foreign Office and its German Consuls before 1914', *Journal of Modern History*, 50:1 (March 1978), On Demand Supplement, D1001–D1034 (D1004).

McDougall, W., *Promised Land, Crusader State: The American Encounter with the World since 1776* (New York: Houghton Mifflin Harcourt, 1997).

McIntyre, W. D., 'Commander Glover and the Colony of Lagos, 1861–73', *Journal of African History*, 4:1 (1963), pp. 57–79.

McKinnon Wood, H., 'The Treaty of Paris and Turkey's Status in International Law', *American Journal of International Law*, 37:2 (1943), pp. 262–74.

McOmie, W., *The Opening of Japan 1853–1855: A Comparative Study of the American, British, Dutch and Russian Naval Expeditions to Compel the Tokugawa Shogunate to Conclude Treaties and Open Ports to their Ships* (Kent: Global Oriental, 2006).

McPherson, K., 'Port Cities as Nodal Points of Change: The Indian Ocean, 1890s–1920s', in Fawaz and Bayly (eds), *Modernity and Culture*, pp. 75–95.

Makdisi, U., 'After 1860: Debating Religion, Reform, and Nationalism in the Ottoman Empire', *International Journal of Middle East Studies*, 34:4 (2002), pp. 601–17.

Mangiafico, L., 'Joel R. Poinsett: First US Envoy in Latin America', *Foreign Service Journal* (2012), pp. 46–9.

Manley, D. and P. Rée, *Henry Salt: Artist, Traveller, Diplomat, Egyptologist* (London: Libri, 2001).

Mann, K., *Slavery and the Birth of an African City; Lagos 1760–1900* (Bloomington, IL, and Indianapolis, IN: Indiana University Press, 2007).

Manning, W. R., 'Poinsett's Mission to Mexico', *American Journal of International Law* (1913), pp. 781–823.

—, *Diplomatic Correspondence of the United States concerning the Independence of the Latin-American Nations*, 3 vols (New York: Oxford University Press, 1925).

Mansel, P., *Levant: Splendour and Catastrophe on the Mediterranean* (London: John Murray, 2010).

Marcus, H. G. and M. E. Page, 'John Studdy Leigh: First Footsteps in East Africa?', *International Journal of African Historical Studies*, 5:3 (1972), pp. 470–8.

Martin, P. F., *Peru of the Twentieth Century* (London: Edward Arnold, 1911), pp. 311–12.

Martineau, J., *The Life and Correspondence of the Right Hon. Sir Bartle Frere, Bart., G.C.B., F.R.S., etc.*, 2 vols (London: John Murray, 1895).

Martinez, J. S., *The Slave Trade and the Origins of International Human Rights Law* (Oxford: Oxford University Press, 2012).

Masashi, H. (ed.), *Asian Port Cities, 1600–1800: Local and Foreign Cultural Interactions* (Singapore and Kyoto: NUS Press in Association with Kyoto University Press, 2009).

Matar, N., *Turks, Moors and Englishmen in the Age of Discovery* (New York: Columbia University Press, 1999).

Matthews, J. F., 'Little Favours from my Government: United States Consuls in Mexico, 1821–1865' (PhD dissertation, Texas Christian University, 1993).

Mattox, H. E., *The Twillight of Amateur Diplomacy: The American Foreign Service and its Senior Officers in the 1890s* (Kent, OH: Kent State University Press, 1989).

Mattingly, G., *Renaissance Diplomacy* (Boston, MA: Mifflin, 1955).

Mees, W. C., 'Debat in the Tweede Kamer der Staten-Generaal over onze Consuls', *De Economist*, 45 (1891), pp. 797–802.

Meissner, K., *Deutsche in Japan* (Wiesbaden and Tokyo: Kommissionsverlag Otto Harrassowitz, 1961).

Melissen, J. and A. M. Fernández, *Consular Affairs and Diplomacy* (Leiden and Boston, MA: Martinus Nijhof Publishers, 2011).

Message from the President of the United States in Relation to the Consular Establishment of the United States, Communicated to the Senate, March 2, 1833 (Washington, DC: F. P. Blair, 1833).

Meyer, A., 'Service consulaire er archéologie', in Ulbert and Prijac (eds), *Consuls et services consulaires*, pp. 36–45.

Mézin, A., *Les Consuls de France au Siècle des Lumières (1715–1792)* (Paris: Imprimerie Nationale, 1997).

Miller, M. B., 'Pilgrims' Progress: The Business of the Hajj', *Past & Present*, 191 (2006), pp. 189–229.

Miller, R. H., *The United States and Vietnam 1787–1941* (Washington, DC: National Defense University Press, 1990).

Ministerie van Buitenlandsche Zaken, *Verzameling van consulaire en andere berigten en verslagen over nijverheid, handel en scheepvaart* (Den Haag: Van Weelden en Mingelen, 1874), pp. 515–26 (report W. Hanegraaff).

—, *Verzameling van consulaire en andere berigten en verslagen over nijverheid, handel en scheepvaart* (Den Haag: Gebroeders Van Cleef, 1884), pp. 28–31 (Report consul J. A. Kruijt).

—, *Verzameling van consulaire en andere berigten en verslagen over nijverheid, handel en scheepvaart* (Den Haag: Gebroeders Van Cleef, 1884) (R. C. Burlage, Consul Generaal New York, Verslag over 1882, 23 mei 1883).

Mitani, H., *Escape from Impasse: The Decision to Open Japan* (Tokyo: I-House Press, 2006).

Mitchell, A., *The Amazon Journal of Roger Casement* (Dublin: Anaconda Editions, 1997).

Miyake, M., 'German Cultural and Political Influence on Japan, 1870–1914', in J. A. Moses and P. M. Kennedy (eds), *Germany in the Pacific and Far East, 1870–1914* (St Lucia: University of Queensland Press, 1977), pp. 156–85.

Molhuysen, P. C. and P. J. Blok (eds), 'Bake, Mr. Rudolph Willem Johan Cornelis de Menthon', *Nieuw Nederlandsch biografisch woordenboek. Deel 8* (Leiden: A. W. Sijthoff, 1930).

Morel, E. D., *Red Rubber: The Story of the Rubber Slave Trade which Flourished on the Congo for Twenty Years, 1890–1910*, rev. edn (1906; Manchester: National Labour Press, 1919).

Muhd Khairudin Aljunied, S., 'Western Images of Meccan Pilgrims in the Dutch East Indies, 1800–1900', *Sari*, 23 (2005), pp. 105–22.

Mülinen, E. Von, 'De Nomaden Abschied: Eine Erinnerung an Konsul Dr. Johann Gottfried Wetzstein', *Zeitschrift der Deutschen Morgenländischen Gesellschaft*, 19 (1925), pp. 150–61.

Muller, H., *Muller. Een Rotterdams zeehandelaar Hendrik Muller Szn (1819–1898)* (Schiedam: Interbook International BV, 1977).

Müller, L., *Consuls, Corsairs, and Commerce: The Swedish Consular Service and Long-Distance Shipping, 1720–1815* (Uppsala: Uppsala universitet, 2004).

Müller, L. and J. Ojala, 'Consular Services of the Nordic Countries during the Eighteenth and Nineteenth Centuries: Did They Really Work?', in G. Boyce and R. Gorski (eds), *Resources and Infrastructures in the Maritime Economy, 1500–2000*, Research in Maritime History Vol. 22, International Maritime Economic History Association (St John's Newfoundland, 2002), pp. 23–43.

Murray, D. R., *Odious Commerce: Britain, Spain and the Abolition of the Cuban Slave Trade* (Cambridge: Cambridge University Press, 2002).

Naff, T., 'Reform and the Conduct of Ottoman Diplomacy in the Reign of Selim III, 1789–1807', *Journal of the American Oriental Society*, 83:3 (1963), pp. 295–315.

—, 'The Ottoman Empire and the European States', in Bull and Watson (eds), *The Expansion of International Society*, pp. 143–71.

Naranch, B. D., 'Between Cosmopolitanism and German Colonialism: Nineteenth-Century Hanseatic Networks in Emerging Tropical Markets', in A. Gestrich and M. Schulte Beerbühl (eds), *Cosmopolitan Networks in Commerce and Society 1660–1914* (London: German Historical Institute, 2011), pp. 99–133.

Nasution, K. S., *More than Merchants: A History of the German-Speaking Community in Penang, 1800s–1940s* (Penang: Areca Books, 2006).

Neel, J. L., *Phineas Bond: A Study in Anglo-American Relations, 1786–1812* (Philadelphia, PA: University of Pennsylvania Press, 1968).

Neumann, L., *Handbuch des Consulatwesens* (Vienna: Von Tendler & Comp., 1854), pp. 1–11.

Neumann, W. L., 'United States Aid to the Chilean Wars of Independence', *Hispanic American Historical Review*, 27:2 (1947), pp. 204–19.

Newbury, C. W., 'General Introduction', in C. W. Newbury, *British Policy towards West Africa: Select Documents 1786–1874*, 2 vols (Oxford: Clarendon Press, 1965), vol. 1, p. 3–44.

Newman, J. L., *Paths without Glory: Richard Francis Burton in Africa* (Washington, DC: Potomac Books, 2010).

Nichols, R. F., 'Trade Relations and the Establishment of the United States Consulates in Spanish America, 1779–1809', *Hispanic American Historical Review*, 13:3 (1933), pp. 289–313.

—, *Advance Agents of American Destiny* (Philadelphia, PA: University of Philadelphia Press, 1956).

North, D. C., *Understanding the Process of Economic Change* (Princeton, NJ: Princeton University Press, 1997).

Northrup, D., 'The Compatibility of the Slave and Palm Oil Trades in the Bight of Biafra', *Journal of African History*, 17:3 (1976), pp. 353–64.

Nwulia, M. D. E., *Britain and Slavery in East Africa* (Washington, DC: Three Continents Press, 1952).

Nzemeke, A. D., 'Local Patronage and Commercial Enterprise in Lagos 1850–1861', *Africa: Rivista trimestrale di studi e documentazione dell'Istituto italiano per l'Africae l'Oriente*, 47:1 (1992), pp. 105–14.

Ó Siocháin, S., *Roger Casement: Imperialist, Rebel, Revolutionary* (Dublin: The Lilliput Press, 2008).

Oosterwijk, B., *Ik verlang geen dank. Lodewijk Pincoffs (1827–1911)* (Rotterdam: Uitgeverij Douane, 2011).

Oren, M. B., *Power, Faith, and Fantasy: America in the Middle East, 1776 to the Present* (New York: W. W. Norton & Company, 2007).

Osgood, J. B. F., *Notes of Travel; or, Recollections of Majunga, Zanzibar, Muscat, Aden, Mocha, and Other Eastern Ports* (Salem: G. Creamer, 1854).

Osiander, A., 'Before Sovereignty: Society and Politics in Ancien Régime Europe', *Review of International Studies*, 27 (2001) pp. 119–45.

—, 'Sovereignty, International Relations, and the Westphalian Myth', *International Organization*, 55:2 (2001), pp. 251–87.

Osterhammel, J., 'In Search of a Nineteenth Century', *GHI Bulletin*, 32 (Spring 2003), pp. 9–28.

Pamuk, Ş., 'Institutional Change and the Longevity of the Ottoman Empire, 1500–1800', *Journal of Interdisciplinary History*, 35:2 (2004), pp. 225–47.

Panzac, D., *Barbary Corsairs: The End of a Legend 1800–1820* (Leiden and Boston, MA: Brill, 2005).

Parton, D. M., *The Diplomatic Career of Joel Roberts Poinsett* (Washington, DC: The Catholic University of America, 1934).

Paske-Smith, M., *Western Barbarians in Japan and Formosa in Tokugawa Days, 1603–1868* (Kobe: J. L. Thompson, 1930).

Paterson, T. G., 'American Businessmen and Consular Service Reform, 1890s to 1906', *Business History Review*, 40:1 (1966), pp. 77–97.

Paulus, J., 'Ons Consulaatwezen en de Consuls', *De Economist*, 41 (1888), pp. 621–53.

Paxson, F. L., *The Independence of the South Republics: A Study in Recognition and Foreign Policy*, 2nd edn (Philadelphia, PA: Ferris & Leach, 1916).

Pearson, M. N., *Pious Passengers: The Hajj in Earlier Times* (London: Sterling Publishers, 1994), pp. 37–64.

Penkwitt, W., *Preußen und Brasilien. Zum Aufbau des preußischen Konsularwesens im unabhängigen Kaiserreich (1822–1850)* (Wiesbaden: Franz Steiner Verlag GmbH, 1983).

Pennell, C. R., 'The Origins of the Foreign Jurisdiction Act and the Extension of British Sovereignty', *Historical Research*, 83:221 (2010), pp. 465–86.

Peterson, H. F., *Argentina and the United States: 1810–1960* (New York: University Publishers Inc., 1964).

Pierson, G. J., 'US Consuls in Zanzibar and the Slave Trade, 1870–1890', *Historian*, 55 (Autumn 1992), pp. 53–68.

Pine, J. C., 'William G. D. Worthington: United States Special Agent, 1817–1819', *Arkansas Academy of Science Proceedings*, 12 (1958), pp. 46–7.

Platt, D. C. M., 'The Role of the British Consular Service in Overseas Trade, 1825–1914', *Economic History Review*, 15:3 (1963), pp. 494–512.

—, *The Cinderella Service: British Consuls since 1825* (London: Longman, 1971).

Playfair, R. L., *The Scourge of Christendom: Annals of British Relations with Algiers prior to the French Conquest* (London: Smith Elder, 1884).

Porter, A., 'Sir Roger Casement and the International Humanitarian Movement', *Journal of Imperial and Commonwealth History*, 29:2 (2001), pp. 59–74.

Porter, J. L., *Five Years in Damascus: Including an Account of the History, Topography, and Antiquities of that City*, 2 vols (London: John Murray, 1855), vol. 1, p. 45.

Pouwels, R. L., 'Eastern Africa and the Indian Ocean to 1800: Reviewing Relations in Historical Perspective', *International Journal of African Historical Studies*, 35:2/3 (2002), pp. 385–425.

Powell, B. E., 'Jefferson and the Consular Service', *Political Science Quarterly*, 21:4 (1906), pp. 626–38.

Prentiss, C., *The Life of the Late Gen. William Eaton; Several Years an Officer in the United States' Army, Consul at the Regency of Tunis on the Coast of Barbary ... Principally Collected from his Correspondence and Other Manuscripts* (Brookfield: E. Merriam & Co., 1813).

Pryor, J. H., *Geography, Technology, and War: Studies in the Maritime History of the Mediterranean 649–1571* (Cambridge: Press Syndicate University of Cambridge, 1992).

Ptak, R., 'Ming Maritime Trade to Southeast Asia, 1368–1567: Visions of a "System"', in C. Guillot et al. (eds), *From the Mediterranean to the China Sea: Miscellaneous Notes* (Wiesbaden: Otto Harrassowitz, 1998), pp. 157–92.

Puente, J. I., 'The Nature of the Consular Establishment', *University of Pennsylvania Law Review*, 78 (1929–30), pp. 321–45.

Putten, F. P. van der, 'Small Powers and Imperialism: The Netherlands in China, 1886–1905', *Itinerario*, 20 (1996), pp. 115–31.

Rabino, J., 'The Statistical Story of the Suez Canal', *Journal of the Royal Statistical Society*, 50:3 (September 1887), pp. 495–546.

Rafeq, A.-K., 'Damascus and the Pilgrim Trade', in Fawaz and Bayly (eds), *Modernity and Culture*, pp. 130–44.

Rajanubhab, H. R. H. Prince Damrong, 'The Introduction of Western Culture in Siam', *Journal of the Siam Society*, 20:2 (1926–7), pp. 89–101.

Rajo Sathian, M., 'Suzerain–Tributary Relations: An Aspect of Traditional Siamese Statecraft (c. 19th century)', *JATI – Journal of Southeast Asian Studies*, 11:1 (2006), pp. 108–25.

Rankin, F. H., *The White Man's Grave: A Visit to Sierra Leone in 1834* (London: Richard Bentley, 1836).

Reid, A., 'Early Chinese Migration into North Sumatra', in J. Ch'en and N. Tarling (eds), *Studies in the Social History of China and South-East Asia: Essays in Memory of Victor Purcell* (Cambridge: Cambridge University Press, 1970).

Reimer, M. J., 'Colonial Bridgehead: Social and Spatial Change in Alexandria, 1850–1882', *International Journal of Middle East Studies*, 20:4 (1988), pp. 531–3.

Reinhardt, C. and A. S. Travis, *Heinrich Caro and the Creation of Modern Chemical Industry* (Dordrecht: Kluwer Academic Publishers, 2000).

Report and Special Report from the Select Committee on Putumayo, together with the Proceedings of the Committee, Minutes of Evidence and Appendices (London: Wyman and Sons, 1913).

Reports Received from Her Majesty's Consuls Relating to the Condition of Christians in Turkey, 1860 (London: Harrison and Sons, 1861).

Ridley, R. T., *Napoleon's Proconsul in Egypt: The Life and Times of Bernardino Drovetti* (London: David Brown Book Company, 1998).

Roberts, E., *Embassy to the Eastern Courts of Cochin-China, Siam, and Muscat: In the US Sloop-of-War Peacock, David Geisinger, Commander, during the Years 1832-3-4* (New York: Harper & Bros., 1837).

Roberts, E. and W. S. W. Ruschenberger, *Two Yankee Diplomats in 1830s Siam by Edmund Roberts and W. S. W. Ruschenberger M.D.*, ed. and intro. M. Smithies (Bangkok: Orchid Press, 2002).

Roberts, P. H. and R. S. Roberts, *Thomas Barclay (1728–1793): Consul in France, Diplomat in Barbary* (Bethlehem, PA: Associated University Presses, 2008).

Robertson, W. S., 'The First Legations of the United States in Latin America', *Mississippi Valley Historical Review*, 2:2 (1915), pp. 183–212.

—, 'Documents Concerning the Consular Service of the United States in Latin America, with Introductory Note', *Mississippi Valley Historical Review*, 2:4 (1916), pp. 561–8.

—, 'The Recognition of the Hispanic American Nations by the United States', *Hispanic American Historical Review*, 1:3 (1918), pp. 239–69.

Rodkey, F. S., 'The Attempts of Briggs and Company to Guide British Policy in the Levant in the Interest of Mehemet Ali Pasha, 1821–41', *Journal of Modern History*, 5:3 (1933), pp. 324–51.

Rodogno, D., *Against Massacre: Humanitarian Interventions in the Ottoman Empire 1815–1914* (Princeton, NJ, and London: Princeton University Press, 2012).

Rodriguez, J. P., *Slavery in the Modern World: A History of Political, Social, and Economic Oppression* (Santa Barbara, CA: ABC Clio, 2011).

Roe, H., *West African Scenes: Descriptions of Fernando Po* (London: Elliot Stock, 1874).

Rogan, A., *De Arabieren; een geschiedenis* (Amsterdam: De Bezige Bij, 2010).

Rogan, E. L., 'Sectarianism and Social Conflict in Damascus: The 1860 Events Reconsidered', *Arabica*, 51:4 (2004), pp. 493–511.

Roosevelt, T., 'The Present Position of Civil Service Reform', *New Princeton Review*, 1:3 (1886), pp. 362–72.

—, 'Six Years of Civil Service Reform', *Scribner's Magazine*, 18 (1895), pp. 238–48.

Ross, F. E., 'The Mission of Joseph Donaldson, Jr., to Algiers, 1795–1797', *Journal of Modern History*, 7:4 (1935), pp. 422–33.

Ruangsilp, B., 'Dutch East India Company Merchants at the Court of Ayutthaya: Dutch Perceptions of the Thai Kingdom, *c.* 1604–1765' (PhD dissertation, Leiden University, 2007).

Ruete, E., née Princess of Oman and Zanzibar, *Memoirs of an Arabian Princess: An Autobiography* (New York: D. Appleton and Company, 1888).

—, *An Arabian Princess between Two Worlds: Memoirs, Letters Home, Sequels to the Memoirs Syrian Customs and Usages by Sayyida Salme/Emily Ruete*, ed. and intro. E. van Donzel (Leiden: E. J. Brill, 1993).

Ruschenberger, W. S. W., *Narrative of a Voyage Round the World during the Years 1835–36–37, Including a Narrative of an Embassy to the Sultan of Muscat and the King of Siam* (Philadelphia, PA: Carby, Lea, & Blanchard, 1838).

Sadosky, L. J., 'Revolutionary Negotiations: A History of American Diplomacy with Europe and Native America in the Age of Jefferson' (PhD dissertation, University of Virginia, 2003).

Salvucci, R. J., 'The Origins and Progress of US–Mexican Trade, 1825–1884: "Hoc opus, hic labor est"', *Hispanic American Historical Review*, 71:4 (1991), pp. 697–735.

Satow, E. M., *A Diplomat in Japan* (London: Seeley, Service & Co. Ltd., 1921).

Sawyer, R. (ed.), *Roger Casement's Diaries – 1910: The Black and the White* (London: Pimlico, 1997).

Schatkowski Schilcher, L., 'Review of Ingeborg Huhn, Der Orientalist Johann Gottfried Wetzstein als preussischer Konsul in Damaskus (1849–1861)', *Middle East Studies Association Bulletin*, 27:2 (1993), pp. 266–7.

Schölch, A., 'The "Men on the Spot" and the English Occupation of Egypt in 1882', *Historical Journal*, 19:3 (1976), pp. 773–85.

Schramm, P. E., *Deutschland und Übersee. Der deutsche Handel mit den andere Kontinenten, insbesondere Afrika, von Karl V. bis zu Bismarck* (Braunschweig: Georg Westermann Verlag, 1950).

Schrecker, J. E., 'Kiautschou and the Problems of German Colonialism', in Moses and Kennedy (eds), *Germany in the Pacific and Far East, 1870–1914*, pp. 185–209.

Schultz, K., 'The Transfer of the Portuguese Court and Ideas of Empire', *Portuguese Studies Review*, 15:1–2 (2007), pp. 367–91.

Scully, E. P., *Bargaining with the State from Afar: American Citizenship in Treaty Port China 1844–1942* (New York: Columbia University Press, 2001).

Shaikh, F., 'Judicial Diplomacy: British Officials and the Mixed Commission Courts', in Hamilton and Salmon (eds), *Slavery, Diplomacy and Empire*, pp. 42–65.

Shaler, W., 'Journal of a Voyage between China and the North-Western Coast of America, Made in 1804', *American Register*, Volume 3, Part 1 (Philadelphia, PA: C. & A. Conrad, 1808), pp. 137–75.

Shaw, S., *The Journals of Major Samuel Shaw, the First American Consul at Canton, with a Life of the Author*, ed. J. Quincy (Boston, MA: Wm. Crosby and H. P. Nichols, 1847).

Sheriff, A., *Slaves, Spices, and Ivory in Zanzibar: Integration of an East African Commercial Empire into the World Economy, 1770–1873* (Athens, OH: Ohio University Press, 1987).

Sherwood, M., 'Perfidious Albion: Britain, the USA, and Slavery in the 1840s and 1860s', *Contributions in Black Studies*, 13/14 (1995), pp. 174–200.

Shreeve, W. W., *Sierra Leone: The Principal British Colony on the Western Coast of Africa* (London: Simmonds & Co., 1848).

Shun Liu, S., *Extraterritoriality: Its Rise and its Decline* (London: P. S. King & Son, Ltd, 1925).

Singha, R., 'Passport, Ticket, and India-Rubber Stamp: "The Problem of the Pauper Pilgrim" in Colonial India *c.* 1882–1925', in A. Tambe and H. Fischer-Tiné (eds), *The Limits of British Colonial Control in South Asia: Spaces of Disorder in the Indian Ocean Region* (New York: Routledge, 2009), pp. 49–84.

Slater, S. E., 'The British Consulate at Fernando Po: 1854–1879' (MA Thesis, University of Calgary, 1983).

Smith, M., 'The Myth of American Isolationism: Commerce, Diplomacy, and Military Affairs in the Early Republic', Special report from the B. Kenneth Simon Center for Principles and Politics, 134 (2013), pp. 5–47.

Smith, R., 'Peace and Palaver: International Relations in Pre-Colonial West Africa', *Journal of African History*, 14:4 (1973), pp. 599–621.

Smith, R. S., 'The Institution of the Consulado in New Spain', *Hispanic American Historical Review*, 24:1 (1944), pp. 61–83.

—, 'A Research Report on Consulado History', *Journal of Inter-American Studies*, 3:1 (1961), pp. 41–52.

—, *The Lagos Consulate 1851–1861* (London: The Macmillan Press, 1978).

Smith, W. B., *America's Diplomats and Consuls of 1776–1865: A Geographic and Biographic Directory of the Foreign Service from the Declaration of Independence to the End of the Civil War* (Washington, DC: US Department of State, 1987).

Smout, T. C., 'American Consular Reports on Scotland', *Business History*, 23:3 (1981), pp. 304–9.

Snouck Hurgronje, C., 'De Hadji-politiek der Indische regeering', *Onze Eeuw*, 9 (1909), pp. 332–61.

Southall, A., 'State Formation in Africa', *Annual Review of Anthropology*, 4 (1974), pp. 153–65.

—, 'The Segmentary State in Africa and Asia', *Comparative Studies in Society and History*, 30:1 (1988), pp. 52–82.

Spruyt, H., 'The Origins, Development, and Possible Decline of the Modern State', *Annual Review of Political Science*, 5 (2002), pp. 127–49.

Stahncke, H., *Die diplomatische Beziehungen zwischen Deutschland und Japan 1854–1868* (Stuttgart: Franz Steiner Verlag, 1987).

Stansfield, M. E., *Red Rubber, Bleeding Trees: Violence, Slavery, and Empire in Northwest Amazonia, 1850–1933* (Albuquerque, NM: University of New Mexico Press, 1998).

State Papers and Publick Documents of the United States, 10 vols, 2nd edn (Boston, MA: T. B. Wait and Sons, 1817).

State Papers and Publick Documents of the United States, 12 vols, 3rd edn (Boston, MA: T. B. Wait and Sons, 1819).

Stewart, I., 'Consular Privileges and Immunities under the Treaties of Friendship, Commerce and Consular Rights', *American Journal of International Law*, 21:2 (1927), pp. 257–67.

Stillé, C. J., *The Life and Services of Joel R. Poinsett, the Confidential Agent in South Carolina of President Jackson during the Nullification Troubles of 1832* (Philadelphia, PA: The Pennsylvania Magazine of History and Biography, 1888).

Stillman, N. A., *The Jews of Arab Lands: A History and Source Book* (Philadelphia, PA: The Jewish Publication Society of America, 1979).

Stoecker, H., *Deutschland und China im 19. Jahrhundert. Das Eindringen des deutschen Kapitalismus* (Berlin: Rütten & Loening, 1958).

—, 'Germany and China, 1861–94', in Moses and Kennedy (eds), *Germany in the Pacific and Far East, 1870–1914*, pp. 26–40.

Strupp, C., 'Das US-amerikanische Konsularwesen im 19. Jahrhundert', in Ulbert and Prijac (eds), *Consuls et services consulaires*, pp. 218–34.

Stuart, G., *American Diplomatic and Consular Practice* (New York: Appleton-Century-Crofts, 1952).

Sumner, C., *White Slavery in the Barbary States* (Boston, MA: John P. Jewett and Company, 1853).

Sundiata, I. K., *From Slaving to Neoslavery: The Bight of Biafra and Fernando Po in the Era of Abolition, 1827–1930* (Madison, WI: The University of Wisconsin Press, 1996).

Suret-Canale, J., *Essays on African History: From the Slave Trade to Neo-Colonialism* (London: C. Hurst & Co., London, 1988).

Suzuki, S., *Civilization and Empire: China and Japan's Encounter with European International Society* (London and New York: Routledge, 2009).

Szipple, R. F., 'Max von Brandt and German Imperialism in East Asia in the Late Nineteenth Century' (PhD dissertation, University of Notre Dame, 1989).

Tagliacozzo, E., 'Ambiguous Commodities, Unstable Frontiers: The Case of Burma, Siam, and Imperial Britain, 1800–1900', *Comparative Studies in Society and History*, 46:2 (2004), pp. 354–77.

—, *The Longest Journey: Southeast Asians and the Pilgrimage to Mecca* (Oxford: Oxford University Press, 2013).

Takao, S., 'Murder of Ludwig Haber, German Consul at Hakodate', *Journal of Konan University: Research Institute*, 95 (January 2008), pp. 113–48.

Tamse, C. A., 'The Netherlands Consular Service and the Dutch Consular Reports of the Nineteenth and Twentieth Centuries', *Business History*, 23:3 (1981), pp. 271–7.

Tarazi Fawaz, L., *An Occasion for War: Civil Conflict in Lebanon and Damascus in 1860* (London and New York, I. B. Taurus Publishers, 1994).

Taussig, M., 'Culture of Terror – Space of Death: Roger Casement's Putumayo Report and the Explanation of Torture', *Comparative Studies in Society and History*, 26:3 (1984), pp. 467–97.

Teetor, P. R., 'England's Earliest Treatise on the Law Merchant: The Essay on Lex Mercatoria from The Little Red Book of Bristol (Circa 1280 AD)', *American Journal of Legal History*, 6:2 (1962), pp. 178–210.

Thayer, L. E., 'The Capitulations of the Ottoman Empire and the Question of their Abrogation as it Affects the United States', *American Journal of International Law*, 17:2 (1923), pp. 213–14.

Thornton, J., 'Early Kongo–Portuguese Relations: A New Interpretation', *History in Africa*, 8 (1981), pp. 183–204.

—, *Africa's Discovery of Europe, 1450–1850* (New York: Oxford University Press, 2002).

Tinniswood, A., *Pirates of Barbary: Corsairs, Conquests, and Captivity in the Seventeenth-Century Mediterranean* (New York: Random House, 2010).

Tuchscherer, M., 'Trade and Port Cities in the Red Sea-Gulf of Aden Region in the Sixteenth and Seventeenth Century', in Fawaz and Bayly (eds), *Modernity and Culture*, pp. 28–46.

Tully, J., *The Devil's Milk: A Social History of Rubber* (New York: Monthly Review Press, 2011).

Ulbert, J. and G. Le Bouëdec (eds), *La fonction consulaire à l'époque moderne. L'Affirmation d'une institution économique et politique (1500–1700)* (Rennes: PUR, 2006).

Ulbert, J. and L. Prijac (eds), *Consuls et services consulaires au XIXème siècle – Die Welt der Konsulate im 19. Jahrhundert – Consulship in the Nineteenth Century* (Hamburg: DOBU, Dokumentation & Buch, 2009).

United States Department of State, *Slavery In Peru: Message from the President of the United States, Transmitting Report of the Secretary of State, with Accompanying Papers, Concerning the Alleged Existence of Slavery in Peru* (Washington, DC: Government Printing Office, 1913).

—, *A Short Account of the Department of State of the United States* (Washington, DC: Government Printing Office, 1922).

Vanthemsch, G., *Belgium and the Congo, 1885–1980* (New York: Cambridge University Press, 2012).

Varg, P. A., 'The Myth of the China Market, 1890–1914', *American Historical Review*, 73:3 (1968), pp. 742–58.

Veenendaal, A. J., *Slow Train to Paradise: How Dutch Investments Helped Build American Railroads* (Stanford, CA: Stanford University Press, 1995).

Viaene, V., 'King Leopold's Imperialism and the Origins of the Belgian Colonial Party, 1860–1905', *Journal of Modern History*, 80:4 (December 2008), pp. 741–90.

Viana Pedreira, J. M., 'From Growth to Collapse: Portugal, Brazil, and the Breakdown of the Old Colonial System (1750–1830)', *Hispanic American Historical Review*, 80:4 (2000), pp. 839–64.

Vivian, C., *Americans in Egypt, 1770–1915: Explorers, Consuls, Travellers, Soldiers, Missionaries, Writers and Scientists* (Jefferson, NC: MacFarland and Company Publishers, 2012).

Von Brandt, M. A. S., *Dreiunddriessig Jahre in Ost-Asien. Erinerungen eines deutschen Diplomaten* (Leipzig: Georg Wigand Verlag, 1901).

Vuurde, R. van, *Nederland en de Monroeleer, 1895–1914: Europese belangenbehartiging in de Amerikaanse invloedssfeer* (Amsterdam: De Bataafsche Leeuw, 1998).

Waley-Cohen, J., *The Sextants of Beijing: Global Currents in Chinese History* (New York and London: W. W. Norton & Company, 1999).

Ward, A. W. and G. P. Gooch (eds), *The Cambridge History of British Foreign Policy 1783–1919*, 3 vols (New York: The MacMillan Company, 1922).

Watson, A., *The Evolution of International Society: A Comparative Historical Analysis* (London and New York: Routledge, 2009).

Webster, A., *Gentlemen Capitalists: British Imperialism in South East Asia 1770–1890* (London: I. B. Taurus, 1998).

Weinstein, B., *The Amazon Rubber Boom, 1850–1920* (Stanford, CA: Stanford University Press, 1983).

Wells, C. B., *Bescheiden betreffende de Buitenlandse Politiek van Nederland 1848–1919* (Den Haag: Martinus Nijhoff, 1972).

—, *Aloofness and Neutrality: Studies on Dutch Foreign Relations and Policy-Making Institutions* (Utrecht: Hes Publishers, 1982).

Werking, R. H., 'The Foreign Service in the 1890s: The Diplomat as Revisionist', *Reviews in American History*, 18:3 (1990), pp. 376–82.

Westermann, J. C., *The Netherlands and the United States: Their Relations in the Beginning of the Nineteenth Century* (Den Haag: Martinus Nijhoff, 1935).

Wetzstein, J. G., 'Der Markt in Damascus', *Zeitschrift der Deutschen morgenländischer Gesellschaft*, 11 (1857), pp. 475–525.

—, *Reisebericht über Hauran und die Trachonen* (Berlin: Dietrich Reimer Verlag, 1860).

White, L. A., 'The United States in the 1850s as Seen by British Consuls', *Mississippi Valley Historical Review*, 19:4 (1933), pp. 509–36.

—, 'The South in the 1850s as Seen by British Consuls', *Journal of Southern History*, 1:1 (1935), pp. 33–48.

Willink, R. J., *Stages in Civilisation: Dutch Museums in Quest of West Central African Collections (1856–1889)* (Leiden: CNWS Publications, 2007).

Wilson, H. H., 'Some Principal Aspects of British Efforts to Crush the African Slave Trade, 1807–1929', *American Journal of International Law*, 44:3 (1950), pp. 505–27.

Windler, C., 'Tributes and Presents in Franco-Tunisian Diplomacy', *Journal of Early Modern History*, 4 (2000), pp. 168–99.

—, 'Diplomatic History as a Field for Cultural Analysis: Muslim–Christian Relations in Tunis, 1700–1840', *Historical Journal*, 44:1 (2001), pp. 79–106.

—, 'Representing a State in a Segmentary Society: French Consuls in Tunis from the Ancien Régime to the Restoration', *Journal of Modern History*, 73:2 (2001), pp. 233–74.

Wippich, R., *"Strich mit Mütze". Max von Brandt und Japan – Diplomat, Publizist, Propagandist* (Tokyo: OAG, 1995).

Witlox, M., 'Als waakhond en beschermer: het Nederlandse consulaat in Djeddah, 1872–1889', in P. Luykx and A. Manning (eds), *Nederland in de wereld 1870–1950* (Nijmegen: SUN, 1988), pp. 65–85.

Woodfork, J., 'The Omani Empire', in Falola (ed.), *Africa*, vol. 1 (African History before 1885), pp. 321–35.

Wriston, H. M., *Executive Agents in American Foreign Relations* (Baltimore, MD: The Johns Hopkins University Press, 1929).

Yasuaki, O., 'When was the Law of International Society Born? An Inquiry of the History of International Law from an Intercivilizational Perspective', *Journal of the History of International Law*, 2 (2000), pp. 1–66.

Yen Ching-hwang, *Coolies and Mandarins: China's Protection of Overseas Chinese during the Late Ch'ing Period (1851–1911)* (Singapore: Singapore University Press, 1985).

Yokota, K. Akemi, *Unbecoming British: How Revolutionary America Became a Postcolonial Nation* (Oxford: Oxford University Press 2011).

Youngquist, E., 'United States Commercial Treaties: Their Role in Foreign Economic Policy', *Studies in Law and Economic Development*, 2:1 (1967), pp. 72–90.

Zacks, R., *The Pirate Coast: Thomas Jefferson, the First Marines, and the Secret Mission of 1805* (New York: Hyperion, 2005).

Zambon, A., 'Louis François Sébastien Fauvel, le consul antiquaire (1753–1838)', in Ulbert and Prijac (eds), *Consuls et services consulaires*, pp. 139–57.

Zhang, Y., 'System, Empire and State in Chinese International Relations', *Review of International Studies*, 27 (2001), pp. 43–63.

Zielke, E., 'Konsul Louis Kniffler – Der Pionier des deutschen Japanhandels. 1859 Gründete er das erste deutschen Unternehmen in Japan', *Zeitschrift für Unternehmensgeschichte*, 25:1 (1980), pp. 1–11.

Zourek, J., 'Consular Intercourse and Immunities', *Yearbook of the International Law Commission*, 2 (1957), pp. 72–7.

Zwi Werblowsky, R. J., *The Beaten Track of Science: The Life and Work of J. J. M. de Goot*, ed. H. Walravens (Wiesbaden: Harrassowitz Verlag, 2002).

INDEX